Competition Laws of Europe

Competition Laws of Europe

Edited by

Julian Maitland-Walker

Solicitor; Partner, Charles Russell

Butterworths
London, Charlottesville, Dublin, Durban, Edinburgh, Kuala Lumpur,
San Juan, Singapore, Sydney, Toronto, Wellington
1995

United Kingdom	Butterworths, a Division of Reed Elsevier (UK) Ltd, Halsbury House, 35 Chancery Lane, LONDON WC2A 1EL and 4 Hill Street, EDINBURGH EH2 3JZ
Australia	Butterworths, SYDNEY, MELBOURNE, BRISBANE, ADELAIDE, PERTH, CANBERRA and HOBART
Canada	Butterworths Canada Ltd, TORONTO and VANCOUVER
Ireland	Butterworth (Ireland) Ltd, DUBLIN
Malaysia	Malayan Law Journal Sdn Bhd, KUALA LUMPUR
New Zealand	Butterworths of New Zealand Ltd, WELLINGTON and AUCKLAND
Puerto Rico	Butterworth of Puerto Rico, Inc, SAN JUAN
Singapore	Reed Elsevier (Singapore) Pte Ltd, SINGAPORE
South Africa	Butterworths Publishers (Pty) Ltd, DURBAN
USA	Michie Butterworth, CHARLOTTESVILLE, Virginia

A CIP Catalogue record for this book is available from the British Library.

ISBN 0 406 03325 0

Typeset by Columns Design and Production Services Ltd, Reading
Printed by Mackays of Chatham plc, Chatham, Kent

Preface

Comparative law is a fascinating field of study. The enormous increase in international trade in an ever more interdependent and shrinking world has changed the nature of the subject from being the purview of the more academically inclined lawyers amongst us to an area of law which practitioners, certainly in Europe, are being confronted with on a daily basis. This is nowhere more true than in relation to competition law where any lawyer advising on any form of agreement whether it be agency or distribution, intellectual property licensing, or a merger or acquisition must have regard to the competition laws within the jurisdictions in which the transaction is to take effect.

Whereas 20 years ago, members of the European Community, with the exception of Germany and the UK, had either a relatively under-developed competition law or no competition law at all, the position in recent years has transformed. All the Member States now have in place national competition laws which apply in parallel to those competition laws of the European Union, or of what remains of the European Economic Area. In many cases these laws are drawn in very similar terms to the competition laws of the EU, but there are often differences sometimes of substance and always of procedure which in any relevant transaction a practising lawyer needs to address.

So far as I am aware, this is the first attempt to offer a practical overview of the current national competition laws of the states of Western Europe to fill this important gap in the transactional lawyer's library and I hope that it will provide a useful source of reference for those advising on multi-national transactions in the future.

This work does not seek to provide a detailed commentary on the laws of the 19 jurisdictions covered. This would obviously be impossible in a book of this size. What we have tried to do is to provide a basic introduction to the national laws linked with a practical appraisal of the consequences of their application in relation to specific types of agreement. Where possible, we have adopted a uniform structure for each chapter so that the user will be able to make a swift comparison as to the application of national competition laws in specific areas in different countries.

In compiling this work, I must express a debt of gratitude to all those busy lawyers who have accepted the task of providing me with a summary of competition law within their jurisdictions within the constraints of the regime which I offered to them. Each of these contributors are specialist practitioners in the field and their patience and understanding in the completion of this publication is very much appreciated.

Although each country chapter does provide limited references to the relevant legislation and some case law, the scope of the publication does not allow for a comprehensive review of case laws and if the reader requires specific guidance on particular issues, there is no substitute for instructing local lawyers within the jurisdiction concerned.

I must also express a debt of thanks to my secretary, Hilary Cripps, for her hard work in assembling the copy and typing manuscripts and the staff of Butterworths for making this publication possible. The law is stated as at July 1995.

Julian Maitland-Walker

Contributors

Contributors' addresses, telephone and fax numbers are given at the beginning of their chapters.

Luis-Ignacio Alonso-Martinez
Madrid, Spain

Knut Bachke
Oslo, Norway

Ivo Van Bael
Brussels, Belgium

Hermann Beythan
Luxembourg

Pierre V F Bos
Brussels, Belgium

Davide Braghini
Milan, Italy

Freddy Brausch
Luxembourg

Andreas Diem
Brussels, Belgium

Nuno Gonçalves
Lisbon, Portugal

Philipp Kaenzig
Zürich, Switzerland

Mats Koffner
Gothenberg, Sweden

Julian Maitland-Walker
London, England

Philippe Matignon
Paris, France

John Meade
Dublin, Ireland

Erik Mohr Mersing
Copenhagen, Denmark

Oppenhoff & Rädler
Cologne, Germany

Julia Pournara
Athens, Greece

Friedrich Schwank
Vienna, Austria

Costas Vainanidis
Athens, Greece

Dominique Voillemot
Paris, France

Carl-Henrik Wallin
Helsinki, Finland

Contents

Table of National Legislation

References in **bold** type indicate where a provision is set out in part or in full.

Table of European Legislation

References in **bold** type indicate where a provision is set out in part or in full.

Table of Cases

In the following table case references are listed according to the chapters in which such cases are cited.

CHAPTER I. European Community, and
CHAPTER II. European Economic Area

CHAPTER IV. Belgium

CHAPTER IX. Greece

CHAPTER X. Ireland

CHAPTER XI. Italy

CHAPTER XIX. United Kingdom

CHAPTER I

European Community

Julian Maitland-Walker

Charles Russell Solicitors
8–10 New Fetter Lane
London EC4A 1RS
England

Tel   ++44 171 203 5000
Fax   ++44 171 203 0200

CHAPTER I

European Community

1 EUROPEAN COMPETITION LAW

1.1 Background

1.1.1 The source of competition law of the European Community is found principally in the Treaty establishing the European Community (the 'EEC Treaty') signed at Rome in 1957 between the original six Member States – the Federal Republic of Germany, France, Italy and the Benelux countries,[1] as amended by the Single European Act[2] and most recently by the Treaty on European Union signed at Maastricht in February 1992.[3] The European Coal and Steel Community Treaty ('ECSC Treaty') and the Euratom Treaty contain special rules for certain products, respectively coal and steel and nuclear energy, and are not dealt with in this chapter.[4]

1.1.2 Most national competition or anti-trust legislation is concerned exclusively with the maintenance of effective competition and the principle of fair trading as a mechanism for the protection of the consumer. In this respect EC competition law can be distinguished from national competition law in that whilst maintenance of competition in general and of 'fairness' in trading are significant secondary considerations, the primary objective of the EC rules on competition is to help bring about Community integration. Thus free competition represents one of the 'freedoms' forming the basis of the EEC Treaty in common with the free movement of workers, freedom of establishment, freedom to provide services and free movement of capital. Article 3 of the Treaty indicates how this objective is to be achieved and refers in particular to:

> '(f) the institution of a system ensuring that competition in the Common Market is not distorted.'

1.1.3 The Commission has defined the objectives of competition policy as the prevention of:

> 'companies ... re-establishing frontiers abolished 25 years ago through the less visible but equally effective means of market sharing agreements and export bans. Both consumers and traders benefit from this policy: consumers because they can enjoy the lowest prices available in any of the Member countries; traders because they have access to a market on a European scale;'

---

1 Under the various Accession Treaties, the United Kingdom, Denmark and Ireland acceded to the EEC with effect from 1 January 1973, Greece with effect from 1 January 1981, Spain and Portugal with effect from 1 January 1986 and Austria, Sweden and Finland with effect from 1 January 1995.
2 Signed in February 1986.
3 For a text of the Maastricht Treaty see (1993) 1 CMLR 573.
4 For an annotated text of the ECSC Treaty and Euratom see Vaughan, *Law of the European Communities Service*, Parts 9 and 10 (Butterworths).

and of

'excessive concentrations of economic power from damaging the interests of consumer (or competitors . . .'.[5]

It is important to note from this quotation that the interests of consumers and competitors is secondary to the need to break down national trade barriers, and this does explain why in some cases Commission Decisions appear to advocate solutions which may not be the most desirable solution on purely competitive criteria but further the interests of the European Single Market, eg Distillers.[6]

1.2   Anti-competitive agreements and concerted practices

1.2.1   *Article 85 – restrictive agreements*

Article 85(1)[7] prohibits agreements or concerted practices between undertakings which may affect trade between Member States and which restrict or distort competition within the Common Market. There are, therefore, three elements:

(a)   an agreement or concerted practice between undertakings;
(b)   which affects trade between Member States; and
(c)   which restricts or distorts competition within the Common Market.

1.2.2   *Undertakings*

The term 'undertaking' includes any legal or natural person carrying on activities of an economic nature. It has been held to include an opera singer,[8] an inventor,[9] a state-owned corporation[10] to the extent that they carry on economic or commercial activities.[11] Individual employees are not, however, undertakings and groups of companies are treated as a single undertaking where the subsidiary is controlled by the parent. The test in each case is whether the subsidiary has autonomy of action.[12]

1.2.3   *Agreements*

Article 85(1) refers to agreements, decisions by associations of undertakings and concerted practices. Thus the definition is not limited to agreements which are legally binding but would include a 'gentleman's agreement' or 'arrangements' binding in honour only. Furthermore, the extension of the prohibition to 'concerted practice' shows that 'conscious parallelism' by competitors will also be caught.[13]

---

5 European Competition Policy 2/83 January 1983.
6 *Distillers* 1978 OJ L50/16; (1978) on appeal – *Distillers v Commission* [1980] ECR 2290.
7 Full text at Annex 1.
8 *RAI/UNITEL* 1978 OJL157/39.
9 *Vaessen/Moris* 1979 OJ L19/32.
10 *Sacchi*: 1155/73 [1974] ECR 409.
11 Note limited exception to this rule under Article 90(2) which excludes the application of the competition rules to undertakings entrusted with the operation of services of general economic interest or having the character of a revenue-producing monopoly to the extent that such rules do not obstruct the performance of the tasks assigned to them.
12 *BMW Belgium v Commission*: 32/78, 36–82/78 [1979] ECR 2435.
13 See *Polypropylene* 1986 OJ L230/1 and on appeal to the Court of First Instance [1991] ECR II-499–1833.

1.2.4 The effect on trade between Member States

An agreement or concerted practice no matter how restrictive of competition will not fall within Article 85(1) unless it can be shown that it *may* effect trade between Member States. This essential procedural requirement will be satisfied if the agreement is likely to produce an appreciable alteration in the natural flow of trade between Member States[14] and will include an actual or potential effect which may be direct or indirect and need not necessarily be detrimental.

1.2.5 The restriction of competition

Article 85(1) itself lists examples of possible restriction on competition as follows:

'(a)   directly or indirectly fix purchase or selling prices or any other trading conditions;
(b)   limit or control production, markets, technical development, or investment;
(c)   share markets or sources of supply;
(d)   apply dissimilar conditions to equivalent transactions with other trading parties, thereby placing them at a competitive disadvantage;
(e)   make the conclusion of contracts subject to acceptance by the other parties of supplementary obligations which, by their nature or according to commercial usage, have no connection with the subject of such contracts.'

The list is illustrative only and any agreement which restricts the parties to the agreement from competing with one another or competing with third parties will be caught and the restriction may be direct or indirect. Thus, for example:

(a)   the grant of exclusive distribution rights for a territory will restrict competition since by definition it precludes the grantor from appointing other distributors within the exclusive territory;[15]
(b)   an undertaking by the vendor of a business not to compete with the purchaser in the same field for a period of time over a given territory will be a restriction on competition imposed on the vendor;[16]
(c)   resale price maintenance will be a restriction on competition since it fetters the freedom of the customer to sell in the market place;[17]
(d)   an agreement between competitors to enter into a joint venture for the development and production of a joint product may restrict competition between the parties.[18]

1.2.6 De minimis

An agreement which effects trade between Member States and restricts competition may nevertheless not fall within Article 85(1) if it can be shown that neither is effected to an appreciable extent.[19]

In 1970 the Commission published its Notice concerning agreements of minor importance and this was amended in December 1994.[20] The Notice indicates that the

14   *AOIP/Beyrard* 1976 OJ L6/8; c/f *Hugin v Commission*: 22/78 [1979] ECR 1869.
15   Regulation 1983/83 1983 OJ L173/1 – see section 3.2.3 below.
16   *AOIP/Beyrard* (ibid).
17   *Groupement des Fabricants de Papiers peints de Belgique v Commission*: 73/74 [1975] ECR 1491.
18   *VW/Man* 1983 OJ L376/11.
19   *Volk v Vervaecke*: 5/69 [1969] ECR 295.
20   (1994) OJ C368/20.

Commission holds the view that agreements between undertakings engaged in the production or distribution of goods do not fall under the prohibition of Article 85(1) if:

(a)   the products which are the subject of the agreement and other products of the participating undertakings considered by consumers to be similar by reason of their characteristics, price or use do not represent in the substantial part of the Common Market more than 5% of the total market for such product; and

(b)   the aggregate annual turnover of the participating undertakings does not exceed 300 million units of account (currently approximately £200 million).

This Notice should be treated with caution:

(a)   the definition of the product and/or its geographical market may not be clear and the Commission has a reputation for defining markets narrowly. Accordingly, the parties may find themselves over the market share threshold with a narrowly defined market;

(b)   the turnover assessment is based on the worldwide turnover of the group of which the particular undertaking may form part. Companies within the same group are widely defined;

(c)   market share and turnover may change through business expansion, merger or acquisition so that reliance upon the Notice in the context of medium- to long-term planning may not be possible.

1.2.7   Article 85(2) – infringing agreements shall be void

Agreements which infringe Article 85(1) and are not eligible for exemption under Article 85(3) (as to which see below) are void from their inception under Article 85(2) and as such unenforceable in the civil courts of the Member States. In addition, parties to such an agreement are exposed to the risk of fines being imposed by the European Commission and (possibly) claims for damages before the national courts (see section 2.6.4 below).

1.2.8   Nullity applies only to those clauses of the agreement which fall within the prohibition of Article 85(1). Thus to the extent that the anti-competitive restrictions are severable from the agreement as a whole, then the remainder of the agreement will be valid. Whether the agreement will survive the deletion of the anti-competitive provisions is a matter to be determined by the relevant national law. Under English law, the issue is whether the deleted clauses so alter the terms of the agreement between the parties that it ceases to be the sort of contract that the parties intended to enter into at all. If such a change is involved, then severance will not be available (*Chemidus Wavin v Teri*).[21]

1.2.9   Article 85(3) exemptions

Article 85(3) provides that Article 85(1) may be 'declared inapplicable' in respect of an agreement:

'Which contributes to improving the production or distribution of goods or to promote technical or economic progress whilst allowing consumers a fair share of the resulting benefit, and which does not:

21 [1978] 3 CMLR 514, CA.

(a) impose on the undertakings concerned restrictions which are not indispensable to the attainment of these objectives;

(b) afford such undertakings the possibility of eliminating competition in respect of a substantial part of the products in question.'

1.2.10 The authority with *sole* power to grant exemption under Article 85(3) is the European Commission in Brussels. There are two types of exemption:

(a) an individual exemption;

(b) a group or block exemption.

1.2.11 Individual exemptions

An individual exemption is granted by the Commission after examining the agreement in question and giving a ruling on the application of the economic benefits described in Article 85(3). The Commission's ruling is then normally published in a formal Decision in the Official Journal of the European Communities.[1]

1.2.12 Notification and negative clearance

With one exception, an agreement will only qualify for an exemption under Article 85(3) if it is notified to the Commission. Parties to an agreement can also make an application for 'negative clearance', ie that the agreement does not fall within Article 85(1) independently of notification, but in practice the official Form A/B provides for an application for negative clearance and for exemption under Article 85(3) expressed in the alternative.

1.2.13 The exception to the notification rule is found in Article 4(2) of Regulation 17/62 which gives the right to the application of Article 85(3) without notification where:

'(1) the only parties thereto are undertakings from one Member State and the agreements, decisions or practices do not relate either to imports or to exports between Member States;

(2) not more than two undertakings are party thereto, and the agreements only:

    (a) restrict the freedom of one party to the contract in determining the prices or conditions of business upon which the goods which he has obtained from the other party to the contract may be resold; or

    (b) impose restrictions on the exercise of the rights of the assignee or use of industrial property rights – in particular patents, utility models, designs or trade marks – or of the person entitled under a contract to the assignment, or grant, of the right to use a method of manufacture or knowledge relating to the use and to the application of industrial processes;

(3) they have as their sole object:

    (a) the development or uniform application of standards or types; or

    (b) joint research and development;

---

1 Rather than proceed to a formal decision, the parties may agree to accept an informal 'comfort' letter confirming the Commission's view that the agreement in question does not infringe.

(c)   specialisation in the manufacture of products, including agreements necessary for the achievement of this; whether the products which are the subject of specialisation do not in a substantial part of the Common Market, represent more than 15% of the volume of business done in identical products or those considered by the consumers to be similar by reason of their characteristics, price and use, and where the total annual turnover of the participating undertakings does not exceed 200 million units of account.'

1.2.14   Group exemptions

To reduce the administrative burden of individual examination of every application for exemption, the Commission has power to introduce group exemptions, exempting categories of agreements which satisfy established criteria.

Current group exemptions

1983/83 — exclusive distribution
1984/83 — exclusive purchasing
2349/84 — patent licensing[2]
1475/95 — selective distribution for motor vehicles and spare parts
417/85 — specialisation agreements
418/85 — joint research and development
4087/88 — franchise agreements
556/89 — know-how licensing agreements[2]
3932/92 — insurance agreements.

1.3   Abuse of market power

1.3.1   Article 86 prohibits the abuse by one or more undertakings of a dominant position within the Common Market or in a substantial part of it in so far as it may affect trade between Member States. Thus it is necessary to establish:

(a)   the existence of a dominant position within the Common Market or in a substantial part of it;
(b)   an effect on trade between Member States (see criteria under Article 85);
(c)   an abuse of the dominant position.

1.3.2   The existence of a dominant position

The term 'dominant position' is not defined in the Treaty but was defined by the Commission in *United Brands*[3] as follows:

'Undertakings are in a dominant position when they have the power to behave independently, without taking into account to any substantial extent their competitors, purchasers and suppliers. Such is the case where an undertaking's market share either in itself or when combined with its know-how, access to raw materials, capital or other major advantages such as trade mark ownership, enables it to determine the price or to control the production or distribution of a significant part of the relevant goods it is not necessary for

2 These Regulations will expire on 31 December 1995 and are to be replaced by a single Technology Transfer Regulation.
3 *United Brands* 1976 OJ L95/1; on appeal *United Brands v Commission*: 27/76 [1978] ECR 207.

the undertaking to have total dominance such as would deprive all other market participants of their commercial freedom as long as it is strong enough in general terms to
devise its own strategy as it wishes, even if there are differences in the extent to which it
dominates individual sub-markets.'

1.3.3 Defining the market

Market share is clearly an important factor in determining dominance although it is
not necessarily conclusive. Relative market share is as important as absolute market
share. Thus, a company with considerably less than 50% of the relevant market may
be dominant if all its competitors have very much smaller market shares. Similarly,
dominance can exist in relation to an extremely narrowly defined product group, eg
spare parts for the main product,[4] or may be exerted over a specific group of customers during a period of emergency.[5] In general terms it may be said that the
Commission invariably define product markets narrowly so that it should not be
assumed that dominance is a risk only for a few multi-national monopolists.[6]

1.3.4 To establish the existence of a dominant position, there must be a definition
of the product market and of the geographical market and in this analysis consideration must be given to the economic tests such as market substitutability, cross
substitutability of demand, barriers to entry. So far as the geographical market is
concerned, the boundaries will be delineated by the area within which market conditions are broadly similar. As in the case of product market definition the
Commission and the Court has shown a willingness to define geographical market
and what constitutes a 'substantial part' of the market very narrowly.[7]

1.3.5 The abuse

Article 86 sets out examples of conduct which may be deemed abusive:

'(a) directly or indirectly imposing unfair purchase or selling prices or other unfair trading conditions;
(b) limiting production, markets or technical development to the prejudice of consumers;
(c) applying dissimilar conditions to equivalent transactions with other trading parties,
thereby placing them at a competitive disadvantage;
(d) making the conclusion of contracts subject to acceptance by the other parties of
supplementary obligations which, by their nature or according to commercial
usage, have no connection with the subject of such contracts.'

These examples are for the purpose of illustration only and any conduct which is
perceived as improper exploitation of the market power of a dominant enterprise,
will be found to infringe. For example:

4 *Hugin/Lipton* (ibid) (Hugin was found to be dominant in the market for spare parts in its own cash
  registers).
5 *ABG/BP* 1977 OJ L117/1; on appeal *BP v Commission*: 77/77 [1978] ECR 1513; [1978] 3 CMLR 174.
6 See, for example, *BSI / Boosey & Hawkes* 1987 OJ L286/36 (British style brass band instruments
  distinguished from ordinary brass band instruments), *Michelin* 1981 OJ L353/33 (new replacement
  tyres for cars distinguished from new tyres for OEM, remould tyres and tyres for vans), *Charles
  Jourdan* 1989 OJ L35/31 (expensive men's shoes).
7 *Sugar Cartel* OJ 1973 L140/17 CMLR D65 (Bavaria constitutes a substantial part of the Common
  Market); *British Midland v Aer Lingus* [1993] 4 CMLR 596 (scheduled flights between Dublin and
  English Airports), *Sealink / B & I* (1992) 5 CMLR 255 (Holyhead harbour).

(a) refusals to supply;
(b) excessive discriminatory and predatory pricing;
(c) tie in sales and purchases;
(d) loyalty rebates.

1.3.6 Negative clearance

As in the case of Article 85, it is possible (although unusual) for a company to seek a negative clearance to the effect that any particular action by it will not infringe Article 86.

1.4 The relationship with the national laws of Member States

1.4.1 Articles 85 and 86 are directly applicable in Member States and as such the national laws are required to apply them as part of domestic law.[8] In the event of conflict between national law and EEC law, it is well established that EEC law will prevail.

1.4.2 National courts must therefore consider issues of EC competition law; in cases of doubt they *can* (and in the case of the ultimate Court of Appeal, *must*) refer questions of the interpretation of Community law to the European Court of Justice under Article 177 of the EEC Treaty for a preliminary ruling.

1.4.3 There is therefore clear jurisdiction for the national courts to determine whether an agreement infringes Article 85 or a particular course of conduct infringes Article 86 and therefore to declare the agreement void or order that the abuse cease[9] as the case may be. It seems also that national courts would be competent to award damages or other remedies for infringements of EC competition law although this will depend on whether national law allows a claim in damages for breach of statutory duty (see section 2.6.4 below).

2 ENFORCEMENT

2.1 Enforcement authorities

2.1.1 The EC Commission

Primary responsibility for the enforcement of EC competition law rests with the EC Commission based in Brussels. The Commission has the duty to ensure the proper functioning and development of the Common Market and the compliance with the rules established under the EEC Treaty (Article 155, EEC Treaty). It is divided into a number of Directorates General, Directorate General IV being responsible for the application of the EC rules of competition. DG IV is itself divided into a number of Directorates:

---

8 *BRT v SABAM*: 127/73 [1974] ECR 51, [1974] 2 CMLR 238.
9 See, for example, *Chemidus Wavin v Teri* [1978] 3 CMLR 514, CA; *ECS/Akzo*.

Directorate A — policy
Directorate B — deals with cartels, dominant positions and discriminatory or restrictive practices generally (but excluding energy and steel)
Directorate C — joint ventures, mergers, steel etc
Directorate E — state aids.

2.1.2   The Merger Task Force

A separate division within DG IV with responsibility for applying and enforcing Merger Regulation under Council Regulation 4064/89 (see section 4 below).

2.1.3   The Court of First Instance

The first tier of appellate jurisdiction with power to hear appeals from the decision of the Commission under Article 173 of action against the Commission based on its failure to act under Article 175.

2.1.4   The European Court of Justice

The Supreme Court with power (inter alia) to hear appeals from the Court of First Instance and to give preliminary rulings concerning the interpretation of the EEC Treaty from the national courts.

2.1.5   The national courts of the Member States

The EC rules of competition are directly effective within each of the Member States and breach of such rules accordingly give rise to a cause of action before national courts for breach of statutory duty.[10]

2.2   Jurisdictional rules

2.2.1   The Commission has jurisdiction to investigate competition law infringements giving rise to anti-competitive effects on trade between Member States. It has *exclusive* jurisdiction in connection with the granting of exemptions under Article 85(3). Because the competition rules are directly effective within the Member States, the national courts of the Member States have concurrent jurisdiction with the Commission in relation to all aspects of the enforcement of EC competition rules save for exemptions under Article 85(3) referred to above.[11]

2.2.2   In cases of conflict, Community law takes precedence over the domestic law of a Member State and Member States are obliged to ensure that such rights can be freely exercised.

2.2.3   The Commission Notice on co-operation between national courts and the

---

10 As to remedies before national courts see section 2.6.4 below.
11 Further special exemptions to this rule are agreements having 'provisional validity' (ie agreements entered into prior to 13 March 1962 or before the relevant accession date) and agreements relating to air transport within third countries.

Commission[12] sets out the approach to be adopted by the courts in dealing with cases involving Community law with the emphasis on seeking to avoid inconsistent decisions. This Notice followed the judgment of the ECJ in the *Delimitis* case[13] in which the national court was advised to adopt the following approach in considering the application of Article 85:

(a)   if Article 85(1) is manifestly *not* applicable, and there is no *real risk* of the Commission taking a different view, the court may proceed to give its ruling;

(b)   if there has been a *clear* infringement of Article 85(1) and, in the light of relevant block exemptions and previous decisions and practice of the Commission, an Article 85(3) exemption *would not possibly* be available, the court may proceed to give its ruling;

(c)   if the action under review *might* benefit from an exemption the national court may stay proceedings or adopt interim measures to maintain the status quo pending such exemption;

(d)   even if the grant of an exemption is unlikely, the national court *may* still elect to grant a stay or grant interim measures or an injunction where it considers that there is a *risk of inconsistent decisions*, eg by reason of notification of the agreement under review or of a complaint having been lodged with the Commission.

2.3   Commission investigations

2.3.1   A Commission investigation can be triggered by:

(a)   *notification* of a particular agreement or conduct; or

(b)   *complaint* by a third party alleging an infringement; or

(c)   *own motion investigation* by the Commission acting on its own initiative.

2.3.2   In practice, much of the investigatory process is carried out informally with the Commission requesting and receiving information concerning the infringement from the alleged infringer and from third parties.

2.3.3   Nevertheless, Regulation 17/62 confers wide powers of investigation on the Commission and in particular:

(a)   to *request information* from any national authority or undertaking (Article 11); and

(b)   to make *on-the-spot enquiries* for the purpose of examining business records and taking copies thereof and to ask for all explanations (Article 14).

Example:

National Panasonic[14] – on-the-spot investigation carried out without prior warning, *AM & S Europe*[15] – request for information – extent of legal professional privilege.

---

12   1993 OJ C39/6.
13   C-234/89: [1991] I ECR I-935.
14   *National Panasonic v Commission*: 155/79 [1980] ECR 2033.
15   *AM & S Europe Ltd v Commission*: 155/79 [1982] ECR 1575.

2.3.4 The Statement of Objection

Having established the alleged infringement to its satisfaction, the Commission may then proceed to prepare a Statement of Objection which will be sent to the enterprises concerned informing them of the objections and the facts upon which the Commission is to base its decision.

2.3.5 The Oral Hearing

The Commission is obliged to grant an Oral Hearing if it intends to impose a penalty but in practice it invariably holds such a hearing in any case. The hearing is very much part of the administrative process. It is held at the Commission offices and presided over by the hearings officer appointed by the Commission. National representatives on the Advisory Committee attend and are able to ask questions. Furthermore, the Complainant (if any) will normally be invited to attend the hearing except for those parts in which confidential information of the alleged infringer is to be discussed.

2.3.6 The Advisory Committee on Restrictive Practices and Monopolies

Following the Oral Hearing, the Commission will prepare a draft Decision which must be submitted to the Advisory Committee on Restrictive Practices and Monopolies. The Committee is comprised of experts in the field appointed by each of the Member States usually on secondment from the national cartel authorities. Although the Commission is not bound to follow the Opinion of the Committee, it does ensure that the views of the Member States are considered.

2.3.7 The Decision

The Opinion of the Advisory Committee together with the draft Committee decision is then submitted to the Commissioners who must give their final approval. On being approved, the final Decision is then sent to the infringer. The Commission has wide power to order fines up to 10% of turnover, the termination of practices, reinstatement of suppliers and even divestiture.

2.3.8 The appeal

The undertakings affected by the Decision have the right to appeal against the Commission Decision to the European Court under Article 173 of the EEC Treaty but this does not have suspensory effect. In order to postpone the effect of the Decision, the defendant must, after lodging the appeal, make a separate application for interim measures to the court, seeking suspension of the effects of the Decision pending the hearing.

2.4 Fines and other sanctions

The Commission has power under Article 15(2) of Regulation 17/62 to impose fines of up to one million units of account or 10% of the turnover for the previous year for deliberate or negligent infringements of Article 85 or 86. It is extremely difficult in decided cases to determine the basis upon which the Commission's calculation of fines is made although it is clear that fines are getting heavier. In the *Pioneer* case[16] for example, Pioneer and its European distributors were fined a total of nearly ECU 9 million (approximately £4.5 million) for the maintenance of export bans. More recently, in *Tetrapak*,[17] an Article 86 case, the company was fined ECU 75 million (approximately £47 million) for various anti-competitive abuses.

2.5   Exemptions

Agreements may be exempted from the prohibition under Article 85(1) by individual exemption on notification or by application of one of the group exemptions (see section 1.2.14 above).

2.6   Third party rights

2.6.1   A third party suffering damage as a result of an infringement of the EC competition rules has three options available to him:

(a)   he may lodge a complaint with the Commission relating to the alleged infringement;
(b)   issue proceedings in the national court of a Member State; or
(c)   take action under (a) and (b) above concurrently.

2.6.2   *Complaint*

Article 3(2) Regulation 17/62 provides that Member States or any national or legal person claiming 'a legitimate interest' is entitled to lodge a Complaint with the Commission in respect of an alleged infringement of Article 85 or 86. The Complaint need not be in any particular form and can be by way of a simple letter.

The Commission has a legal duty to investigate all Complaints and the Complainant is entitled to demand that the Commission adopt a formal Decision on the Complaint which is capable of judicial review under Article 173. If the Commission fails to do so then the Complainant can bring proceedings under Article 175 on the basis of the Commission's failure to act. It is important to note that in proceedings under Article 173 or 175 the aggrieved party must bring their action within two months of the offending Decision or within two months of the Commission having failed to act after having been invited to do so within a period of two months.

2.6.3   *Interim measures*

In the *Camera Care* case,[18] the ECJ held that the Commission has power to grant interim measures which are broadly equivalent to an injunction obtainable in a national court. Interim measures may be specifically applied for by a Complainant

---

16 *Pioneer* 1980 OJ L60/21; [1980] 1 CMLR 457.
17 *Tetrapak* 1992 OJ L290/35; [1992] 4 CMLR M81.
18 *Camera Care v Commission*: 792/79R [1980] ECR 119.

or granted by the Commission on its own initiative. The criteria applied by the Commission in granting interim measures are as follows:[19]

(a) prime facie infringement of Community competition rules;
(b) proven urgency;
(c) serious and irreparable damage or damage intolerable for the public interest.

The measures must be temporary and conservatory and must not exceed what is necessary to achieve that objective.

2.6.4 *Proceedings in the national courts*

As stated above, the national courts have concurrent jurisdiction with the Commission in cases involving the EC rules of competition. The pleading of a breach of EC competition rules will adopt the form appropriate within the relevant jurisdiction for a breach of statutory duty.

The EEC Treaty makes no provision for third party remedies in respect of a breach of the EC rules of competition. Accordingly the nature and extent of remedies for such breach is a matter for determination in accordance with the national law in the jurisdiction in which the action is pursued.[20]

3 CHECKLIST OF POTENTIAL INFRINGEMENTS

3.1 Agency

3.1.1 A commercial agency agreement will exist where the supplier (principal) appoints an agent to procure business or to transact business for and on behalf of the principal. The Commission's Notice on Exclusive Agency Contracts with commercial agents published in 1962[1] indicated that agency agreements would not normally be caught by Article 85(1) because the agent is not acting as an independent trader but is essentially an extension of the principal's sales operation. As such, the agent could not be treated as an independent 'undertaking' and thus there is no agreement between 'undertakings' as is required under Article 85(1).

3.1.2 This reasoning was endorsed by the *Sugar Cartel* case.[2] Subsequent decisions of the Commission and the ECJ have, however, shown a retreat from this liberal approach towards agency. Article 85(1) may apply if the agent in fact acts as an independent entity in relation to the agency. Thus in *Pittsburgh Corning*[3] the Commission held that Article 85(1) would only not apply if the agent was a true auxiliary fully integrated into the principal's sales operation. Similarly, in

---

19 *La Cinq v Commission*: T-44/90 [1992] ECR II-1.
20 In *Garden Cottage Foods v Milk Marketing Board* [1984] AC 130, the English House of Lords indicated by a majority that a remedy in damages was likely to arise in respect of a breach of Article 86. An injunction for breach in a number of English cases, eg *Cutsforth v Mansfield Inns* [1986] 1 WLR 558.
1 1962 OJ L139/2921. The Commission is in the process of preparing a fresh Notice on commercial agency which is likely to restrict the extent of non-application of Article 85(1) to agents integrated into the principal's marketing system.
2 OJ 1973 L140/17 [1973] CMLR D65.
3 OJ 1972 L272/35 [1973] CMLR D2.

VVR v Social Dienst,[4] the ECJ found that travel agents acting for large numbers of tour operators were acting as independent traders and agreements between travel agents and tour operators fell within Article 85(1).

The fact that an agent represents more than one principal does not necessarily prevent the agent being treated as an auxiliary of his principals in relation to each agency. In each case it is necessary to consider the degree of economic independence enjoyed by the agent in the context of the particular agency.

3.1.3 To the extent that an agency falls within Article 85(1), the following restrictions are likely to be restrictions in competition with the definition set out in Article 85(1):

(a)   territorial exclusivity;
(b)   restriction on sales by agent out of territory;
(c)   restriction on sales by principal in territory;
(d)   customer allocation provisions;
(e)   imposition of variable commission rates to discourage extra-territorial sales;
(f)   unreasonable restraint of trade provisions both pre- and post-termination.

3.2   Distribution

3.2.1 A distribution agreement is distinguished from an agency agreement by virtue of the fact that the distributor purchases the contract products for resale as distinct from an agent who does not purchase stock but merely procures sales for his principal in return for a commission.

3.2.2 A distribution agreement will normally be seen to enhance rather than restrict competition by increasing the sources of outlets for a particular product. Typically, the following provisions in distribution agreements will involve restrictions on competition:

(a)   territorial exclusivity;
(b)   restriction on supplier's sales in territory;
(c)   restriction on distributor's sales out of territory;
(d)   restriction on distributor manufacturing or selling competing goods;
(e)   pre- and post-termination non-compete provision.

3.2.3 The Commission has long recognised the positive benefits of exclusive distribution in the efficient marketing of products and accordingly Regulation 1983/83 grants a group exemption to exclusive distribution agreements which satisfy the following conditions:

(a)   only two parties (company and principal shareholder and parent and subsidiary are treated as one party for this purpose);
(b)   goods for resale;
(c)   grant of exclusivity (ie the group exemption does not apply to non-exclusive distributorship agreements which will have to be individually notified if they contain anti-competitive restrictions);
(d)   agreement does not involve the granting of reciprocal distribution rights between

4   311/85: [1987] ECR 3801.

actual or potential competitors or a non-reciprocal distribution agreement where the distributor has a turnover in excess of ECU 100 million (£70,000).

3.2.4 Regulation 1983/83 permits the following obligations:

On supplier — not to appoint other distributors or sell to users in the territory.
On distributor — not to manufacture or distribute competing goods;
— to obtain contract goods for resale only from supplier;
— to refrain from active selling outside territory;
— to purchase minimum quantities and maintain stock;
— to use supplier's trademark, get-up and packaging etc;
— to promote.

3.2.5 Provided the distribution agreement satisfies the criteria for the application of Regulation 1983/83 described in section 3.2.3 and does not contain restrictions on competition beyond those outlined in section 3.2.4 the group exemption will apply without the need for notification. In all other cases, if the agreement involves restrictions on competition and the parties seek an exemption, the agreement will have to be notified.

3.3 Selective distribution

3.3.1 Selective distribution arises where a supplier wishes to restrict the number of dealers who may sell his goods whether to limit the quantity of outlets or to ensure the quality of outlets.

3.3.2 In general terms, selective distribution systems will not infringe Article 85(1) if the selection is based solely on *objective qualitative criteria*, ie that the dealer has the sales facilities, sales staff and expertise 'appropriate' to the nature and quality of the contract goods. If selection extends to *quantitative* criteria which limit the number of dealers to a given territory, eg by imposing minimum ordering levels or restricting appointment by sales area, Article 85(1) will apply but, provided that the contract goods 'justify' selective distribution treatment, an individual exemption under Article 85(3) may be granted.

3.3.3 The Commission has approved the use of selective distribution systems in relation to luxury products such as perfumes, expensive watches and china.[5] Selective distribution has also been permitted in relation to 'high tech' products with significant post-sales servicing requirements such as TVs, cars and personal computers.[6] On the other hand, selective distribution has been refused for plumbing equipment and moisturising cream.[7]

3.3.4 The only group exemption for selective distribution is for motor vehicles, EC Regulation 1475/95.[8] In all other cases of selective distribution imposing

5 *The Perfume cases* [1980] ECR 2327, 2481 and 2511 (luxury perfume); *Omega* (1970) JO L242/22 (watches); *Villeroy & Boch* (1985) OJ L376/15 (china).
6 *Metro v Commission*: 26/76 [1977] ECR 1875 (televisions); *BMW* (1975) OJ L29/1 (cars); *IBM Personal Computer* (1984) OJ L118/24 (PC's).
7 *Ideal - Standard* (1985) OJ L20/38 (plumbing equipment); *Vichy* (1991) OJ L75/57.
8 (1995) OJ C145/25.

restrictions on competition, an exemption will require notification for individual exemption unless Article 4(2) of Regulation 17/62 applies.[9]

3.3.5 Regulation 1475/95 permits the following obligations on selective distribution for motor vehicles:

On supplier	— to supply within a defined territory of the Common Market only to one or a number of specified resellers motor cars or spare parts therefor; — not to supply within territory direct.
On distributor	— restriction on resale to 'unauthorised' resellers (except spare parts for repairs to subject cars); — restriction on sales to 'intermediaries' for customers without written authorisation; — restriction on manufacturing contract goods or selling competing goods; — actively seeking sales out of territory; — obligation to observe minimum sales standards; — obligation to maintain stock and achieve minimum sales; — obligation to carry out guarantee work.

3.4   Exclusive purchasing

3.4.1 An exclusive purchasing agreement imposes on a reseller the obligation to buy certain goods for resale only from the supplier. Such a restriction is an anti-competitive restriction but may be exempted under EC Regulation 1984/83 or by individual exemption on notification.

3.4.2 Regulation 1984/83 grants a group exemption for general forms of exclusive purchasing (Title I) and for two special forms of exclusive purchasing: beer supply agreements (Title II) and service station agreements (Title III). Title I sets out criteria for the application of the block exemption virtually identical to that for exclusive distributions under Regulation 1983/83[10] with the added requirements that

(a)   the exclusive purchasing obligations must be limited to products by their nature or commercial usage 'connected' to each other; and
(b)   the agreement is concluded for five years or less.

3.5   Franchising

3.5.1 Franchising involves the grant of a licence by the owner of a marketing system of the right to exploit that marketing system and is often granted with an exclusive purchasing obligation in respect of proprietary products supplied by the licensor and sold under the marketing system, eg McDonald's Restaurant, Benetton Knitwear.

9 See section 1.2.13 above.
10 See section 3.2 above.

3.5.2 In the *Pronuptia* case,[11] the ECJ held that the grant of a licence in respect of the franchise marketing system with all intellectual property rights coupled with the necessary obligations designed to preserve confidentiality and those proprietary rights did not infringe Article 85(1). Similarly, obligations designed to maintain the reputation of the marketing system would not infringe Article 85(1). On the other hand, the grant of territorial exclusivity for franchisees and restrictions preventing franchisees from competing on price will be caught by Article 85(1). Following the ECJ judgment in *Pronuptia*, the Commission introduced a group exemption for franchising EC Regulation 4087/88.[12]

3.5.3 Regulation 4087/88 provides a group exemption for franchise agreements (and master agreements) as defined which include the following obligations:

On franchiser — not to sell or exploit franchise into franchisee's territory;
— not to appoint others to do so.
On franchisee — not to exploit franchise outside contract premises or contract territory;
— not to manufacture or sell competing goods or services;
— to comply with quality standards;
— to sell only franchiser's goods or services where impracticable to apply objective quality specification;
— not to engage in a competing activity during the period of the franchise and for 12 months thereafter;
— not to sell other than to the end consumer and other network franchisees;
— to purchase minimum quantities and maintain stock.

Other obligations relating to confidentiality, maintenance of standards and non-assignment are also permissible.

3.5.4 Article 5 contains a list of prohibited clauses which include a no-challenge clause in respect of intellectual property rights, restriction on pricing, a tie in respect of goods not justified on objective grounds and franchises between competing suppliers.

3.6 Intellectual property licensing

3.6.1 National laws concerning intellectual property rights, eg trademarks, patents, copyright and similar rights, are laws restricting the import and export of goods across national boundaries. As such they must be considered first of all under Community law in the context of Articles 30–36 of the EEC Treaty which deals with the free movement of goods.

3.6.2 Article 30 prohibits quantitative restrictions and measures having equivalent effect on imports and exports between Member States. National laws protecting intellectual property rights do fall within the prohibition under Article 30 but are excluded by virtue of Article 36 which provides that if the measure is justified on grounds of the protection of 'Industrial and Commercial Property' the

11 161/84: [1986] ECR 353.
12 (1988) OJ L359/46.

prohibition under Article 30 will not be applicable provided that 'the prohibitions or restrictions shall not . . . constitute a means of arbitrary discrimination or a disguised restriction on trade between Member States'.

3.6.3 The European Court of Justice has reconciled the apparent conflict between national laws protecting intellectual property rights and Article 30 by distinguishing between the 'existence' and the 'exercise' of such rights. The application of rules protecting the existence of rights is permissible under Article 36 but the exercise of such rights may be qualified by the provision of the Treaty.[13]

3.6.4 So far as the competition rules are concerned, the licensing of intellectual property rights will most frequently give rise to potential restrictions under Article 85(1). There is a group exemption for patent licensing agreements (EC Regulation 2349/84) and a very similar group exemption for know-how licences (EC Regulation 556/89).[14] No group exemption yet exists for other forms of intellectual property right licensing such as trademarks and copyright so that licences containing restrictions on competition would normally require notification to the Commission if an exemption is sought. However, the restriction permitted in the context of patents and know-how may provide guidance as to the Commission's likely response.

3.6.5 Regulation 2349/84 applies to patent licences which may also include ancillary know-how. Regulation 556/89 applies to industrial/technical know-how licences which may also include ancillary patents. As stated above, both group exemptions are similar but the main restrictions permitted in the context of patent licensing are as follows:

Obligations as licensor — not to license others in the licensed territory whilst patents subsist;
— not to exploit in licensed territory himself whilst patents subsist.
Obligations as licensee — not to exploit in territories reserved to licensor or other licensees whilst patents subsist;
— not to actively market outside licensed territory;
— not to sell in territories licensed to other licensees for a period not exceeding five years from the date when the product is first put on the EC market by the licensor or with his consent provided products covered by patents in the territory.

3.6.6 Article 2 of Regulation 2349/84 lists further permissible obligations on the basis that they do not generally restrict competition. These include obligations to tie purchase of products to supplier where essential for 'technically satisfactory' exploitation patent, an obligation to pay minimum royalties or produce minimum stock, to restrict field of use, to grant non-exclusive licences on improvements and to apply 'most favoured licensee' provisions.

3.6.7 Article 3 of Regulation 2349/84 sets out a list of clauses which would result

---

13 *Consten & Grundig v Commission*: 56, 58/64 [1966] ECR 299.
14 These Regulations are due to expire on 31 December 1995 and are to be replaced by a single 'Technology Transfer' Group Exemption.

in the licence being excluded from the group exemption. These include a no-challenge clause (but without prejudice to the right of the licensor to terminate in the event of challenge) the extension of the licence beyond the life of the patents (unless subject to an annual right of termination for the licensee), restrictions on prices, production volumes or categories of customer to whom the licensee may sell, the imposition of royalties on products not covered by the patents.

3.6.8 Article 4 involves an opposition procedure conferring the benefit of the group exemption on licences with restrictions going beyond those expressly permitted but which are not included in Article 3. In such cases, the licence must be notified but exemption can be assumed if the Commission fails to respond within six months.

3.6.9 Although the holding of an intellectual property right will not, of itself, constitute a dominant position, the exercise of intellectual property rights may constitute an abuse of a dominant position under Article 86. Thus, the refusal of a television company to grant a copyright licence for advance programme information has been held to be a breach of Article 86.[15]

3.7 Refusals to supply

3.7.1 A refusal to supply will not of itself constitute a breach of Article 85 unless it can be shown to have been brought about by the existence of an agreement to impede trade between Member States which is not the subject of an individual or group exemption.[16]

3.7.2 A truly unilateral refusal to supply may, however, constitute an infringement of Article 86 if it cannot be justified on objective grounds.[17]

3.8 Price restrictions

3.8.1 As indicated above, both Articles 85(1) and 86 include amongst listed examples of restrictions of competition or abuse:

(a) directly or indirectly fixing purchase or selling prices or any other trading conditions;
(b) applying dissimilar conditions to equivalent transactions.

3.8.2 Resale price maintenance which in any event is likely to be illegal for most products under the laws of most Member States will infringe both Article 85(1) and 86 and is unlikely to merit exemption under Article 85(3).

3.8.3 Price fixing between competitors is an obvious and serious breach of

15 *Magill TV Guide/ITP, BBC & RTE* 1989 OJ L78/43; *Radio Telefis Eireann v Commission*: T-69/89 [1991] ECR II-485.
16 See, eg, *Ford v Commission*: 25, 26/84 [1985] ECR 2725 in which the apparently unilateral sales policy of Ford in restricting sales of cars to certain dealers was deemed to give rise to an implied agreement within Article 85(1).
17 *Commercial Solvents v Commission*: 6, 7/73 [1974] ECR 223; *United Brands v Commission*: 27/76 [1978] ECR 207.

Article 85(1) often giving rise to the protection of national markets or the effective allocation of customer markets. Price recommendations may also have a similar effect and to the extent that they do will also be treated as an infringement.[18]

3.8.4 Discriminatory pricing, ie the offering of different prices to customers at the same level of distribution, will not ordinarily infringe Article 85(1) unless coupled with other restrictions designed to isolate national markets. This is because in a competitive environment such discriminatory pricing would be limited by parallel imports of products from the low price to high price territories. If, however, such a market mechanism is not available by reason, eg of other trade restrictions or the application of tariff or non-tariff barriers, taxation or duties, differential or discriminatory pricing is likely to infringe.[19]

3.8.5 Discriminatory pricing is more likely to give rise to problems in the context of Article 86 where the existence of a dominant position means that the corrective mechanisms in a normal competitive environment are not present. In particular, the extremes of pricing discrimination such as excessive pricing (pricing in excess of 'economic value')[20] or predatory pricing (pricing designed to eliminate a competitor)[1] or loyalty rebating (discounts linked to purchasing loyalty as compared with volume purchases).[2]

3.9   Tie in sales

The tying of an obligation to purchase a product or service in an agreement in respect of the supply of other products or the licensing of intellectual property rights may be an infringement of Article 85(1) where the products are neither by their nature nor according to commercial usage connected to each other or are not necessary for the effective technical satisfactory exploitation of the licensed rights. Tie in sales may also constitute an infringement of Article 86 and have been the subject of heavy fines.

3.10   Information exchange

Agreements providing for the exchange of information on such matters as costs, prices, customers etc which would ordinarily be considered confidential business information are likely to infringe Article 85(1), whether between actual or potential competitors,[3] between supplier and distributor[4] or between distributors.[5] However, there would be no objection to the collection or exchange of general information and statistics whether directly or indirectly through a trade association provided that the exchange of such information does not enable actual or potential competitors to anticipate the market behaviour of others.

18 *ICI v Commission*: T-13/89 [1992] ECR II-1021.
19 *Distillers v Commission*: 30/78 [1980] ECR 229.
20 *British Leyland v Commission*: 226/84 [1986] ECR 3263.
 1 *Akzo v Commission*: C-62/86 [1991] ECR I-3359.
 2 *Hoffman La Roche v Commission*: 102/77 [1978] ECR 1139.
 3 *ICI v Commission*: 48/69 [1972] ECR 619.
 4 *SABA* (1976) OJ L28/19.
 5 *Hasselblad* (1982) OJ L161/18.

3.11 Joint buying and selling

Agreements between competitors to establish joint purchasing or selling will invariably require examination under Article 85(1) since they will usually involve the surrender by participants of all or part of their freedom to act in the market. Joint purchasing or selling by a number of small enterprises on a co-operative basis may not give rise to the necessary effect on trade between Member States to give rise to an infringement. Even if the jurisdictional test is satisfied, the chance of an individual exemption for such an agreement between relatively small players in a market are good on the basis that joint purchasing or selling may enable them to compete more effectively against competitors with substantial market shares. On the other hand, joint purchasing by competitors with substantial market shares is unlikely to obtain exemption under Article 85(3).[6]

3.12 Market sharing

Agreements whereby competitors agree to share markets whether territorially or by customer type will invariably infringe Article 85(1) and are unlikely to be exempted.[7] The highest fines have been imposed for infringements of this type and in the recent European *Cement* case[8] fines totalling ECU 248 million were imposed on 30 European cement manufacturers.

3.13 Joint ventures

3.13.1 A distinction must be drawn between 'concentrative' joint ventures which are effectively mergers and are dealt with under the Merger Regulation (see section 4 below) and 'co-operative' joint ventures which fall to be examined under Article 85(1).

3.13.2 A joint venture will be 'concentrative' if it 'performs on a lasting basis all the functions of an autonomous entity'.[9] In addition the joint venture must not involve the co-ordination of competitive behaviour. In the absence of both these criteria, the joint venture will be deemed co-operative and as such governed by Article 85(1).

3.13.3 A co-operative joint venture between actual or potential competitors whether involving joint research and development, specialisation or joint market-ing is likely to fall within Article 85(1) since the co-ordination of competitive behaviour is implicit. The Commission generally takes a positive view towards joint ventures in granting individual exemptions particularly where joint research and development is involved or the opportunity for technology transfer for the ben-efit of Community industry. There are group exemptions for specialisation joint ventures (Regulation 417/85) and for research and development joint ventures (Regulation 418/85).

---

6 *National Sulphuric Acid Association* (1980) OJ L260/24; *CSV* (1978) OJ L242/15.
7 *BP Kemi / DDSF* (1979) OJ L286/32.
8 *Cement* (1994) OJ L343/1.
9 For a detailed commentary on the distinction between concentrative and co-operative joint ventures see the Commission Notice on the subject: (1994) OJ C385/1.

4   CONCENTRATIONS, MERGERS AND ACQUISITIONS

4.1   Introduction

4.1.1   Merger control on an EC wide basis was introduced by Council Regulation 4067/89[10] 'on control of concentrations between undertakings' which was adopted on 21 December 1989 and came into force on 21 September 1990.

4.1.2   The Merger Regulation lays down the substantive rules for Community merger control but is supplemented by Commission Regulation 2367/90[11] ('the Administrative Regulation') which deals with the administration of the control system in respect of notifications, time limits and hearings. Annex 1 to the administration Regulation contains Form CO, setting out the information required by the Commission on a pre-merger notification.

4.1.3   The Commission has also published two Notices providing guidance on the interpretation of the Merger Regulation:

(a)   a Notice on ancillary restrictions;[12]
(b)   a Notice regarding concentrative and co-operative operations.[13]

Such Notices do not have the force of law. However, they do indicate the policy of the Commission and will be factors of which a national court may take note.

4.1.4   In contrast to the European Steel and Coal Treaty,[14] the EEC Treaty contains no specific merger control provision. Prior to the adoption of the Merger Regulation a limited opportunity to review mergers existed under Article 86 through the principles established by the European Court of Justice in the *Continental Can* case.[15] In that case, the ECJ held that the acquisition by a dominant firm of a competitor was capable of constituting an abuse of a dominant position within Article 86. More recently, in the *Phillip Morris* case,[16] the ECJ approved the Commission's use of Article 85 in relation to mergers adopting the view that in certain circumstances an agreement to acquire a competitor might well give rise to restrictions on competition even in a non-dominant situation. These judgments, and particularly the most recent *Phillip Morris* case, provided the necessary impetus to the Council of Ministers to adopt a comprehensive EC merger control system and as will be seen, a condition of the adoption of the Merger Regulation was that Articles 85 and 86 would be largely disapplied from merger situations.

4.1.5   The Community authority with responsibility for applying the Merger Regulation is the 'Merger Task Force' which although within Directorate General IV is a

10   1989 OJ L395/1.
11   1990 OJ L219.
12   1990 OJ C203.
13   (1994) OJ C385/1.
14   ECSC Treaty, Article 66 provides that any transaction shall, subject to certain exceptions, require prior authorisation of the Commission if it has in itself the direct or indirect effect of bringing about a concentration between undertakings at least one of which is an undertaking to which the ECSC Treaty applies.
15   *Europemballage Corp and Continental Can v Commission*: 6/72 [1973] ECR 215.
16   *BAT and Reynalds v Commission*: 142, 156/84 [1987] ECR 4487.

separate Directorate operating as a discrete and fully independent section. The Merger Task Force is always willing to provide informal guidance on the scope and application of the Merger Regulation and operates a helpline for such enquiries in Brussels (tel: 32 2 236 5040).

4.2 The scope of the regulation

4.2.1 The Merger Regulation will apply to those concentrations having 'a community dimension'. The word concentration includes all mergers, acquisitions and takeovers and joint ventures of a 'concentrative' nature. Concentrations not having a Community dimension will continue to be regulated only by the national authorities of the Member States. The point at which jurisdiction over concentrations passes from national authorities to the European Commission is obviously a crucial element. The Merger Regulation adopts a turnover criteria on the basis that it represents the most objective and readily ascertainable measure of size. There are, however, special rules governing banking and insurance institutions.

4.2.2 The turnover threshold is set out in Article 1(2) of the Merger Regulation and breaks down into three separate elements. In order for a concentration to qualify as a Community dimension concentration, the following must be satisfied:

(a)   the combined aggregate worldwide turnover of all undertakings concerned must be at least ECU 5,000 million; and
(b)   the Community wide turnover of each of at least two of the undertakings concerned must be more than ECU 250 million; UNLESS
(c)   each of the undertakings concerned achieves more than two thirds of its aggregate Community wide turnover within one and the same Member State.

Accordingly, even if (a) and (b) above are satisfied, the concentration may still not qualify as a Community dimension merger if all the participating undertakings with a turnover within the Community achieve more than two thirds of that turnover within one Member State.

4.3 Appraisal of concentrations

4.3.1 The criteria set by the Regulation for the appraisal of mergers is, on the face of it, exclusively competition related. Article 2(3) of the Regulation, echoing the phraseology of Article 86, provides that a concentration will not be permitted if it:

'creates or strengthens a dominant position as a result of which effective competition would be significantly impeded in the Common Market or in a substantial part of it . . .'

4.3.2 This approach is entirely consistent with the judgment of the court in *Continental Can*. By using a competition law test as opposed to a public interest or economic test, the Regulation takes up the criterion of a 'dominant position', a notion which has been tried and tested before in the context of Article 86.[17]

---

17 For a definition of the term 'dominant position' see section 1.3.2 above.

4.3.3   Whilst the creation or strengthening of a dominant position is the precondition to the Commission opposing a concentration, this does not mean that it is sufficient on its own. Article 2(1) provides that in making an appraisal as to whether a concentration is compatible with the Common Market, the Commission must have regard to the factors listed in sub-paragraphs (a) and (b). These factors include not only those related to the competitive environment within the Community but also include:

(a)   the state of competition from outside the Community;
(b)   the interests of intermediaries and consumers; and
(c)   the development of technical and economic progress.

Thus a concentration which does result in the creation or strengthening of dominance may nevertheless be sanctioned by the Commission if it is judged necessary to secure the survival of a lone Community producer seeking to keep pace with the non-EEC competition. Similarly, evidence that a merger will lead to benefits in terms of the transfer of technology or improved distribution might override the dominance test in appropriate cases.

4.4   Definition of concentration

4.4.1   As stated above, the definition of 'concentration' will include mergers and takeovers whether hostile or friendly and will also include a change in control. Article 3(2) illustrates how widely the concept of change of control is to be interpreted. It is not dependent on legal control and is established where there is the possibility of 'exercising decisive influence on an undertaking'.

4.4.2   Article 3(1)(b) refers to the assumption of control of an undertaking by 'one or more persons'. Thus the assumption of joint control of an undertaking can constitute a concentration. However, the creation of joint control of another undertaking will not by itself give rise to a concentration. Article 3(2) draws a distinction between joint ventures which co-ordinate the competitive behaviour of undertakings which remain independent ('co-operative joint ventures') and those joint ventures 'performing on a lasting basis all the functions of an economic entity' ('concentrative joint ventures'). The former are potentially anti-competitive agreements which would need to be considered under Articles 85 and 86 of the EEC Treaty, the latter are concentrations to be considered only under the Merger Regulation. The distinction between concentration and co-operative joint ventures is frequently a difficult one and reference should be made to the Commission's Notice on concentration and co-operative operations referred to above in cases of doubt.

4.5   Prior notification of concentrations

4.5.1   Concentrations with a Community dimension must be notified not more than one week after the conclusion of the agreement or the announcement of public bid or the acquisition of a controlling interest. In the case of a consensual merger or joint acquisition, the obligation to notify rests on the parties jointly. Where there is a takeover, then the bidder company is responsible to notify. Failure to notify a qualifying concentration may give rise to substantial fines.

4.5.2 The procedure on notification and the form of notification is dealt with in detail in the administrative regulation.

4.6 The calculation of turnover

4.6.1 Article 5 provides the detailed rules for calculating turnover for the purpose of meeting the Community dimension thresholds contained in Article 1(2) of the Merger Regulation. Turnover is defined as follows:

'... the amounts derived by the undertaking concerned in the preceding financial year from the sale of products and the provision of services falling within the undertaking's ordinary activities after deduction of sales, rebates and of value added tax and other taxes directly related to turnover.'

4.6.2 The turnover figure must exclude the sale of products or the provision of services between associated companies whose turnover is aggregated with the target company.

4.6.3 Where part only of an undertaking is to be acquired, then Article 5(2) provides that only the turnover attributable to the parts being acquired is taken into account for the purposes of establishing whether the turnover thresholds have been met.

4.6.4 Article 5(3) adopts different criteria for the calculation of turnover of credit or financial institutions and insurance undertakings in which turnover will clearly be an inappropriate basis of assessment. With regard to credit and financial institutions, the calculation is based on total worldwide assets. In place of the worldwide turnover criteria used in Article 1(2)(a), one must take one tenth of total assets. To determine the Community and individual significance of the undertakings within the Member State, the one tenth asset value must be multiplied by the ratio between loans and advances to credit institutions and customers in transactions with residents in the relevant territory. With regard to insurance undertakings, the turnover threshold is replaced by the value of gross premiums written.

4.7 Procedure

4.7.1 Timing is invariably critical in mergers and to avoid the danger of delay, the Regulation sets out specific time limits for each stage of the procedure for which the Commission is required to comply.

4.7.2 The Commission is required to examine the notification 'as soon as it is received'. There are then three options available to it. The Commission may decide:

(a) that the concentration falls outside the Regulation;
(b) that the concentration falls within the Regulation but does not raise serious doubts as to the compatibility with the Common Market;
(c) that the concentration falls within the Regulation and does raise serious doubts as to the compatibility within the Common Market, in which case it shall decide to initiate proceedings.

These decisions must be notified to the undertakings concerned and the competent authorities of the Member States 'without delay'. Details of notifications received and of the decisions described above are also published in the Official Journal (C series) and third parties are invited to submit observations.

4.7.3   A concentration having a Community dimension must not be put into effect prior to notification or within three weeks following notification. The Commission has power to continue the suspension of the concentration beyond the three week period where it is 'necessary in order to ensure the full effectiveness of any decision . . .'

4.7.4   The Commission is required to conclude any proceedings initiated pursuant to Article 6(1)(*c*) by a 'Decision'. Article 189 of the Treaty provides that a Decision of the Commission is binding in its entirety on those to whom it is addressed. Such Decisions are usually published in the Official Journal although publication is not obligatory.

4.7.5   Where the Commission finds that a concentration is incompatible with the Common Market it shall issue a Decision accordingly. Parties putting into effect such a concentration would then be liable to the imposition to fines. Where a concentration has already been implemented, the Commission may order divestiture or the cessation of joint control or order other action 'that may be appropriate in order to restore conditions of effective competition'.

4.8   Referrals to Member States

4.8.1   One of the principal objectives of the Merger Regulation is to confer on the Commission exclusive jurisdiction to regulate qualifying concentrations. This principle of 'one-stop shopping' involves Member States giving up the right themselves to regulate such concentrations. This rule is, however, qualified by two important exceptions:

(i)   Article 9 – distinct market exception;
(ii)   Article 21(3) – legitimate interest exception.

4.8.2   *The distinct market exception*

Article 9 provides that if within three weeks of receiving a copy of the notification from the Commission, a Member State informs the Commission that a concentration:

> '. . . threatens to create or strengthen a dominant position as a result of which effective competition would be significantly impeded on a market, within that Member State, which presents all the characteristics of a distinct market . . .'

The key element therefore is the existence of a 'distinct market' which is determined by reference to the factors set out in Article 9(7). If the Commission finds there is no distinct market it must inform the Member State concerned. Even if it accepts that there is a distinct market, it may nevertheless elect to deal with the matter itself.

4.8.3 The legitimate interest exception

Article 21(3) permits Member States to apply national merger legislation to Community dimension mergers if necessary to protect 'legitimate interests' to the extent compatible with Community law. 'Legitimate interests' include public security, plurality of the media and prudential rules. In a joint statement made by the Commission and the Council of Ministers[18] at the time that the Regulation was adopted, it was stated that Article 21(3) permits Member States only to exercise negative control so that if a concentration has been forbidden by the Commission under the Merger Regulation it cannot be approved by a Member State. However, a Member State may prohibit a concentration to the extent that it has an effect within the national jurisdiction and provided that it does not give rise to arbitrary discrimination or a disguised restriction on trade between Member States.

4.9 Application of the Regulation

4.9.1 As mentioned above, the Regulation effectively disapplies the competition rules by excluding the application of the implementing legislation. Theoretically, however, Articles 85 and 86 remain in force although the Commission/Council statement has indicated that the Commission would not seek to apply the competition rules to Community dimension mergers. However, the Commission reserved the right to do so in relation to mergers below the thresholds but where worldwide turnover exceeded ECU 2 billion and Community turnover exceeded ECU 100 million.

4.9.2 Exceptionally a Member State can invite the Commission to intervene under the Merger Regulation where the turnover does not meet the thresholds where the concentration may create or strengthen a dominant position in the Member State concerned.

4.10 Timetable

4.10.1 The Commission is given a maximum period of one month within which to give its decision under Article 6(1). This period is increased to six weeks where a Member State makes an application under Article 9.

4.10.2 Having decided to initiate proceedings, the Commission is required to make a final decision on the concentration within four months. The Commission has only limited powers to extend this period and if the Commission fails to take a decision within the time limits set, the concentration will be deemed to have been declared compatible with the Common Market.

4.11 Requests for information

The Merger Regulation confers upon the Commission a general power to obtain all 'necessary' information similar to the powers existing in relation to competition enquiries.

18 (1990) CMLR 314.

4.12   Fines

The Commission has power by formal decision to impose fines against both under-takings and individuals for failure to notify, the supply of incorrect information and failure to comply with decisions.

4.13   Judicial review

The unlimited power of the European Court of Justice as provided by Article 172 of the EEC Treaty in relation to acts of the Commission, to review any decision of the Commission imposing a fine or periodical penalty payments is confirmed by Article 16. The right of review extends to cancelling, reducing or increasing the amount involved.

CHAPTER II

European Economic Area

Andreas Diem

Gleiss Lutz Hootz Hirsch & Partners
Avenue Louise 475
Boîte 13
1050 Brussels
Belgium

Tel   ++32 2 647 6374
Fax   ++32 2 640 9231

CHAPTER II

European Economic Area

1 EEA COMPETITION LAW

1.1 EEA Agreement

1.1.1 The Agreement on the European Economic Area (EEA Agreement)[1] came into force on 1 January 1994. The Contracting Parties are, in addition to the EC, the European Coal and Steel Community (ECSC), the 15 Member States of the European Union, and three of the seven EFTA States[2] (just as in the EEA Agreement itself, the three EFTA States which are Contracting Parties to the EEA will be termed as the EFTA Contracting Parties or the EFTA States).[3]

1.1.2 The EEA Agreement seeks to create an area similar to the Internal Market, in which the four basic freedoms of the EC Treaty (free movement of goods, persons, services and capital) shall likewise apply. The EEA is equipped with its own institutions. However, unlike in the EC, the EEA Contracting Parties do not pursue a common policy in the areas of foreign trade (they do not, therefore, form a customs union), agriculture, fishing, taxation and the reduction of regional disparities. Nor were the institutions of the EEA vested with any legislative powers.

1.2 Institutions

Some of the EEA institutions are joint institutions of all the Contracting Parties, while others are institutions of either just the EC Member States or the EFTA Contracting Parties. The joint institutions include the EEA Council, the EEA Joint Committee, the EEA Joint Parliamentary Committee and the EEA Consultative Committee, which are mainly responsible for political co-ordination. All decisions taken by these institutions require unanimity between the Community on the one hand and the EFTA States on the other. The implementation of the EEA Agreement and the related judicial functions are incumbent upon parallel institutions of the EC and the EFTA States respectively. On the EC side these functions are performed by the European Commission, the European Court of Justice (ECJ) and the European Court of First Instance (CFI), on the EFTA side by two newly-established institutions, the EFTA Surveillance Authority (ESA) and the EFTA Court of Justice.[4] Whilst the EFTA institutions apply EEA law only, the

---

1 (1994) OJ L 1/3.
2 Originally Austria, Finland, Iceland, Norway and Sweden have become members of the EEA. In a referendum on 6 December 1992 the Swiss people had voted against joining the EEA. On 1 January 1995 Austria, Finland and Sweden joined the EU thus reducing the number of EFTA States being members of the EEA Agreement to two. On 1 May 1995 Liechtenstein became a new Contracting Party to the EEA Agreement, (1995) OJ 140/30.
3 The Protocol adjusting the EEA Agreement provides that the term 'EFTA States' used in Article 2(2) of the Agreement shall mean only the EFTA Contracting Parties of the EEA.
4 The EFTA States also set up a Standing Committee of the EFTA States and a Committee of Members of Parliament of the EFTA States to co-ordinate their policy in respect of the EEA.

Commission, the ECJ and the CFI will act partly as EC institutions and partly as EEA institutions and will apply different law in each case. However, in practice, these differences will not be significant since the EEA provisions – in so far as they relate to areas which were also regulated in the EC – essentially mirror the relevant provisions of EC law and are (to be) interpreted in the same way.

1.3   Statutory sources

1.3.1   The Contracting Parties agreed on the 129-article EEA Agreement, which includes 48 Protocols,[5] 22 Annexes[6] and a large number of Declarations. The Annexes and the acts referred to therein, as adapted for the purposes of the Agreement, as well as the Protocols form an integral part of the EEA Agreement (Art 119).

1.3.2   The EEA competition rules are mainly contained in Part IV of the Agreement (Articles 53–60), and in Protocols 21–25. Article 60 of the EEA Agreement refers to Annex XIV, which contains a long list of EC regulations, EC directives, High Authority decisions, and Commission notices relating to competition law. These acts include, in addition to the Merger Regulation (Regulation 4064/89), the block exemption regulations for exclusive distribution agreements (Regulation 1983/83), exclusive purchasing agreements (Regulation 1984/83), certain categories of motor vehicle distribution and servicing agreements (Regulation 123/85), patent licensing agreements (Regulation 2349/84), specialization agreements (Regulation 417/85), research and development agreements (Regulation 418/85), franchising agreements (Regulation 4087/88), know-how licensing agreements (Regulation 556/89) and regulations in the areas of transport, directives in the areas of public undertakings and all Commission notices that bear relevance to EC competition law.[7] These EC texts were adapted to the changed personal and geographical scope of application by means of 'horizontal adaptations'[8] and 'sectoral adaptations'.[9]

1.3.3   In so far as the provisions of the EEA Agreement are 'identical in substance' to the provisions of the EEC Treaty or the Treaty establishing the European Coal and Steel Community (ECSC Treaty), they will be interpreted in accordance with the judgments issued by the ECJ prior to the signing of the EEA Agreement, ie before 2 May 1992. Although the future case law of the ECJ, like the entire case law of the CFI, cannot be used as a binding basis when interpreting the provisions of the EEA Agreement, it does have to be duly complied with by the EFTA institutions.[10]

---

5   The Protocols deal mainly with more specific subjects, such as horizontal adaptations of secondary legal provisions of the EEC Treaty and the ECSC Treaty (Protocol 1) and the implementation of competition rules applicable to undertakings (Protocol 21).

6   The Annexes contain references to secondary law of the EC and the ECSC, as well as the necessary textual adaptations. Reference is made to a total of 1,600 acts, which fill approximately 12,000 pages in the Official Journal and are termed as the *acquis communautaire*. On 21 March 1994 the EEA Joint Committee adopted the *Interim Package of Additional EC Acquis* incorporating references to an additional 485 legal acts of the EC, (1994) OJ L 160/1.

7   On 12 January 1994 the EFTA Surveillance Authority adopted ten Commission Notices relating to competition law, (1994) OJ L 153/1, and on 6 April 1994 another three, (1994) OJ L 186/57. The Notice on co-operation between national courts and the EFTA Surveillance Authority in applying Article 53 and 54 of the EEA Agreement has been issued only on 4 May 1995, (1995) OJ C 112/7.

8   See Protocol 1 of the EEA Agreement, which lays down general rules for the application of the acts to which the EEA Agreement, its Protocols or Annexes refer.

9   See Annex XIV of the EEA Agreement, which provides, for example, that the term 'common market' is to read 'the territory covered by the EEA Agreement'.

10   Article 3(2) of the Treaty between the EFTA States regarding the establishment of a Surveillance Authority and a Court of Justice.

1.3.4 Differences of opinion between the EC and EFTA regarding the interpretation of the EEA Agreement will be settled in accordance with the dispute settlement procedure laid down in Articles 111ff. Either party may refer the matter to the EEA Joint Committee, which will try to reach agreement. In the event of a dispute concerning the interpretation of provisions of the EEA Agreement which are identical in substance to the corresponding provisions of the EC Treaty, the ECSC Treaty or their secondary legal provisions, the matter may be referred to the ECJ if no agreement has been reached within three months after the matter was brought before the EEA Joint Committee and if the Contracting Parties involved in the dispute agree to the matter being referred to the ECJ.

1.4 Substantive EEA competition law

1.4.1 Like EC competition law, EEA competition law is divided into three areas: the prohibition of restrictive agreements, the prohibition of an abuse of a dominant position and merger control.

1.4.2 Article 53 of the EEA Agreement prohibits restrictive agreements between undertakings, decisions by associations of undertakings and concerted practices. Article 54 contains provisions concerning the abuse of a dominant position. The substantive prerequisites for prohibition of a merger are laid down in Article 57(1). These provisions correspond almost word for word to the parallel provisions in Articles 85 and 86 of the EC Treaty and in Regulation 4064/89, any changes stemming from the fact of the different Contracting Parties or the different geographical area of application. There are no material differences between the competition laws of the EEA and of the EC.

1.5 Relationship between EEA, EC and national competition laws

1.5.1 With the entry into force of the EEA Agreement a third set of competition rules was added to the existing competition rules of the EC and the national competition laws. In principle, every competition case with effects in an EC or EFTA State must be examined under all three legal systems. In practice, however, there are only one or two competition laws applicable.

1.5.2 As to the relationship between EEA and EC competition law on the one hand and national competition law on the other EEA and EC law only apply where a case has effects beyond the territory of one Contracting Party.[11] EC law on agreements between undertakings (Article 85(1) of the EC Treaty) and the abuse of a dominant position (Article 86(1) of the EC Treaty) only applies if a conduct may affect trade between Member States. This so-called inter-state clause is interpreted very broadly by the Commission and the courts. It depends on whether a direct or indirect, actual or potential effect on trade between Member States can be assumed with a sufficient degree of probability.[12] An indirect influence is enough, eg if agreements between manufacturers about conditions of sale could mean that there

---

11 The ECSC Treaty, on the other hand, does not require, for its application, a (possible) negative effect of trade between Member States (see Articles 65, 66 ECSC Treaty). There is no room for the application of national law alongside the competition rules of the ECSC Treaty (see, for Germany, Section 101(3) GWB (Law against Restraints on Competition)).

12 *Coöperative Stemsel- en Kleurselfabriek v Commission*: 61/80 [1981] ECR 851, 867.

is no incentive for distributors to promote the sale of imported products.[13] EEA law also contains an inter-state clause in Articles 53(1) and 54(1). These provisions only apply if a conduct is likely to have an effect on trade between the EEA Contracting Parties.[14] If the inter-state requirement is fulfilled, then all three may apply – national, EEA and EC competition law.

1.5.3 The relationship between EC and national competition law is based on the general relationship between EC and national law.[15] National competition law is applicable as long as it is not inconsistent with EC competition law. A practice which is prohibited under EC law is unlawful even if the practice is permissible under the national law of a Member State. A practice which is permitted by a positive act of the Commission[16] may not be prohibited by national competition authorities. This does not apply to the relationship between EEA law and the national law of the EEA Contracting Parties.[17] To ensure the primacy of EEA law over national law, the EFTA states have undertaken to introduce, if necessary, a statutory provision to the effect that EEA rules prevail in the case of conflict (Protocol 35).

1.6   Relationship between EEA and EC competition law

1.6.1 Articles 85 and 86 of the EEC Treaty apply when trade between Member States is affected. Articles 53 and 54 of the EEA Agreement apply when trade between the Contracting Parties is affected. There is no overlap between the scope of EEA and EC competition law. The only Contracting Parties for Articles 53–60 of the EEA Agreement are the EC (and the ECSC) on the one hand and the three EFTA States on the other. Thus, Articles 53 and 54 of the EEA Agreement apply only if the conduct in question is likely to affect trade between the EC (or the ECSC) and one or more EFTA States or between different EFTA States, while Articles 85 and 86 of the EC Treaty apply if trade between EC Member States is affected.

1.6.2 The thresholds for the applicability of Article 53 of the EEA Agreement are specified in the Notice of the ESA on agreements of minor importance:[18] the prohibitions do not take effect unless the goods or services affected by the restraint on competition account for more than five per cent of the total market for said goods or services and the aggregate turnover of the undertakings involved exceeds ECU 200 million[19] in one year.

---

13 *Heintz van Landewyck v Commission*: 209–215, 218/78 [1980] ECR 3125, 3275.
14 Pursuant to Article 6 of the EEA Agreement, its provisions are to be interpreted in conformity with rulings of the ECJ existing at the time of signing of the EEA Agreement on provisions of the EC Treaty which are identical in substance. The inter-state clause of the EEA is therefore also to be interpreted broadly.
15 Established decision-making practice of the ECJ, see only *Walt Wilhelm*: 14/68 [1969] ECR 1.
16 Ie by an individual or block exemption pursuant to Article 85(3) of the EEC Treaty.
17 *Cf Diem*, EEA Competition Law, (1994) ECLR 263.
18 (1994) OJ L 153/32.
19 The EC has amended its Notice on agreements of minor importance, (1986) OJ C 231/2 in December 1994, raising the threshold to ECU 300 million, (1994) OJ C 368/20. The ESA is planning to amend its Notice in the same way in June 1995.

2 ENFORCEMENT

2.1 Enforcement authorities

2.1.1 A 'two-pillar system' has been created to implement EEA competition law. As a rule of thumb the Commission is responsible for the area of the Community and the ESA is responsible for the EFTA States.[20] The law applied by both institutions is in substance the same.

2.1.2 The ESA is headed by a College of three members, one from each EFTA State. This College is the equivalent of the European Commission. The administrative body of the ESA is divided into eight organisational units, one of which deals with issues of competition and another with state aid and monopolies. The working language of the ESA is English. It can be addressed, however, in any of the 12 official languages of the EEA.

2.2 Jurisdictional rules

2.2.1 There is no overlap between the jurisdiction of the Commission and that of the EFTA Surveillance Authority. Only one authority is competent to decide on a case (so-called 'one-stop-shop' principle). The attribution rules are contained in Articles 56 and 57.

2.2.2 With respect to cartel agreements there are two criteria which can be of importance when deciding whether a case is to be attributed to the Commission or the ESA, namely (a) the potential effects on trade, ie whether only trade between EFTA States is affected, or between the EC and EFTA States as well, and (b) the share of EEA turnover made in the EC and in the EFTA States. The Commission as an EEA institution only has jurisdiction if the cartel agreement has effects on trade 'between the Contracting Parties'. Contracting Parties as defined by Article 53 of the EEA Agreement are the EC and the ECSC (but not the EC Member States) and the EFTA States. Where only trade between EC Member States is affected, Article 53 EEA Agreement does not apply, but Article 85 of the EC Treaty, for whose enforcement the Commission is competent. According to Article 56 of the EEA Agreement, the EC Commission has jurisdiction for all cases which are caught by Article 53 and which are not expressly attributed to the ESA. The ESA has jurisdiction when:

(a) trade between EFTA States only is affected; or
(b) trade between the EC and at least one EFTA State is affected and the participating undertakings achieve 33% or more of their total EEA turnover in EFTA States; or
(c) the effects on trade between EC Member States or on competition within the Community are not appreciable.[1]

2.2.3 The Commission has jurisdiction if trade between the EC and at least one EFTA State is affected, and:

20 Article 109(1) EEA Agreement and Protocol 21.
 1 Article 56(3) of the EEA Agreement states that the ESA has jurisdiction in these cases, too, if the effects on trade between EC Member States are not appreciable. Since only the second alternative requires an effect on intra-Community trade, Article 56(3) of the EEA Agreement refers only to this alternative. This means that the ESA always has jurisdiction if trade between EC Member States is (also) affected, but not appreciably.

(a)   although the agreement does not affect trade between EC Member States, more than 67% of the EEA turnover is achieved in the EC;[2] or

(b)   trade between EC Member States is affected.

2.2.4   As regards the definitions of the terms 'undertaking' and 'turnover', Article 56(4) refers to Protocol 22, according to which an undertaking is 'any entity carrying out activities of a commercial or economic nature'. For cartel agreements (and the abuse of a dominant position), there is no clause corresponding to Article 5(4) of Regulation 4064/89, according to which turnover of associated undertakings has to be included. For distribution and supply agreements and know-how agreements, the relevant turnover is not the total turnover of the undertaking, but only the turnover made with the goods or services concerned, or like goods or services (Article 4 of Protocol 22). Like in Regulation 4064/89, for credit institutions and insurance companies, their total assets and gross premiums, respectively, are used instead of turnover, these to be calculated as specified (Article 3 of Protocol 22). In the coal and steel area, the relevant turnover is only that made with coal and steel products (Article 5 of Protocol 22). It should be noted that, for the purposes of determining turnover made in the EFTA States, turnover in Switzerland is to be disregarded.[3]

2.2.5   As regards the abuse of a dominant position the Commission is competent as an EC institution for cases in which an abuse of a dominant position can only affect trade between EC Member States (Article 86 of the EEC Treaty). In cases of abuse which may affect trade between the EC (or ECSC) and at least one EFTA State, either the Commission or the ESA may have jurisdiction. The division of jurisdiction in cases of abuse of a dominant position is based on three parameters:

(a)   the geographical market in which a dominant position is found to exist;

(b)   the potential effects on trade; and

(c)   the shares of turnover in the EC and EFTA.

Cases are attributed to one or the other authority on the basis of a combination of two or all three parameters. In principle, that surveillance authority 'in whose territory a dominant position is found to exist' has jurisdiction. If a dominant position is found to exist in both the EFTA States and the EC, the rules mentioned above under sections 2.2.2 and 2.2.3 apply:[4] the EFTA Surveillance Authority has jurisdiction only if trade between the EC and at least one EFTA State is affected (but not trade between EC Member States) and if the undertaking achieves at least 33% of its aggregate EEA turnover in the territory of the EFTA States. The Commission has jurisdiction if:

(a)   the undertaking achieves more than 67% of its aggregate EEA turnover in the territory of the EC Member States; or

(b)   the practice affects trade between EC Member States.

---

2 According to the wording of Article 56(3) of the EEA Agreement, this rule applies regardless of the turnover made within the Community. However, this would lead to the contradictory result that the ESA has jurisdiction in the event of effects on trade between an EC Member State and at least one EFTA State only if the EEA turnover in the EC is less than 67% (Article 56(1)), EEA Agreement), but, in the same situation regardless of turnover in the EC, if trade between EC Member States is affected, too, but not appreciably. For this reason, Article 56(3) is to be interpreted restrictively as meaning that the EEA turnover made in the EC may not amount to more than 67%.

3 Agreed Minutes of the Contracting Parties on Annex XIV, printed at: Federal Law Gazette 93 II, p 1307.

4 Article 56(2).

The last-mentioned rule also applies when trade between EC Member States is not appreciably affected.[5]

2.3 Duties and powers of ESA

2.3.1 Pursuant to Article 108 of the EEA Agreement, the EFTA States have undertaken to establish an independent surveillance authority. The ESA[6] is the Commission's counterpart and its task is, inter alia, to ensure the application of the principles laid down in Articles 53 and 54.[7]

2.3.2 The legal basis for the establishment of the ESA is an Agreement between the EFTA States.[8] This Agreement gives the ESA 'equivalent powers and similar responsibilities' to those which the Commission had in respect of the application of the competition rules of the EEC Treaty and the ECSC Treaty at the time when the EEA Agreement was signed.[9]

2.3.3 In addition to the acts listed in Annex XIV, the Commission regulations and the High Authority decisions listed in Article 3 of Protocol 21 reflect the powers and functions of the Commission for the application of the competition rules of the EEC Treaty and the ECSC Treaty. From the area of the law relating to restrictive agreements, for example, Regulations 17/62[10] and 27/62[11] apply; from the area of merger control, Articles 6–25 of Regulation 4064/89,[12] and Regulation 2367/90.[13] Both surveillance authorities are therefore equally empowered to conduct investigations, to grant negative clearances or individual exemptions, or pronounce prohibitions. They can impose fines and periodic penalty payments.

5 Article 56(3) EEA Agreement refers only to Article 56(1), ie to the division of jurisdiction in case of cartel agreements.
6 Address: EFTA Surveillance Authority, Rue de Trèves 74, 1040 Brussels, Belgium.
7 Article 55(1). In the first six months of its existence the ESA has received some 60 complaints against EFTA States as had adopted 76 formal decisions. It was examining more than 5,000 notifications on the implementation of EEA-relevant legal acts in the EFTA States along with over 400 state aid schemes, ESA Press Release 27 June 1994.
8 Article 1 Protocol 21; Agreement between the EFTA States dated 2 May 1992 regarding the establishment of a Surveillance Authority and a Court of Justice (ESA/Court Agreement), amended by the Protocol adapting the Agreement between the EFTA States regarding the Establishment of a Surveillance Authority and a Court of Justice dated 17 March 1993. Detailed rules concerning the powers and areas of responsibility of the EFTA Surveillance Authority in the area of competition can be found in Protocol 4 to the ESA/Court Agreement.
9 Although the legal foundations for the Commission's activities have changed since the signing of the EEA Agreement on 2 May1992, the vast majority of the legal acts adopted by the EC thereafter have been included in the *Interim Package of Additional EC Acquis*, adopted by the EEA Joint Committee on 21 March 1994, (1994) OJ L 160/1. Thus the legal basis of the ESA mirrors that of the Commission.
10 (1962) OJ 13/204.
11 Commission Regulation 27/62 of 3 May 1962, (1962) OJ L35 11.5.62 p 118; on the EC side, this Regulation has been replaced by Commission Regulation (EC) No 3385/94 of 21 December 1994 on the form, content and other details of applications and notifications provided for in Council Regulation No 17/62, (1994) OJ L 377/28 (Article 5). The EEA Joint Committee is planning to adopt this Regulation in the summer of 1995.
12 (1989) OJ L 395/1.
13 Commission Regulation (EEC) No 2367/90 of 25 June 1990 on the notifications, time limits and hearings provided for in Council Regulation (EEC) No 4064/89 on the control of concentrations between undertakings, (1990) OJ L 219/5. In the EC, this Regulation has been replaced by Commission Regulation (EC) No 3384/94 of 21 December 1994 on on the notifications, time limits and hearings provided for in Council Regulation (EEC) No 4064/89 on the control of concentrations between undertakings, (1994) OJ L 377/1. The EEA Joint Committee is planning to adopt this regulation in the summer of 1995.

2.4   Co-operation between the surveillance authorities

The Commission and the ESA liaise with each other regarding the treatment of competition law cases. If competitive conditions in the EC are (also) affected, the authorities will forward each other copies of notifications and complaints and inform each other when opening *ex officio* procedures.[14] If one of the authorities intends to grant a negative clearance or an individual exemption or to send a statement of objections to the undertakings involved, it has to consult with the other authority before doing so. The authority not dealing directly with a case has the right to attend meetings of the Consultative Committee, but has no voting right. The co-operation between the authorities also extends to investigations and the enforcement of decisions.

2.5   Judicial relief in the EEA

2.5.1   The ECJ having declared that the establishment of a joint EEA court would be incompatible with Community law,[15] the Contracting Parties agreed on the establishment of an EFTA Court of Justice (EFTA Court) to exist alongside the two EC courts. It has its seat in Geneva.[16] In the same way as competition law will be enforced by two authorities working in parallel, two parallel courts will supervise their actions. The two courts will exchange information about the development of their case law.

2.5.2   The scope of the jurisdiction of the EFTA Court corresponds to Article 169ff of the EEC Treaty[17] limited, however, to cases concerning EFTA States or acts of the ESA. The EFTA Court consists of three judges, one from each EFTA State.[18] Unlike the ECJ, which can refer a case to a Chamber, the EFTA Court sits only in plenary session.[19] There are no Advocates-General.

2.5.3   The EFTA Court has established its own rules of procedure.[20] The language of proceedings is always English, with the exception of proceedings for preliminary rulings.

3   CHECKLIST OF POTENTIAL INFRINGEMENTS

3.1   Commercial agency

3.1.1   Contracts with commercial agents as defined by the ESA do not fall under Article 53(1). A commercial agent is to be distinguished from an independent trader. The distinguishing criteria have been spelled out in the Notice of the ESA on exclusive dealing contracts with commercial agents.[1] This notice mirrors the

---

14   Article 2 of Protocol 23.
15   Advisory Opinion 1/91 of 14 December 1991.
16   Address: EFTA Court, 4, Ave des Morgines, 1213 Petit Lancy (GE), Switzerland.
17   Articles 31ff of the ESA/Court Agreement.
18   Article 28 of the ESA/Court Agreement as amended by the Protocol adjusting the ESA/Court Agreement.
19   Article 29 of the ESA/Court Agreement.
20   However, these still have to be approved by the EFTA States. In substance, they are based on the rules of procedure of the ECJ and the CFI.
 1   (1994) OJ L 153/23.

Notice of the Commission on exclusive dealing contracts with commercial agents.[2] The ECJ held that Article 85(1) of the EEC Treaty does not apply to clauses in a contract with a commercial agent which are restricting the agent's competitive behaviour if the agent is merely an auxiliary organ forming an integral part of the principal's undertaking.[3] This applies equally to Article 53(1).

3.1.2 A commercial agent may be obliged to observe the prices and conditions set by the principal without infringing Article 53(1). The principal may not prohibit the commercial agent from sharing the commission paid in respect of sales with his clients or granting rebates to his clients.[4] It should be noted that the Commission's notice is currently under review with the aim of incorporating in particular the ECJ's judgment in *VVR v Sociale Dienste*.[5]

3.2 Distribution agreements

3.2.1 Exclusive distribution agreements typically require one party to supply only to the other party goods within a defined geographical area. Such agreements are subject to examination under Article 53.

3.2.2 Exclusive distribution agreements will fall under Article 53(1) but may be exempted under Article 53(3). Pursuant to Article 60 of the EEA Agreement, provisions implementing the principles of Article 53 are contained in Annex XIV. This Annex refers to Regulation 1983/83 on exclusive distribution agreements. It is adapted to the particularities of the EEA by horizontal and vertical adaptations. Exclusive distribution agreements may thus benefit from a block exemption under Regulation 1983/83 as adapted by the EEA Agreement. Guidance as to the interpretation of these Regulations is provided by the ESA's Notice on the application of Article 53(3) to categories of exclusive distribution and exclusive purchasing agreements.[6] Often goods are not bought for resale but as raw material or components in the production process of the purchaser. Such agreements do not fall under Regulation 1983/83.

3.3 Selective distribution systems

3.3.1 A manufacturer may want to have his products sold by certain dealers only. Where the nature of the product is such that the dealer and his staff need special professional qualifications or the store has to be specially equipped, the manufacturer may permit only those dealers who fulfil certain objective criteria to become part of his selective distribution system and exclude those who do not. In order to

---

2 (1962) OJ L 139/2921.
3 *Sugar*: 40–48/73 [1975] ECR 1663, 2007.
4 *VVR v Sociale Dienste*: 311/85 [1987] ECR 3801, 3828.
5 311/85: [1987] ECR 3801, 3828; Article 25 (2) of the Court Agreement obliges the ESA to adopt acts corresponding to i.a. the Commission's Notice on exclusive dealing contracts with commercial agents of 1962. In view of the principle of homogeneity, Articles 98 and 102(1) of the EEA Agreement require the EEA Joint Committee to adopt new Community legislation. Even though the ESA is only required to adopt notices and guidelines issued by the EC Commission before 31 July 1991, it will also adopt new notices to improve homogeneity within the EEA. Thus the ESA will most likely adopt the amended Notice on exclusive dealing contracts with commercial agents once the Commission has published it.
6 Adopted on 1 January 1994, (1994) OJ L 153/13 and modified by the Notice of the ESA of 6 April 1994, (1994) OJ L 186/69.

set up a closed distribution system, he may prohibit his authorized dealers from supplying to non-authorized dealers who do not belong to his distribution system. A system of this kind is not considered a violation of Article 53(1) only provided the manufacturer does not use these criteria as a way of discriminating against some dealers, ie supplies to every dealer who fulfils the objective qualitative criteria.

3.3.2   If the dealers are selected on the basis of quantitative criteria, this is normally deemed a violation of Article 53(1). In particular, a manufacturer may not refuse authorization to a dealer on the grounds that he is already supplying to another dealer in that same area. In these cases, an individual exemption is necessary pursuant to Article 53(3).

3.3.3   As yet, no block exemption regulation exists for selective distribution systems. There is only one for motor vehicle distribution and servicing agreements (Regulation 123/85).[7] This regulation is part of EEA law as adopted.[8] Regulation 123/85 was replaced on the EC side by Regulation 1475/95 on 1 July 1995.[9] The EEA Joint Committee plans to adopt a regulation mirroring the new EC regulation in summer 1995. The ESA also adopted a Notice on the interpretation of Regulation 123/85[9] and a Clarification supplementing this Notice as to the scope of the activities of motor vehicle intermediaries.[10]

3.4   Exclusive purchasing

3.4.1   Exclusive purchasing agreements typically require one party to purchase certain goods only from the other party. They are likely to constitute an infringement of Article 53(1).

3.4.2   Agreements to purchase certain goods for resale exclusively from the other party may benefit from block exemption under Regulation 1984/83[11] as adapted by the EEA Agreement.[12] Special rules apply to beer supply agreements[13] and to service-station agreements.[14] If the goods are materially altered by the purchaser prior to resale, Regulation 1984/83 does not apply.

3.5   Franchising

3.5.1   Franchise agreements consist essentially of licences of industrial or intellectual property rights relating to trade marks or signs and know-how, which can be combined with restrictions relating to supply or purchase of goods. There are three types of franchise agreements:

(a)   service franchising concerning the supply of services;

---

7 (1984) OJ L 15/16.
8 Annex XIV, no 4.
9 (1995) OJ L 145/25.
10 The Notice was adopted on 1 January 1994, (1994) OJ L 153/20; the clarification was adopted on 6 April 1994, (1994) OJ L 186/70.
11 (1983) OJ L 173/4; Corrigendum (1983) OJ L 281/24.
12 Annex XIV, no 3. See also Notice of the EFTA Surveillance Authority on the application of Article 53(3) of the EEA Agreement to categories of exclusive distribution and exclusive purchasing agreements, adopted on 1 January 1994, (1994) OJ L 153/13.
13 Article 6ff Regulation 1984/83, as adapted.
14 Article 10ff Regulation 1984/83, as adapted.

(b)   production franchising concerning the manufacturing of goods; and
(c)   distribution franchising concerning the sale of goods.[15]

3.5.2   Distribution and/or service franchise agreements which contain clauses intended to prevent the franchisor's competitors from benefiting directly or indirectly from the know-how being transferred to the franchisee or which serve to protect the identity or the reputation of the network bearing the franchisor's business name or symbol (eg homogeneity, quality control) do not infringe Article 53(1). Clauses which seek to share markets between franchiser and franchisees or between franchisees or to prevent franchisees from engaging in price competition with each other are restricting competition in the sense of Article 53(1).[16] They may benefit from a block exemption under Regulation 4087/88[17] as adapted by the EEA Agreement.[18]

3.5.3   Industrial franchise agreements do not fall under Regulation 4087/88. Although they may be exempted in some cases by Regulation 2349/84 on patent licensing agreements[19] or Regulation 556/89 on know-how licensing agreements[20] as adapted by the EEA Agreement,[1] the majority of such agreements will require individual exemption under Article 53(3).

3.6   Intellectual property licensing

3.6.1   Intellectual property rights comprise rights conferred mainly by national law[2] such as patents, trade marks, copyrights or registered designs. The intellectual property right affords protection against exploitation, eg of the patented invention, or use of the trade mark by third parties without the consent of the holder of the intellectual property right. Such consent is typically given in licensing agreements whereby the licensor grants the right to the licensee to exploit his intellectual property right. Licensing agreements often contain clauses restricting the freedom of the licensee, eg to supply certain customers or to sell into certain areas or to determine prices and conditions of sale. Such clauses are likely to infringe Article 53(1).

3.6.2   Patent licensing agreements may benefit from a block exemption under Regulation 2349/84[3] as adapted by the EEA Agreement.[4] Licensing of a patent is often coupled with licensing of know-how. Therefore know-how licensing agreements are commonly dealt with in the context of intellectual property licensing

---

15 *Pronuptia*: 161/84 [1986] ECR 353, 381; Regulation 4087/88, Rec (2) and (3), (1988) OJ L 359/46.
16 *Pronuptia*: 161/84 [1986] ECR 353, 381ff.
17 (1988) OJ L 359/46.
18 Annex XIV, no 8.
19 (1984) OJ L 219/15; *Corrigendum* (1985) OJ L 280/32; Regulation 2349/84 will be replaced by a Commission Regulation on the application of Article 85 (3) of the Treaty to certain categories of technology transfer agreements, a preliminary draft of which has been published in (1994) OJ C 178/3.
20 (1989) OJ L 61/1; Regulation 556/89 will be replaced by a Commission Regulation on the application of Article 85(3) of the Treaty to certain categories of technology transfer agreements, a preliminary draft of which has been published in (1994) OJ C 178/3.
1   Annex XIV, no 5 and no 9.
2   In the EC Regulation 40/94 of 20 December 1993 on the Community trademark, (1994) OJ L 11/1, entered into force in March 1994. This Regulation is not referred to in Annex XVII nor in the *Interim Package of Additional EC Acquis* and therefore is not part of EEA law.
3   (1984) OJ L 219/15; *Corrigendum* (1985) OJ L 280/32.
4   Annex XIV, no 5.

agreements, even though there is no intellectual property right protecting know-how. Know-how licensing agreements may benefit from an exemption under Regulation 556/89[5] as adapted by the EEA Agreement.[6] The Commission has published a draft Regulation on the application of Article 85(3) to certain categories of technology transfer agreements,[7] which will replace Regulations 2349/84 and 556/89 and extend their scope to Community patents, European patents as well as mixed patent licensing and know-how licensing agreements. After this new block exemption regulation has entered into force, it will also be made part of EEA law.

3.7   Refusal to supply

3.7.1   In principle, Article 53(1) does not prohibit refusals to supply, for in a free market economy a manufacturer is usually free to decide to whom he wishes to supply his products. However, this does not apply if he refuses, within the framework of a selective distribution system, to supply to dealers who fulfil all the objective, qualitative selection criteria without having an objectively legitimate reason for doing so (quantitative selection).[8] A refusal to supply is also unlawful if it is based on a decision by a dealer association not to supply to other dealers who have not agreed to comply with fixed prices.[9]

3.7.2   An objectively unjustifiable refusal to supply will infringe Article 54(1) if the supplier has a dominant position on the market.[10]

3.8   Price restrictions

3.8.1   Agreements between competitors to fix purchase or selling prices are very likely to violate Article 53(1). The same applies to horizontal price 'recommendations', ie in the form of target prices.

3.8.2   Resale price maintenance may constitute an infringement of Article 53(1). Exemptions under Article 53(3) will be granted only for few products such as magazines.[11] Vertical price recommendations are only objectionable if they lead to identical prices, in particular because the manufacturer puts pressure on dealers.[12] Collective vertical resale price maintenance constitutes by its very nature an infringement of Article 53(1).[13]

3.8.3   An undertaking having a dominant position within the EEA or in a substantial part of it may infringe Article 54(1) by imposing directly or indirectly unfair purchase or selling prices. Unreasonably high or unreasonably low prices, discriminatory pricing as well as predatory pricing (in order to undercut prices of a competitor) or discriminatory loyalty rebates may also constitute an infringement of Article 54(1).

---

5 (1989) OJ L 61/1.
6 Annex XIV, no 9.
7 (1994) OJ C 178/3.
8 Eg *SABA* (1976) OJ L 28/19, 25; *Peugeot v Commission*: T-23/90 [1991] ECR II-653.
9 *Cementhandelaren* (1972) OJ L 13/34, 40.
10 *Polaroid/SSI Europe*, Thirteenth Report on Competition Policy (1983), point 157.
11 *Binon v AMP*: 243/83 [1985] ECR 2015.
12 *AEG v Telefunken*: 107/82 [1983] ECR 3151.
13 *VBVB*: 43, 63/82 [1984] ECR 19.

3.9 Tie in sales

3.9.1 Tie in sales are forced, combination or package sales. A tie in arrangement between the seller and the purchaser will not normally infringe Article 53(1). Agreements between competitors to engage in tie in sales are, however, likely to violate Article 53(1) if the supplementary obligation has no connection with the subject of the sale. A connection between the subject of the sale and the supplementary obligation exists, if, from an objective point of view, the tie in of products or services is necessary for the use, the safety, the warranty or legitimate economic interests of the vendor.

3.9.2 If the seller has a dominant position on the market, a tying clause whereby the seller agrees only to supply a product for which he holds a dominant position if the purchaser agrees to buy another product as well may be caught by Article 54(1) if no connection exists between the subject of the sale and the supplementary obligation.

3.10 Information exchange

In principle, undertakings are free to exchange information. Article 53(1) only objects to the exchange of information between competitors on prices, sales conditions, customers, ie information usually considered as business secrets and which may enable competitors to engage in parallel behaviour. In contrast, the exchange of information of a general or statistical nature or information which is necessary to check the adherence of another party to admissible obligations will not infringe Article 53(1).[14]

3.11 Joint buying and selling

3.11.1 Joint selling arrangements between competing enterprises may not entail an appreciable restraint of competition if such enterprises are small or medium-sized.

3.11.2 Joint buying does not infringe Article 53(1) if the participating enterprises are free to buy directly for their own use only and are not forced always to buy collectively.

3.12 Market sharing

3.12.1 Article 53(1) prohibits agreements relating to the allocation of markets. This includes agreements in which the parties agree to do business predominantly in their home market. Such agreements have little chance of being granted an exemption.

3.12.2 Vertical agreements restricting the freedom to export to certain areas may be used as a means of attributing markets between competitors. Such agreements are likely to infringe Article 53(1) and will not easily be granted an exemption.

---

14 Art II.1 Notice of the EFTA Surveillance Authority concering agreements, decisions and concerted practices in the field of co-operation between enterprises of 12 January 1994, (1994) OJ L 153/25.

3.13   Joint ventures

3.13.1   Joint ventures of a concentrative nature may fall under Regulation 4064/89[15] as adapted by the EEA Agreement,[16] joint ventures of a co-operative nature are subject to examination under Article 53(1).[17] Some guidance as to whether a joint venture is concentrative or co-operative in nature is provided by the ESA's Notice on concentrative and co-operative joint ventures.[18]

3.13.2   The view of the ESA on the application of Article 53(1) to co-operative joint ventures is delineated in its Notice concerning agreements, decisions and concerted practices in the field of co-operation between enterprises[19] and in its Notice on the assessment of co-operative joint ventures.[20] Joint ventures between non-competitors rarely constitute a restriction of competition. As to joint ventures between competitors, the following rules apply.

3.13.3   Research and development joint ventures are likely to restrict competition if the joint venture also assumes distribution or other exploitation of the newly developed products. Sales joint ventures will usually infringe Article 53(1) even without an exclusivity clause, because they restrict competition on the supply side. The application of Article 53(1) on buying joint ventures depends on the individual case. Exclusivity will most likely infringe Article 53(1).[1] Buying joint ventures may lead to a weakening of price competition between the participating undertakings, particularly when the cost of the jointly bought products makes up a significant part of the total cost of the products sold by the participants. High market shares or a commitment for more than five years might be seen as anti-competitive behaviour under Article 53(1).[2] The assessment of manufacturing joint ventures producing only products which are to be further processed by the parent companies follows the same lines. Joint ventures processing half-finished into fully-finished products which will be distributed by the parent companies are likely to infringe Article 53(1).

3.13.4   Co-operative joint ventures may benefit from block-exemption Regulation 417/85 on specialisation agreements[3] as adapted by the EEA Agreement,[4]

15 (1989) OJ L 395/1.
16 Annex XIV, no 1.
17 For a co-operative joint venture examined under both Article 85 EEC Treaty and Article 53 EEA Agreement see eg *BT-MCI* (1994) OJ L 223/36.
18 Notice of the EFTA Surveillance Authority regarding the concentrative and co-operative operations under the act on the control of concentrations between undertakings referred to in point 1 of Annex XIV to the EEA Agreement (Regulation 4064/89) of 12 January 1994, (1994) OJ L 153/7. The new Commission Notice on the distinction between concentrative and co-operative joint ventures under Council Regulation (EEC) No 4064/89 of 21 December 1989 on the control of concentrations between undertakings, (1994) OJ C 385/1, is planned to be adopted by the ESA in June 1995.
19 Art II.6.(a) Notice of the EFTA Surveillance Authority concerning agreement, decisions and concerted practices in the field of co-operation between enterprises of 12 January 1994, (1994) OJ L 153/25.
20 Notice of the EFTA Surveillance Authority concerning the assessment of co-operative joint ventures pursuant to Article 53 of the EEA Agreement of 6 April 1994, (1994) OJ L 186/58.
 1 Eg *National Sulphuric* (1980) OJ L 260/24.
 2 *Coöperateive Stremsel-en Kleurselfabriek v EC Commission*: 61/80 [1981] ECR 851; *EBU-Eurovisions-System* (1993) OJ L 179/23.
 3 (1985) OJ L 53/1.
 4 Annex XIV, no 6.
 5 (1985) OJ L 53/5.

Regulation 418/85 on research and development agreements[5] as adapted by the EEA Agreement,[6] Regulation 2349/84 on patent licensing agreements[7] as adapted by the EEA Agreement[8] and Regulation 556/89 on know-how licensing agreements[9] as adapted by the EEA Agreement.[10]

4 CONCENTRATIONS, MERGERS AND ACQUISITIONS

4.1 Introduction

The EEA Agreement also covers merger control. Merger control provisions are contained in Article 57 as well as in Regulation 4064/89 as adapted by the EEA Agreement.[11] On account of the allocation of competence between the Commission and the ESA, most mergers in the EEA fall under the purview of the Commission.

4.2 Scope of EEA merger control law

As regards the implementation of merger control, there is no clear delimitation between the scope of EEA law and that of EC law. EEA merger control covers mergers with a Community dimension as well as those with an EFTA dimension. If a merger has a Community dimension, then the Commission applies both Regulation 4064/89 and the corresponding EEA merger control provisions.[12]

4.3 Thresholds

All mergers with a Community or an EFTA (not EEA!) dimension are subject to EEA merger control and have to be notified on Form CO.[13] A merger has a Community or an EFTA dimension if:

(a) all participating undertakings together have an aggregate worldwide turnover[14] of more than ECU 5 billion;

6 Annex XIV, no 7.
7 (1984) OJ L 219/15; *Corrigendum* (1985) OJ L 280/32.
8 Annex XIV, no 5.
9 (1989) OJ L 61/1.
10 Annex XIV, no 9.
11 Cf Annex XIV, no 1. See also Notice of the EFTA Surveillance Authority regarding the concentrative and co-operative operations under the act on the control of concentrations between undertakings referred to in point 1 of Annex XIV to the EEA Agreement. (Regulation 4064/89) of 12 January 1994, (1994) OJ L 153/7 and Notice of the EFTA Surveillance Authority regarding restrictions ancillary to concentrations of 12 January 1994, (1994) OJ L 153/3.
12 Eg *Neste/Statoil*, Commission Decision of 17 February 1994 (not published).
13 Annex to Commission Regulation (EEC) No 2367/90 of 25 June 1990 on the notifications, time limits and hearings provided for in Council Regulation (EEC) No 4064/89 on the control of concentrations between undertakings, (1990) OJ L 219/5. In the EC, this Regulation has been replaced by Commission Regulation (EC) No 3384/94 of 21 December 1994 on the notifications, time limits and hearings provided for in Council Regulation (EEC) No 4064/89 on the control of concentrations between undertakings, (1994) OJ L 377/1. The EEA Joint Committee is planning to adopt this regulation in the summer of 1995.
14 The Commission has issued a Notice on calculation of turnover under Council Regulation (EEC) No 4064/89 of 21 December 1989 on the control of concentrations between undertakings, (1994) OJ C 385/21. Even though the ESA has not yet published such a Notice, there is an informal policy to take due account of it.

(b)   at least two participating undertakings have an aggregate Community- or EFTA-wide turnover of more than ECU 250 million each; and

(c)   the undertakings participating in the merger do not each make more than two-thirds of their total Community- or EFTA-wide turnover in one and the same Member State.[15]

4.4   Jurisdictional rules

4.4.1   Mergers with a Community dimension and mergers with an EFTA dimension are subject to EEA merger control. Mergers are subject to the jurisdiction of the Commission if they have a Community dimension, and to the jurisdiction of the ESA if they have an EFTA dimension, but no Community dimension. Thus, the ESA only has subsidiary competence. Two of the three criteria named in Article 1(2) of Regulation 4064/89 as amended (aggregate worldwide turnover of ECU 5 billion, not more than two-thirds of turnover in one and the same state) have to be met in both cases. Only the third criterion decides whether a merger has a Community or an EFTA dimension. A merger has a Community dimension if at least two participating undertakings each have a turnover of more than ECU 250 million either only in the EC or both in the EC and in EFTA. A merger has an EFTA dimension if these thresholds are only exceeded in EFTA, ie if at least two participating undertakings each have a turnover of more than ECU 250 million in EFTA, and not both more than ECU 250 million in the EC.

4.4.2   Therefore the thresholds laid down in Regulation 4064/89 as adapted by the EEA Agreement are not fulfilled if the ECU 250 million turnover is achieved by an undertaking only in the EC and EFTA States together, or if one participating undertaking has the required turnover in the EC only and the other in EFTA only. According to the wording of the Merger Control Regulation as adapted, which is quite clear in this respect, it covers only two types of mergers: mergers with a Community dimension and mergers with an EFTA dimension, but not mergers with an EEA dimension. To have a Community dimension, a merger has to involve at least two undertakings with an aggregate Community-wide turnover of at least ECU 250 million each; to have an EFTA dimension, a merger has to involve at least two undertakings with an aggregate EFTA-wide turnover of at least ECU 250 million each (Article 1(2), sub-para (b) of Regulation 4064/89 as adapted). A merger which exceeds the turnover threshold of ECU 250 million for two of the participating undertakings only in the EC and the EFTA States together is not caught by Regulation 4064/89 as adapted.

4.4.3   A merger has to be prohibited by the Commission if the dominant position significantly impedes effective competition in the EEA or a substantial part of it (Article 57(1) of the EEA Agreement). This means that the Commission will have to take market conditions in the EFTA States into consideration in the future, too, as the prerequisites for a prohibition are also fulfilled if the merger does not lead to a dominant position in the Community, but creates or strengthens a dominant position in the EFTA territory or a substantial part of it.[16] The same applies to the EFTA Surveillance Authority for the territory of the EC.

15 Article 1 of Regulation 4064/89, as amended by Article 57(2)(a) of the EEA Agreement in conjunction with Annex XIV, no 1(b).

16 In *Electrolux/AEG*, the Commission investigated whether the merger was liable to create a dominant position on the Swedish market, Commission decision of 21 June 1994, point 6 (not published).

4.5 Co-operation between the enforcement authorities

4.5.1 The Commission and the ESA will co-operate in merger cases where the Commission has jurisdiction, but the merger is of significant relevance for EFTA. This is essentially the case if:

(a) the aggregate turnover of the participating undertakings in the territory of the EFTA States is 25% or more of their total EEA turnover; or
(b) if at least two participating undertakings have a turnover of more than ECU 250 million in the territory of the EFTA States; or
(c) if the merger creates or strengthens a dominant position and if effective competition in the territory of the EFTA States or a substantial part thereof is thereby significantly impeded;[17] or
(d) if effective competition in a distinct, geographical market in one EFTA State is potentially significantly impeded by a dominant position.

The intensive co-operation is intended to make up for the fact that the Commission clearly has overriding competence in the case of merger control.

4.5.2 The co-operation procedures provide for the forwarding of documentation and an exchange of ideas and information. In certain cases, it is intended that the ESA will send representatives to the hearings before the Commission and to consultations of the EC Advisory Committee on Concentrations. The EFTA representatives will not, however, have the right to vote.[18]

4.6 Relationship between EEA and national competition authorities

4.6.1 If the ESA is competent, the national authorities of the EC Member States remain competent although the national competition authorities of the EFTA States are no longer competent.[19] If, on the other hand, the merger comes under the jurisdiction of the Commission, then its competence displaces that of all EC Member States and all EFTA States.[20]

4.6.2 The Commission can refer a notified merger to the competent national authority of an EFTA State if the merger threatens to create or strengthen a dominant position in a geographical reference market in that EFTA State.[1]

---

17 Eg *Electrolux/AEG*, Commission Decision of 21 June 1994.
18 Article 5(3) of Protocol 24.
19 Article 57(2)(b) of the EEA Agreement and Article 21, Part III, Chapter XIII of Protocol 4 of the ESA/Court Agreement.
20 Article 57(2)(a).
 1 Article 6(1) of Protocol 24.

CHAPTER III

Austria

Dr Friedrich Schwank

Law Offices Dr F Schwank
Stock Exchange Building
34 Wipplingerstrasse
Vienna 1010
Austria

Tel   ++43 1 533 5704
Fax   ++43 1 533 5706

CHAPTER III

Austria

1 AUSTRIAN COMPETITION LAW

1.1 Background

Austrian competition law is divided into distinct sections of legislation. One area of legislation is the regulation of the market as such by way of controlling restrictive practices, cartels, abuse of market power, concentration and mergers. This is the anti-trust legislation comprised in the cartel act. The other area of competition law is the rules against unfair competition which are the rules of conduct of the competitors on the market place between themselves and vis-à-vis the consumer. The main piece of legislation in that area is the act against unfair competition.

1.2 The anti-trust rules are comprised in the Cartel Act 1988, as amended in 1993. The present Act is a thoroughly revised and adapted Act with a view to comply with the EEA requirements and is based on its predecessors the Cartel Act 1951 and the Cartel Act 1972. Anti-trust legislation was already in force during the Austro-Hungarian monarchy. As early as 1838 a decree declared all agreements controlling offers at public auctions null and void. In 1870 an Act was promulgated which made illegal all agreements of either employers or employees with an intention to control the labour market. But not until 1951 was a comprehensive Cartel Act introduced upon recommendation of the Johnston Report on competition in Austria which was commissioned by the Marshall Plan and was a pre-condition of aid under the Marshall Plan with the view to introduce a free market economy in Austria.

1.3 The development of the Cartel Act had to take into account the various stages of progress of Austria's integration in the European market. The first step was the Free Trade Agreement with the EEC in 1972. As a result cartels offending the rules of the Free Trade Agreement were not admissible though being otherwise compatible with the Austrian rules. The membership of the EEA which became effective as from 1 January 1994 required further adaptation of the Cartel Act under which the *acquis communautaire* was adopted. As these amendments were far reaching no further amendments were required upon Austria's accession to full membership of the EU effective as of 1 January 1995.

1.4 The Unfair Competition Act 1984 is an updated version of the same Act of 1923 and regulates conduct between competitors as well as which practices are acceptable for the purposes of marketing. Its basic rules are fairness, business ethics and absence of deception.

1.5 In contrast to the Cartel Act, the Unfair Competition Act has not been amended in view of Austria's progressive integration into the European market. To what extent the rules against unfair competition and, in particular, the admissibility of marketing practices are affecting the free movement of goods and services on the European market will certainly be tested in the courts once defences based on EU law are raised against unfair competition actions.

2   ANTI-COMPETITIVE AGREEMENTS AND CONCERTED PRACTICES

2.1   Cartels within the meaning of the Cartel Act are as follows:

(a)   cartels by way of agreement (Article 10);
(b)   cartels by way of concerted practices (Article 11);
(c)   cartels by way of recommendation (Article 12).

2.2   Cartels by way of agreements are any agreements between economically independent entrepreneurs or an association of entrepreneurs which, in pursuance of the common interest, aim at restricting competition, in particular with regard to production, sales, demand or prices or, if it has not been aimed for, that it is actually accomplished.

2.3   Understandings between entrepreneurs are exempt if there is an express agreement that such understandings are non-binding and if there is no economical social pressure applied or to be applied for the purpose.

2.4   The exchange of information on prices is expressly defined as a cartel by agreement irrespective of whether the prices are communicated directly or indirectly. However, an exchange of information on prices which have become obsolete for at least one year is permitted.

2.5   Concerted practice is conduct by entrepreneurs which is neither accidental nor incidental to the market situation and creates the effect of restricting competition.

2.6   Concerted practices are allowed in the following instances:

(a)   if they are based on a permissible recommendation;
(b)   if they have been created within the framework of a statutory trade association;
(c)   if they are the result of compliance with legal provisions; or
(d)   if they have been expressly and jointly approved by the Chamber of Commerce, the Chamber of Labour, the Agricultural Representative Organisation and the Association of Trade Unions.

2.7   Cartels by recommendation are recommendations to observe fixed prices, price limits, costing directives, mark ups for trade or rebates and have the effect of or the intention of restricting competition. Also advertising, including retail prices, of goods or services is considered as a cartel by recommendation unless such advertising emanates from the retailer.

2.8   Recommendations are allowed if they are expressly designated as non-binding and if there is no economic or social pressure to be applied or intended to be applied.

2.9   Petty cartels which do not supply more than 5% of a national, and not more than 25% of a regional, market at the time of the creation can be carried on without prior registration. However, the Cartel Court has the power to forbid the continued implementation of petty cartels.

2.10   Exemption by special ordinance of the Ministry of Justice

The ministry, after consultation with the social partners, the official representatives of employers and employees, has the authority to issue exemption regulations in respect of:

(a)   certain forms of inter-company co-operation or announcements of prices in respect of goods and services; and
(b)   certain types of cartels to the extent that they are obviously in the interest of the national economy.

2.11   The authority to issue such exemption regulations is restricted mainly to:

(a)   joint R & D activities;
(b)   the creation and the use of joint transport, shipping and warehousing facilities, joint exhibition rooms and a joint commercial agent task force;
(c)   joint advertising of entrepreneurs who in respect of the goods and services to be advertised have an aggregate share of the total domestic market of less than five per cent;
(d)   joint advertising of all other entrepreneurs provided no prices are being advertised;
(e)   the joint use of book-keeping and accounting facilities;
(f)   creation and use of joint information systems;
(g)   advertising of prices of goods and services by the tourist and transport industry;
(h)   offering of tied services of different entrepreneurs in the area of transport and tourism at single prices (eg package tours).

2.12   Even the partial implementation of cartels is forbidden if one of the following conditions is met:

(a)   before the final approval by the Cartel Court; or
(b)   to the extent that the Cartel Court has forbidden the implementation of the cartel or renounced its permission; or
(c)   upon the expiry of its approved term.

2.13   Forfeiture of gains

Ill-gotten gains from the implementation of a forbidden cartel are to be declared as forfeited by the Cartel Court. The Cartel Court can refrain in part or in whole from forfeiting the ill-gotten gains if this is equitable in respect to the economic consequences.

2.14   Cartel agreements are ineffective to the extent as the implementation is forbidden.

2.15   The Cartel Court will approve cartels on application if all of the following conditions are met:

(a)   if the cartel does not contain any of the following restrictions:

   (i)   to deal exclusively only in goods or to provide exclusively only those services which are the subject matter of the cartel;
   (ii)   to deal in substitute goods or to provide substitute services which are similar to those covered by the cartel only at fixed prices or in limited quantities;
   (iii) to boycott in whole or in part certain persons or groups of persons;

(b)   the cartel must not violate a legal provision or offend good ethics;
(c)   the cartel is justified from the point of view of national economy.

2.16   The Cartel Court will determine the term of the validity of the cartel which must not exceed five years. An extension of the term is possible upon application.

2.17   The Cartel Court also has the power to withdraw or restrict the ambit of cartels already approved.

3   ABUSE OF MARKET POWER

3.1   Pre-condition for the abuse of market power is a dominant position

Dominant positions are defined by the Cartel Act as enterprises being either on the supply or the demand side of the market and:

(a)   which are exposed to no competition at all or only to a non-substantive extent; or
(b)   which have a market share on the whole domestic market of more than 5% and are exposed to the competition of not more than two other enterprises; or
(c)   which are one of the four biggest enterprises having an aggregate market share on the domestic market of at least 80% provided that the enterprise concerned has at least a share of more than 5%; or
(d)   which have in relation to the other competitors an eminent position on the market having regard in particular to the following: the financial means, the relations to other enterprises, the access to supply and distribution markets and other circumstances which restrict the access to the market for other enterprises.

3.2   In addition an enterprise is also considered to have a dominant position if it has an eminent position in the market in respect to either its suppliers or its customers. This is particularly the case if customers and suppliers are dependent on the maintenance of the business relationship with the enterprise as they will suffer considerable economic disadvantages otherwise.

3.3   Upon application the Cartel Court can order the enterprise in question to discontinue the abuse of a dominant position.

3.4   An abuse of a dominant position is in particular seen in the following instances:

(a)   direct or indirect imposition of unfair purchase or sales prices or other unfair conditions of contract;
(b)   the restriction of production, distribution or technical development to the detriment of the consumers;

(c) the discrimination of trading partners in the area of competition by way of applying different conditions for the same services;
(d) tying in with the contract additional services which have no reasonable or customary relation to the main object of the contract.

3.5 An application to the Cartel Court for issuing an order against an enterprise to discontinue its abuse of the dominant position can be made:

(a) by four official bodies:

    (i)   the Republic represented by the Attorney General;
    (ii)   the Federal Chamber of Commerce;
    (iii) the Federal Chamber of Labour;
    (iv)   the Conference of the Presidents of the Agricultural Chambers;

(b) by trade associations affected by the abusive conduct;
(c) by any other enterprise which is affected in its legal or economic interest by the abusive conduct.

4 CHECKLIST OF POTENTIAL INFRINGEMENTS

4.1 Agency

4.1.1 Agency agreements are not covered by the Cartel Act and are, as a general rule, not considered as restrictive practices. The relationship between principal and agent is regulated in the Act on Commercial Agents.

4.1.2 In extreme circumstances and applying the substance over form rule an agency could be caught by the Cartel Act provision. But there has not yet been a precedent of a reclassification of an agency as a cartel.

4.2 Distribution

4.2.1 Vertical restrictions on distributions are defined by the Cartel Act as contracts between one enterprise (restricting enterprise) with one or more economically independent enterprises (restricted enterprises) by means of which the latter are restricted in the supply or the distribution of goods or services.

4.2.2 Restrictions on prices are expressly excluded from this provision as they are cartels anyway.

4.2.3 Vertical restrictions on distributions have to be notified to the Cartel Court prior to the implementation by the restricting enterprise.

4.2.4 Together with the notification a sample contract with the restricted enterprises has to be submitted. As only a sample of the agreement has to be submitted and not the full agreement any trade or business secrets can be excluded from the sample.

4.2.5 Upon application the Cartel Court has to forbid the implementation of a vertical restriction on distribution if one of the following conditions is met:

(a)   the vertical restriction on distribution violates a legal provision or offends good ethics;

(b)   the vertical restriction on distribution is not justified from the point of view of national economy. When checking the justification from the point of view of national economy the Cartel Court has to take into account justified interests of the restricting enterprise, and of the restricted enterprise and the consumers to an equal extent. In addition, the freedom of making economic decisions on the part of the restricted enterprise must not be limited to an unreasonable extent and also the access to the market for other competitors must not be made unreasonably too difficult.

4.2.6   An application to forbid the implementation of vertical restriction of distribution can be made by the following:

(a)   the four official authorities (see section 3.5);

(b)   the trade associations affected by the vertical restriction;

(c)   each enterprise with economic or legal interest affected by the vertical restriction.

4.2.7   To the extent that the Cartel Court has either by way of a final decision or by way of injunction forbidden the implementation of a vertical restriction on distribution its implementation is illegal and the agreement is ineffective.

4.2.8   The Ministry of Justice can issue ordinances stating that certain groups of vertical restrictions on distributions are allowed and are not to be forbidden by the Cartel Court. An ordinance has been released by the Ministry of Justice which states that the rules of the EC block exemptions on exclusive distribution (1983/83) and on automotive distribution (1475/95) will be applicable within Austria for the purposes of the Austrian Cartel Act. This has been criticised as being legislation by reference only.

4.3   Exclusive purchasing

Exclusive purchasing agreements are considered as vertical restrictions on competition and follow the rules set out in section 4.2 above. An ordinance on exclusive purchasing has been issued by the Ministry of Justice exempting all agreements which meet the rules of the EC block exemption on exclusive purchasing (1984/83).

4.4   Franchising

To the extent that franchise agreements are vertical restrictions on distribution or supply they require notification prior to their implementation. The Ministry of Justice has issued an ordinance exempting all agreements complying with the EC block exemption on franchising (4087/88).

4.5   Intellectual property

The use of intellectual property for the purposes of competition has not yet given rise to any anti-trust action in Austria. The Act against Unfair Competition affords special protection against unlicensed use of intellectual property rights.

4.6 Refusals to supply

4.6.1 A refusal to supply could be considered an abuse of market power which can be committed only by an enterprise having a dominant position on the market; see section 3 above. The enterprise concerned can be forced by a Cartel Court order to supply the enterprises affected by its abuse of market power.

4.6.2 A special act secures local distribution.

4.6.3 Entrepreneurs who are otherwise free in the choice of their retailers can be forced to supply a particular retailer if that retailer is otherwise not able to satisfy local demand.

4.6.4 The satisfaction of local demand is seen to be in jeopardy if a reasonable amount of consumers is not able to buy the goods for satisfying the necessary needs of daily life in a reasonable manner without using a car or public transport.

4.7 Price deductions

Price deductions are permissible if they are granted within the limits of good business ethics (see section 4.13.1). Price deductions which are outside commercial reasonableness and granted for the sole purpose of destroying a competitor on the market would be considered to be outside good business ethics. Advertising of price reductions for commerce is expressly allowed; see section 4.13.6.(e).

4.8 Tie in sales

As a general rule tie in sales are permitted. Only in extreme circumstances, where the buyer is induced to purchase the tied in product although he is only interested in the main product, could the tie in be considered as violating good business ethics. If the tie in results in a deception about the real price of the goods or a concealing of a non-permitted incentive (see section 4.13.6) this would constitute a violation of the Act against Unfair Competition.

4.9 Information exchange

An exchange of information on prices is a cartel under the Act unless the prices are obsolete for more than one year (see section 2.4 above). An exchange of other information could give rise to a cartel depending on the circumstances (see sections 2.3 and 2.5 above).

4.10 Joint buying and selling

Joint buying and selling will be considered as a cartel as it is aimed at restricting competition in the mutual interest of the enterprises taking part. On the basis of an ordinance of the Ministry of Justice an exception exists which permits joint buying provided there are no restrictions imposing exclusivity of purchasing, minimum quantities to be bought resulting in economic dependence, fixed prices or other fixed terms of sale.

4.11   Market sharing

Agreements on sharing the market are clearly anti-competitive and will be considered as cartels.

4.12   Joint ventures

As joint ventures are in general anti-competitive they will be caught by the wide definition of cartel (see section 2.2). Certain joint ventures might qualify for exemption by special ordinance of the Ministry of Justice (see sections 2.10 and 2.11). These are in particular joint ventures in the narrow sense of jointly carrying out a specified project.

4.13   Unfair competition

4.13.1   Any conduct on the market within the framework of competition violating the good ethics is forbidden and can be stopped by the Commercial Court which can also award damages to the injured party.

The reference to good ethics is a rather general reference and therefore the courts have over the years established certain rules on good ethics. However, it is often very difficult to predict what the courts will state in a given case as good ethics depend on the particular circumstances, trade usages, customs, the particular market etc.

4.13.2   Unfair competition is also the deception or generally the misleading of customers. This is particularly the case if the advertising of an enterprise is misleading as to the nature, origin, way of production or price calculation of goods and services. Advertising of comparative prices is allowed provided it does not violate good ethics.

Apart from a court order to stop such advertising and the exposure to the liability for damages, there is also the risk of criminal prosecution if the deception was intentional.

4.13.3   A special provision of the Act Against Unfair Competition forbids the use of deceptive packaging where the size of the packaging does not bear reasonable relation to its contents unless there are special reasons due to the nature of the goods or for reasons of packaging technology.

4.13.4   The dissemination of demeaning information about another enterprise, its owners or managers, its goods or services results in a claim for damages if such information damages the other enterprise or its credit, unless the information can be proven to be true.

4.13.5   The Act also forbids the use of names or descriptions which can result in confusion with the names and descriptions of another enterprise. If this is done intentionally then it can also result in a claim for damages.

4.13.6 The offering, advertising and granting of incentives or free additional goods or services to the consumer are only allowed if they consist of:

(a) the usual attachments to goods or the customary subordinated services;
(b) samples of goods;
(c) advertising articles provided they show clearly and permanently a relation to the enterprise;
(d) incentives or goods of petty value;
(e) a determined or determinable sum of money which is not attached to the goods;
(f) a determined and according to fractions computable amount of the same merchandise;
(g) provision of information and advice;
(h) a chance to win provided that the aggregate value of the prizes does not exceed ATS 300,000 and the ticket has no greater value than ATS 5.00 taking into account the total amount of the tickets issued and the aggregate amount of the prizes.

4.13.7 Bribery of employees or agents of enterprises by way of providing gifts or other advantages for the purpose of obtaining preferential treatment in an unethical manner is a criminal offence carrying a sentence of up to three months' imprisonment or a fine of up to 180 daily rates. In the same manner, employees or agents of an enterprise are punishable who demand gifts or other advantages.

4.13.8 In the same manner, the violation of trade or business secrets or the misuse of documents or technical drawings is punishable.

4.13.9 There is no special legal provision against passing off. An action of passing off has therefore to be based on one or more of the provisions of the Act Against Unfair Competition. However, the reliance on a violation of good business ethics alone is not enough unless it can be proved that the violating enterprise is exploiting the breach of contract of somebody else, eg a former employee of the other enterprise.

5 CONCENTRATIONS, MERGERS AND ACQUISITIONS

5.1 Definition of a merger

5.1.1 The acquisition of an enterprise in its entirety or of a significant part thereof by another enterprise, particularly by merger or reorganisation.

5.1.2 The acquisition of a right by an enterprise at the premises of another enterprise by means of business surrender or plant management agreements.

5.1.3 The direct or indirect acquisition of shares in a company by another enterprise if this results in achieving or exceeding a threshold shareholding of either 25% or 50%.

5.1.4 A situation in which at least one-half of the members of the management bodies or supervisory boards of two or more companies are the same persons.

5.1.5   Any other links between enterprises by virtue of which one enterprise directly or indirectly is able to exercise a dominating influence over another enterprise.

5.1.6   The formation of a joint venture as an independent economic unit where there is no regulation of the competition between the founding members themselves or between the founding members and the joint venture.

5.2   Definition of enterprise

The term *enterprise(s)* includes everything from a business which is a part of a company through to a group of companies. A *group* is defined very broadly. Members of a group can be:

(a)   legally independent enterprises grouped together for economic reasons under central governance of a company; or
(b)   legally independent enterprises grouped together either on the basis of equity participation or, due to any other reasons, are under the direct or indirect controlling influence of another enterprise.

Therefore, acquisitions within an existing group fall outside the definition of merger and are therefore not subject to any merger control.

5.3   Threshold requirements

The threshold requirements for the application of the merger control of the Cartel Act are based on the worldwide turnover of the enterprises party to the transaction provided that an Austrian enterprise is being affected. In case of merger the turnover of both parties including their related companies, ie the turnover of both groups counts towards the threshold. In the case of an acquisition the group turnover of the buyer and the turnover of the actual target enterprise count towards the threshold.

5.4   Pre-merger registration

5.4.1   Intended mergers have to be filed with the Austrian Cartel Court *prior to their implementation* (execution) if the following conditions are met:

(a)   the aggregate turnover of all enterprises taking part in the merger is ATS 3.5 billion or more; and
(b)   at least two enterprises taking part in the merger have a turnover of ATS 5 million or more each.

Considerably lower thresholds are applicable if the merger is in the area of media (press, radio, television) or enterprises serving the media (publishers, printers, advertising agents, wholesale distribution of media products).

5.4.2 Pre-merger registration application

The registration has to contain a description of all circumstances relevant to the increase of the dominant position created or enhanced by the proposed merger. In that respect the following details have to be supplied to the Cartel Court:

(a) the ownership structure of the respective enterprises before and after the proposed merger (organisational charts of the respective undertakings are useful);
(b) turnover of the enterprises broken down into the various markets of goods and services, as applicable, and also broken down into domestic Austrian and foreign turnover. Some indication of the market concentration after the merger in respect to the same goods or services of the enterprises merged is required;
(c) market shares of the participating enterprises in Austria for the relevant goods and services;
(d) general description of the structure of the Austrian market, including in particular:

  (i) the top four competitors and their respective market shares of the relevant goods or services in Austria, or, in the alternative, all enterprises with a market share in excess of 5%;
  (ii) if the merger results in an increase in the market share of the merging enterprises in excess of 5% on the domestic market, the entry barriers into that specific market should be described in general terms.

5.4.3 Pre-merger registration procedure

Once the registration has been submitted, the Cartel Court publishes the names of the participating enterprises, a description of the proposed merger and the affected business area in an official gazette.

Copies of the registration are served by the Cartel Court upon the following public bodies:

(a) the Republic, represented by the Attorney General;
(b) the Federal Chamber of Commerce;
(c) the Federal Chamber of Labour;
(d) the Conference of the President of the Agricultural Chamber.

Within four weeks of service these official bodies are entitled to request that the Cartel Court scrutinise the merger. If no such application is received within four weeks from any of these official bodies, the Cartel Court will issue a clearance and the merger can be consummated.If an application is received, then the Cartel Court has to make further investigations and eventually publish its findings on whether or not the merger is allowed.

In practice, it is possible to shorten the four-week waiting period by way of obtaining statements from the respective official bodies beforehand that they will refrain from making an application. Upon production of these statements to it, the Cartel Court issues an informal clearance. Once the clearance is obtained the merger can proceed in a legal manner.

5.4.4   Violation of registration requirement

If no clearance is obtained, the merger will be null and void and the contracts relating to the merger will be invalid under Austrian law.

If a merger which is subject to registration has been carried out without obtaining a prior clearance, the Cartel Court has to determine upon application whether the merger is legal. The application to the Cartel Court to issue a statement that a merger is illegal can be made by the following:

(a)   the official bodies mentioned above;
(b)   organisations which represent the economic interest of enterprises affected by the merger; and
(c)   any entrepreneur whose legal or economic interests are affected by the merger.

As a result the consummation of a merger which should have been registered exposes the merger to direct attack by competitors. Apart from the risk of the merger being invalid, the parties taking part in it expose themselves to fines.

5.5   Post-merger notification

If the gross turnover of the parties to a merger does not meet the threshold requirements for registration, then only post-merger notification has to be submitted to the Cartel Court. Post-merger notification is required if the joint turnover of the enterprises involved is between ATS 150 million and 3.5 billion or one party has a turnover in excess of ATS 3.5 billion and the target enterprise has a turnover below ATS 5 million.

5.6   Exempted merger

No notification whatsoever is required in the following instances:

(a)   if the combined turnover of the enterprises taking part in the merger is less than ATS 150 million;
(b)   if the target has a turnover of less than ATS 5 million, unless the acquiring group has a turnover of ATS 3.5 billion or more.

CHAPTER IV

Belgium

Ivo Van Bael

Van Bael & Bellis
Avenue Louise 165
1050 Brussels
Belgium

Tel   ++32 2 647 7350
Fax   ++32 2 640 6499

CHAPTER IV

Belgium

1 BELGIAN COMPETITION LAW

1.1 Background

1.1.1 Belgian competition law is contained primarily in the Law of 5 August 1991 on the Protection of Economic Competitions[1] (hereinafter the 'Competition Law'). The Competition Law entered into force on 1 April 1993, which marked an important step in the development of the rules of Belgian competition law. The Competition Law replaces the Law of 27 May 1960 on the Protection against the Abuse of a Dominant Position which was generally considered ineffective.[2]

1.1.2 The Competition Law is, in large measure, modelled on the EC competition rules and draws heavily on the relevant treaty provisions and implementing regulations for both substantive and procedural matters. Moreover, according to the legislative history of the Competition Law, the case law developed by the EC Court of Justice and the EC Commission is relevant for the purpose of interpreting the Competition Law.

1.1.3 In addition to the Competition Law, the Belgian law of unfair trade practices is also aimed at protecting free competition. The fundamental concept of the Belgian unfair trade practices law is set forth in Article 7 of the French Decree of 2–17 March 1791 which was incorporated into Belgian law through a 1795 Decree (at the time when Belgium was under French control). It establishes the principle that all persons, at their own discretion, should be free to enter any business and to compete in any market. Certain methods of competing are none the less prohibited.

1.1.4 The Belgian law on unfair trade practices originated with the Royal Decree No 55 of 23 December 1934, which has been amended by the Law of 14 July 1971 on Trade Practices and by the Law of 14 July 1991 on Trade Practices and Consumer Information and Protection[3] (hereinafter the 'Trade Practices Act'). The law of unfair trade practices was originally used to protect competitors and other traders. The interests of consumers were, as a result, generally ignored. Since the adoption of the Law of 14 July 1971 on Trade Practices, however, the law on unfair trade practices has increasingly been used by the Belgian courts as an

---

1 Loi sur la protection de la concurrence économique/Wet tot bescherming van de economische mededinging.
2 The reasons for this ineffectiveness were, inter alia, the requirement that the public interest had to be infringed for the law to apply, the complex and lengthy procedure and the absence of effective sanctions.
3 Loi sur les pratiques du commerce et sur l'information et la protection du consommateur/Wet betreffende de handelspraktijken en de voorlichting en bescherming van de consument.

instrument of consumer protection. The Trade Practices Act, which came into effect on 29 February 1992, formally introduced the interests of consumers amongst the interests protected by Belgian unfair trade practices law.

1.2   Differences between Belgian and EC competition law

1.2.1   The following is a non-exhaustive list of the more salient differences between the Belgian competition law and the competition law of the European Community:

(a)   agricultural products are included in the scope of the Belgian Competition Law;

(b)   the *de minimis* concept in Belgian Competition Law does not include any reference to market share;

(c)   the exemption criteria under Belgian Competition Law include an express provision designed to foster the competitive position of small and medium sized companies;

(d)   enforcement of the Belgian Competition Law has a quasi-judicial character in that the Administration, ie the Competition Service, can only propose measures for approval by the Competition Council, an administrative tribunal;

(e)   the powers of investigation of the Belgian Competition Service extend to the private dwellings of executives, employees and advisers of the company concerned, provided a prior authorization is obtained from a judge;

(f)   the Brussels Court of Appeals has full powers of review, ie they go beyond a mere review of the legality of the decisions adopted by the Competition Council.

1.2.2   In the area of merger control, the more important differences are, that:

(a)   the Belgian Competition Law provides for a shorter time limit (105 days) within which a final decision must be adopted;

(b)   among the criteria for assessment, the Belgian Competition Law includes a reference to the general economic interest;

(c)   the Belgian Competition Law does not specifically address the question of ancillary restrictions.

1.3   Anti-competitive agreements, decisions and concerted practices

1.3.1   General principle

Article 2(1) of the Competition Law, which is set forth in terms very similar to Article 85(1) of the EEC Treaty, prohibits all agreements between undertakings, decisions by associations of undertakings and concerted practices which have as their object or effect the prevention, restriction or distortion of competition to an appreciable extent within the relevant Belgian market, or a substantial part thereof.

While the Competition Law provides little guidance as to the interpretation of the key concepts contained in Article 2(1), the case law of the EC Commission and the Court of Justice provides assistance in this respect.

1.3.2 Undertakings

Article 2(1) of the Competition Law applies only to 'undertakings' which term must be given the same broad meaning as under EC competition law. In general, 'undertakings' covers all individuals and legal entities which pursue an economic objective on a lasting basis.[4] The broad definition of 'undertaking' contained in the Competition Law implies that the nationality or domicile of the individual or legal entity is not relevant to the application of Article 2(1).

1.3.3 Agreement, decision of an association and concerted practice

Article 2(1) of the Competition Law refers to agreements, decisions by associations of undertakings and concerted practices. The terms 'agreement', 'decision of an association' and 'concerted practice' cover a wide range of actions involving at least two independent undertakings acting in concert. As confirmed by the case law relating to Article 85 of the EEC Treaty, agreements within the meaning of Article 2(1) of the Competition Law need not necessarily be legally binding contracts. The reference in Article 2(1) of the Competition Law to decisions of associations of undertakings indicates that the prohibition can also apply to situations where undertakings act in concert through the intermediary of an association. In general, the notion of concerted practices refers to behaviour whereby the undertakings concerned replace independent competitive behaviour by some form of co-operation or co-ordination.

1.3.4 Prevention, restriction or distortion of competition

Article 2(1) of the Competition Law contains the following non-exhaustive list of practices which prevent, restrict or distort competition:

(a)   directly or indirectly fixing purchase or selling prices or any other trading conditions;
(b)   limiting or controlling production, markets, technical development or investment;
(c)   sharing markets or sources of supply;
(d)   applying dissimilar conditions to equivalent transactions with other trading parties, thereby placing them at a competitive disadvantage;
(e)   making the conclusion of contracts subject to acceptance by the other parties of supplementary obligations which, by their nature or according to commercial usage, have no connection with the subject of such contracts.

This is the same list as is included in Article 85(1) of the EEC Treaty.

1.3.5 De minimis

The prohibition contained in Article 2(1) of the Competition Law applies only to practices which restrict competition to an appreciable extent. As a result, *de minimis* restrictions of competition are not caught by the prohibition of Article 2(1).

4   Article 1(a) of the Competition Law.

According to Article 5 of the Competition Law, restrictive practices are presumed to be *de minimis* if they are entered into by undertakings which, individually, do not exceed more than one of the following thresholds:

(a)   average number of employees during the relevant period: not more than 50. However, if the average number of employees during the relevant period exceeds 100, then the presumption does not apply regardless of (b) and (c) below;

(b)   annual turnover, excluding VAT: not more than BEF 145 million. In this regard, the annual turnover must be calculated on the basis of the total turnover on export markets as well as the Belgian domestic market;[5]

(c)   total assets: not more than BEF 70 million.

The presumption established in Article 5 of the Competition Law is rebuttable. The Competition Council may hold that a restrictive practice has an appreciable effect on competition, and is therefore caught by the prohibition of Article 2(1) of the Competition Law, even though the above thresholds are not exceeded. In such cases, the burden of proof will be on the Competition Council to demonstrate that the effect on competition cannot be considered *de minimis*. Conversely, even if undertakings do not meet the conditions of Article 5 of the Competition Law, they may still demonstrate that the effect of a particular practice is nevertheless de *minimis*. In such cases, the burden of proof will rest on the undertakings concerned.

1.3.6   The relevant Belgian market or a substantial part thereof

Article 2(1) of the Competition Law applies to practices which prevent, restrict or distort competition on the relevant Belgian market or a substantial part thereof. In other words, Article 2(1) is only concerned with the anti-competitive impact of certain practices within Belgium and cannot be invoked in order to prohibit conduct the anti-competitive effects of which are only felt outside Belgium.

Article 2(1) of the Competition Law refers not only to the relevant Belgian market, but also to a substantial part of that market. Legislative history indicates that a city, and certainly a province, may qualify as a substantial part of Belgium for the purposes of the application of Article 2(1) of the Competition Law.

1.3.7   Sanctions

Agreements which infringe Article 2(1) of the Competition Law and which are not eligible for an exemption under Article 2(3) of the Competition Law (see below) are void pursuant to Article 2(2) and therefore unenforceable. In addition, the Competition Council may impose fines up to 10% of the annual turnover upon each of the undertakings concerned when it establishes the existence of a restrictive practice.

1.3.8   Severability

Unenforceability as a result of Article 2(2) only applies to those provisions or features of an agreement or practice which violate Article 2(1). As a result, the

---

5   Article 46(1) of the Competition Law.

remaining provisions are unaffected by the nullity sanction, provided the unenforceable provisions are severable.

1.3.9 Negative clearance

At the request of the undertakings or associations of undertakings concerned, the Competition Council may issue a decision stating that, on the basis of the information available, there are no grounds for taking action pursuant to Article 2(1) of the Competition Law.[6] Such a 'negative clearance' implies that one or more of the essential elements of Article 2(1) are not present in the situation reviewed by the Competition Council. In its decision granting negative clearance, the Competition Council must provide adequate reasons.[7]

The formal requirements relating to requests for a negative clearance are laid down in a Royal Decree of 23 March 1993. A request for a negative clearance can be made jointly or separately by the undertakings involved. In case of a joint application, the request must be filed by a joint representative.[8] If the application is only filed by certain undertakings or associations of undertakings, these undertakings or associations of undertakings must inform the other undertakings or associations involved. The parties must use form CONC E/A-1[9] in order to apply for negative clearance with the Competition Service.

1.3.10 Exemptions

Even if a practice is deemed to violate Article 2(1) of the Competition Law, there are three ways in which such a practice can escape the prohibition contained in that provision: (i) through an individual exemption granted by the Competition Council, (ii) through the application of a group exemption issued by Ministerial Decree and (iii) by the granting of an exemption pursuant to Article 85(3) of the EEC Treaty.

1.3.11 Individual exemption by the Competition Council

Conditions An exemption will only be granted by the Competition Council if the following conditions, listed in Article 2(3), are satisfied:

(a) the practice must contribute to improving the production or distribution of goods or to promoting technical or economic progress, or it must offer small and medium-sized undertakings the possibility of strengthening their competitive position on the relevant market or on the international market;
(b) consumers must obtain a fair share of the resulting benefits;
(c) the practice may not entail the imposition of restrictions on the undertakings concerned which are not indispensable to the attainment of these objectives; and
(d) the practice may not afford such undertakings the possibility of eliminating competition in respect of a substantial part of the products in question.

6 Article 6(1) of the Competition Law.
7 Article 30 of the Competition Law.
8 Article 2(3) of the second Royal Decree of 23 March 1993.
9 Annex to the second Royal Decree of 23 March 1993.

With the exception of the reference to the strengthening of the competitive position of small and medium-sized undertakings, the conditions for an exemption pursuant to Article 2(3) of the Competition Law are identical to those contained in Article 85(3) of the EEC Treaty. Consequently, the relevant EC case law will be the principal guide in the interpretation of the conditions set forth in the Competition Law.

Notification requirement Generally, an individual exemption cannot be granted by the Competition Council acting on its own initiative. In order to obtain an individual exemption pursuant to Article 2(3) of the Competition Law, the restrictive practice must be notified.[10]

As an exception to this general rule, Article 7(2) of the Competition Law lists a number of practices which need not necessarily be notified in order to obtain an exemption pursuant to Article 2(3). The undertakings concerned are, however, entitled to notify these enumerated practices should they so desire. The practices listed in Article 7(2) of the Competition Law are those:

(a)   to which not more than two undertakings are a party and which only:

    (i)   restrict the freedom of one party in determining the prices or conditions of business upon which the goods which he has obtained from the other party to the contract may be resold; or

    (ii)   impose restrictions on the exercise of the rights of the assignee or user of industrial property rights – in particular patents, utility models, designs or trade marks – or of the person entitled under a contract to the assignment or grant, of the right to use a method of manufacture or knowledge relating to the use and the application of industrial processes; or

(b)   which have as their sole object:

    (i)   the development or uniform application of standards or types; or

    (ii)   joint research and development concerning technical improvements provided that all the parties have access to the results and are free to exploit such results.

Since the EC Commission and the EC Court of Justice have adopted a narrow interpretation of a similar list of practices contained in Article 4(2) of Council Regulation No. 17/62, it is advisable not to place too much emphasis on the exemption from notification provided in Article 7(2) of the Competition Law.

Notification formalities The formal requirements relating to notifications are laid down in a Royal Decree of 23 March 1993. Notification of a practice for the purposes of obtaining an individual exemption must be made to the Competition Service.[11] The notifying parties must use form CONC E/A-1.[12]

Decision An individual exemption pursuant to Article 2(3) of the Competition Law can only be obtained by way of a decision adopted by the Competition Council. The Competition Council is the only body which has the authority to make such a decision. As under EC competition law, the Competition Law does not provide for

10 Article 7(1) of the Competition Law.
11 Article 7(1) of the Competition Law.
12 Annex to the second Royal Decree of 23 March 1993.

any time limit within which the Competition Council must adopt an exemption decision.

The Competition Council's authority to grant an individual exemption is subject to certain conditions.[13] The Competition Council must fix the term for which an individual exemption is granted, as well as the date from which it starts running.[14] This date may not be earlier than the date of notification. Individual exemptions may not be given for an indefinite period of time. At the request of the undertakings concerned, the Competition Council may extend an individual exemption upon its expiry, provided the conditions of Article 2(3) continue to be satisfied.

Article 29(2) of the Competition Law entitles the Competition Council to withdraw or alter an individual exemption under circumstances similar to those under which the EC Commission may withdraw or alter an exemption decision taken pursuant to Article 85(3) of the EEC Treaty. Such a withdrawal or alteration is possible:

(a)   where there has been a change in any of the circumstances which were essential to the making of the decision;
(b)   where the parties commit a breach of any obligation attached to the decision;
(c)   where the decision is based on incorrect information or was induced by fraud; or
(d)   where the parties abuse the exemption granted to them.

1.3.12   Application of a group exemption issued by Ministerial Decree

Pursuant to Article 28(l) of the Competition Law, the Minister of Economic Affairs is authorised to adopt Ministerial Decrees providing for an automatic exemption of certain categories of practices. The Minister acts upon a proposal from the Competition Council, based upon a report from the Competition Service and after consultation with the Competition Commission.

The most important feature of such group exemptions is that practices which meet their requirements benefit from an automatic exemption pursuant to Article 2(3) of the Competition Law and need not be notified to the Competition Service. The group exemptions referred to in Article 28 of the Competition Law are similar to the block exemption regulations which exist in EC competition law. The Minister of Economic Affairs has not yet adopted, as of November 1995, any group exemption for certain categories of practices.

1.3.13   Application of an exemption pursuant to Article 85(3) of the EEC Treaty

The prohibition contained in Article 2(1) of the Competition Law is inapplicable to practices which benefit from an exemption pursuant to Article 85(3) of the EEC Treaty. It is immaterial whether the exemption stems from an individual exemption rendered by the EC Commission or from the application of an EC block exemption regulation. Practices which benefit from an EC exemption need not be notified under the Competition Law and the Competition Council may not further review them.[15]

---

13 Article 29(2) of the Competition Law.
14 Article 29(3) of the Competition Law.
15 Articles 8 and 32 of the Competition Law.

1.4   Prohibition against the abuse of a dominant position

1.4.1   General principle

Article 3 of the Competition Law provides that any abuse by one or more under-takings of a dominant position on the relevant Belgian market or a substantial part thereof is prohibited. The wording of Article 3 of the Competition Law is very similar to that of Article 86 of the EEC Treaty.

1.4.2   Dominant position

Article 3 of the Competition Law only applies to undertakings which enjoy an individual or collective dominant position. Any finding of dominance requires the prior definition of a relevant market, both in relation to the product or service involved and in relation to the geographic territory concerned. The economic strength of the undertaking concerned must be assessed within the product and geographic market as defined. The legislative history of Article 3 makes it clear that the market definition and the dominance assessment required under the Competition Law must be made in accordance with the relevant EC competition law principles.

As a result, market share figures are bound to play an important role. Thus, a market share of 40% or more will constitute an important factor in the dominance analysis necessary for the application of Article 3 of the Competition Law.

1.4.3   Abuse

Article 3 of the Competition Law contains the following non-exhaustive list of abusive conduct:

(a)   imposing directly or indirectly unfair purchase or selling prices or other unfair trading conditions;
(b)   limiting production, markets or technical development to the prejudice of consumers;
(c)   applying dissimilar conditions to equivalent transactions with other trading parties, thereby placing them at a competitive disadvantage;
(d)   making the conclusion of contracts subject to acceptance by the other parties of supplementary obligations which, by their nature or according to commer-cial usage, have no connection with the subject of such contracts.

1.4.4   Negative clearance

Undertakings are entitled to request the Competition Council to confirm that a par-ticular practice does not constitute an abuse of a dominant position. Any negative clearance by the Competition Council must be granted by way of a reasoned deci-sion.[16] The formal requirements relating to requests for a negative clearance are laid down in a Royal Decree of 23 March 1993.

16 Articles 6 and 30 of the Competition Law.

2   ENFORCEMENT

2. 1   Enforcement authorities

2.1.1   Institutions responsible for the application and enforcement of the Competition Law

Competition Service[17]   The Competition Service, a service within the Ministry of Economic Affairs, is primarily responsible for investigating cases covered by the Competition Law and ensuring the proper enforcement of any decisions adopted pursuant to the Competition Law. The Competition Service also operates as the secretariat of the Competition Council.

Competition Council[18]   The Competition Council is an administrative tribunal. Its primary task is to adopt decisions pursuant to the Competition Law (negative clearances, exemption decisions and decisions relating to concentrations). In addition it enjoys broad advisory powers. Each year, it is obliged to present a report on the application of the Competition Law to the Minister of Economic Affairs.

Competition Commission[19]   The Competition Commission is a joint committee, with advisory powers, which comprises part of the Central Economic Council.[20] It may exercise its advisory powers either upon its own initiative or at the request of the King, the Minister of Economic Affairs or the Competition Council.

President of the Competition Council   The President of the Competition Council is a magistrate who is a member of the judiciary. Aside from his function as President of the Competition Council, he has particular powers regarding requests for information[1] and may order interim measures in cases which are being investigated under the Competition Law.[2] In both instances, the President may impose periodic penalty payments.

Minister of Economic Affairs[3]   The Minister of Economic Affairs is authorized to adopt Ministerial Decrees which would provide for the automatic exemption of certain categories of practices from the provisions of the Competition Law. The Minister will act on a proposal from the Competition Council, based upon a report from the Competition Service, and after consultation with the Competition Commission.

Brussels Court of Appeals[4]   The Brussels Court of Appeals hears appeals against decisions of the Competition Council and its President. In addition, it will give preliminary rulings on issues of law concerning the Competition Law at the request of other courts and tribunals.

17 Articles 14 and 15 of the Competition Law.
18 Articles 16 to 20 of the Competition Law.
19 Articles 21 and 22 of the Competition Law.
20 The function of the Central Economic Council is to submit to a Minister or to the Parliament, upon its own initiative or at their request, reports or proposals relating to issues regarding the economic life of the country.
1 Article 23(2)(l) of the Competition Law.
2 Article 35 of the Competition Law.
3 Article 28(1) of the Competition Law.
4 Article 43 of the Competition Law.

2.1.2 *Other enforcement authorities*

President of the Commercial Court Article 95 of the Trade Practices Act provides that a party seeking relief against an unfair trade practice may apply to the President of the Commercial Court for a cease and desist order. Following a special summary proceeding, a cease and desist order may be granted.[5]

Commercial courts and courts of first instance Apart from the summary procedure provided for by Article 95 of the Trade Practices Act, any unlawful restraints of trade may also be the subject of a tort action brought before ordinary courts under Article 1382 of the Civil Code.

Pursuant to Article 1382 of the Civil Code, proceedings may be brought either before the Courts of First Instance or the Commercial Courts. However, as far as the Commercial Courts are concerned, the defendant must qualify as a merchant within the meaning of Belgian law.

2.2 Jurisdictional rules

2.2.1 *Procedural rules provided for by the Competition Law*

Investigative powers of the Competition Service The Competition Service has wide investigative powers which are comparable to those of the EC Commission. Under Article 23(2) of the Competition Law, the Competition Service is empowered to request undertakings and associations of undertakings to provide information.[6] If, within the specified time limit, the undertakings or associations do not supply the information requested or if the information they provide is incorrect, incomplete or misleading, the President of the Competition Council may, at the request of the Competition Service, order that the information be supplied. In addition, if the information is not supplied accurately or within the appropriate time limit, the Competition Council is authorised to impose fines ranging from BEF 20,000 to BEF 1,000,000.[7] Furthermore, the President of the Competition Council may impose periodic penalty payments of up to BEF 250,000 per day, if undertakings or associations do not comply with decisions requiring them to supply specific information.

The Competition Service is also empowered to gather all information, take written or oral testimonies, obtain all necessary documents or information and make all necessary findings on the spot. It is authorised to carry out an investigation at the undertaking's premises to examine the books and other business records and take copies of same. Moreover, provided it has obtained the prior authorization of a judge, it is entitled to undertake investigations at the dwellings of company managers, directors and staff, as well as all other internal and external persons entrusted with the commercial, accounting, administrative, financial and fiscal management of the undertaking.

Anti-competitive practices The Competition Service may start an investigation of anti-competitive practices as a result of one of the following actions:

---

5 Action en cessation/vordering tot staking.
6 Article 23(2) of the Competition Law.
7 Article 37 of the Competition Law.

(a) requests by undertakings involved for a negative clearance or an exemption decision;

(b) complaints lodged by interested parties demonstrating a direct and immediate interest;

(c) requests by the Minister of Economic Affairs or the Competition Council where there are serious indications of the existence of a restrictive practice or in connection with a proposal for a group exemption. In both cases the Competition Service may also start an investigation on its own initiative;

(d) requests by public institutions responsible for supervising a particular economic sector such as the Banking and Finance Commission;

(e) requests by the Brussels Court of Appeals in the context of a request for a preliminary ruling.

The procedure before the competition service and the Competition Council is as follows:

(a) before starting an investigation, the Competition Service must first examine whether the request is admissible.[8] If the Competition Service concludes that the request is inadmissible it will propose to the Competition Council not to act upon the request. The Council must then decide whether or not to follow this proposal;

(b) if the request is held to be admissible by the Competition Service or if the Competition Council rejects the conclusion of inadmissibility reached by the Competition Service, the Competition Service must start its investigation;[9]

(c) on completion of its investigation, and prior to drafting its report – which must indicate the grounds on which it is based – the Competition Service must grant the parties involved an opportunity to submit their views.[10] At this stage of the procedure, the parties do not have access to the file;

(d) the Competition Service then submits the file to the Competition Council, together with its report which may include:

  (i) a proposed decision;
  (ii) a proposal that the Competition Council should not act upon the complaint (if the Competition Service finds that the complaint is unfounded);
  (iii) a proposal for a group exemption;
  (iv) a reply to the Court of Appeals;

(e) on receipt of the report from the Competition Service, the Competition Council is to inform the undertakings whose activities are the subject of the investigation of the fact that the report has been completed and, if deemed appropriate, of the identity of the complainant. The Competition Council must also send a copy of the report to the undertakings at least one month before the hearing at which the case will be examined.[11] This must be done even if the Competition Service proposes in its report that the Competition Council should not act upon the request;

(f) the Competition Council informs the Competition Commission of the cases

8 Article 24(1) of the Competition Law.
9 Article 24(2) of the Competition Law.
10 Article 24(3) of the Competition Law.
11 Article 27(1) of the Competition Law.

that have been initiated and communicates the identity of the parties and the provisions of the Competition Law on which the file is based;

(g)   the undertakings involved are given an opportunity to consult a non-confidential version of the administrative file held by the Competition Council and to obtain copies of same;

(h)   the Competition Council examines the case at a hearing where the undertaking whose activities have been investigated will be heard, as well as the complainant, should they so request. The Competition Council may also hear other persons or undertakings if they provide evidence of sufficient interest;

(i)   the Competition Council may adopt any of the following decisions:

   (i)   *a negative clearance*   This is a decision, issued at the request of the undertakings concerned, stating that, on the basis of the information available, there are no grounds for taking action pursuant to Articles 2(1) or 3 of the Competition Law;

   (ii)· *an individual exemption*   Such a decision may be issued where the undertakings involved have requested an exemption of the prohibition on restrictive practices contained in Article 2(1) of the Competition Law. If the necessary conditions are fulfilled, the Council may grant an individual exemption. This exemption may contain conditions and obligations and is granted for a definite period, with the possibility of renewal on request;

   (iii) a decision establishing the existence of an anti-competitive practice and ordering the termination of this practice in the way set forth by the Competition Council;

   (iv) a decision that there is no infringement of the Competition Law;

   (v)   a proposal for a group exemption addressed to the Minister of Economic Affairs.

Concentrations   As regards concentrations, the Competition Law provides for a fast two-step procedure. The first stage comprises a preliminary examination of the concentration which must be completed by the Competition Council within a period of one month following the notification by the parties involved. Upon receipt of the notification, the Competition Service starts its investigation although it may ask for additional information. Subsequently, the Competition Service hears the parties and submits its report to the Competition Council. Within ten days of receiving the report, the Council must send a copy of same to the undertakings concerned. The Council must allow the parties involved to be heard. At the latest within one month following the notification or receipt of the additional information requested, the Council must adopt one of the following decisions:

(a)   the notified transaction is not covered by the Competition Law; or

(b)   the notified transaction is covered by the Competition Law but does not raise serious doubts as to its compatibility with the standards set forth in the Competition Law. In such cases, the Competition Council may not oppose the concentration; or

(c)   the notified transaction is covered by the Competition Law and raises serious doubts as to its compatibility with the Competition Law. In such cases, the Competition Council must initiate further proceedings.

In the latter case, the Competition Council begins the second stage of the procedure and instructs the Competition Service to undertake an additional inquiry and, as a result, to draft a new report, a copy of which is sent to the parties.

After hearing the parties, the Competition Council must adopt a final decision on the admissibility of the concentration within a period of 75 days following the day on which the decision to initiate a second step proceeding was taken.

This decision will determine either that:

(a) the concentration is admissible; or that
(b) the concentration is not admissible. In this case, the Competition Council may provide for additional measures necessary to restore effective competition, such as the divestiture of certain undertakings or assets or the termination of situations of joint control.

If the Competition Council fails to take a decision within either the one-month period or the 75-day period, the concentration will be deemed to be approved.

The Royal Decree of 23 March 1993 relating to the notification of concentrations of undertakings sets out the notification formalities. If the concentration results from an agreement, the notification must be made jointly. In all other cases, the notification will be made by the undertaking that effects the concentration.[12] All notifications are to be made using form CONC C/C-1.[13] At the request of the undertakings involved, the notification of a concentration may be converted into an application for a negative clearance or a notification in order to obtain an exemption[14] if upon examination of the transaction it appears that there is no concentration.

Appeals An appeal may be lodged against a decision adopted by the Competition Council, or its President, with the Brussels Court of Appeals within 30 days from the date of the decision's publication in the Belgian Official Journal, or from the date of its notification (depending on the type of decision). The appeal may be lodged either by the undertakings that were subject to the investigation, by the complainant, or by any of the parties that appeared before the Competition Council. Although the appeal has no suspensory effect, the Brussels Court of Appeals may, upon request, suspend the obligation to pay fines or penalties until the date of its judgment on the merits. The decisions of the Brussels Court of Appeals are published in the Belgian Official Journal.

2.2.2 The cease and desist order provided for by the Trade Practices Act

A party, seeking relief against an unfair trade practice that is specifically prohibited by a provision of the Trade Practices Act or that falls under the catch-all provisions of Articles 93 and 94 of that Act, may apply to the President of the Commercial Court for a cease and desist order. Articles 93 and 94 of the Trade Practices Act contain a general prohibition against all unfair trade practices whereby a trader injures or attempts to injure the professional interests of one or more traders or the interests of one or more consumers.

Such cease and desist order must be granted, following a special summary proceeding, if the following criteria are satisfied:

12 Article 12(2) of the Competition Law and Article 2 of the first Royal Decree of 23 March 1993.
13 Annex to the first Royal Decree of 23 March 1993.
14 Article 6 of the first Royal Decree of 23 March 1993.

(a)   the petitioner must have a personal interest in the termination of the practice at issue.

Under the Trade Practices Act the following persons or entities may also apply for a cease and desist order:[15]

(i)   the Minister of Economic Affairs;

(ii)   trade associations, provided that they have legal personality, and have an interest in obtaining the termination of the alleged unfair trade practice; and

(iii) consumer associations, provided that they have legal personality and that they are represented at the Consumer Council; and

(b)   the activity alleged to constitute an unfair trade practice must not have been discontinued before the suit was brought, unless such practice may be repeated.

Where the President of the Commercial Court determines that an unfair trade practice has been engaged in, he may forbid such action in the future. In addition, the President's cease and desist order may be accompanied by the imposition of periodical penalty payments for non-compliance with the cease and desist order. However, the President is not authorized to award damages. Decisions taken by the President of the Commercial Court may be appealed to the Court of Appeals within one month following the formal notification of the judgment prohibiting the unfair trade practice.

The President of the Commercial Court who issues a cease and desist order may also order the posting of the judgment within or outside the premises of the offender and/or the publication of the judgment in newspapers or otherwise, at the offender's expense.

2.2.3   Other procedures under the Trade Practices Act

Warning procedure   The Trade Practices Act provides for a warning procedure[16] whereby the Minister of Economic Affairs may formally notify a trader that he is in breach of the Trade Practices Act and that, if he does not cease the violation, the Minister of Economic Affairs will initiate legal proceedings against the alleged offender.

Investigation   Officers of the General Economic Inspection appointed by the Minister of Economic Affairs may investigate those infringements of the Trade Practices Act which are subject to criminal sanctions.[17] To that end, they are entitled to carry out on-the-spot investigations. Other officers appointed by the Minister of Economic Affairs may, on the basis of the aforesaid investigation reports, make administrative settlement offers. These settlement offers prevent a criminal case from being brought in relation to the infringement concerned.[18]

---

15 Article 98 of the Trade Practices Act.
16 Article 101 of the Trade Practices Act.
17 Article 113 of the Trade Practices Act.
18 Article 116 of the Trade Practices Act.

2.3 Fines and other sanctions

2.3.1 *Under the Competition Law*

The Competition Council is empowered to impose fines on each of the undertakings concerned of up to 10% of their annual turnover in the following cases:

(a) when it determines the existence of a restrictive practice;
(b) upon breach of a condition or obligation attached to an exemption decision;
(c) when an exemption decision has been obtained on the basis of incorrect information or by fraud;
(d) when the parties abuse the exemption granted to them;
(e) upon breach of a condition or obligation attached to a decision by which a concentration is approved;
(f) when the undertakings concerned, prior to the adoption of a decision by the Competition Council on the compatibility of a concentration with the Competition Law, take steps which impede the reversibility of the concentration or bring about a lasting change in the market structure.

Fines may not be levied for acts taking place between the notification of a restrictive practice with a view to obtaining an exemption (as distinct from a negative clearance) and the adoption of a decision by the Competition Council, provided these acts have been described in the notification.[19]

The Competition Council is also entitled to impose fines of between BEF 20,000 and BEF 1,000,000 on persons, undertakings and associations of undertakings in the following circumstances:

(a) when incorrect or misleading information is supplied in a notification or in reply to a request for information;
(b) when incomplete information is supplied;
(c) when information is supplied late;
(d) when the investigation by the Competition Service is resisted;
(e) when a concentration is realised without prior notification.

Finally, in several other cases described in the Competition Law, periodic penalty payments of up to BEF 250,000 per day may be imposed by the Competition Council or by its President.

2.3.2 *Under the Trade Practices Act*

Pursuant to the Trade Practices Act, persons who intentionally infringe the provisions of that Act are liable to receive fines ranging from BEF 500 to BEF 20,000 (to be multiplied by 100).[20]

The violation of a cease and desist order issued by the President of the Commercial Court constitutes an offence punishable by a fine of BEF 250 to BEF 20,000 (to be multiplied by 100).[1]

---

19 Article 39 of the Competition Law.
20 Article 103 of the Trade Practices Act.
1 Article 104 of the Trade Practices Act.

2.4   Third party rights

2.4.1   Under the Competition Law

A third party suffering damages as a result of an infringement of the Competition Law has the following three options:

(a)   lodge a complaint with the Competition Service relating to the alleged infringement;
(b)   initiate proceedings before the courts; or
(c)   take action under (a) and (b) above at the same time.

Right of third parties to lodge complaints, to ask for provisional measures and to be heard by the Competition Council   The Competition Service may begin an investigation of anti-competitive practices or concentrations as a result of a complaint submitted by a natural or legal person demonstrating a direct and actual interest. The complainant may request the President of the Competition Council to adopt provisional measures so as to suspend the restrictive practices (not the concentrations) under investigation when this is necessary to avoid serious, immediate and irreparable harm to the undertakings whose interests are affected by the practices. The plaintiff must demonstrate the urgency of the matter and all of the conditions must be fulfilled. The complainant may also claim that the general economic interest is suffering damage. The President will request the Competition Service to submit a report containing the measures it considers necessary. This report must be submitted to the President within a period of maximum 15 days. The President must reach his decision within a period of 15 days after the submission of the report. The report must be accessible to all parties who must be given an opportunity to make their views known. The decision will be notified to the undertaking concerned and to the complainant.

During the proceedings, the Competition Council may also hear third parties, at their request, provided they show a sufficient interest. In merger control cases, this may include members of the boards of the undertakings concerned and workers' representatives in these undertakings.

Right of third parties to initiate proceedings before the courts   Third parties may also invoke the prohibition of anti-competitive practices directly before the ordinary courts. These courts are entitled to establish the invalidity of cartels and decisions prohibited pursuant to Article 2(1) of the Competition Law as well as to condemn the abuse of a dominant position in accordance with Article 3 of the Competition Law. Courts do not have competence to grant exemptions.

Article 42 of the Competition Law provides that any court or tribunal, if it considers that a decision on the compatibility of a practice with the Competition Law is necessary in order to enable it to give judgment, may suspend the case and request the Brussels Court of Appeals to give a preliminary ruling. Such ruling is not subject to appeal and is, as to the legal issue that it addresses, binding upon the court or tribunal that made the request. The Court of Appeals may ask the Competition Service to conduct an investigation in order to enable it to give its preliminary ruling.

2.4.2 Under the Trade Practices Act

A third party which suffers damage as a result of an infringement of the Trade Practices Act has the following three options:

(a) request the President of the Commercial Court to issue a cease and desist order forbidding the restrictive practice;
(b) initiate proceedings before the ordinary courts on the basis of a cease and desist order issued by the President of the Commercial Court in order to obtain compensation for the damage suffered;
(c) bring infringements of the Trade Practices Act to the attention of the General Economic Inspection which may start an investigation.

3 CHECKLIST OF POTENTIAL INFRINGEMENTS

3.1 Agency

3.1.1 Under Belgian law, a commercial agent is normally defined as an independent intermediary who has the authority to negotiate, and possibly to conclude, agreements in the name and on behalf of the principal. Commercial agents are different from commercial representatives in that while both parties have lasting links with their respective principal and act in his name and on his behalf, a commercial agent is nevertheless an independent intermediary whereas a commercial representative is subordinate to his principal. Commercial agents are also different from distributors in that a commercial agent acts in the name and on behalf of his principal while a distributor acts in his own name.

3.1.2 As the Competition Law is generally based on the EC competition rules, the case law developed by the EC Court of Justice and the European Commission relating to agency agreements is relevant for the purposes of interpreting the Competition Law.

3.1.3 Agency agreements may come within the scope of Article 2(1) of the Competition Law. However, exclusive dealing contracts with commercial agents would not have a restrictive effect on the market for the provision of goods, provided the agent does not assume any financial risk resulting from the transaction. The commercial agent in that case would only perform an auxiliary function, acting on the instructions and in the interest of the company for which he is operating. Nevertheless, the case law of the European Commission and the EC Court of Justice shows that care should be exercised when seeking to rely on these principles.

3.1.4 Agency agreements may come within the scope of Article 3 of the Competition Law as well. For example, a contractual clause prohibiting competition between a dominant principal and his agent could constitute an abuse within the meaning of Article 3 when this agent has duties which from an economic point of view are approximately the same as those of an independent dealer.

3.2 Distribution

3.2.1 Under Belgian law, distribution agreements are usually defined as agreements whereby one party (the supplier) agrees with another (the distributor) to supply the latter with products or services for the purpose of resale. Distribution agreements may be entered into at different levels in the distribution chain: between manufacturer and importer, between importer and wholesaler, or between wholesaler and retailer.

3.2.2   Provisions in distribution agreements such as territorial restrictions which can take a variety of forms ranging from outright bans on exports to differential pricing or restrictions on the provision of after sales service, resale price maintenance, customer restrictions, restrictions on use, pre- and post-termination non-compete provisions, etc may be restrictive of competition and consequently may come within the prohibition of Article 2(1) of the Competition Law.

3.2.3   As mentioned above, the case law of the EC Court of Justice and the European Commission relating to distribution agreements may be relevant in order to interpret the Competition Law.

3.2.4   Under Article 28(1) of the Competition Law, the Minister of Economic Affairs may adopt Ministerial Decrees providing for a group exemption for certain categories of practices. It is expected that the Minister will adopt a Ministerial Decree similar to Regulation No 1983/83 on exclusive distribution agreements.

3.3   Selective distribution

3.3.1   Selective distribution is a form of distribution in which a supplier limits the sale of its products to a limited class of wholesalers and/or retailers.

3.3.2   The existing EC case law is relevant for the purpose of interpreting the Competition Law. This is evidenced by the fact that Article 85(1) of the EC Treaty has been used by the Belgian courts to assess whether a refusal by a supplier to admit a new distributor in a selective distribution system was lawful.[2]

3.3.3   A selective distribution system may be based upon three broad categories of requirements:

(a)   objective qualitative requirements, ie requirements concerning the nature of the product which may call for specific technical qualifications of the distributor, his staff and business premises;

(b)   qualitative requirements combined with additional obligations. This category covers situations in which selection is not based solely on the technical expertise of the distributor but, in addition, on his willingness to assume certain other obligations (eg his co-operation in sales promotion);

(c)   quantitative requirements. This category consists of the quantitative limits that a manufacturer may choose to impose on the authorised distributors.

3.3.4   As far as the objective qualitative criteria are concerned, these criteria would not violate Article 2(1) of the Competition Law provided that there is no discrimination in the application of such criteria and that the system is open to all potential dealers who meet the criteria. With regard to qualitative requirements

---

2   Pres Comm Brussels, 23 October 1985, *RDC*, 1987, 293; Pres Comm Charleroi, 14 June 1993, RG 2708; Pres Comm Brussels, 8 March 1993. RG AC 13342/92.

combined with additional obligations, such additional obligations would normally fall within the prohibition of Article 2(1), but may be exempted pursuant to Article 2(3) in some cases. Finally, with regard to quantitative requirements, they are usually seen as being restrictive of competition and will be exempted pursuant to Article 2(3) only in exceptional circumstances.

3.4 Exclusive purchasing

3.4.1 Exclusive purchase agreements are agreements under which the purchaser accepts an obligation to purchase particular goods from one supplier only over a relatively long period. Such agreements may be entered into by purchasers who use the product in order to produce another product or by purchasers intending to resell the product. Exclusive purchase agreements may fall within the prohibition of Article 2(1) of the Competition Law, in addition to the prohibition of Article 3 of the Competition Law when the supplier is in a dominant position. Individual exemptions may be granted in certain circumstances if a notification is made.

3.4.2 It is expected that the Minister of Economic Affairs will adopt a Ministerial Decree similar to Regulation No 1984/83 in respect of exclusive purchase agreements.

3.5 Franchising

3.5.1 Franchising may be described as a form of commercial marketing whereby goods and/or services are distributed at the retail level under the same trade mark or trade name through a network of similar, yet economically independent, retail outlets.

3.5.2 Franchising agreements in general have positive effects as they increase competition and contribute to the creation of a unified market. Nevertheless, such agreements can have a negative effect on competition if they contain restrictions of competition such as market sharing and resale price maintenance. Such restrictions are not justified by the need to protect the franchisor's know-how or preserve the identity and reputation of the franchise system. Consequently, such restrictions fall under the prohibition of Article 2(1) of the Competition Law.

3.5.3 The Minister of Economic Affairs may adopt a Ministerial Decree similar to the already existing Regulation No 4087/88 on franchising agreements.

3.6 Intellectual property licensing

3.6.1 Assignments or licensing agreements involving intellectual property rights should be drafted having regard to the provisions of EC law governing the free movement of goods as well as the provisions of Belgian competition law.

3.6.2 As far as the provisions of EC law governing the free movement of goods is concerned, the EC Court of Justice has created rules concerning so-called 'Community-wide exhaustion' of intellectual property rights which affect the right of the owner of an intellectual property right to oppose the import of goods protected by that intellectual property right. Under the exhaustion doctrine, the owner of an intellectual property right will be unable to rely on his right to prohibit the importation of products which have been placed on the market by himself or with his consent in another Member State.

3.6.3   As far as Belgian competition rules are concerned, the licensing of intellectual property rights frequently gives rise to potential restrictions under Article 2(1) of the Competition Law. For example, clauses in intellectual property licensing agreements dealing with exclusivity, restrictions on the licensee's activities outside the licensed territory, the use of trademark and get-up, tying, field of use, no challenge, grant back, non-competition, price restrictions, royalties, post-term bans on use, duration, etc may fall within the prohibition of Article 2(1).

3.6.4   The Minister of Economic Affairs may adopt Ministerial Decrees similar to the existing Regulation No 2349/84 and Regulation No 556/89 on patents and know-how licensing agreements.

3.7   Refusals to supply

3.7.1   A refusal to supply does not normally constitute a violation of Article 2(1) of the Competition Law, unless it is shown to be brought about by the existence of an agreement or concerted practice which has as its object or effect the prevention, restriction or distortion to an appreciable extent of competition within the relevant Belgian market, or a substantial part thereof.

3.7.2   Even though the text of Article 3 of the Competition Law does not impose a duty to supply on dominant undertakings, it is likely that, unless objectively justified, refusals to supply by a dominant undertaking will constitute an abuse within the meaning of Article 3.

3.7.3   A refusal to supply may also fall under the prohibition of Articles 93 and 94 of the Trade Practices Act, which prohibit unfair trade practices whereby a trader injures the professional interests of one or more traders or the interests of one or more consumers. Refusals to supply are in principle lawful. Refusals to supply become unlawful only when the refusal is decided arbitrarily[3] when the refusal is applied discriminatorily or when the refusal does not have a legitimate purpose.

3.8   Price restrictions

3.8.1   As indicated above, both Articles 2(1) and 3 of the Competition Law include amongst listed examples of restrictions of competition or abuse:

(a)   directly or indirectly fixing purchase or selling prices or any other trading conditions;
(b)   applying dissimilar conditions to equivalent transactions.

3.8.2   Resale price maintenance is likely to infringe both Articles 2(1) and 3 of the Competition Law.

---

3   Cass, 27 June 1985. Pas, 1985, I.

3.8.3 Price-fixing agreements between competitors will in most cases be held to be incompatible with Article 2(1) of the Competition Law and will generally be denied an exemption. The most obvious type of price-fixing is an agreement between competitors whereby they fix their sale or resale prices. Various other types of conduct which, at first glance, do not appear to constitute price-fixing are likely to be condemned under Article 2(1): agreements fixing discounts to be offered to customers, agreements fixing target prices, agreements setting up a compensation system for equalising proceeds of domestic and foreign sales, agreements restricting or limiting rebates, agreements to refrain from advertising rebates, etc.

3.8.4 Discriminatory pricing, ie agreements or practices whereby competitors undertake to discriminate among their customers as regards pricing terms, will infringe Article 2(1) of the Competition Law.

3.8.5 The charging of discriminatory prices by a dominant undertaking may also constitute an abuse of a dominant position within the meaning of Article 3 of the Competition Law. Article 3(c) provides that an abuse may consist in applying dissimilar conditions to equivalent transactions with other trading parties, thereby placing them at a competitive disadvantage.

3.9 Tie in sales

3.9.1 Under the terms of Article 3 of the Competition Law, the tying of an obligation to purchase a product or a service to the supply of other products or services may be prohibited. Among the examples of an abuse of a dominant position listed in Article 3(d) are the conclusion of a contract subject to the acceptance by the other party of supplementary obligations which, by their nature or according to commercial usage, have no connection with the subject matter of the contract.

3.9.2 A tie in clause may also constitute an infringement of Article 2(1) of the Competition Law.

3.9.3 The Trade Practices Act contains a general prohibition on the tying of products or services that are offered to consumers. A joint offer exists under the Trade Practices Act when the acquisition (with or without consideration) of products, services, other advantages or of vouchers is linked to the acquisition of other products or services.[4] It should be noted, however, that the following exceptions to this rule exist:

(a) a joint lump-sum offer for products or services that constitute a single unit;[5]
(b) a joint lump-sum offer for identical products or services provided that:

    (i) each product and each service can be bought separately at its usual price in the same place;
    (ii) the purchaser is clearly informed of this possibility as well as the separate sale price of each product and service; and
    (iii) the price reduction offered to the purchaser of all the products or

4 Article 54 of the Trade Practices Act.
5 Article 55(1) of the Trade Practices Act.

services does not exceed one third of the total normal price that the customer would have to pay.[6]

The concept of identical products or services has been narrowly interpreted by the Belgian courts. Only products and services which are identical with respect to their form, dimension, quality, measures and characteristics are considered to be identical; products that are merely similar are not. For example, the joint offer for two books having a different title was held not to be covered by the exception;[7]

(c)   the offering for free with a principal product or service, of (i) accessories of the principal product, (ii) packaging of the products, (iii) small products or services accepted by commercial usage including delivery, installation, control and maintenance of the products sold, (iv) samples (to the extent that they are offered in quantities necessary to check the qualities of the product), (v) pictures and other prints of minimal commercial value, (vi) vouchers granting participation in lotteries authorized by law, and (vii) promotional articles that bear a non-erasable message provided that their value does not exceed five per cent of the price of the main product or service;[8]

(d)   the issuing, for free, with a principal product or service, of vouchers entitling the consumer to a discount or a premium provided that the specific requirements laid down in Article 57 of the Trade Practices Act are complied with.

3.10   Information exchange

Information exchange agreements may lead to market co-ordination among those exchanging the information. Violations of Article 2(1) of the Competition Law may consist in the exchange of various kinds of trade information, including cost and production data, sales and business strategies, and prices. The legality of this type of arrangement will be assessed on a case-by-case basis taking into account all the specific circumstances and the case law developed by the EC Court of Justice and the EC Commission.

3.11   Joint buying and selling

3.11.1   Joint purchasing agreements may restrict competition where the participants represent a significant share of the market, thus affecting the competitive position of suppliers.

3.11.2   In their most common form, joint selling arrangements involve the grant to a common agent of the right to sell the products of the participants in specified areas. In order to ensure that all participants receive the same price per unit regardless of the actual selling prices obtained by the joint agent, joint selling arrangements often provide for equalisation systems.

3.11.3   Joint selling and purchasing arrangements are likely to be considered unlawful under Article 2(1) of the Competition Law if the firms involved account for a large share of the market concerned.

---

6   Article 55(2) of the Trade Practices Act.
7   Pres Comm Brussels, 23 May 1981, VCB 1982, 57.
8   Article 56 of the Trade Practices Act.

3.12 Market sharing

Market sharing in its various forms is prohibited under the Competition Law. Article 2(1)(c) expressly mentions the sharing of markets or sources of supply as an anti-competitive practice and Article 2(1)(b) condemns, inter alia, the limitation or control of production.

3.13 Joint ventures

3.13.1 Belgian law draws a distinction between concentrative joint ventures, which are subject to the merger control provisions of the Belgian Competition Law, and co-operative joint ventures which may be subject to the application of Article 2(1) of the Competition Law.

3.13.2 Transactions, including the creation of a joint venture, which have as their object or effect the co-ordination of the competitive behaviour of undertakings which remain independent do not amount to a concentration within the meaning of the Competition Law.[9] Such transactions may be subject to Article 2(1) of the Competition Law.

3.13.3 The creation of joint ventures which perform on a lasting basis all the functions of an autonomous economic entity, and which do not give rise to the co-ordination of the competitive behaviour of the parties amongst themselves or between them and the joint venture are concentrations within the meaning of the Competition Law.

4 CONCENTRATIONS, MERGERS AND ACQUISITIONS

4.1 Introduction

4.1.1 On 1 April 1993, the date of entry into force of the Competition Law, merger control was introduced in Belgium.

4.1.2 The substantive rules for Belgian merger control are set forth in the Competition Law which is complemented by a Royal Decree of 15 March 1993 and by two Royal Decrees of 23 March 1993 all of which deal, inter alia, with the implementation of notifications, time limits and hearings. Form CONC C/C- 1 is contained in the Annex to the first Royal Decree of 23 March 1993 and sets forth the information required by the Belgian competition authorities for a pre-merger notification.

4.1.3 As the system of Belgian mergei control is greatly inspired by the EC Merger Regulation, the case law of the EC Commission may provide assistance in interpreting the Competition Law.

4.1.4 As indicated above, the Competition Council and the Competition Service are the competition authorities with primary responsibility for applying the Belgian merger control provisions.

---

9 Article 9(2) of the Competition Law.

4.2   The scope of Belgian merger control

4.2.1   The Belgian merger control provisions apply to concentrations composed of undertakings whose joint turnover and market share exceed certain quantitative thresholds. The term concentration includes all mergers, acquisitions and takeovers as well as joint ventures of a concentrative nature.

4.2.2   Article 11(1) of the Competition Law contains the appropriate quantitative thresholds. A concentration which fulfils the following conditions will be subject to Belgian merger control:

(a)   the joint turnover of the undertakings concerned must exceed BEF 3 billion; and
(b)   the undertakings concerned must together hold 25% of the relevant market in Belgium.

The turnover mentioned in the Competition Law is the total consolidated turnover achieved during the previous accounting year in Belgium and abroad, calculated in accordance with the principles contained in a Royal Decree of 6 March 1990 on consolidated accounts (see section 4.6.1 below).[10] The quantitative threshold amounts contained in Article 11(1) of the Competition Law may be increased by Royal Decree.

4.3   Appraisal of concentrations

4.3.1   Concentrations are appraised for their compatibility with the Competition Law on the basis of their effect on the Belgian market. Concentrations are compatible with the Competition Law[11] provided that they do not create or reinforce a dominant position restrictive of competition to an appreciable extent on the Belgian market, or a substantial part thereof.

4.3.2   Although the creation or strengthening of a dominant position is the precondition for the Competition Council to oppose a concentration, this does not mean that it is sufficient on its own to warrant opposition. In appraising a concentration for its compatibility with the Competition Law, the Competition Council is obliged to take account of factors such as the general economic interest, the competitiveness of the economic sectors involved compared with international competition and the interests of consumers.[12]

If the Competition Council were to establish that the improvements in production or distribution, the economic or technical progress or the improvements in the market structure created by the concentration outweigh any negative impact on competition, the Competition Council may decide not to oppose a concentration even though it creates or reinforces a dominant position.

4.3.3   A concentration may not be authorised if it imposes restrictions on the undertakings concerned that are not indispensable for the concentration or that

10   Article 46(1) of the Competition Law.
11   Article 10(2) of the Competition Law.
12   Article 10(3) of the Competition Law.

afford the undertakings concerned the possibility of ousting competition in respect of a substantial part of the products or services in question.[13]

4.4   Definition of concentration

4.4.1   Article 9 of the Competition Law defines the notion of 'concentration' in substantially the same way as Article 3 of the EC Merger Regulation. A concentration shall be deemed to arise where:

(a)   two or more previously independent undertakings merge; or

(b)   one or more persons already controlling one or more undertakings acquire, whether by purchase of securities or assets, by contract or by any other means, direct or indirect control of the whole or parts of one or more other undertakings.

4.4.2   The concept of change of control is to be interpreted widely, as illustrated by the Competition Law. The Competition Law provides that control results from rights, agreements or other means which, separately or jointly, in consideration of all factual and legal circumstances, make it possible to exercise a decisive influence on the activities of an undertaking. As a result, the concept of change of control is not dependent on legal control but is established if decisive influence may be exercised over an undertaking.

4.4.3   Arrangements, including the creation of a joint venture, which have as their purpose or effect the co-ordination of the competitive behaviour of undertakings which remain independent of each other do not amount to a concentration within the meaning of the Competition Law.[14] Such transactions may be examined under Article 2(1) of the Competition Law which deals with restrictive agreements and practices. However, the creation of joint ventures which perform all the functions of an autonomous economic entity on a lasting basis, and which do not give rise to the co-ordination of the competitive behaviour of the parties amongst themselves or between them and the joint venture are concentrations within the meaning of the Competition Law.[15]

4.4.4   Exceptionally, the following transactions are not considered concentrations within the meaning of the Competition Law:

(a)   when credit institutions, other financial institutions or insurance companies, the normal activities of which include dealing in securities on their own behalf or on behalf of others, hold on a temporary basis securities which they have acquired in an undertaking with a view to reselling them, provided they do not exercise the voting rights attached to these securities with a view to controlling the competitive behaviour of that undertaking or provided they exercise such voting rights only with a view to preparing the sale of whole or a part of the undertaking concerned, or its assets, or the sale of those securities, and that any such sale takes place within one year of the date of acquisition;[16]

13   Article 10(3) of the Competition Law.
14   Article 9(2) of the Competition Law.
15   Article 9(2) of the Competition Law.
16   Article 9(5) of the Competition Law.

(b)   when control is acquired by a government or court-appointed office holder pursuant to a judicial decision or a compulsory liquidation procedure;[17]

(c)   when the concentration is subject to control by the EC Commission.[18]

4.5   Prior notification of concentration

4.5.1   A concentration must be notified to the Competition Service when turnover and market share exceed the quantitative thresholds defined in the Competition Law. A concentration must be notified within a period of one week from either the conclusion of the agreement, the announcement of the public bid, or the acquisition of a controlling interest.

4.5.2   The first Royal Decree of 23 March 1993 deals in detail with the procedure and form of notification. Form CONC C/C- 1 sets forth the way in which notifications must be submitted.[19]

4.5.3   When the concentration is the result of an agreement, the obligation to notify rests jointly on all parties. In all other cases, the party acquiring control of the whole or parts of others is obliged to make the notification.[20]

4.6   Calculation of turnover

4.6.1   The turnover mentioned in the Competition Law is the total consolidated turnover achieved during the previous accounting year in Belgium and abroad, calculated in accordance with the principles contained in the Royal Decree of 6 March 1990 on consolidated accounts. As a result, the turnover of all the undertakings that belong to the same group should be added to the turnover of the undertaking directly involved. The concept of a group of undertakings must be interpreted in accordance with the Royal Decree of 8 October 1976 on the annual accounts of undertakings, as amended.

4.6.2   If only part of an undertaking is to be acquired, only the turnover of that part of the business which is being acquired will be taken into account as far as the seller is concerned.

4.6.3   Where, within a two-year period, two or more transactions take place between the same undertakings, these transactions shall be treated as one and the same concentration arising on the date of the last transaction.

4.6.4   The Competition Law establishes different criteria for the calculation of turnover of credit institutions, or other financial institutions, insurance undertakings and public undertakings. As regards credit institutions and other financial institutions, turnover is replaced by one-tenth of the total balance sheet of the institution concerned.[1] As regards insurance undertakings, turnover is replaced by

17   Article 9(5) of the Competition Law.
18   Article 13 of the Competition Law.
19   Annex to the first Royal Decree of 23 March 1993.
20   Article 12(2) of the Competition Law.
1   Article 46(3)(a) of the Competition Law.

one-tenth of the gross premiums underwritten,[2] which must comprise all amounts received and receivable in respect of insurance contracts issued by or on behalf of the insurance undertakings, including also outgoing reinsurance premiums, and after deduction of taxes and quasi-fiscal contributions or levies charged by reference to the amounts of individual premiums or the total volume of premiums. As regards public undertakings, the turnover to be taken into consideration is that of all the undertakings forming an economic entity and endowed with autonomous decision-making power, irrespective of who holds their capital or of the rules of administrative supervision applicable to them.

4.7 Procedure

4.7.1 In respect of each stage of the merger control procedure, the Competition Law lays down specific time limits with which the Competition Council must comply.

4.7.2 Within one month following the notification, the Competition Council's preliminary examination of the concentration must be completed. This examination is carried out on the basis of a report prepared by the Competition Service and will result in a decision that:

(a) the notified operation is not covered by the Competition Law (for example, because the concentration does not meet the quantitative thresholds set forth in the Competition Law). As a result, the Competition Council is obliged to decide not to oppose the concentration; or

(b) the notified operation comes within the scope of the Competition Law but does not raise serious doubts as to its admissibility. In this case, the Competition Council is obliged to decide not to oppose the concentration; or

(c) the notified operation is covered by the Competition Law and raises serious doubts as to its admissibility. As a result, the Competition Council must decide to initiate further proceedings.

4.7.3 If the Competition Council were to fail to take a decision within a period of one month following the notification, then the notified concentration will be deemed to be admissible. If further proceedings are initiated by the Competition Council, the Competition Service will be asked to draw up a new report. The Competition Council must take a final decision concerning the admissibility of the notified concentration within 75 days from the day on which further proceedings were initiated. Should the Competition Council fail to take a decision within this period of 75 days, the notified concentration will be deemed to be admissible.

4.7.4 Where the Competition Council establishes that a concentration is incompatible with the Competition Law, it must issue a decision accordingly. A decision by the Competition Council opposing the concentration may also impose conditions which are necessary to restore effective competition, including the divestiture of certain undertakings or assets.

4.7.5 Until the one-month period mentioned above has expired or until the issuance of a decision by the Competition Council, the undertakings concerned are

2 Article 46(3)(b) of the Competition Law.

only allowed to take those measures relating to the concentration which do not impede its reversibility and which do not lead to a lasting change in the structure of the market.[3] One month following the notification, the undertakings concerned may request the Competition Council to decide whether certain proposed measures would impede the reversibility of the concentration or lead to a lasting change in the market structure. The Competition Council may impose certain conditions or obligations, when authorizing these proposed measures.[4]

4.8   Request for information

With a view to obtaining all necessary information, the Competition Service enjoys wide investigative powers under the Competition Law.

4.9   Fines

4.9.1   Fines between BEF 20,000 and BEF 1 million may be imposed on parties which put a concentration into effect without prior notification in accordance with the Competition Law. A fine may be imposed even if the concentration is subsequently found to be admissible.

4.9.2   In addition, the Competition Council may impose fines on each of the undertakings concerned of up to 10% of their annual turnover if, prior to the adoption of a decision by the Competition Council on the admissibility of the concentration, the undertakings concerned take measures which impede the reversibility of the concentration or which bring about a lasting change in the market structure.

4.9.3   In addition to the possible imposition of fines, failure to notify may also result in the enforceability of the transaction being challenged.

4.10   Judicial review

The decisions of the Competition Council may be appealed to the Brussels Court of Appeals. The appeal must be lodged within a period of 30 days of the date of publication of the Competition Council's decision in the Belgian Official Journal.

3   Article 12(4) of the Competition Law.
4   Article 12(5) of the Competition Law.

Denmark

Erik Mohr Mersing

Kromann & Münter
14 Radhuspladsen
1550 Copenhagen V
Denmark

Tel   ++45 33 111110
Fax ++45 33 118028

CHAPTER V

Denmark

1 DANISH COMPETITION LAW

1.1 The law

1.1.1 The Competition Act and previous laws

The Danish Competition Act (Act No 370 of 7 June 1989 with later amendments) became effective on 1 January 1990. The Act repeals a number of previous Acts, including primarily the Danish Monopolies and Restrictive Practices Act (Act No 102 of 31 March 1955 with later amendments) which had been in force since 1955.

The Competition Act to some extent builds on the same principles as the former Monopolies and Restrictive Practices Act, and precedents are therefore still of some relevance for interpretation purposes.

1.1.2 Other relevant law

In a number of areas the Competition Act has been replaced or supplemented by special enactments.

The Competitive Tendering Act (Act No 216 of 8 June 1976) includes special rules governing bidding for building and civil engineering contracts. This industry is basically governed by the Competition Act, but the rules of the Competitive Tendering Act provide that the concept of free competition, on which the Competition Act is based, is to some extent deviated from.

The Danish Medicinal Drugs Act (Act No 327 of 26 June 1975 with later amendments) expressly provides that the pricing of manufactured drugs is comprised by the Competition Act. Consequently, the Act does not include any special regulation of this area and is mentioned only because price control of medicinal products used to be handled by the National Health Board.

The Electricity Supply Act (Act No 54 of 25 February 1976 with later amendments) transfers the control of electricity prices to the Electricity Pricing Committee which shares secretarial facilities with the Danish Competition Council.

The Heat Supply Act (Act No 382 of 13 June 1990) similarly transfers the control of gas and heat prices to the Gas and Heat Pricing Committee which also shares secretarial facilities with the Danish Competition Council.

1.1.3   European Union competition rules

The European Union's competition rules and regulations extend directly to business enterprises and citizens in the various Member States. The rules are administered by the Commission which collaborates with national authorities – in Denmark with the Competition Council secretariat. One of the tasks of this secretariat is to assist the Commission with its inspections in Denmark.

The general assumption is that EU rules prevail over national rules. But fundamentally in the Danish authorities' opinion, the Commission's group exemptions do not prevent intervention by the Competition Council provided the conditions under Danish law are satisfied. In reality, however, the Danish authorities have avoided conflicts between EU rules and Danish competition laws by interpreting the Danish laws in accordance with EU competition rules.

1.2   General principles

1.2.1   Objectives

The ultimate objective of the Competition Act is maximum competition, and thereby *efficiency*. The Act builds on a deregulation principle compared with the previous Monopolies and Restrictive Practices Act because the structural changes in the business world and growing international competition will in future constitute more effective regulators. Within limits acceptable to society, trade and industry are to have a basic freedom to enter into agreements and contracts and to make their own financial arrangements.

1.2.2   Transparency

The primary means to obtaining the ultimate objective of the Competition Act is *transparency*. The Act builds on the assumption that the need for competition regulations will diminish with increasing transparency.

1.2.3   Intervention and control

While transparency is generally expected to reduce the need for regulation aimed at the harmful effects of restrictive practices, the Competition Act also includes rules governing intervention.

Intervention is primarily aimed at agreements and decisions which lock the market structure and obstruct efficiency measures. The basic condition for any regulation is that restrictions of competition which cause or may cause damage to efficiency are practised on the market.

1.2.4   Control principle

The Competition Act builds on a control principle whereby restrictive practices are lawful until terminated by the authorities. It is inherent in the control principle that any intervention or sanction only extends to future infringements.

The Danish Competition Act is thus based on a principle which differs from that of the EU competition rules which build on a prohibition principle. Generally speaking, this principle outlaws certain types of restrictive practices unless an exemption is granted.

The Competition Act has one deviation from the control principle: section 14 prohibits the fixing of *binding resale prices*, but the Competition Council may grant exemptions in particular cases.

1.3 Agreements restricting competition

1.3.1 Notification and intervention

The Competition Council must be notified (section 5) of any agreements or decisions aimed at obtaining a dominant position, or where a dominant influence can be exercised. The Competition Council's and the Competition Appeals Tribunal's existing practice shows that although the wording of the Act provides only *one* condition, the existence of a 'dominant position', in reality notification requires that *two* conditions be satisfied: a dominant position *and* an agreement containing clauses restrictive of competition. These terms are examined in more detail at sections 1.3.3 and 1.3.4.

If a third condition is fulfilled also – ie that the agreement entails or may entail harmful effects on competition – the Competition Council has powers to intervene (sections 11 ff, see sections 4 and 5).

1.3.2 Agreements and decisions

The words 'agreements and decisions' are defined in accordance with the practice that was applied under the Monopolies and Restrictive Practices Act, ie not just explicit, written agreements and decisions but also implicit agreements and concerted practices.

1.3.3 Dominant position

The commentary on the Competition Act does not include an elaborate interpretation of 'dominant position' in relation to agreements. The most important contribution to interpretation concerns dominance in relation to the market power of individual firms; see section 1.4.2.

The Competition Council has published a general review (Documentation from the Competition Council, 1991, p 196) on the agreements of dominant undertakings. It is emphasised that although the agreements of dominant undertakings are normally notifiable, this is not always the case. The determining factor is the contents of the agreements, and the ties and products involved, ie does the agreement concern a principal product, or is it just a sideline or a special product.

This general attitude is reflected in practice. The Competition Council has thus (Documentation from the Competition Council, 1991, p 191) established that an agreement between Enigheden Produktion A/S and MD Foods was notifiable. In its decision the Council stressed that MD Foods had 45% of the market east of the Great Belt and Enigheden 15%, with Kløvermælk accounting for the remaining 40%. In addition, the agreement regulated Enigheden's and MD's principal product, milk.

But in another case the Competition Council (Documentation from the Competition Council, 1991, p 192) found that an agreement between

Havnemøllerne A/S and Drabæks Mølle A/S was not notifiable. From the case file it is seen that Havnemøllerne and its sister companies accounted for approximately 70% of the relevant market. There is no information on Drabæks Mølle's market share. However, the Council decided that the fact that a company's market share on a given market is large, is not in itself enough to make an agreement entered into by that firm notifiable. In other words, there is no duty to notify if the agreement as such has only limited influence on the market.

The Competition Council in its decision pointed out that the agreement between Havnemøllerne and Drabæks Mølle concerned a number of special products and sidelines. In fact the agreement only regulated less than 1% of the relevant markets.

This means that when deciding whether or not a firm has a dominant position, it is not just the market shares of the firms involved which are relevant, but the product areas with which the agreement is concerned.

1.3.4   Restrictions of competition

As mentioned in section 1.3.1 above, market dominance and restraints of trade are the two preconditions for notification and intervention. Practice is very rigorous regarding the question of restrictions of competition, the presumption being that market-dominant agreements also contain restraints of trade. However, there are a number of appeal decisions which demonstrate that the existence of restrictions of competition is a real precondition for notification and intervention.

This precondition is mentioned in a decision (Documentation from the Competition Council, 1991, p 302) from the Appeals Tribunal in respect of an agreement between Bang & Olufsen A/S and Philips A/S. The Appeals Tribunal determined that the agreement was not notifiable. The Tribunal did not attach importance to the market shares of the parties, but to the precise wording of their agreement. The Tribunal emphasised that there were no elements in the particular agreement which had so far affected marketing, and that it had not been proved that the agreement contained elements which would be of special importance to marketing. Based on its wording, section 5 of the Competition Act must in the Tribunal's opinion be construed to concern marketing conditions rather than research advantages or financial positions, at least if there is no reason to assume that these matters would materially affect marketing.

1.3.5   Notification

If the conditions for notification are satisfied, an agreement is notifiable within 14 days after the particular agreement or decision has been made. The Competition Act leaves it to the Competition Council to frame rules governing notification. In its rules (Competition Council Executive Order No 56 of 1 February 1990) the Competition Council prescribes that written agreements with annexes are to be submitted by one of the parties (Section 2(1) of the executive order).

As regards implicit agreements or concerted practices, a summary of such agreement or practice is to be submitted by either party, with the date of commencement (Section 2(3) of the executive order).

Neither the wording of the Competition Act nor the Competition Council's executive order allows for the fact that only certain clauses are notifiable for the majority of notifiable agreements. Section 5 implies that the entire agreement is notifiable. However, the precondition for notification is always the existence of restrictions of competition. In practice it is in many cases coincidental whether an agreement is contained in one document or whether there are two or more separate agreements. In the latter instance, only the agreements containing restrictions of competition will be notifiable. This was seen from a decision by the Competition Council (Documentation from the Competition Council, 1991, p 102) on IATA resolutions in the travel agency business.

Under section 5 the Competition Council demanded that a number of IATA resolutions be notified, partly because IATA airlines have a dominant position on the market for sale of international scheduled flight tickets and partly because of the concrete wording, ie the restrictions of competition of the IATA sales system. However, the Competition Council found that only *a number* of the resolutions were notifiable. This applies although it is logical to assume that the dominant position of IATA airlines applies to all their resolutions.

This leads to the conclusion that if dominance is established in respect of an agreement, only the clauses containing restrictions of competition will be notifiable. On the other hand, any notification must be so broad as to give the reader the required basis for assessing the significance of the agreement in terms of competition. But it should be noted that under section 6 of the Competition Act, the Competition Council can demand that all necessary information be given. Consequently, the Council is likely to ask that additional clauses of the agreement be submitted – possibly the entire agreement. Such additional information, which is not comprised by the duty to notify, is not covered by the rules governing free access to public records, see section 3.6.

1.3.6 Altering notified agreements

Alterations to notified agreements are to be reported within 14 days (section 5(2) of the Competition Act).

1.3.7 Validity

Notifiable agreements and decisions are not valid unless they are notified within the prescribed time limit (section 5(3)). But failure to notify only invalidates the agreement between the parties, which means that it can be ratified by the parties (entered into again), for subsequent notification of the renewed agreement.

Deliberate or negligent infringement of the duty to notify is punishable with a fine (section 20(1)). Experience shows that an infringement must be extremely grave to be punishable.

As mentioned at section 1.3.5 above, the presumption is that notification only extends to the clauses of an agreement containing restrictions of competition as well as any clauses required to assess the importance of such restrictions. Similarly, the validity provisions of section 5(3) are presumed to extend only to the clauses of a non-notifiable agreement which include restrictions of competition. But as yet there are no precedents.

1.3.8 Intervention

As mentioned in section 1.3.1 above, the same basic conditions are applicable to notification of agreements and decisions as to intervention. The preconditions for notification are dominant position and restrictions of competition, and intervention additionally requires that the restrictions will or may entail harmful effects. Any harmful effects of restrictions of competition are assessed in the light of the objectives of the Act to promote efficiency in production and distribution. Intervention and harmful effects are considered in more detail in sections 4 and 5.

1.4   Abusive exploitation

1.4.1   No duty to notify

Under section 5 of the Competition Act notification only extends to agreements and decisions. As opposed to the legal position under the previous Monopolies and Restrictive Practices Act, the Competition Act does not provide for a register of dominant firms – a so-called monopolies register.

The fact that dominant undertakings are not notifiable means that their normal business terms and conditions or agreements with their customers are not notifiable either. But based on the merits of a particular agreement, the Council can decide that agreements with customers are separately notifiable, if the agreements *themselves* satisfy the conditions for notification of restrictions of competition.

The provisions in respect of intervention included in sections 11ff of the Competition Act are applicable to both individual undertakings and agreements containing restrictions of competition.

1.4.2   Dominant position

Although it is not seen from the explicit wording of the Competition Act, it follows from the commentary that the provisions of intervention can only be enforced vis-a-vis individual undertakings with a 'dominant position'. The authorities attach importance to a number of indicators when deciding the question of market dominance, as follows:

Market share   The most important criterion in practice is the market share. The commentary on the Act provides that 'the market share has to be so large as to give the undertaking power to an appreciable degree independently of its competitors to fix the prices of its own production'. This implies that 'the market share criterion alone should not automatically be applied to market shares under 40–45%'.

Precedents do not suggest where the market share criterion is today. Statements from the Competition Council seem to give the impression that the authorities will consider the dominance requirement to be satisfied with market percentages of 30% or over.

Market form   The various market forms are also important in practice – monopoly, duopoly, oligopoly etc. Traditionally, authorities would view duopolies and oligopolies as an expression of neutralisation of competition.

Undertaking-related matters   In addition to the above criteria also undertaking-related matters such as capital strength, financial connections, availability of raw materials etc play some part in the weighing of market dominance. This also applies to the end result, ie the particular undertaking's earnings over a number of years.

1.4.3 The relevant market

An anti-competitive practice must be exercised in a 'particular market' (section 11). The market concept is two-dimensional. First the authorities must define the *territory*, on the basis of which an anti-competitive practice is to be assessed, and secondly, the *product* or product group constituting the market.

In practice defining the relevant geographical market has not attracted much attention. It is seen from the commentary on the Competition Act that the relevant geographical market territory may also be a local market area. The Competition Council has for instance distinguished between the markets east and west of the Great Belt.

On the product-related definition of the relevant market, the theoretical starting point is the cross price elasticities, ie the relative effects of a price change on the consumption of a substitute.

In reality calculating cross price elasticities is not possible, and instead a number of cross elasticity indicators are used – thereby revealing the substitute options:

(a) *statutory rules* or other regulations may rule out substitution;
(b) *technical conditions* may rule out substitution;
(c) *price differences* between a particular product and its technical substitute may prohibit substitution;
(d) *subjective factors* may be decisive, such as fashion, taste, identification or other consumer preferences.

In practice the subjective factors are probably the single factor which has caused the greatest uncertainty. The commentary on the Competition Act seems to suggest that, especially in cases of refusals to supply, it may be necessary to use fairly narrow and short-term criteria for defining the market, to allow for changes in fashion and taste etc. But particularly when it comes to intervention in profits and prices, authorities are reluctant to apply a product-based market definition building on short-term consumer preferences.

The practical application of competition rules has shown that competition authorities are inclined to define the relevant market rather narrowly – also in cases with suitable substitutes on the supply or demand sides.

In connection with an exclusive distribution agreement for telephone switchboard systems, the Competition Appeals Tribunal has thus (Documentation from the Competition Council, 1991, p 103) attached importance to the significance of the agreement to so-called PABC systems and other major systems although the complainants had emphasised that there was no technical delimitation between the small and the large systems, and that the agreement should therefore be assessed on the basis of the market for all systems.

1.4.4 Examples of harmful effects of the dominance of individual firms

Section 5 gives a number of examples of the harmful effects of individual firms' market dominance.

1.5 Amendments or reform

1.5.1 Although the Danish Competition Act took effect on 1 January 1990 and is thus a fairly new law, there are already deliberations for amending its basic principles.

In June 1993 the Danish Minister of Industry set up a committee to identify advantages and drawbacks by introducing a change from the existing control principle to a prohibition principle. The committee was set up in the light of international developments, many countries having changed their national competition rules so that they are based on a prohibition principle in similarity with EU competition law. In a few years Denmark will, if the Competition Act is not amended, in all probability be the only EU Member State whose competition law builds on a control principle.

In addition, the committee is to look into the pros and cons of implementing rules on control of mergers and acquisitions in Danish competition law.

1.5.2 The committee submitted its report in June 1995. It recommends the Danish Competition Act be changed from the present control principle to a mixed principle, where agreements are ruled by the prohibition principle and individual undertakings by the control principle. The committee recommends that no specific Danish rules on merger control be introduced.

2   ENFORCEMENT

2.1   Authorities

2.1.1   *The Competition Council*

The Competition Act is administered by an independent body, the Competition Council. The Council consists of 15 members, seven members being appointed on the recommendation of trade and consumer organisations. The members meet once a month and only consider cases involving fundamental principles. Other cases are determined by the Council Secretariat, see section 2.1.2.

Undertakings whose affairs are being considered are not entitled to appear before the Council. It bases its decisions on written statements prepared by the Secretariat, in which the Secretariat describes factual circumstances, relevant problems and the viewpoints of the affected firms.

The Competition Council is independent, which means that it does not accept instructions from other authorities or from the Minister of Industry whose department is competent in matters relating to the Competition Act.

2.1.2   *The Secretariat*

The Competition Council is assisted by a Secretariat with 100 staff. Formally, the Secretariat is a directorate under the Ministry of Industry. The Competition Act does not confer any independent competence on the Secretariat, and any powers exercised by the Secretariat are based on authorisation by the Competition Council. It can be confusing that the Competition Council – ie the 15 members – and the Secretariat are both called the 'Competition Council'.

The Secretariat is responsible for day-to-day management, ie collecting information and presenting cases to the Council. The Secretariat negotiates with the firms involved and arranges for the written presentation of cases in the Council. In addition, the Competition Council Secretariat can decide less important cases, and it may also decide to present urgent matters to the Competition Council Executive Committee only. This committee consists of a chairman and two members.

The Secretariat publishes a number of publications explaining the decisions of the Council, in particular:

(a) Competition Bulletin, a four-page leaflet published once or twice a month;
(b) Documentation, a quarterly 100-page review, with mention of all decisions made by the Competition Council and the Competition Appeals Tribunal (see section 2.1.3 for more information on the Appeals Tribunal).

2.1.3 The Competition Appeals Tribunal

A Council decision can be brought before a special appeals board, the Competition Appeals Tribunal (section 18) within four weeks. The Tribunal has three members. Its chairman must satisfy the qualifications for being a supreme court judge and the two other members must have economic and legal professional qualifications. In practice a supreme court judge and two professors of law and economics will always be appointed for the positions as chairman and members.

The Competition Act contains a number of restrictions on appeal access, ie neither the rejection of a case nor the refusal of confidentiality of business secrets can be appealed.

The Competition Appeals Tribunal has *full* competence of examination and investigation. This means that the Appeals Tribunal can not only decide formal questions but also questions of competition policy. This is remarkable because the Competition Council is composed of a wide circle of professionals and representatives to ensure a particular expertise in its decisions, but a decision by the three members of the Appeals Tribunal will nevertheless override Council decisions.

Undertakings which have submitted cases for consideration by the Competition Council and the Appeals Tribunal are sometimes of the opinion that the Tribunal is characterised by a more typical law and order approach. This may be because, as opposed to the Council, the Tribunal has a more court-like function where both parties – the Competition Council and the affected undertakings – are entitled to appear.

2.1.4 The courts

The decisions made by the Competition Appeals Tribunal may be brought before the Danish High Court, within eight weeks of notification of the party involved (section 18(4)). High Court appeals are rare.

An examination by a court follows the usual pattern of hearing of administrative cases where the courts are reluctant to reject politically influenced assessments. This means that a court examination is more in the nature of a control of legality.

High Court decisions in competition cases can be brought before the Danish Supreme Court in accordance with the normal rules of procedure.

2.2 Sanctions

2.2.1 The control principle

As already mentioned in section 1.2.4 above, the control principle of the Competition Act means that intervention by the authorities is only effective for any future infringements. Sanctions are therefore only possible in special cases.

2.2.2   *Penalties*

The Competition Council has wide powers to request information. Failure to comply with such request enables the Council to impose daily or weekly fines on the party involved (section 19). This provision has only seldom been used, but the Council has imposed a fixed weekly fine of 5,000 Danish kroner.

2.2.3   *Penalty clauses*

A party who deliberately or negligently ignores the duty to notify anti-competitive practices (section 5) or infringes the prohibition (section 14) not to fix binding resale prices (section 20, paragraphs 1 and 2) is punishable with a fine. Similarly, a party giving incorrect information, ignoring agreements made with the Competition Council or failing to comply with an order issued by the Council (section 20, paragraphs 3, 4 and 5) is punishable with a fine.

The penalty provisions are more or less a continuation of the corresponding provisions of the Monopolies and Restrictive Practices Act. Practice shows that infringements must be very grave before a fine is imposed. So far there are no instances of application of the penalty provisions under the existing Competition Act.

2.3   Damages

2.3.1   *The control principle*

Also in relation to the question of damages to other undertakings for competition-restricting conduct, it is crucial that the Danish Competition Act builds on a control principle. Competition-restricting conduct is legal and valid until terminated by the authorities based on their demonstration of its harmful effects. Then the conduct must be changed or the restrictions removed, but such orders are *only effective for future infringements*.

2.3.2   *Duty to contract*

In legal literature it has from time to time been asserted that there is a duty to contract even without mediation by the authorities – so that refusal to contract may trigger liability for damages under civil law. But the area in which a duty to contract exists by virtue of unwritten rules of law is extremely narrow. Existing precedents are fairly old, and are all based on a severe scarcity of goods and an existing business relationship between the affected parties. The relevant judgments all date from the time immediately after the Second World War when there was a widespread shortage of goods and subsequent rationing which made it impossible to secure supplies from suppliers other than those a buyer had dealt with previously. The conclusion is therefore that for many years there have been no examples in practice which suggest the existence of a duty to contract without a prior decision by the Competition Council.

3   TRANSPARENCY

3.1   The transparency concept

The Competition Act operates with transparency as an essential means to achieving its ultimate objective, maximum competition, and thereby efficiency. The need for regulation of competition is deemed to diminish with an increasing degree of transparency in the market. The transparency concept of the Competition Act is reflected in a number of provisions included in the Act which will be considered in the following.

3.2   Duty to notify

Transparency is sought by virtue of section 5 which prescribes a duty to notify anti-competitive agreements and decisions aiming to ensure a dominant position. The provision was considered at section 1.3.5 above.

3.3   Duty to disclose

Under section 6 the Competition Council can demand that all information deemed necessary be provided. The Council has extremely wide powers, and the commentary on the Act shows that in reality there are very few restrictions on the access to obtain information under section 6.

3.4   Duty to report

Under section 7 the Competition Council can order selected undertakings to report their prices, discounts and other terms of business for periods of up to two years at a time. Such duty to report can be imposed where competition is not sufficiently effective, or where there are other special reasons for wishing to observe the competitive situation or create transparency of pricing conditions.

It is not a condition for invoking this provision that the affected undertakings are dominant – and thereby comprised by the intervention regulations of the Act.

The former monopolies register has not been continued under the Competition Act (see section 1.4.1 above). On commencement of the Act, attention was therefore focused on the administration of the duty to report under section 7. At the beginning it seemed as if section 7 was invoked on many of the firms which used to be comprised by the duty to report to the monopolies register. The commentary on the Act seems to indicate that the provision aims to throw light on the market conditions, not on the *internal* affairs of individual firms. But a number of firms were none the less asked to provide information on their budgets etc, ie information on purely internal matters.

Some of the Competition Council's decisions on the duty to report were appealed to the Competition Appeals Tribunal. The Tribunal's decisions followed the pattern that it almost always seemed to uphold the duty to report but that it based its decisions on the commentary on the Act so that the duty to report was restricted to comprise information serving to elucidate market conditions only. The Competition Council therefore had to restrict its reporting procedures to include *external* matters only.

3.5   Investigations

3.5.1   Under section 8 of the Act, the Competition Council is to undertake such investigations as are suitable to promote transparency of competitive conditions. The commentary points out that these investigations are the most important form at all of free access to public records.

3.5.2   Investigations may be published, and normally are. They are fairly comprehensive, at times up to several hundred pages.

3.5.3   In 1993 the Competition Council published investigations of the following areas:

(a)   mergers and acquisitions in 1992 (with figures relating to mergers and acquisitions in Danish business);

(b)   energy (with details of structure, agreements and competitive conditions);

(c)   personal tax-deductible pension schemes (with a description of matters of relevance to transparency in this area, including structure, rules of law, offered products, comparison of pension policies from banks and insurance companies, agreements and practice);

(d)   home insurance (describing market structure, products and premiums);

(e)   means of payment on travels abroad (describing applications and costs);

(f)   the steel trade (detailing structure and pricing systems as well as public regulation); and

(g)   the electricity companies' use of time-dependent rates (describing the theoretical basis of time rating and the practical use of the rates).

3.6   Public access and confidentiality

3.6.1   Amendment of the Act in 1992

When the Competition Act became operative, its transparency concept was extremely wide, the principle being that all information given to the Competition Council should be freely accessible. There were only particular, restricted exemptions concerning actual business secrets.

This almost unrestricted transparency soon caused a number of problems. In relation to the affected *undertakings* the problem was that the competition laws of other countries did not comprise a similar transparency concept. The Act therefore meant that the business secrets of Danish firms were revealed to foreign competitors without the firms getting a similar insight into the affairs of their foreign competitors.

In relation to the *Competition Council* the transparency provisions caused problems because firms were very reluctant to give the Council the desired information, and transparency also caused difficulties in connection with the Council's administration of free access to public records.

Consequently, the Competition Act was amended with effect from 1 June 1992 (Act No 280 of 29 April 1992). The amendment limited transparency, but the principle of free access to public records remains fairly wide.

3.6.2 Free access to public records

Free access to public records is first of all ensured under the Act on Free Access to Public Records 1985, see section 10(1) of the Competition Act. However, this free access applies only to:

(a) notifiable agreements under section 5; and
(b) information reported under paragraph 1 of section 7 'where competition is not sufficiently effective'.

The latter restriction refers to paragraph 1 of section 7 under which reporting obligations can be imposed:

(a) where competition is not sufficiently effective;
(b) 'where for particular reasons it is necessary to observe the competitive conditions or create transparency of pricing conditions'.

The latter situation most often arises in markets with aggressive competition, where the Competition Council wants information on discounts and rebates to ensure that active competition does not set the stage for a price war. In such circumstances such information would not be available under the public access rules.

The Competition Council decides what information is to be freely accessible. But both information to which there is public access and other information are subject to the restrictions considered at section 3.6.3.

3.6.3 Confidentiality and secrecy

There are two areas in which the affected undertakings can demand that the information provided be kept confidential and this applies both to information with free access and information which, based on a Council decision, is made freely accessible.

First of all, there are particular restrictions regarding *technical matters*. The commentary on the Competition Act emphasises that to satisfy the objectives of the Act for creation of transparency, it is not information on technical production details which is relevant, but information on the firm's conduct on the market. An undertaking can therefore demand that its technical data be kept confidential if these data are of crucial financial importance to the particular undertaking (section 10(2), cf paragraph 2 of section 12 of the Act on Free Access to Public Records). Similarly, an undertaking can demand that information on its relations with banks or insurance companies be kept confidential (section 10(2) of the Competition Act).

It is more difficult to demand that business secrets be kept confidential if they are not of a technical nature. But under section 10(3) an undertaking can demand that business secrets be kept confidential if, firstly, the particular undertaking may suffer substantial financial losses through publication, and secondly, if publication would give other undertakings an unjustified competitive advantage, or if there are other special circumstances. 'Special circumstances' aim particularly at confidentiality in connection with public interests, such as major import or export interests.

In the commentary on the Act it is emphasised that the exemptions under section 10(3) can be invoked only if the significance of the information to competition is out of proportion to the risk of substantial financial losses.

4   POWERS OF INTERVENTION

4.1   Secondary measures

As mentioned at section 1.2.2 above, the most important means of achieving competitive efficiency as provided for in the Act is transparency. Accordingly, the powers of intervention are *secondary* compared with the transparency provisions. But this does not mean that invocation of the general provisions of the Act (transparency) is to precede the powers of intervention. A specific measure is chosen by the Competition Council based on its estimation of the effectiveness of the measure for achieving the objectives of the Act.

4.2   De minimis rule

4.2.1   Under section 11 of the Competition Act, the Competition Council may intervene if it finds that harmful anti-competitive restrictions are practised, thereby reducing efficiency. The Council is thus *not obliged* to intervene. This provision is new compared with the previous Monopolies and Restrictive Practices Act. If the former Monopolies Commission found that an anti-competitive practice caused unreasonable effects, it was obliged to seek to remedy the situation. In the commentary on the Competition Act, it is mentioned that as a result of this provision the Monopolies Commission had too many minor cases to consider straining the resources which from a more general politico-competitive viewpoint could have been used more wisely.

4.2.2   Consequently, the presumption in the commentary is that only cases of fundamental importance to the social economy or individual trades weighing heavily in the economy as such, are to be considered by the Competition Council. The Council is to consider individual cases only if it is deemed an expedient approach to attack widespread anti-competitive practices.

4.2.3   The Competition Council's decision to reject a case is final and cannot be appealed to the Competition Appeals Tribunal (section 18(1)).

4.3   Negotiations

4.3.1   Alternatives to intervention

If the Competition Council decides to terminate a harmful anti-competitive practice, the primary measure is *negotiation* with the affected undertakings (section 11). This negotiation is carried through because – should it fail – the Competition Council has powers to issue an order by virtue of sections 12 and 13 of the Competition Act, see sections 4.5 and 4.6. Negotiations are therefore often perceived by the affected undertakings as a kind of 'lenient' intervention under the above provisions.

4.3.2   Agreements with the Competition Council

It is clear from the commentary on the Act that negotiations between the Competition Council and the affected undertakings can be a real alternative to intervention under sections 12 and 13. Through its negotiations, the Competition

Council has powers to intervene in a different manner than provided for in the Act. Such solutions will of course require the consent of the particular firm.

The authority to depart from the general powers of intervention is particularly practical where the Council wishes to prescribe specific changes to agreements, decisions, stipulations or business secrets. The right to enter into such agreements means that the Competition Council can suggest changes that will be acceptable to the authorities.

From an administrative point of view, the right to enter into deviating agreements is problematic. These powers must be administered in such a way that the Council carefully informs the affected undertakings of their rights and obligations so that they know exactly when they enter into an agreement which goes beyond the powers of intervention contained in the Act.

4.4 Orders

4.4.1 Formal conditions

In order to invoke sections 12 and 13, it is a condition that negotiations have been unsuccessful. Negotiations are to be in the nature of a verbal discussion, ie a telephone conversation does not suffice.

4.4.2 Nature of order

In pursuance of section 12(1) the order can comprise 'complete or partial termination of agreements, decisions, stipulations and business conditions'. But the Council has no authority to order *concrete changes*. In reality however, the authorities will often suggest changes which they expect to be accepted. This should be viewed in the light of section 4.3.2 above, from which it appears that authorities can negotiate solutions other than those described in sections 12 and 13.

4.5 Duty to supply

4.5.1 Ranking

Where harmful anti-competitive practices are not discontinued following an order under section 12(1), the Competition Council can issue an order by virtue of section 12 (2) to a firm to supply specific buyers with goods on its normal conditions for similar sales. In addition to the general conditions applicable to intervention, there are special conditions for invoking a supply order. A list ranking the various intervention options has been drawn up, and duty-to-supply orders are only invoked where other orders are deemed to fail.

4.5.2 Conditions for a duty-to-supply order

A duty-to-supply order is an extraordinary type of sanction by the authorities because most sanctions are prohibitory, ie they order firms *not* to do something, whereas a duty-to-supply order is a positive order to *do* something. All interventions under sections 11 and 12 require the existence of anti-competitive practices on the relevant market. The requirements in respect of the strength of a particular practice are the same, irrespective of the nature of intervention. But based on the commentary on the Act, it is possible to apply a narrower definition of relevant market in the case of refusals to supply, see section 1.4.2.

A number of conditions must be satisfied by the undertaking where a refusal to supply is exercised before a duty-to-supply order will be invoked. The particular undertaking must have a considerable commercial interest in obtaining supplies, and the products in question shall be goods coming within the natural range of products required by the firm, the type of product shall be significant in terms of turnover, and there must be no obvious substitution possibilities.

Practice seems to indicate that the requirements in respect of the above conditions are not very strict.

The *grounds* for the supplier refusing to supply are also important, and traditionally the following will not be accepted:

(a)   the refusal to supply may involve an exclusive agreement which has formally been terminated, but is in fact still complied with;
(b)   suppliers sometimes claim that they are short of production or storage capacity. The competition authorities state that such situations must be accommodated through an equal reduction of all orders;
(c)   a refusal to supply is often an attempt to enforce recommended resale prices and thus contradictory to section 14 of the Competition Act;
(d)   a refusal to supply is often explained by untraditional forms of business. But a duty-to-supply order is specifically aimed to enable trade and industry to develop freely so that traditional trading does not obstruct the appearance of new and untraditional sales channels;
(e)   a supplier sometimes explains his refusal to supply by claiming that the number of distributors is adequate (the demand point of view). The authorities always reject this argument.

A number of reasons for refusing to supply will be accepted based on the merits of the case. But the authorities normally regard these 'creditable' reasons with some scepticism, as they often conceal the real and often less creditable reason.

Among the reasons that may merit an exemption are:

(a)   a refusal to supply is sometimes explained by the potential buyer not satisfying the conditions of the supplier's *selective sales systems*. The precondition is however that the particular sales systems build on objective criteria, and that they are always observed;
(b)   a refusal to supply may also be due to *existing exclusive distribution rights*. Exclusive distribution systems may be acceptable and so will be refusals to supply based thereon;
(c)   a refusal to supply is often explained by an undertaking not wishing to *supply a competitor*. Over the years authorities have been very reluctant to issue duty-to-supply orders in such cases.

4.6   Control of prices and profits

4.6.1   Ranking

Government intervention in respect of prices and profits (section 13 of the Competition Act) is the last step on the intervention ladder. Such intervention is thus conditional upon the other remedies of law not providing the desired results.

4.6.2 *Conditions for price and profit control measures*

Price and profit control presumes that an anti-competitive practice will invariably result in a price or profit which clearly exceeds the *level* and *duration* obtainable in a market with effective competition. In principle, price control builds on the fundamental viewpoint of the Competition Act to focus on the market rather than on individual firms. This is among other things reflected in the commentary on the Act:

> 'An assessment of reasonable earnings is based on the market conditions. If an undertaking under conditions of free pricing and competition can maintain a particular price level, the price cannot be excessive.'

The Competition Act provides that the *principle of calculating prices on a product by product basis* is to be applied, ie prices and profits are also assessed on a product by product basis. On the computation of earnings and returns on capital, the *cost principle* is applied which means that production factors are included at actual cost – as opposed to the replacement principle, where costs are included at their estimated prices on replacement.

4.6.3 *Practice*

Under the previous Monopolies and Restrictive Practices Act, government price control measures used to attract much attention, not least the discussion of whether such control measures were reasonable, and this lead to a law reform and the introduction of the new Competition Act. The business community viewed the wide transparency concept of the Act as part of a 'barter' where price and profit control was given lower priority, but where it had to accept a transparency concept which was problematic but which most businessmen thought they would be able to live with.

Practice since the commencement of the Competition Act in January 1990 shows that the preconditions for this bartering held good: price and profit control has, generally speaking, not been important under the Act. In a few cases the Competition Council has touched upon the question of prices and profits, but in all essentials section 13 of the Competition Act is not invoked.

5 CHECKLIST OF POTENTIAL INFRINGEMENTS

A Vertical Agreements

5.1 Exclusive distributors

5.1.1 In practice the Council has intervened extremely rarely in connection with exclusive distribution agreements. But with the introduction of the Competition Act the formal possibilities of disrupting these agreements have been increased with the issuance of duty-to-supply orders which break up existing agreements.

5.1.2 However, this does not mean that the Competition Act excludes exclusive distribution agreements, even where anti-competitive practices exist. Exclusive agreements will in many cases contribute to efficiency in sales and distribution, and thus be in line with the ultimate objectives of the Act. This is indeed the reason why the authorities continue to pursue a cautious policy of regulating exclusive agreements.

5.1.3   Traditionally, agreements concerning commercial agency have been met with little interest from the Danish competition authorities as the general point of view is that these agreements are of minor importance for the competition. Agreements on commercial agencies are neither mentioned in the competition law itself nor the commentary of the Act.

5.2   Selective distributors

5.2.1   General requirements

The starting point is that all qualified distributors should have equal access to buy a particular product, and that restrictions on distribution for the purposes of costs or sales should be based on objective and reasonable criteria.

Concrete, objective conditions   Authorities demand concrete, precise and preferably quantified acceptance requirements, and attach tremendous importance to the requirements being available in written form, thereby being able to establish their extent and scope. Vague or unspecific expressions such as 'reasonable, proper' etc provide suppliers with too wide a scope for discrimination.

Reasonable conditions   In addition, acceptance requirements should be of relevance to the particular product. There are therefore major differences between what is acceptable from one group of products to the next. These are typically quality requirements in respect of shop standard, assortment and professional training or know-how.

Consistently applied conditions   Finally, acceptance conditions should be applied consistently. In the cases where a duty-to-supply order is issued, the reason is often that the supplier's official acceptance criteria are more or less considered unreasonable, but that he has not applied them consistently.

5.2.2   Concrete examples

The demand criterion   The Council always intervenes in cases of restrictions on the number of distributors in a geographic area based on an evaluation of the demand in the particular area.

Professional qualification requirements   A supplier can set up requirements for professional qualifications if they are significant to the marketing of his products.

Nature of business   A special much-discussed aspect is to what extent acceptance requirements can be made, for instance that the business appears as a specialist shop in the particular trade. Demands as to the nature of the shop are considered to be an exception, but were actually accepted in a case where the Danish Bang & Olufsen audio/video suppliers refused to supply goods to two shops which in their opinion did not live up to the required standards (Documentation, 1991, p 214).

Range   Reasonable demands may be made, for instance that the distributor is to take a representative selection of the supplier's goods.

Stocks The supplier can make it a condition that the distributor has a particular assortment of his goods in stock.

Shop arrangement The supplier can demand that the shop displays his goods neatly and systematically. In this area there has been a tremendous development in recent years. The demands in respect of shop arrangement can – just as the demands for the nature of the shop – normally only be made for that *section* of the shop which is to sell the particular products.

Professional training Professional qualifications are accepted in respect of the distributor's or his staff's knowledge of a particular product area. But the requirements may not exceed what is considered necessary to serve the customers properly. Neither can it be made a condition that it is the shop owner himself who has the required qualifications. It suffices if his staff have the desired qualifications.

5.3 Exclusive purchasing

The Competition Council always intervenes in respect of exclusive purchasing agreements where an agreement stipulates that purchases be made from a single or a limited circle of suppliers. If the granting of discounts or bonuses is tied with an exclusive purchasing obligation, the starting point is that the agreement is harmful to competition. But the competition authorities have also intervened in a number of cases where there has been no financial consideration in return for exclusive purchasing obligations.

5.4 Franchising

In many cases franchising can be viewed as a qualified form of exclusive distribution agreement. An evaluation from a competition point of view must therefore have the same starting point. There are not many precedents in Denmark on the evaluation of franchising agreements. An evaluation under the Danish Competition Act will presumably in all essentials observe the same principles as apply in the European Commission's group exemptions for franchise agreements (Commission Regulation 4087/88 of 30 November 1988).

5.5 Non-competition clauses

5.5.1 It is uncontested that competition clauses in connection with the sale of firms restrict the seller's commercial freedom. But on the other hand, some restrictions are necessary to ensure that the acquired goodwill exists also after the assignment. The competition authorities will therefore always accept competition clauses, but as regards geographical territory and product range they should be limited to the areas where the undertaking operated prior to assignment. As regards time scale a competition clause should be restricted to the period considered necessary for the buyer through an active effort to retain the acquired firm's position. Consequently, the scope of a competition clause is decided on a case by case basis, geographically and in terms of products and duration.

5.5.2 In a decision from the Competition Appeals Tribunal's predecessor, the Monopolies Appeals Tribunal (Monopolies Commission bulletin 1978, p 100) this

Tribunal cancelled a decision made by the Monopolies Commission which had issued an order to the effect that a competition clause was to be limited to three years instead of five years as agreed between the parties. In this case the Monopolies Appeals Tribunal did not consider that there were grounds for setting aside the agreement between the parties. The decision was criticised by the then chairman of the Monopolies Commission who among other things found that 'if a purchaser (a bread factory) could not over two or three years convince his customers that his bread was better, it would probably be because the customers did not share his view.'

5.5.3   Since this decision in 1978 the competition authorities have been very reluctant to criticise the duration of competition clauses. On an evaluation of competition clauses today, there is no reason to believe that the Competition Council would hold opinions differing widely from that of the European Commission as expressed in the Commission bulletin of 14 August 1990 on ancillary restrictions in connection with mergers and acquisitions (OJ C 203/5 1990). The Commission here considers a period of five years reasonable when the assignment of a firm comprises clientele and know-how, whereas a two-year period is considered reasonable if only the clientele is involved. But there is nothing to prevent that under specific circumstances, a longer period would be accepted.

5.6   Intellectual property licensing

5.6.1   There are only a few precedents on the application of the Danish Competition Act to patent licences. The starting point for an evaluation must always be that with a patent the patentee obtains a legal exclusive right – in principle an anti-competitive restraint – which must be respected by the competition authorities. However, if any additional competition restraints included in a licence are considered to be unreasonable – ie be harmful to competition, and thereby to efficiency, they should be decided on a case by case basis.

5.6.2   The theoretical discussion in Denmark concerning intellectual property licensing has focused solely on patent licensing agreements. Patent licensing must in this respect be seen as representing all sorts of commercial and industrial property rights. There are no reasons to expect the competition authorities to have a different point of view on other sorts of industrial property licensing than those on patents.

5.7   Tie in sales

Over the years the authorities have decided cases concerning tie in sales and have intervened in a number of cases. Based on previous practice it is difficult to set out general guidelines, but in the light of the general principles of the Competition Act, the assumption is that today authorities would almost always intervene in combined sales practised by dominant individual firms.

5.8   Refusals to supply

As mentioned at section 4.5.2 above, the material conditions for issuing a duty-to-supply order are to a wide extent identical with the conditions for intervening in agreements, decisions, stipulations and business conditions. For details on duty-to-supply orders, reference is made to section 4.5.

5.9 Price control

It is mentioned, at section 4.6 above, that the provisions of the Competition Act in respect of price and profit control (section 13) are generally speaking not invoked in practice. Reference is made to section 4.6.

5.10 Discounts and bonuses

5.10.1 General requirements

The commentary on the Competition Act mentions that inequality of terms extended to firms may be an example of the harmful effects of anti-competitive practices. Discrimination is often caused by differences in costs of supplying small or large quantities. A cost-related inequality for small and large buyers will always develop in an effective competitive environment. It is one of the advantages of large-scale operations, and it is said in the commentary that it would obstruct production efficiency if authorities would intervene in such situations. The presumption is therefore that there is no unreasonable discrimination if discounts or bonuses are based on cost-related factors.

For a number of years the authorities have on their assessment of discounts and bonuses attached particular importance to the following:

(a) if the discount or bonus is based on objective criteria;
(b) if the discount system is consistently applied;
(c) if the size of discounts is the same for all;
(d) if buyers and competitors are familiar with the discounts and the size thereof on delivery;
(e) if discounts or bonuses are cost-related; and
(f) if discounts or bonuses are reflected in the consumer prices.

5.10.2 Specific examples

From practice concerning categories of discounts or bonuses the following can be mentioned:

Annual bonus Over the years authorities have scrutinised annual bonus terms on a specific and individual assessment basis. Scrutiny seems to have focused on whether a particular annual bonus was cost-related.

Membership rebates It has been an established custom for authorities to intervene in connection with rebate schemes conditional upon membership of associations whether or not the rebate was cost-related.

Loyalty bonus It has been an established custom for authorities to intervene in connection with loyalty bonuses which entail an exclusionary obligation for the buyer to purchase all his requirements from the particular supplier.

Aggregated sales bonus   In the authorities' opinion this type of bonus with suppliers undertaking to grant customers a discount based on their aggregate purchases is always harmful.

Progressive rebates   It has been an established custom for authorities to intervene in connection with progressive rebates which depend on the customer increasing his purchases compared with a previous period from a particular supplier.

Chain bonus   In a number of cases authorities have intervened in connection with retail chain bonuses given on the basis of a chain's or wholesale society's total purchases from a single supplier. This type of bonus is similar to the aggregated sales bonus. But sometimes the chains undertake some of the supplier's normal functions in connection with buying and selling (distribution etc). In such cases a function rebate may be acceptable.

Special bonus   Conceptually, special bonus plays a special role because it is debatable if a special bonus is comprised by the concept of 'business conditions'. Experience shows that it is difficult to decide if actual business conditions are involved – where the authorities would normally always intervene – or if it is a matter of a single departure from normal conditions which the authorities would not generally act upon. Importance should presumably be attached to the volume of business, with the supplies accounting for a large part of the supplier's total sales, or whether the departures are of a more permanent nature, which will also pull in the direction of considering them comprised by the concept of 'business conditions', probably resulting in a regulation.

Campaign discount   It is arguable whether campaign discounts are a special category. They are typically short-term and granted if the retail link – typically a wholesale society – wishes to carry through a short-term price reduction. Authority action is marked by the fact that campaign discounts seem to be an inevitable phenomenon in active competition areas, such as the sale of convenience goods and staples. Efforts have not concentrated so much on removing campaign discounts but rather on limiting their use and making it more objective.

5.10.3   Meeting the competition defence

It is seen in the commentary on the Competition Act that the granting of discounts and bonuses is *a natural part of competition*, often similar to price competition. This is the reason why the commentary first seems to suggest that there should be no control of cost-related discounts. But elsewhere it appears that this does *not* mean that the Competition Council has to intervene in connection with discounts which are not granted on a cost-related basis. It is mentioned that the Competition Council's predecessor – the Monopolies Commission – was reluctant to intervene in connection with competition-related discounts which did not give rise to discrimination, primarily of small firms. This is typically the case where large undertakings compete for market shares by means of discounts or bonuses, and where these are reflected in consumer prices. This practice is approved by the drafters of the bill. In other words, the Competition Act should be administered in accordance with the international development where the concept of 'meeting the competition defence' is accepted.

5.10.4 The Competition Council's 1993 bulletin

The Competition Council has published a general review of certain types of discounts and bonuses (Documentation from the Competition Council, 1993, p 429). The Council distinguishes between cost-related discounts and discounts not related to costs (demand-dependent discounts). It is recognised that cost-related discounts are basically in harmony with the Competition Act although in the Council's opinion it is up to the affected firms themselves to substantiate that a discount is cost-related. But it is fairly negative towards demand-dependent discounts as the Council emphasises that the purpose of these discounts is to induce the buyer to make all his purchases from a particular supplier whether in the form of a few large orders or a number of small orders. It is pointed out that one of the harmful effects of this type of discount is that it weakens the buyer's motivation to change supplier, including switching to new entrants on the market.

It is very remarkable that the review does not consider the problems linked to 'meeting the competition defence'.

With the unambiguous statement in the Competition Act in favour of campaign discounts, it is possible that the Competition Appeals Tribunal will disagree with the Competition Council in its rather rigorous handling of all demand-dependent discounts.

B   Horizontal Restrictions

5.11   Pricing cartels

The horizontal fixing and pricing between competitors is an anti-competitive practice which will normally be opposed. For many years there was a precedent from the Monopolies Appeals Tribunal (Monopolies Commission bulletin, 1967, p 231) which attached importance to the participants being able to withdraw from a price agreement with a reasonable notice, and accordingly, authorities for a number of years concentrated their efforts on altering price agreements so that binding prices were made recommended.

The commentary on the Competition Act seeks to tighten the reins so that it does not always suffice for parties to an agreement to be able to withdraw from that agreement or to depart from its recommendations. Practice seems to develop accordingly.

5.12   Other horizontal agreements

Market-sharing and production-sharing agreements are considered forms of cartel whose harmful effects are indisputable, and which will therefore be accepted only in quite exceptional cases. There are a few cases of acceptance by the authorities if the restrictive agreements promote rationalisation efforts, however on condition that the advantages could not be achieved through less restrictive measures. This is the case where the productive capacity of the parties to an agreement is adjusted to suit altered (deteriorated) market conditions.

5.13   Trade organisation agreements

5.13.1   A number of horizontal anti-competitive practices stem from decisions made by trade organisations. The overriding consideration of an assessment of such competitive restrictions is that they must not be too difficult to comply with for new entrants, particularly in cases where membership of an organisation is of vital importance to the practising of a particular trade.

5.13.2 Entry conditions must be objective, professional, reasonable and consistently applied. There must be no resolutions which directly or indirectly prevent free competition, or which weaken or prevent mutual competition.

5.13.3 In recent years the Competition Council has focused on the resolutions of the liberal professions. The Competition Appeals Tribunal agrees with the more critical approach by the Competition Council to restrictions on advertising where previously relatively comprehensive advertising restrictions were accepted (Documentation from the Competition Council, 1993, p 175).

5.14 Joint ventures

5.14.1 Joint ventures are considered on a concrete basis. Practical experience has focused on two types of joint activities: agreements for joint selling and purchasing. Previous practice in respect of *joint selling* gives rise to the general conclusion that the question of rationalising or obstructing rationalisation has weighed heavily in connection with the decision.

5.14.2 Agreements for *joint purchasing* can both restrict and strengthen competition: often such agreements limit the participants' mutual competition, purchasing prices being the same for all, and the suppliers' possibilities are also restricted in connection with such joint purchasing. On the other hand, joint purchasing can increase competition by enabling the parties to influence the market through a joint effort. Authorities have been fairly reluctant to intervene in respect of agreements for joint purchasing, attaching importance among other things to how easy it is to become a member of a purchasing organisation.

6 MERGERS AND ACQUISITIONS

6.1 No rules on control of mergers and acquisitions in the Danish Competition Act

The Act does not contain any provisions on control of mergers and acquisitions. Prior to passing the bill, it was considered whether to include a general provision in respect of control of mergers and acquisitions, but in the end it was not included. Special business sectors have rules governing mergers and acquisitions based on considerations other than competition. This is the case for banking and insurance.

6.2 General provisions of the Competition Act

6.2.1 It has been said on many occasions by the Competition Authorities that the general provisions of the Competition Act cannot be applied to mergers and acquisitions. This was clarified in 1974 (Monopolies Commission bulletin, 1974, p 68) in connection with an agreement for collaboration between two cement factories on the manufacture, sale and distribution of cement in Denmark. One of the manufacturers transferred its production facilities and all its tank truck fleet to the other in a way which in practice was irrevocable, and which in reality amounted to a merger of the production link.

6.2.2 Despite the fact that the authorities had to accept that the existing anti-competitive practices in cement production had been reinforced, the merger could not be opposed based on the general provisions of law.

6.2.3 As regards the duty to notify mergers and acquisitions the authorities have followed the guideline (Monopolies Commission bulletin, 1986, p 292) that agreements for mergers or acquisitions are not directly notifiable if they only involve two firms and a regulation of the shareholders' mutual relationship. But if the merger agreement also contains provisions of material anti-competitive effects, these parts of the agreement may become notifiable.

6.2.4 After commencement of the Competition Act, the Competition Council confirmed (Documentation from the Competition Council, 1990, p 98) that the Act does not contain any provisions regarding the control of mergers or acquisitions, and that in themselves these are not notifiable under section 5 of the Act. As in the case of the Monopolies and Restrictive Practices Act, a merger agreement will only be notifiable if it contains other anti-competitive restrictions and if so, only the relevant provisions are notifiable.

6.3 Reform of the Competition Act

As mentioned in section 1.5 above, a committee under the Ministry of Industry has considered reform but recommended that no rules governing control of mergers and acquisitions be incorporated into Danish competition law.

CHAPTER VI

Finland

Carl-Henrik Wallin

Hannes Snellman
Attorneys at Law
Eteläranta 8
00130 Helsinki
PL 333
Finland

Tel   ++358 0 228841
Fax ++358 0 636992

CHAPTER VI

Finland

1 FINNISH COMPETITION LAW

1.1 Background

1.1.1 The history of the Finnish competition law dates back to the 'Cartel Act' of 1957.[1] This Act and its successors[2] until 1988 were largely based on the belief that gathering information on restrictions on competition and publishing the information would discourage undertakings from entering into such arrangements. Though the 'Cartel Act' and its successors until 1988 introduced competition law aspects into the Finnish legal system, their effect was fairly limited due to the lack of effective enforcement procedures.

1.1.2 The Act on Restrictions on Competition,[3] which came into force in 1988, significantly changed the above-described situation. It created a new competition authority, the Office of Free Competition, and this authority was given increased powers to effectively eliminate the harmful effects of restrictions on competition.

1.1.3 Though the Act on Restrictions on Competition 1988 did function fairly well, it had already, in 1990, become obvious that the intensified process of European integration required further changes in the Finnish Competition legislation. As a result of this commonly recognised need, the present Act on Restrictions on Competition[4] came into force on 1 September 1992. Since this date the material rules of Finnish competition law are to be found in the said Act.[5]

1.1.4 The objective of the Act on Restrictions on Competition 1992 (hereinafter the 'Competition Act') has been both to improve the protection of sound and effective economic competition and to narrow the gap between Finnish and EC competition law.[6]

As for the implementation of the objective, the second paragraph of Section 1 of the Competition Act states that:

> 'In the application of this Competition Act, special attention shall be paid to the interests of consumers and the protection of the freedom of trade from unjustified barriers and restraints.'[7]

---

1 147/57.
2 1/64 and 423/73.
3 709/1988.
4 480/1992.
5 See, however, section 1.2 ff below.
6 Government proposal for an Act on Restrictions on Competition 162/1991.
7 All quotations of the Competition Act in this presentation are unofficial translations.

1.1.5   The Finnish competition law thus gives first priority to consumer interests and freedom of trade. Despite the unquestionable objective to narrow the gap between Finnish and EC competition law, the Competition Act says nothing explicit about the possible need to break down the national trade barriers versus the EU.[8]

1.1.6   The Competition Act is largely based on the 'principle of prohibition'. It prohibits consequently per se resale price maintenance, tendering cartels, horizontal agreements on prices, restrictions of production, market sharing and abuse of dominance. Other restrictions on competition are judged on the basis of the 'principle of abuse'.

1.1.7   Since the Competition Act has been in force for only some three years, there exists so far very little practice on the material rules of the Act. The cases referred to below have been decided by the Competition Council and the Supreme Administrative Court whereas the decisions taken by the Office of Free Competition have not been dealt with here.

1.2   The European Union

1.2.1   Finland has been a member of the European Union since 1 January 1995. As a consequence of this, the territorial scope of EC competition law rules has now been extended to the Finnish territory.[9]

1.2.2   Since the EC competition law has been presented in Chapter I, the presentation below does not include the relevant EC aspects at any length. It is, nevertheless, important to note the EC competition law dimension when analysing Finnish restrictions on competition.

1.3   Anti-competitive agreements

1.3.1   The Competition Act contains several sections (4, 5, 6, 9) regulating the use of anti-competitive agreements. These sections deal with specific types of anti-competitive agreements; the presentation below is structured accordingly.

1.3.2   Resale price maintenance

Section 4 of the Competition Act prohibits resale price maintenance. The section provides:

> 'It shall be forbidden in trade to require that the next sales level shall not undercut or exceed a certain price, consideration, or basis for its determination when offering a commodity for sale or rent in Finland.'

Though the Competition Act does not explicitly define the concept 'trade', it is possible to get some guidance from the definition of 'undertaking' in the first paragraph of section 3 of the Competition Act:

---

8 Compare with the EC competition law standpoint.
9 Due to the EEA Agreement, the EC competition law rules have largely been in force in Finland already since 1 January 1994.

'In this Act, an undertaking shall refer to a natural person or a private-law or public-law legal person, who offers for sale, buys, sells or otherwise for consideration acquires or disposes of goods or services (commodities), on a professional basis.'

The concept 'trade' should consequently be given a wide definition.

Prohibited resale price maintenance is defined in section 4 as an arrangement whereby the 'principal' requires that the 'distributor' abides by a certain price level. The use of both minimum and maximum prices is thus prohibited. The prohibition covers both normal sales, renting and leasing. The prohibition does not cover price recommendations. Such recommendations are allowed provided that the 'next sales level' is not de facto forced to follow them.[10]

Arrangements infringing section 4 may upon application be exempted, as described below in section 2.5 ff.

1.3.3   Tendering cartels

Section 5 of the Competition Act prohibits tendering cartels. The section provides:

'It shall be forbidden in trade to apply a contract or other mutual arrangement under which competitive bidding for the sale or purchase of a commodity or the rendering of a service shall take place so that:

1   a party shall refrain from making a tender; or
2   a party shall tender a higher or lower offer than another; or
3   the price tendered or the advance or credit term set is based on collaboration of the tenderers in question.

The provisions in paragraph 1 do not apply to a contract or arrangement according to which the tenderers have joined in order to make a joint offer for joint performance.'

Prohibited tendering cartels are here defined as arrangements whereby the parties somehow agree on their tendering tactics in a way described in sub-paras 1–3. The tendering may concern sales, purchasing or rendering of a service.

According to the second paragraph of section 5, the prohibition does not concern joint tendering for joint performances. This refers to the situation where the parties concerned agree on offering a joint performance, which could not be performed by one of the parties alone.

Arrangements infringing section 5 may upon application be exempted, as described below in section 2.5 ff.

1.3.4   Horizontal agreements

Section 6 of the Competition Act prohibits certain types of horizontal agreements between undertakings or associations of undertakings. The section provides:

'Undertakings or associations of undertakings operating on the same level of production or distribution may not, by contract, decision or other comparable measures:

1   fix or recommend the prices or consideration charged or payable in trade; or
2   restrict production, or share the markets or sources of supply, unless this is necessary for arrangements that contribute to the efficiency of production or distribution or

---

10 See decision by the Competition Council 29 October 1993, d:o 6/359/93.

further technical or economic progress and which mainly benefit the customers or consumers.'

The definition of prohibited horizontal agreements (ie agreements between actual or potential competitors) is fairly extensive and covers price fixing and recommendations, restrictions of production and market sharing.

The prohibition concerns except explicit contracts also decisions by associations of undertakings and concerted practices, including so called 'gentlemen's agreements'. Conscious parallelism in pricing behaviour by competitors will consequently be caught by this prohibition.

Price fixing and recommendations   The prohibition against price fixing and recommendations concerns both prices to be paid and prices to be charged by undertakings. In addition to actual prices, discounts and guidelines for pricing are also covered by the prohibition.

Restrictions of production   The prohibition concerning restrictions of production covers both production quotas and other comparable arrangements. The said prohibition is, however, not without exceptions. Where it is possible to show that the restriction of production is necessary in order to contribute to the efficiency of production or distribution or to further technical or economic progress and that customers or consumers are the beneficiaries of the arrangement, the restriction might be approved. A prerequisite for this is that the arrangement does not contain any elements of price fixing.

According to the government proposal for an Act on Restrictions on Competition,[11] one should take into account the EC group exemptions and case law when considering whether an arrangement fulfils the criteria set out in section 6 for the approval of a restriction of production.

Sharing markets or sources of supply   Section 6 also prohibits arrangements whereby the parties share markets or sources of supply. Market sharing is prohibited regardless of whether it is implemented through agreed market shares, territorial division or customer allocation. Correspondingly, sharing of sources of supply is prohibited regardless of the way of implementation. The prohibition against sharing markets or sources of supply is not absolute. The possibilities for an 'exception', described above, applies also to market sharing and sharing sources of supply.[12]

1.4   Abuse of a dominant position

1.4.1   Section 7 of the Competition Act prohibits abuse of a dominant position by an undertaking or association of undertakings. The section provides:

'An abuse of a dominant position by an undertaking or association of undertakings shall be forbidden.
    The following shall, among other things, be deemed to constitute an abuse of a dominant position:

---

11 162/1991.
12 See decision by the Competition Council 27 January 1994, d:o 5/359/93.

1 refusal of entering into a business relationship without justifiable cause;
2 use of business terms which are not based on good business practice and which restrict the freedom of the customer;
3 use of exclusive sales or purchase agreements without special reason;
4 application of a pricing practice, unreasonable or evidently aimed at restricting competition; or
5 abusing a dominant position in order to restrict competition in the production or marketing of other commodities.'

If section 7 is to apply it is necessary to establish:

(a) the existence of a dominant position on the relevant market, and
(b) an abuse of the dominant position.

1.4.2 The existence of a dominant position

The second paragraph of section 3 of the Competition Act defines a 'dominant position' as follows:

> 'An undertaking or association of undertakings shall be deemed to have a dominant position if the undertaking or association of undertakings, either on the national market for a commodity or in a certain area of the market concerned, has an exclusive right or other corresponding dominant position which allows it to control the price level or delivery terms of the relevant commodity or has another equivalent effect on the conditions of competition on a certain level of production or distribution.'

Market shares of more than 50% are considered to indicate dominance.

1.4.3 Defining the market

When establishing the existence of a dominant position, one must define both the relevant product market and the relevant geographic market. As for defining the relevant product market, supply and demand substitutability must be analyzed. Highly substitutable products are likely to belong to the same product market.

The relevant geographic market consists of the area where the dominant undertaking can control the market conditions. Areas consisting of less than the whole of Finland may be defined as a relevant geographic market.[13]

1.4.4 The abuse

As presented above, section 7 contains a list of examples of conduct deemed abusive. The list is not exhaustive. Consequently, any conduct which is perceived as improper exploitation of market power of a dominant undertaking, will infringe section 7. The following are examples of abusive practices:

(a) discrimination;
(b) predatory pricing;

---

13 See decision by the Supreme Administrative Court 30 August 1993, 15094, 1397, 1398, 1641 and 3156/1/93.

(c) tie-in sales;
(d) refusal to supply.

1.5 General prohibition against harmful restrictions on competition

1.5.1 Section 9 of the Competition Act consists of a provision which at first sight gives the impression of a mere definition of 'harmful restrictions on competition'. The section provides:

'A restriction on competition shall be deemed to have harmful effects if it, in a way incompatible with sound and effective economic competition,

1 affects price formation; or
2 decreases or is likely to decrease the efficiency of trade; or
3 prevents or hinders the trade of another; or
4 is incompatible with an international convention binding on Finland.'

1.5.2 Due to the wording of section 16 of the Competition Act, section 9 does, however, become a material 'prohibition section'. Section 16 provides:

'If a restriction on competition has a harmful effect referred to in section 9, the Competition Council may:

1 prohibit an undertaking or association of undertakings from applying an agreement or other arrangement restricting competition or other corresponding practice; or
2 oblige an undertaking to supply a commodity to another undertaking under similar terms as those applied to other undertakings in a corresponding position.

A decision by the Competition Council shall be complied with irrespective of appeal unless otherwise ordered by the Supreme Administrative Court.'

The general prohibition against harmful restrictions on competition stipulated through sections 9 and 16 is, however, unlike the prohibitions stipulated in sections 4, 5, 6 and 7, not an absolute prohibition.[14] It is instead based on the 'principle of abuse'. This means that possible restrictions on competition are not necessarily prohibited according to section 9. Only if the relevant restrictions also are 'incompatible with sound and effective economic competition' will section 9 be infringed. The general prohibition covers all types of restrictions on competition not explicitly covered by sections 4, 5, 6 or 7. It applies, consequently, to both anti-competitive agreements and abuses of dominance not covered in the respective sections.

---

14 The prohibitions stipulated in sections 5 and 6 are to a certain extent conditional as described above in sections 1.3.3 and 1.3.4.

2 ENFORCEMENT

2.1 Enforcement authorities

2.1.1 Primary responsibility for the enforcement of the Finnish competition law rests with the Office of Free Competition, the Competition Council, the county governments and the regular courts of law.[15]

2.1.2 The Office of Free Competition

The principal tasks of the Office of Free Competition are to investigate the conditions of competition and to undertake the measures necessary in order to eliminate harmful restrictions on competition.[16] Usually this means that the Office gathers information from the market and starts negotiations with the relevant undertakings supposed to be in breach of the provisions of the Competition Act.

If it is necessary to prevent the application or implementation of a restriction on competition without delay and this cannot be achieved on a voluntary basis, the Office may issue an interlocutory injunction to this effect.

The Office does also in certain cases grant exceptions from the prohibitions in sections 4–6 of the Competition Act and finally if it has not been possible to eliminate a harmful restriction on competition on a voluntary basis, it refers matters to the Competition Council.

2.1.3 The Competition Council

If the Office of Free Competition has not succeeded in eliminating the harmful effects of a restriction on competition through negotiations, the Office shall refer the matter to the Competition Council. A matter may also be referred to the Council by an undertaking directly affected by the relevant restrictions on competition or by an organization representing the interests of undertakings or consumers. The Council can not by itself decide to start investigations/proceedings if the matter has not been referred to it as described above.

The Council is organized like a regular court of law. The members of the Council act under equivalent responsibility as regular judges.

The principal task of the Competition Council is to decide whether a restriction on competition has harmful effects; to prohibit the application of a restriction on competition; to decide whether a penalty shall be imposed upon an undertaking or association of undertakings that infringes the provisions of sections 4–7 of the Competition Act and finally to decide whether a conditional fine shall be imposed.

The decisions taken by the Competition Council can be appealed to the Supreme Administrative Court.

---

15 A restriction on competition may be taken up also by the Financial Supervision when the restriction mainly concerns an activity under its supervision or by the Ministry of Social Affairs and Health when the restriction mainly concerns insurance activities.
16 Act on Office of Free Competition 711/88, 482/1992, section 2.

2.1.4   The county governments

The county governments investigate restrictions on competition and their effects on a local level, and upon referral by the Office of Free Competition, undertake measures to eliminate the harmful effects of restrictions on competition.[17]

2.1.5   The regular courts of law

Disputes concerning restrictions on competition can also come up in and be decided by regular courts of law. Section 18 of the Competition Act provides:

'A term contained in a contract, by-laws, decision or other judicial measure or arrange-ment, which violates the provisions of sections 4–7 or which violates an order, injunction, or obligation issued by the Competition Council or an interim injunction or obligation issued by the Office of Free Competition, shall not be applied or implemented.'

The courts of law must respect section 18 when deciding disputes.

2.2   Notification of restrictions on competition

The Finnish competition law does not require systematic notifications of restric-tions on competition. According to section 11 of the Competition Act, the Office of Free Competition may, however, order an undertaking with a dominant position to notify any contracts concerning the acquisition of firms, the purchase of a majority holding or other acquisition of dominance with regard to the operations of another undertaking which may be deemed to have a significant effect on the conditions of competition. This obligation may for specific reasons also be imposed on other than dominant undertakings.

2.3   Investigations

2.3.1   The Office of Free Competition is the main investigating body. Its investi-gations can be triggered by:

(a)   the Office's own initiative;
(b)   complaint by a third party; or
(c)   notification of a particular agreement or examples of conduct.

The investigations conducted by the Office are mainly carried out informally with the Office requesting and receiving information on the alleged restriction on competition.

2.3.2   The right to request and receive information is based on section 10 of the Competition Act. The section provides:

'An undertaking or association of undertakings shall be compelled, at the request of the Office of Free Competition, to submit to the Office all information and documents necessary to investigate the contents, purpose and effect of a restriction on competition as well as the conditions of competition.

17 Section 12 of the Competition Act.

An undertaking or association of undertakings shall, at the request of the Office of Free Competition, also submit information and documents to the Office in order to make possible investigation of whether the undertaking or association of undertakings has a dominant position.

The corresponding information and documents shall be submitted to the County Government when it investigates restrictions or conditions of competition.

The information shall be given in writing when so required.'

2.3.3 Section 20 of the Competition Act does, in addition to this, provide the Office and the county governments with extensive powers to conduct inspections on-the-spot. The section provides:

'A competent civil servant of the Office of Free Competition or the County Government shall be empowered to conduct an inspection to supervise compliance with this Act and with provisions and orders issued thereunder. The Office of Free Competition has a duty to carry out, on the request of the EC Commission, inspections, which are prescribed in the EC provisions.

The Office of Free Competition shall assist the EC Commission in carrying out inspections in a manner prescribed in the EC provisions.

For the purposes of an inspection, an undertaking or association of undertakings shall allow a civil servant referred to in paragraphs 1 and 2 access to all business and storage premises, land areas and means of transport in its possession. The civil servant conducting the inspection or investigation has the right to investigate the business correspondence, accounts, data processing records and other documents of the undertaking or association of undertakings that may be of importance in the supervision of compliance with this Act or with provisions and orders issued thereunder.

The civil servant conducting the inspection or investigation has the right to demand oral explanations on location and take copies of the documents being examined.

When needed the police shall at request give executive assistance, in a manner prescribed separately, for conducting the inspection and investigation referred to in paragraphs 1 and 2.'

Inspections conducted with the support of section 20 must have a specific purpose related to a suspected restriction on competition. Consequently, the Office or the county governments can not go on mere 'fishing expeditions'.

As for the competence of the EC Commission, please see Chapter I.

2.4 Penalties and other sanctions

2.4.1 *Penalty*

The Competition Council has power under section 8 of the Competition Act to impose penalties up to FIM 4 million or 10% of the total turnover for the preceding year for infringement of the provisions of sections 4–7 of the Competition Act. Section 8 of the Competition Act provides:

'A penalty shall be imposed upon an undertaking or association of undertakings that infringes the provisions of sections 4–7 unless the infringement is deemed minor or the imposition of a penalty is otherwise deemed unnecessary in order to safeguard competition. In determining the amount of the penalty, attention shall be paid to the nature and scope as well as to the duration of the restriction on competition. The penalty shall be between five thousand and four million marks. Where the restriction on competition and the circumstances of the case so warrant, the maximum amount may be exceeded. The maximum penalty shall however, not exceed 10 per cent of the total turnover from the preceding year of the undertaking or association of undertakings participating in the restriction on competition.

The penalty shall be imposed by the Competition Council upon a proposal by the Office of Free Competition. The penalty shall be ordered payable to the State.

The Competition Council may order that an undertaking or association of undertakings terminate an activity referred to in sections 4–7.'[18]

The Competition Council has so far not imposed any penalties.

2.4.2   Conditional fines

The Office of Free Competition may in certain cases impose conditional fines in order to enforce the duty to submit information or to make documents available. The conditional fine shall be ordered payable by the Competition Council.

2.4.3   Competition restriction offences

Anyone who wilfully submits a false notification or false information to the Office of Free Competition, the county governments or the Competition Council shall be sentenced for a 'competition restriction offence' to a fine or imprisonment not exceeding six months. When a regular court of law handles such matters, it shall reserve to the Office of Free Competition or the Competition Council a right to be heard.

2.5   Exemptions

Arrangements formally infringing the prohibitions stipulated in sections 4–6 of the Competition Act may upon application be exempted by the Office of Free Competition under section 19 of the said Act. An exemption should be granted if the relevant restriction on competition contributes to an increase in the efficiency of production or distribution or the furtherance of technical or economic progress and if it mainly benefits the customers or consumers. It is important to note that no exemption can be granted if the relevant arrangement constitutes an abuse of a dominant position (section 7).

2.6   Third party rights

2.6.1   A third party suffering from an infringement of the Competition Act has three options available to him:

(a)   he may file a complaint with the Office of Free Competition;
(b)   he may refer the matter to the Competition Council;[19] or
(c)   start proceedings in a regular court of law.

---

18 A penalty imposed under section 8 is by its nature an 'administrative' penalty. It is consequently not a fine for a criminal offence.
19 This possibility is open only to undertakings directly affected by the infringement and organisations looking after the interests of undertakings or consumers, if the Office of Free Competition has not referred the matter to the Competition Council.

The possible outcomes of alternatives 1 and 2 have been described above.[20]

2.6.2 As for proceedings before a regular court of law, the courts are bound by section 18 of the Competition Act. Section 18 stipulates that arrangements infringing the prohibitions in sections 4–7 may not be applied or implemented and consequently, not upheld by courts of law.

2.6.3 The Competition Act does not contain any provisions regarding the possible liability to pay damages due to a restriction on competition. It is, nevertheless, theoretically possible to sue for damages in a regular court of law on the basis of the 'general' Act on Damages.[1] In such a case the plaintiff would have to prove the actual damages suffered by him due to the relevant restriction on competition.

3   CHECKLIST OF POTENTIAL INFRINGEMENTS

3.1   Agency

3.1.1 The principal appoints the agent to procure business or to transact business for and on behalf of the principal in an agency agreement. Since the agent normally acts as an extension of the principal's sales arm, agency agreements do not normally present any problem from a competition law point of view due to the fact that they do not involve an agreement between fully separate undertakings from an economic point of view.

3.1.2. The Finnish law contains a specific act concerning agency agreements, the Act on Commercial Representatives and Salesmen.[2] This Act as well as the Competition Act does, however, not contain any provisions particularly related to competition law aspects of agency agreements. Neither has the case law developed any definite competition law standpoint regarding agency agreements.

3.1.3 Due to the nature of the agency agreements, it is fairly unlikely that such agreements would be challenged on the basis of the prohibitions stipulated in the Competition Act. In cases where the agent de facto acts as a relatively independent entity in relation to the principal and where the agency element therefore is 'watered down', the arrangements might, however, be caught by the prohibitions in sections 4, 6 or 9 of the Competition Act.

3.1.4 The possibility of obtaining an exemption has been described in section 2.5.

3.2   Distribution

3.2.1 A distribution agreement differs from an agency agreement in that the distributor purchases the contract products for resale whereas the agent only procures sales for his principal.

---

20 See sections 2.1.2 and 2.1.3.
 1 412/74.
 2 417/92.

3.2.2 Since distribution agreements, by increasing the sources of outlets, normally further competition, the Finnish competition law generally approves of the use of such agreements. Exclusive distribution agreements concluded by dominant undertakings are, however, an exception to this rule. As described in section 1.4 above, the Competition Act prohibits the use of 'exclusive sales agreements' by dominant undertakings 'without special reason'. The prohibition applies regardless of whether the dominant undertaking is principal or distributor.

3.2.3 There exists so far no practice defining the concept 'special reason'. Situations where the particular nature of the product results in exceptionally high costs for establishing a distribution system have though been mentioned as potential 'special reason' cases.[3]

3.2.4 In cases where none of the undertakings involved has a dominant position, the competition restricting elements of the distribution agreement should be judged on the basis of the prohibitions stipulated in sections 4, 6 and 9 of the Competition Act. An arrangement obstructing parallel imports will always be prohibited.

3.2.5 The possibility of obtaining exemption has been described in section 2.5.

3.3   Selective distribution

3.3.1 Selective distribution arises where a principal uses certain criteria for choosing the distributor or dealers entitled to sell the relevant product. The objective of the principal is usually to make distribution more effective, to protect the image or the trade mark of the product, etc. He may further wish to deal only with distributors prepared to undertake sales promotion or after sales service obligations.

3.3.2 The Finnish competition law generally approves of the use of selective arrangements as long as they are based on non-discriminatory qualitative criteria and the nature/quality of the products justifies the use of such an arrangement. If a selective arrangement is based on other than non-discriminatory qualitative criteria, section 9 of the Competition Act is likely to apply and the arrangement likely to be considered as a 'prohibited harmful restriction on competition'. If the principal is a dominant undertaking, section 7 might also apply.

3.3.3 The possibility of obtaining exemption has been described in section 2.5.

3.4   Exclusive purchasing

3.4.1 In an exclusive purchasing agreement the buyer commits himself to buy products for resale only from one specific supplier. Such agreements restrict competition since third party suppliers are excluded from selling their products to the relevant buyer.

3.4.2 The use of exclusive purchasing agreements might, however, in some cases be motivated by, for example, extensive investments in distribution facilities made by the supplier or the need to protect the product development.

---

3 See government proposal for an Act on Restrictions on Competition 162/1991, p 13.

3.4.3 The Finnish competition law contains no general prohibition against the use of exclusive purchasing agreements. As described in section 1.4ff above, the Competition Act does, however, prohibit dominant undertakings from using 'exclusive purchasing agreements without special reason' through section 7. The prohibition applies regardless of whether the dominant undertaking is 'supplier' or 'buyer'. The 'special reasons' are likely to be the type of reasons indicated above (see section 3.2.2), ie extensive investments etc.[4]

3.4.4 In cases where none of the undertakings involved have a dominant position, the competition restricting elements of the exclusive purchasing agreement should be judged on the basis of the prohibitions stipulated in sections 4, 6 and 9 of the Competition Act.

3.4.5 The possibility of obtaining exemption has been described in section 2.5.

3.5 Franchising

3.5.1 Franchising refers to an arrangement where the franchisor licenses the franchisee the right to use a particular trade mark or name and where he obligates the franchisee to arrange his marketing system in a way associated with the franchisor. Franchising agreements often contain conditions restricting competition such as prohibition to sell competing products, sales territories etc.

3.5.2 The Finnish competition law generally approves of the use of franchising agreements since such agreements usually enhance efficiency. The Competition Act does not contain any provisions concerning specifically franchising agreements. It should, however, be noted that a franchising agreement still must respect the prohibitions provided for in sections 4 and 6 of the Competition Act and that the other possible competition restricting elements of such an agreement will be judged on the basis of section 9 of the same Act.

3.5.3 The possibility of obtaining exemption has been described in section 2.5.

3.6 Intellectual property licensing

3.6.1 The Finnish competition law generally approves of the use of intellectual property licensing arrangements. Despite the fact that the Competition Act does not contain any provisions relating specifically to intellectual property licensing, the particular prohibitions stipulated in sections 6 and 7 of the Competition Act must, nevertheless, be observed when concluding, for example, patent licensing agreements.

3.6.2 The possibility of obtaining exemption has been described in section 2.5.

3.7 Refusals to supply

3.7.1 Refusals to supply usually exist in connection with dominance, but may also do so where several undertakings have agreed on common behaviour, eg a collective boycott.

4 See decision by the Competition Council 17 March 1993, d:o 2/359/92.

3.7.2 According to Finnish competition law a refusal to supply is generally prohibited. A refusal to supply 'without approvable cause' by a dominant undertaking constitutes an infringement of section 7 of the Competition Act. Approvable causes are for example lack of capacity, known financial problems of the buyer etc. Where several undertakings have commonly agreed not to supply, section 6 of the said Act will, with the same exceptions as for dominant undertakings, be infringed. Single non-dominant undertakings refusing to supply only risk infringing Section 9 of the Competition Act.

3.7.3 The possibility of obtaining exemption has been described in section 2.5.

3.8 Price restrictions

3.8.1 The common forms of price restrictions are resale price maintenance, price fixing between competitors and discriminatory pricing.

3.8.2 Finnish competition law prohibits all sorts of absolute price restrictions. The prohibitions against resale price maintenance and price fixing between competitors have, together with the lawfulness of price recommendations, been described above in sections 1.3.2 and 1.3.4 respectively.

3.8.3 Discriminatory pricing, ie offering different prices to similar customers, usually occurs in connection with dominant undertakings. Section 7 of the Competition Act prohibits, as presented above in section 1.4 abuses of a dominance, including discriminatory pricing. In cases where dominance cannot be established, the lawfulness of discriminatory pricing should be judged on the basis of the General prohibition stipulated in Section 9 of the Competition Act. In such cases the discriminatory element is not likely to infringe the said section.

3.8.4 The possibility of obtaining exemption has been described in section 2.5.

3.9 Tie-in sales

3.9.1 Tie-in sales refer to the situation where the supply of one product A is made conditional upon the supply of another product B. Tie-in sales present a problem from a competition law point of view where the relevant products are neither by their nature nor commercial usage connected to each other.

3.9.2 Finnish competition law prohibits, through section 7 of the Competition Act, tie-in sales where the supplier has a dominant position and where the products are unconnected with each other.

3.9.3 The lawfulness of tie-in sales conducted by non-dominant undertakings should be judged on the basis of the general prohibition stipulated in section 9 of the Competition Act. Such conduct is not likely to infringe the said section.

3.9.4 The possibility of obtaining exemption has been described in section 2.5.

3.10 Information exchange

3.10.1 Agreements between actual or potential competitors concerning exchange of information on prices, customers, costs, investments etc may restrict competition if they *de facto* restrict the freedom of action of the relevant undertakings.

3.10.2 Exchange of confidential information between actual or potential competitors might infringe section 6 of the Competition Act whereas similar exchange of public information is not likely to do so.

3.10.3 The possibility of obtaining exemption has been described in section 2.5.

3.11 Joint buying and selling

3.11.1 Agreements between competitors to establish joint buying or selling are problematic from a competition law point of view since they usually involve the surrender by participants of their freedom of action.

3.11.2 The lawfulness of joint buying and selling arrangements should primarily be judged on the basis of section 6 of the Competition Act. If the arrangement contains de facto market sharing or price co-operation elements, it is likely to infringe the said section.

3.11.3 Joint buying and selling arrangements may in certain cases also infringe section 9 of the Competition Act.

3.11.4 The possibility of obtaining exemption has been described in section 2.5.

3.12 Market sharing

3.12.1 As described in section 1.3.4 above, market sharing is prohibited regardless of the manner of implementation.

3.12.2 The possibility of obtaining an exemption has been described in section 2.5.

3.13 Joint ventures

3.13.1 Joint ventures can be defined as juridically independent units with separate organisations, formed by two or more undertakings for specific purposes and jointly owned by the undertakings. The purposes of joint ventures are often rationalisation of production, joint R & D, joint selling organisations etc.

3.13.2 The Finnish competition law generally approves of the use of joint ventures. A joint venture might, however, restrict competition in a way prohibited in section 6 of the Competition Act. Section 6 may for example be infringed if the patents restrict their own production, fix prices or undertake not to compete with each other or the joint venture, thereby effectively sharing markets. If the production restricting or market sharing elements are necessary and the joint venture 'contributes to the efficiency of production or distribution or further technical or economic progress and benefits customers or consumers' the joint venture may, according to sub-paragraph 2 of section 6, be permitted.

3.13.3 In cases where the efficiency advantages of an anti-competitive joint venture are more significant than the anti-competitive elements, the joint venture may upon application be exempted under section 19 of the Competition Act as described above in section 2.5.

4   CONCENTRATIONS, MERGERS AND ACQUISITIONS

4.1   Introduction

Finnish competition law does not contain any provisions explicitly regulating concentrations, mergers or acquisitions.[5] Consequently, the Office of Free Competition and the Competition Council lack the kind of 'arsenal' which would make it possible for them to block concentrative arrangements.[6]

4.2   Notifications

Despite the fact that Finnish competition law does not require systematic notifications of restrictions on competition, section 11 of the Competition Act enables the Office of Free Competition to order certain undertakings to notify concentrative arrangements. The section provides:

> 'The Office of Free Competition may order that an undertaking, enjoying a dominant position, notifies any contracts concerning the acquisition of a firm, the purchase of a majority holding, or other acquisition of dominance, with regard to the operations of another undertaking which may be deemed to have a significant effect on the conditions of competition.
>
> The duty of notification may also be imposed on an undertaking other than one referred to in paragraph 1 if the undertaking operates in a commodities market in which free competition is prevented or significantly distorted by the public authorities.
>
> The Office of Free Competition may, where necessary, oblige an undertaking referred to in paragraphs 1 and 2 to submit additional information on the measure being notified.'

The purpose of this section is to improve the competition authorities' ability closely to monitor 'critical' concentrative arrangements.

4.3   Concentrative agreements as abuses of dominance

4.3.1 As mentioned above in section 1.4, section 7 of the Competition Act prohibits abuses of dominant market power. The prohibited abuses are not exhaustively defined in the said section, wherefore any kind of improper exploitation of market power by a dominant undertaking must be considered prohibited.

---

5 Finnish legislation, quite apart from the competition law, contains an Act, the Act on Monitoring Foreign Ownership of Business 16/2/92, which requires post-notification when shares (at least 33%) in the largest Finnish companies are bought by foreigners. This Act, it is believed, will be abolished by 1 January 1996.

6 It should, however, be noted that the EC competition law contains provisions regulating concentrative measures and that these provisions are binding also in Finland. The EC competition law is presented in Chapter I.

4.3.2 The obvious question in connection with concentrative practices is whether section 7 can also be applied to such practices, ie whether for example a merger as such could infringe section 7. The wording of the Competition Act does not indicate that this would be the case. Neither do the government proposals for the Competition Acts (148/87 and 162/1991) say anything to support the applicability of section 7 on concentrative arrangements.

4.3.3 Despite these arguments, it is not impossible that section 7 could be applied on concentrative practices under some circumstances.[7] This could, for example, happen in cases where a dominant undertaking through its market position forces a smaller competitor into a merger.

4.3.4 The question as to the extension of the applicability of section 7 to concentrative arrangements will, however, have to be resolved by case law in the future.

7 Compare with the application of Article 86 on concentrative arrangements within the EC.

France

Dominique Voillemot
Philippe Matignon

Gide Loyrette Nouel
26 Cours Albert 1er
75008 Paris
France

Tel   ++33 1 40 75 60 00
Fax ++33 1 43 59 37 79

CHAPTER VII

France

1 FRENCH COMPETITION LAW

1.1 Background

1.1.1 French competition law was profoundly amended by the Ordinance of 1 December 1986[1] governing price fixing and competition and its implementing decree of 29 December 1986[2] which repealed the two Ordinances of 30 June 1945,[3] the Act of 19 July 1977[4] on economic concentrations and review of anti-competitive agreements and abuses of dominant position.

Certain provisions of the Ordinance concerning unlawful commercial practices were incorporated into the Consumer Protection Code by the Act of 26 July 1993.[5]

1.1.2 The major innovations in the 1986 reform were:

(a) the review of anti-competitive agreements and abuses of dominant position was entrusted to the Competition Council, which replaced the Competition Commission. The Competition Council enjoys independent decision-making and disciplinary powers;

(b) the decriminalisation of discriminatory practices, refusals to supply and tied sales. These practices are, however, decriminalised only to the extent that they do not target consumers;

(c) the definition of a new anti-competitive practice subject to the same legal rules as abuses of dominant position: abuse of economic dependency;

(d) the investigation and recording of violations are conducted under new procedural rules designed to afford defendants better protection.

1.2 Anti-competitive agreements and concerted practices

1.2.1 The prohibition on anti-competitive agreements is imposed by Article 7 of the Ordinance of 1 December 1986, which states:

'Concerted practices, express or tacit agreements and coalitions are prohibited if the object or potential effect thereof is to restrain, limit or distort competition in a market, including in particular when they may:

1 Limit market access or freely competitive behaviour by other undertakings;

---

1 Ordinance no 86-1243 of 1 December 1986 governing price fixing and competition.
2 Decree no 86-1309 of 29 December 1986.
3 Ordinances no 45-1483 of 30 June 1945 governing prices and no 45-1484 of 30 June 1945 governing the 'recording, prosecution and prevention of violations of economic legislation'.
4 Act no 77-806 of 19 July 1977 on economic concentrations and review of anti-competitive agreements and abuses of dominant position.
5 Act no 93-949 of 26 July 1993. Consumer Protection Code.

145

2   Prevent prices from being fixed by the free action of the market, by promoting their artificial increase or decrease;
3   Limit or control production, sales outlets, investments or technical progress;
4   Allocate markets or supply sources.'

1.2.2   Parties to the agreement

Article 7 of the Ordinance does not define precisely who is a party to the agreement. It is clear, however, that an agreement may be between individuals or legal entities. The agreement must involve economically independent undertakings. Therefore, agreements between economically dependent undertakings are not anti-competitive agreements.[6] On the other hand, parties to any agreement may very well be at different levels in the economic process. Anti-competitive vertical agreements as well as anti-competitive horizontal agreements are therefore prohibited by Article 7.[7]

1.2.3   Form of concerted action

Article 7 of the Ordinance of 1 December 1986 makes no reference to the form which prohibited actions or agreements must take. It is now well recognised that the legal form of the agreement has no effect on the applicability of Article 7. The agreement may be express and in writing, or may result from actions bringing together undertakings (company formation, joint subsidiary, co-operative, association, syndicate, etc). The agreement may also be tacit and not legally formalised. Parallelism in behaviour may therefore constitute a prohibited agreement.[8]

1.2.4   Proof of anti-competitive agreements

The Competition Council has on numerous occasions recognised that concerted behaviour may be proved without any written proof, through the presence of serious, specific and consistent indications (the so-called 'set of indications' method).[9]

The Competition Council has gone even further, deducing the existence of concerted practice from the mere similarity of behaviour, even in the absence of consistent presumptions. The Competition Council will find the existence of a tacit agreement if the parallelism cannot be explained by 'either the market conditions to which each undertaking is subject or the pursuit by each of its individual interests'.[10]

1.2.5   Anti-competitive nature of the agreement

By prohibiting agreements 'whose object or potential effect is to impede competition', Article 7 of the Ordinance makes an impediment to competition an

6   1980 Report, p 25.
    Decision of 7 July 1987, BOCCRF 20 October 1987.
7   1988 Report by the Competition Council, p 21.
    Decision of the Competition Council of 9 June 1987 *'competition in pharmacy distribution of certain body-care products'*. Court of Appeal of Paris, 6 December 1988. BOCCRF 29 December 1988.
8   1980 Report of the Competition Commission, p 26.
9   1990 Report, p 27. 1989 Report, p 26. Competition Council, 12 December 1986 'Electrical Equipment', upheld by the Court of Appeal of Paris, 1st Division, 19 September 1990.
10 Competition Council, 'Fuel in the Corsica region'. 25 April 1989, upheld by the Court of Appeal of Paris, 9 November 1989, BOCCRF 18 November 1989.

independent condition to the existence of the violation itself. There are two alternative bases on which an agreement may be found to be anti-competitive:[11]

(a) *the restriction on competition may arise from the object of the agreement* The parties to the agreement may have entered into it with the intent to hinder competition. An agreement may be for the purpose of limiting competition if the parties thereto could not have been unaware of its anti-competitive effects;[12]

(b) *the restriction on competition may also follow from the agreement's effect* It is enough to ascertain the existence of the elements of an anti-competitive agreement without having to show a deliberate intent on the part of the parties to prejudice competition.[13] The restrictive effect on competition may be actual or potential. To establish a potential effect, the nature of the practices and the agreement's impact on the market must be examined.[14]

1.2.6 Main anti-competitive practices

The main practices which may be subject to the prohibition on anti-competitive agreements are:

(a) the fixing of quotas between competitors or market-sharing practices;[15]
(b) agreements governing prices, mark-ups and sale conditions;[16]
(c) coalitions of contract bidders and winners;[17]
(d) barriers to market access or commercial freedom of other players on the market;[18]
(e) the set-up of distribution networks[19] (exclusive, selective, franchise);
(f) the formation of joint subsidiaries;[20]
(g) joint buying.

1.3 Monopoly practices (abuse of market power)

1.3.1 Article 8 of the Ordinance of 1 December 1986 imposes the prohibition on abuses of dominant position and states:

'The improper exploitation of the following by an undertaking or group of undertakings shall be prohibited under the same terms:

1 a *dominant position* on the domestic market or a substantial part thereof;
2 a condition of *economic dependency* on it by a customer or supplier who has no equivalent choice.

11 1990 Report, p 30.
12 See Sélinsky, 'L'entente prohibée' (Prohibited agreements), Litec 1979.
13 1988 Report of the Competition Council, p 22.
14 Competition Council, decision of 13 December 1988.
15 Competition Commission, opinion, 11 December 1980, cycle spare parts wholesalers.
16 Commission opinion of 20 June 1985 *'competition on the market for welded mesh'*. Decision of the Competition Council *'railroad ties'* no 88-D-43 of 8 November 1988, BOCCRF 24 November 1988.
17 Decision of the Competition Council, 16 February 1989, BOCCRF 1 March 1988, p 68.
18 Decision of the Competition Council relating to competition on the hearing-aid market, 15 March 1988, BOCCRF, 16 April 1988, p 96.
19 Decision of the Competition Council, 9 June 1987 *'Cosmetic and body-care products'*.
20 Competition Council, 13 June 1989 *'competition in the semolina industry'*.

These abuses shall include in particular refusals to supply, tie-in sales and discriminatory sale conditions, as well as the termination of established commercial relationships on the sole ground that the partner refuses to accept unjustified sale terms.'

Dominant positions, whether held by an undertaking or a group of undertakings, are prohibited only when their activities hinder or are liable to hinder competition.

1.3.2   Abusive exploitation of a dominant position

(1)   § 1   Three elements must be present for a *dominant position* to exist:

An undertaking or a group of undertakings   The notion of a group of undertakings is quite broad because it covers undertakings linked together either by common control[1] (a group of parent and subsidiary companies) or by *'financial or family'* links creating interlocking interests among the companies in question.[2] It is sufficient that the links between the companies are sufficiently *'stable, substantial and direct'*.[3] The Competition Commission went even further by holding that a certain economic complementarity between undertakings was sufficient to constitute a group of undertakings, even without a showing of any formal agreement. In this case, however, the undertakings must *consciously* adopt common behaviour or strategy (1979 Report, p 196).

A relevant market   This is defined by:

(a)   the nature of the product or service: the market must be defined 'based on the substitutability of the products or services for a specified clientele'.[4] This substitutability may be determined on the basis of various criteria, such as the features of the products, the technical conditions under which they are used, the costs incurred in using them or furnishing them, the strategy employed by the products' manufacturers,[5] as well as technical recommendations for their use, their size and price;[6]

(b)   geographical area: the market may be national or merely regional or local. It suffices that it cover 'a substantial part of the national territory'. The geographical market may be determined on the basis of such varying factors as the degree of protection (by tariff or otherwise) imposed at the border, the magnitude of imports, the transport costs and possibilities, the importance of accessory services accompanying the supply of the product;

(c)   the nature of the customers: the customers may be determined by analysing, inter alia, their location, specific needs, buying power, professional position, etc;

(d)   the marketing methods and conditions of use for the products.[7]

Market dominance   Market dominance is characterised by a 'monopoly situation' or a 'patent concentration of economic power'. Thus, any undertaking which is

1 Technical Commission on Anti-competitive Agreements, 18 March 1966 *'water meters'*.
2 Opinion of 27 January 1983 *'Brick and tile market in Alsace'*.
3 Opinion of 17 October 1973 *'PVC pipes'*.
4 1991 Report, p 47.
5 1989 Report, p 33.
6 Competition Council, 18 November 1992. *'Biwater'*.
7 Competition Council, 28 November 1989 *'bookclub sales'*, upheld by the Court of Appeal of Paris, 21 May 1990 BOCCRF, 1 June 1990, D 1990 p 523 Ch Gavalda note.

'able to play a leading role on the market to the extent that its competitors are as a practical matter forced to follow its behaviour'[8] is in a dominant position, as is one which has 'the ability to avoid constraints imposed by real competition'.[9] Market domination may be found on the basis of various criteria: the main criterion is market share, but other factors must also be taken into account such as technical or sales advantages, ease of market access, the magnitude of investments necessary in the business, etc.

(2)   § 2   Abusive exploitation

A dominant position is not in itself prohibited. It is merely the *sine qua non* to a finding of abuse, as prohibited by Article 8 of the Ordinance of 1 December 1986. The factors constituting abuse are determined in the discretion of the courts[10] and are shown by both the behaviour adopted by the undertaking in question and the causal nexus between the dominant position and this behaviour. Anti-competitive practices often result from acts which are in and of themselves unlawful. However, a practice which is not in itself an offence may become unlawful if it manifests the actor's intent to hinder competition.

1.3.3   Abusive exploitation of a condition of economic dependency

Economic dependency is 'a commercial relationship in which one of the partners has no alternative in the event that it wishes to refuse to contract under the terms imposed on it by its customer or supplier'.[11] The existence of economic dependency within the meaning of Article 8, paragraph 2 of the Ordinance of 1 December 1986 is determined on the basis of:

(a)   the share of the reseller's turnover represented by the supplier;
(b)   the supplier's brand name recognition;
(c)   the supplier's market share;
(d)   the impossibility for the distributor to find other suppliers of equivalent products.

These criteria must all be satisfied before an abuse of economic dependency may be found.[12]

1.4   Exemptions

1.4.1   Article 10 of Ordinance no 86-1243 of 1 December 1986 provides an exemption from the prohibition imposed in Articles 7 and 8 of the Ordinance for practices:

'1   which result from the application of a statute or a regulation promulgated to implement a statute;
2   which may be shown to result in economic progress and which allow users a fair share of the resulting benefit, without however giving the undertakings in question the

8 Competition Commission, 9 November 1978 *'Rousselot SA'*.
9 Competition Commission, 2 April 1981 *'retreading of tyres'*. 1990 Report, p 34.
10 Cass Crim 21 November 1991, Bull Inf Cass no 340, 15 February 1992, p 31 no 291.
11 Rep min quoted in the J Colon report, p 24.
12 Competition Commission, 3 July 1990 *'JVC Vidéo France'*. 1990 Report, p 73.

possibility of eliminating competition in respect of a substantial part of the products in question. These practices may impose restrictions on competition only to the extent that such restrictions are indispensable to attain this objective of promoting progress.

Certain classes of agreements, including in particular those whose purpose is to improve the management of small or medium-size undertakings, may be recognised as satisfying these requirements by decree issued with the concurring opinion of the Competition Council.'

1.4.2. The anti-competitive agreement or dominant position resulting from application of a statute or regulation (10 §1)

The legal provisions referred to in Article 10 §1 are statutes, decrees and orders (*arrêtés*) issued to implement statutes, and circulars or letters from the Minister of the Economy and Finance,[13] provided that such circulars or letters are formal interpretations of the statutes in force, expressly authorise the challenged practices and, above all, are issued by the Minister of the Economy and Finance. This justification has been applied to extended interprofessional agreements entered into in connection with interprofessional agricultural organisations.[14]

The statutory or other provision in question must result in a restraint on competition.[15] The Competition Council requires that the contested practices be the direct and unavoidable consequence of the regulation cited to justify them.[16]

1.4.3 The economic justification for an anti-competitive agreement or abuse of dominant position (10 §2 paragraph 1)

It is important to note that, unlike Community law, French law provides no notification procedure for exemptions. The economic justification for an anti-competitive agreement or abuse of dominant position on the basis of Article 10.2 may be asserted at any time, without preliminary procedure.

Conditions   Under Article 10 §2 practices complying with two positive requirements and two negative requirements are exempt from the prohibition imposed by Articles 7 and 8.

The two positive requirements are:

(a)   the practices must generate economic progress;[17]
(b)   the contested practices must afford users a fair share of the resulting benefit.[18]

The two negative requirements which are borrowed directly from Community law are:

(a)   the anti-competitive agreement must not impose restrictions which are not strictly indispensable to the achievement of economic progress;

---

13 1975 Report of the Competition Commission, p 989.
14 Competition Commission, 20 November 1980 '*Cahors wine*'.
15 Competition Council, decision 88-D-43 of 8 November 1988, BOCCRF, 24 November 1988, p 301.
16 Competition Council of 1 December 1987, architects' fees, BOCCRF, 16 December 1987, p 360.
17 Decision 88-D-10 of 1 March 1988, BOCCRF, 19 March 1988, p 79.
18 Competition Council decision 90-D-20 of 12 June 1990, BOCCRF, 12 July 1990.

(b)   nor may the anti-competitive agreement afford the parties thereto the possibility of eliminating competition in respect of a substantial part of the products in question.

Economic balancing   The economic advantages and drawbacks of the restraints on competition must be weighed. The restraints are justified only to the extent that the advantages outweigh the drawbacks. The economic progress demonstrated upon completion of this balancing corresponds to improvements in either productivity or market conditions.

1.4.4   Decrees adopted under Article 10 §2 paragraph 2

Just as the Community authorities may issue block exemptions by Regulation, the French authorities may by decree rule that certain classes of agreements comply with the requirements of Article 10.2. No decree has, however, yet been issued.

2   ENFORCEMENT

2.1   Enforcement authorities

2.1.1   The Competition Council

Created by the Ordinance of 1 December 1986, the Council is made up of 16 members appointed for six-year terms. It is presided over by a chairman and two vice-chairmen. The members are assisted by a rapporteur-general, permanent rapporteurs and outside rapporteurs. A Government Commissioner (*Commissaire du Gouvernement*) represents the state's interests.

The Competition Council has both advisory and enforcement functions.

Advisory function   The Competition Council may render its views on any matter involving competition provided that the question has been referred to it, as the legislature did not empower it to take the initiative on advisory matters. The Council may be generally consulted by the government, parliamentary committees and various legal entities such as local authorities, professional organisations and trade unions. Furthermore, it must be consulted on certain draft regulations which are liable to impose serious restrictions on competition.[19]

Moreover, the Council may be consulted by the courts in cases involving anti-competitive practices (Article 26 of the Ordinance) and by the Minister of the Economy and Finance in cases involving concentrations (Article 38 of the Ordinance).

Enforcement powers   Pursuant to Article 11, paragraph 2, the Council:

> 'shall examine practices referred to it to determine whether they fall within the scope of Articles 7 (anti-competitive agreements) or 8 (abuses of dominant position) or may be justified under Article 10'.

The Council may carry out its review in any sector of activity and has jurisdiction with respect to legal entities formed under public law, state-owned undertakings

---

19 Article 5 of the Ordinance of 1 December 1986.

and legal entities formed under private law but providing a public service. The Council has been granted decision-making authority; it may impose 'injunctions and sanctions'.

Article 12 of the 1986 Ordinance empowers the Competition Council to take interim protective measures designed to safeguard the rights of victims of anti-competitive practices in urgent cases.

2.1.2   Court of Appeal of Paris

Council decisions may be appealed within a period of one month from service of the decision to the Court of Appeal of Paris for reversal or revision.

2.1.3   Court of Cassation

Decisions of the Courts of Appeal may be appealed to the Court of Cassation within a period of one month from the service of the decision.

2.1.4   The authorities

The Directorate General for Competition, Consumer Protection and Prevention of Fraud (*Direction Générale de la Concurrence de la Consommation et de la Répression des Fraudes* or 'DGCCRF') is authorised to investigate any behaviour violating the rules governing the transparency and free functioning of the market. It has substantial powers with respect to review of anti-competitive practices, accompanied by investigative powers for identifying and ascertaining unlawful economic practices (see section 2.3).

2.2   Jurisdictional rules

In addition to the Competition Council, the courts of general jurisdiction may apply Articles 7 and 8 of the Ordinance of 1 December 1986.

2.2.1   Powers of the national courts of general jurisdiction

Civil and commercial courts   Actions to void 'commitments, agreements or clauses' connected with unlawful anti-competitive agreements or abuses of dominant position on the basis of Articles 7 and 8 of the Ordinance of 1 December 1986 may be brought before the civil or commercial courts. Similarly, any person who believes he is a victim of an anti-competitive practice may bring an action in the courts of general jurisdiction against the parties engaging in the practice for damages for the prejudice caused thereby on the basis of Article 1382 of the French Civil Code. Only the Competition Council, however, has jurisdiction to impose fines either immediately or upon failure to comply with injunctions. (See the discussion in section 2.4.1 concerning the amount of the fine.) These two procedures, brought before either the judicial courts or the Competition Council, are independent.

Criminal courts   Anti-competitive agreements and abuses of dominant position may constitute criminal offences if a natural person has fraudulently played a decisive personal role in carrying them out (Article 17). Prosecution before the criminal court is independent of proceedings before the Competition Council.

2.2.2 National courts and Community law

The Treaty of Rome established its own legal rules to be integrated into the legal systems of the Member States and imposed on their courts. Thus, as the Court of Justice has reiterated on many occasions, the civil and commercial courts may themselves apply Articles 85 and 86 of the Treaty of Rome. To emphasise this possibility, those responsible for the drafting of the Act of 11 December 1992[20] believed it necessary to specify that matters may be referred directly to the Competition Council on the basis of Articles 85 and 86 of the Treaty of Rome.

It therefore follows that the national authorities must first apply Community standards. Thus, application of the national law is permitted only to the extent that it does not impede the uniform enforcement of the Community rules throughout the Common Market.

2.3 Adversary proceedings (enquiries and investigations)

2.3.1 Administrative enquiry

The Minister of the Economy and Finance, as well as the Competition Council, may trigger administrative enquiries in enforcement of the Ordinance.

Persons empowered to make enquiries The following are empowered to make enquiries:

(a) authorised officials: pursuant to Article 45 of the Ordinance, administrative enquiries are carried out by 'government officials authorised for such purpose by the Minister of the Economy'. These are class A and B officials reporting to the Director of the DGCCRF. Only class A officials are however authorised to conduct site inspections and effect seizures;

(b) rapporteurs of the Competition Council: in matters referred to the Competition Council, the Council's rapporteurs have the same investigative powers as the officials referred to in Article 45.

Simple enquiries Article 47 of the Ordinance empowers the persons conducting the enquiry to undertake certain non-coercive review measures themselves and without judicial authorisation. They may:

(a) enter any buildings, land or means of transport used for business purposes; they may not however inspect or search the premises;

(b) require the production of the books, invoices and other business documents and make copies thereof;

(c) gather information and substantiation, either on-site or pursuant to request;

(d) require an expert's report prepared with the participation of all parties.

---

20 Act no 92.1282 of 11 December 1992.

Enquiries conducted under judicial supervision Before carrying out any site inspections or effecting any coercive seizures (searches) of documents, the investigators must comply with the requirements of Article 48 of the Ordinance. The main requirements are:

(a) the enquiry must have been sought by the Minister of the Economy and Finance or the Competition Council;[1]

(b) the enquiry must have been authorised by order of the Presiding Judge of the competent District Court (*Tribunal de Grande Instance*);

(c) the on-site inspection and seizure must be carried out under the authority and supervision of the court, which appoints one or more judicial police officers to accompany the investigators.

Minutes The investigators' findings are recorded in minutes and, possibly, reports. The minutes are sent to the competent authority: the prosecutor, the Minister of the Economy or the Competition Council.

2.3.2 Investigation before the Competition Council

Upon completion of the administrative enquiry, an administrative report is drawn up and sent to the Competition Council. The Chairman of the Competition Council appoints a rapporteur to investigate the matter. The rapporteur may hold hearings prior to giving notice of the infringements alleged. There are two distinct procedures before the Competition Council: the ordinary procedure and the simplified procedure. Whether the simplified procedure may be used depends on the magnitude of the case.

Ordinary procedure The procedure is as follows:

(a) the Rapporteur gives notice of the alleged infringements to the parties;

(b) the parties file an answer (within two months);

(c) the Rapporteur draws up a report;

(d) the parties file a response (within two months);

(e) a hearing is conducted before the Council.

Simplified procedure Under the simplified procedure, recourse to the procedure described in section 2.3.2 (a) may be avoided whenever the anti-competitive practice appears relatively straightforward or of minor importance.

After notice of the alleged infringements is given to the parties in question, the chairman of the Council may decide to refer the matter to the Permanent Commission, which is made up solely of himself and the two vice-chairmen. The Permanent Commission is then empowered to rule on the merits, in place of the Council, and enjoys all powers of the Council, without having to establish a preliminary report.

If the parties agree to the simplified procedure, they have a period of two months from receipt of notice of the chairman's decision to refer the matter to the Permanent Commission to present their comments on the allegations.

The Permanent Commission makes its decision on the merits without prior hearing.

---

1 Cass Crim, 28 November 1989 and Cass Crim, 12 and 19 December 1989, Petites Affiches 28 March 1992 p 4.

2.4 Fines and other sanctions

2.4.1 Anti-competitive agreements and abuses of dominant position

Fines imposed by the Competition Council   Under the ordinary procedure, the Competition Council may, pursuant to Article 13 of the Ordinance, fine each of the parties engaging in an anti-competitive practice. The maximum amount of the fine on undertakings is 5% of the turnover, net of taxes, made during the last closed financial year. The maximum fine for persons other than undertakings is 10,000,000 francs. The maximum fine under the simplified procedure is 500,000 francs for each party engaging in the prohibited practice.

Damages awarded by the civil and commercial courts   Persons believing themselves victim of an anti-competitive practice referred to in Articles 7 or 8 of the Ordinance and suing in a civil or commercial court may claim damages from the party engaging in the practice on the basis of Article 1382 of the Civil Code.

2.4.2 Criminal sanctions for anti-competitive practices

Under Article 17 of the Ordinance of 1 December 1986 natural persons fraudulently participating in anti-competitive practices may be subject to criminal sanction. This article subjects individuals committing violations to:

> 'imprisonment of six months to four years and a fine of 5,000 to 500,000 francs, or one of these two penalties only, any natural person who fraudulently plays a personal and decisive role in the design, organisation or implementation of practices referred to in Articles 7 and 8'.

Furthermore, under Article 17-1 legal entities may be subject to criminal sanctions beginning 1 March 1994, including in particular a fine of no more than 2,500,000 francs.

2.4.3 Concentrations

The fines are the same as those under Article 13 of the Ordinance (see section 2.4.1).

2.5 Exemptions

See section 1.4.

2.6 Third party rights

2.6.1 Private parties

The victim of an unlawful agreement or abuse of a dominant position may bring the matter before the Competition Council or the civil or commercial courts. The case must be brought by an undertaking or organisation representing collective interests. The complainant must have capacity and standing.

2.6.2   *Public persons*

Applicability of competition law to public persons   Article 53 of the 1986 Ordinance provides that public persons shall be subject to the rules set forth therein whenever engaged in manufacturing, distribution or service activities.

Role of public persons in applying competition law   The prosecutor, Minister of the Economy and chairman of the Competition Council are empowered to pursue parties engaging in anti-competitive practices referred to in Article 36 in the civil or commercial courts. Pursuant to Article 56 of the Ordinance, the Ministry of the Economy may also file pleadings in the civil or commercial courts.

3   CHECKLIST OF POTENTIAL INFRINGEMENTS

A   Vertical Agreements

3.1   Exclusive distribution agreements

3.1.1   *Pre-contract disclosure*

Apart from competition law, it is important to note that a statute enacted on 31 December 1989 requires pre-contract disclosure for certain types of contract. Article 1 of the 1989 Act provides that:

> 'Any person who authorises another person to use a trade name, trade mark or trade sign and requires from such other person a commitment of exclusivity or quasi-exclusivity in the conduct of his business must provide such other person with a document containing truthful disclosure before any contact in the joint interest of the parties is signed, thereby enabling such other person to contract with full knowledge.'

This definition may cover certain exclusive distribution agreements.[2]
The disclosure document must contain information[3] on the supplier, the general and local markets, the general and local markets for the products or services covered by the agreement and growth prospects for this market, the distribution network and the planned transaction (term of the contract in particular).

3.1.2   *Validity under competition law*

The validity of an exclusive distribution agreement must be determined under Community Regulation 1983/83, which is directly applicable in France, and French case law. French law authorises the imposition of a certain number of obligations on the parties:

On the supplier to refrain from appointing other distributors and selling to customers located in the territory.

On the distributor:

2   Act of 31 December 1989, no 89-1008.
3   Decree no 91-337 of 4 April 1991; OJ of 6 April p 4644.

(a) to refrain from distributing competing products;
(b) an exclusive requirements clause provided that the agreement has a limited duration (see section 3.3);
(c) a clause imposing quotas and objectives;
(d) maintenance of a minimum stock;
(e) obligation to comply with the supplier's standards; after-sales service;
(f) distributor's obligation to provide information to the supplier;
(g) non-competition obligation;
(h) to refrain from active competition outside its territory;
(i) the awarding of an exclusive territory is permitted under certain conditions. By forbidding the supplier to contract with any other distributor and prohibiting the distributor from supplying products to customers outside the awarded territory, territorial exclusivity leads to refusals to supply (Article 36).

3.1.3 Justification for exclusive distribution contracts

Exclusivity agreements are valid if they meet the conditions of Article 10 §2 (see section 1.4.3). The Court of Cassation in 1962 laid down the requirements for an exclusive distribution network to be lawful. In order to render the products subject to exclusive distribution agreements legally unavailable to third parties, the exclusive distribution agreement must:

(a) limit the commercial freedom of the parties by imposing reciprocal obligations;
(b) not result directly or indirectly in imposed prices;
(c) provide better service to the consumer;
(d) cover highly technical products or high-quality goods.

The Competition Council bases its determination on an analysis of the exclusivity clause's effect on the free play of competition and on its benefits to customers. If the product does not present any distribution problem (this is the case for example of refillable products),[4] it is difficult to justify exclusivity.

On the other hand, if special expertise or facilities, as well as after-sales service, are required to sell the products, which is the case for the distribution of complicated machinery, the clause is more frequently upheld.[5]

3.2 Selective distribution

3.2.1 Lawfulness of the network

Under the case law, a supplier's qualitative selection of its resellers is lawful if it is made on the basis of objective qualitative criteria which relate to the nature of the products and are consistently applied. The Court of Appeal of Paris explained the conditions on lawfulness of a network in the following terms:[6]

---

4 Competition Commission, opinion of 8 February 1979.
5 Decision of the Competition Council, 14 May 1991, '*Materials for physical therapists*'. Rec Lamy no 477. Similarly, Cass Crim 11 July 1962, Soc Brandt, D 1962 p 497.
6 CA Paris, 28 January 1988. BOCCRF 4 February 1988.

'Although the systems lead by themselves to a certain restriction on competition, they are nevertheless acceptable provided that the choice of resellers is made on the basis of objective qualitative criteria relating to the professional credentials of the reseller and its personnel and the quality of its facilities, *that these criteria must be justified by requirements for the adequate distribution of the products* and must not have the purpose or effect of excluding per se one or more specific forms of commerce which would be appropriate for this distribution and that they are applied in a non-discriminatory manner.'

Criteria related to requirements for the adequate distribution of the product   Selective distribution of a product must be justified by 'the requirements for the adequate distribution' of such a product.[7]

Criteria for selecting distributors   There are both qualitative and quantitative criteria for selecting distributors:

(i)   qualitative criteria: the selection must be made under objective criteria relating to the professional qualifications of the reseller and its personnel, as well as to the quality of its facilities, which are determined in a consistent manner and applied in a non-discriminatory fashion.

The qualitative criteria may relate to the following in particular:

(a)   the point of sale: location, standard and environment of the shop, furnishings and condition of the points of sale;
(b)   the quality of the distributor and its services: the expertise and professional quality of the distributor and its personnel, services and facilities, of repairs and after-sales service.

If a reseller satisfies the criteria, it must not be refused admission to the network. If it is, a supplier who refuses to sell to the distributor could be liable for refusal to supply under Article 36:

(ii)   quantitative criteria: until a few years ago, French case law allowed quantitative selection under certain conditions, on the basis of Article 10 §2.[8] French law has now adopted the Community position, which prohibits quantitative selection criteria.

3.2.2   Anti-competitive nature of the network

If the selection criteria do not satisfy the conditions referred to in section 3.2.1 or if the agreement contains provisions restricting competition, the network falls under Article 7. The courts may however uphold a distribution system on the ground that it contributes to economic progress (Article 10 §2).

3.2.3   Refusal to supply a reseller who is not a member of the network

A refusal to sell products to a reseller who is not a member of the network constitutes a refusal to supply (Article 36). The refusing supplier may, however, avoid the prohibition contained in Article 36 if the selective distribution network is justified under Article 10 §2.

7 Competition Commission, 1 December 1983, ' *Selective distribution of perfumery products*'.
8 Court of Appeal of Paris, 8 July 1983, Gaz Pal 1983, 2 p 566.

3.3   Exclusive requirements contracts

3.3.1   This type of agreement may also fall under the Act of 31 December 1989 (see section 3.1). In addition, the Act of 14 October 1943 limits to a maximum of ten years the term of any exclusivity clause under which a buyer, assignee or lessee of personal property agrees with the seller, assignor or lessor not to use similar or complementary products furnished by another supplier. The Act does not specify the sanctions which apply to violations of its provisions. Under the case law an exclusivity commitment entered into for more than ten years must be reduced to the legal limit but does not result in voiding the clause *ab initio*.[9]

3.3.2   The contract must also comply with the rules established by Community Regulation 1984/83, which is directly applicable in France.

3.3.3   An exclusive requirements contract does not raise any difficulty with respect to the prohibition on refusals to supply because the supplier remains free to sell to other distributors. The exclusive requirements obligation on the reseller may, however, be subject to the prohibition on anti-competitive agreements. The Competition Commission, like the Council, has taken into account the supplier's economic power and the market share held by the reseller in their opinions and decisions.[10]

3.3.4   Thus, consignment contracts imposing an exclusive requirements obligation on distributors of zinc plate were held unlawful because they imposed excessive limitations on the distributor's commercial freedom in light of the predominant position held by the suppliers.[11]

3.4   Franchising

3.4.1   Preliminary disclosure to potential franchisees

Franchise agreements meeting the requirements of the Act of 31 December 1989 must be preceded by the pre-contract disclosure required by this statute (see section 3.1).

3.4.2   Validity of the contract under competition law

In general, franchise agreements must comply with the rules of Community law.[12] This is true of the clauses protecting the identity and reputation of the network, protecting know-how and granting an exclusive territory. Similarly, the characteristic elements of the franchise (assistance furnished to the franchisee, the franchisor's furnishing of distinctive signs and the communication of franchise know-how) looked to under French case law[13] are the same as those taken into account under Community law.

---

9 Cass Crim, 1 December 1981 Bull IV 377.
10 1978 Report of the Commission, p 8.
11 Opinion of the Competition Commission of 8 February 1979 *'Zinc plate market'*. The decision of 29 September 1987 of the Competition Council and the Court of Appeal of Paris, 5 May 1988, *Cuves* case, and BOCCRF 11 May 1988 may also be cited.
12 Exempting Regulation 4087/88 of 30 November 1988. OJ EC no 2359 of 28 December 1988.
13 Court of Appeal of Paris, 28 April 1978, BT 1978, p 277.

It should be noted, however, that under French law the exclusive requirements obligation is limited to ten years (Act of 14 October 1943) (see section 3.3).

3.5   Intellectual property licensing

3.5.1   The effect of competition law on patent licences

Patent licence agreements do not per se escape the application of competition law, ie Article 7 of the Ordinance of 1 December 1986. This principle was established very early on by the Technical Commission for Anti-competitive Agreements (*Commission technique des ententes*), the predecessor to the Competition Commission, which was itself replaced by the Competition Council.[14] This view has never been repudiated.

Patent licence agreement provisions which may constitute restrictions on competition are primarily those related to exclusivity of use and the limitation on the licensee's rights of exploitation.

In addition to French case law, reference should also be made to the Community Regulation of 23 July 1984,[15] which establishes the conditions for exemption of patent licence agreements. Under this Regulation, which is directly applicable in France, clauses which may be incorporated in a patent licence agreement relate, for the most part, to the granting of territorial exclusivity, an obligation on the licensee to purchase from the licensor and the limitation on the exploitation to certain technical applications.

This Regulation excludes clauses extending the term of the agreement beyond the validity of the patent, production limitations and, generally, limitations on the licensee's marketing actions from coverage under the exemption.

3.5.2   Effect of competition law on know-how licensing agreements

Like patent licences, know-how licences do not per se escape the reach of the competition rules. Here again, reference should be made to the Community exemption Regulation adopted on 30 November 1988[16] regarding know-how licences. This Regulation establishes the extent to which the agreement may infringe competition law.

Clauses which may be included without restriction in a know-how licensing agreement relate for the most part to the granting of territorial exclusivity, with the particularity that they may lead to an absolute partitioning of the market for a certain limited period of time.

Certain clauses are authorised under certain conditions. These are in particular those concerning the conditions under which improvements are to be communicated and exploited, compliance with the technical specifications, raw material supplies to the licensee and the terms governing the protection of rights against infringement by third parties.

14 Opinion of 8 October 1955. REC Lamy no 3; concerning an anti-competitive agreement in the magnesium industry.
    Opinion of 22 June 1962. REC Lamy no 35; concerning an anti-competitive agreement in the nylon thread industry.
15 Regulation 2349/84 of 23 July 1984, OJ EC 16 August 1984, no L219 p 15.
16 Regulation 5566/89, 30 November 1988. OJ EC, 4 March 1989 no L61. Amended by Regulation 151/93, 23 December 1992, OJ EC 29 January 1993 no L21 p 8.

Finally, certain clauses amounting to needless and excessive restrictions on competition and whose prohibition does not prevent entry into know-how licensing agreements are prohibited.

3.5.3 Effect of competition law on trade mark licence agreements

An analysis of the decisions of the Competition Commission, and subsequently the Competition Council, show that the French authorities are also careful to prevent trade mark licence agreements from containing restrictions on competition. For example, the Competition Commission held that the authorisation to use a label or certification mark for products may not be made conditional on compliance with very strict requirements relating to internal operation of the undertaking when these requirements are not designed to guarantee the quality of the product.[17]

3.6 Commercial agency

The position of commercial agent is defined by the Act of 25 June 1991,[18] which incorporated the Community Directive of 18 December 1986[19] on independent commercial agents, into French law. Article 1 states that 'the commercial agent is an agent (*mandataire*)'. As such, he acts 'in the name and on behalf of his principal'. He may not therefore be deemed an independent undertaking (see section 1.2.2). Therefore, the relations between the principal and the agent are not, a priori, subject to the regulation of anti-competitive agreements.

3.7 Restrictive trade practices

3.7.1 Practices which restrict competition may occur in connection with the anti-competitive agreements and abuses of dominant position referred to in Articles 7 and 8 of the Ordinance (see section 1.2). Restrictive practices are, however, also subject to their own set of regulations and may be punished even in the absence of an anti-competitive agreement or abuse of dominant position. This is the case for refusals to supply, discriminatory practices, imposed prices, sales at loss and tie-in sales.

3.7.2 Refusal to supply

A supplier must honour all product orders sent to it without discrimination; otherwise, it engages in a refusal to supply.[20] Refusal to supply is prohibited by Article 36 of the Ordinance of 1 December 1986, which provides that:

'any producer, merchant, manufacturer or craftsman who refuses to satisfy orders by buyers of products or services when the orders are not unusual and are made in good faith

---

17 Opinion of 15 April 1980: 'Practices observed on the market for products intended for wood preservation', REC Lamy no 161.
18 Act no 91-593 of 25 June 1991 relating to relations between commercial agents and their principals.
19 Directive no 86/653 of the Council dated 18 December relating to the co-ordination of the laws of the Member States concerning independent commercial agents (OJ EC no L382, 31 December 1986).
20 *Deutsche Grammophon GmbH v Metro-ZB-Großmärkte GmbH & Co KG*: 78/70 [1971] ECR 487, [1971] CMLR 631, ECJ.

and the refusal is not justified under Article 10 shall be liable therefor and shall repair the prejudice caused by him'.

Under Article 36, a refusal to supply may be justified in three cases:

When the order is unusual   The unusual nature of an order was explained in the 'Fontanet' administrative circular dated 31 March 1990, which specifies that the unusual nature may result either from the quantity of goods ordered (a quantity which is too high or too low), the delivery terms (customary terms, refusal by the buyer to perform various services which the supplier demands from all its distributors, etc), the quality of the person placing the order (absence of professional qualification) or the conditions of the facilities maintained by the person placing the order.

In the event of bad faith on the part of the person placing the order   Bad faith presupposes that the person placing the order intended to damage the supplier or that he would use sales methods which are unlawful or contrary to proper commercial practices (such as bait-and-switch prices, loss leaders, etc).

When the supplier invokes the provisions of Article 10 of the Ordinance (see section 1.4):

(a)   application of a statute or regulation;
(b)   justification by economic progress.

Sanctions may be imposed on a refusal to supply on the basis of Article 36 of the Ordinance or, if the refusal results from an anti-competitive agreement, on the basis of Article 7.

Sanctions under Article 36   A refusal to supply is not subject to criminal sanction unless the refusal is made to a consumer. It nevertheless gives rise to civil liability; the supplier may be ordered to repair the prejudice suffered by the person placing the order (this prejudice may be represented in particular by the profit margin which the distributor would have realised on the products which the supplier refused to sell).

Sanctions on prohibited agreements (see section 2.4)   The distributor may bring an action before the court or refer the matter to the Competition Council if he can cite an anti-competitive agreement.

3.7.3   Discriminatory practices

Under Article 36.1 of the Ordinance of 1 December 1986:

'any producer, merchant, manufacturer or craftsman who, with respect to an economic partner, charges or obtains discriminatory prices, payment terms, or purchase or sale conditions not justified by real consideration, and thereby creates a disadvantage for such partner or a competitive advantage shall be liable therefor and shall repair the prejudice caused'.

There must be *discrimination*. Discrimination consists of affording different treatment to two buyers 'who are similarly situated and conduct a transaction at a comparable time for identical products or services'.[1] Discrimination is determined by analysis of terms offered in comparable circumstances. It cannot be justified by taking an economic overview and balancing sales across a group of customers.

Since 1 December 1986, discriminatory practices have not been subject to criminal sanctions. The sanction for these practices is the civil liability of the party engaging in them on the basis of Article 1382 of the French Civil Code.

3.7.4   Resale price maintenance

In 1986 the legislature wished to maintain in force criminal sanctions for the practice of imposing minimum prices. Article 34 of the Ordinance of 1 December 1986 makes it a criminal offence for 'any person to impose, directly or indirectly, a minimum resale price for a product or goods, or a minimum price for a service or a minimum profit margin'. As there is no exception to the prohibition on this practice, the prohibition has now become absolute.

The criminal sanction for imposing minimum prices is a fine of between 5,000 and 100,000 francs. As to civil liability, it is clear that a contractual clause setting a minimum price is deemed null and void.[2]

3.7.5   Sales at a loss

Under Article 32 of the 1 December 1986 Ordinance, sales at loss are defined as resales of a product 'as is at a price less than its actual purchase price'. The Ordinance specifies that 'the actual purchase price is presumed to be the price indicated on the purchase invoice', including all taxes. This provision then lists six cases in which 'these provisions do not apply':

(a)   the sale of perishable products 'beginning at the time they become subject to rapid deterioration';
(b)   liquidating sales;
(c)   the sale of seasonal products at the end of the season;
(d)   the sale of outmoded or obsolete products;
(e)   the sale of products 'the replacement of which was or may be accomplished at a lower price';
(f)   the sale of 'products whose resale price is set to match the price legally charged for the same products by another merchant in the same business area'; this exception is justified by the need to match the competition.

The prohibition does not apply to the rendering of services. As the legislature referred only to the resale of a 'product', the prohibition covers only products resold 'as is', which therefore eliminates any product which has undergone processing. This offence therefore applies essentially to undertakings in the distribution business which resell at a loss, whether to consumers or merchants.[3]

The Court of Cassation has ruled that Article 32 of the Ordinance of 1 December 1986 is compatible with Articles 85 and 86 of the Treaty of Rome,[4] as 'resales at a loss' are an unfair practice 'because they generate inequality between merchants

---

1 Selinzky and Mousseron: the new French law of competition, Litec, 1987, no 147.
2 Court of Appeal of Paris, 28 April 1966, D67, p 373.
3 Court of Appeal of Paris, 9th Ch A, 12 November 1991, Gaz Pal, 23 April 1992, Jur, p 35, Marché note.
4 Cass Crim 28 September 1992, BID 1993, no 2 p 30.

and enable a party to eliminate a competitor'. Thus, reselling at a loss is in itself illegal and need not occur as part of an anti-competitive agreement or abuse of dominant position.

Sanctions for resale at a loss   The fine for 'resales at a loss' is 100,000 francs, whether the sale is to the end customer or a merchant. From a civil law perspective, since resales at a loss are acts of unfair competition, the merchant who is the victim thereof may sue for reparation and be awarded damages.

3.7.6   Tie in sales

Article 36 paragraph 3 of the Ordinance of 1 December 1986 and Article L 122-1 of the Consumer Protection Code forbid tie in sales of products or services. They distinguish tie in sales from a professional to a consumer, which are subject to criminal sanction (fifth-class minor offences), from those between professionals, which give rise only to civil sanctions. Several kinds of violations of Article 30 are possible:

(a)   an obligation imposed on the purchaser to buy a minimum quantity (required quantity sale);
(b)   the sale of different products in a single lot, without enabling the buyer to divide up the lot and buy only certain articles (sale by lot);
(c)   the refusal to fill the order of a buyer or service user unless he purchases another product or service at the same time (conditional product or service sale).

There are, however, exceptions to the prohibition on tie in sales of products and services:

(a)   if each of the products in the lot may be purchased separately;
(b)   if trade practices have established the sale in groups of certain identical products (eggs for example) or different products (a stereo system for example);[5]
(c)   if the required quantity is sold in a single package prepared by the manufacturer and the quantity in the package does not exceed the needs of an individual consumer;[6]
(d)   in the hotel industry.

B   Horizontal Restrictions

3.8   Information exchange

3.8.1   Agreements providing for the exchange of information between competitors regarding their current or future prices may constitute anti-competitive practices. Thus, information exchanges regarding price increases before they take effect or just after they have taken effect 'constitute a substitute for and sometimes an addition to a price-fixing agreement'[7] and fall under the prohibition of Article 7 of the Ordinance. Information exchange agreements are improper when two conditions are met:

5 Cass Crim 30 November 1981, D 1982, IR p 151.
6 Cass Crim 29 October 1984, Bull Crim p 859, JCP ed G 1985, II, no 20489, G Heidsieck note.
7 1985 Report of the Competition Commission, p 20.

'the information exchanged is sufficiently individualised and precise to enable the undertakings receiving it to identify the parties to the transactions, the products in question are sufficiently homogenous and substitutable for there to be price competition'.[8]

3.8.2 Conversely, dissemination of price information in the form of market reports, or *a fortiori* an information system used occasionally and on request from a centralised point, regarding prices charged or discounts granted are not incompatible with the legal provisions if the data are recorded after the fact and represent market results and if these results are not individualised and do not enable each participant to adjust its price policy on the basis of the price policy followed by its competitors.[9]

3.9 Joint buying and selling

3.9.1 Joint buying by distributors, wholesalers or retailers may be unlawful under Articles 7 and 8 of the Ordinance. The Competition Commission[10] and the *Conseil d'Etat* have held that the process of removing buyers or sellers from the approved list may be restrictive of competition when it results in eliminating new suppliers from the market or preventing the supply of competing distributors.

3.9.2 However, the mere fact that a group of merchants recommends certain suppliers or certain products to its members does not result in impeding, restricting or distorting competition.[11]

3.9.3 The Council condemns the practice of improper withdrawal of approval when it constitutes the reply to a supplier's refusal to extend unjustified terms. When distributors acting together in a joint buying unit take advantage of the reinforcement of their position on a market to demand that suppliers grant them such terms, this behaviour may constitute an abuse of economic dependency as referred to in Articles 8, 2 and 43 of the Ordinance.

3.9.4 Nevertheless, joint buying may contribute to economic progress as a result of real services offered to the industry (assurance of sources, consolidation of delivery or billing) or when it enables distributors to improve their operating conditions by offering them technical services.[12] Furthermore, joint selling by competing undertakings may lead to creation of a prohibited anti-competitive agreement.

3.10 Fixing prices and conditions of sale

In order to preclude a fall in prices, undertakings sometimes agree to fix them at a certain level. For this purpose they may act at the price level itself, in particular by setting a minimum price or a floor price which they agree not to go below,[13] or by

8 Competition Commission, 15 April 1980, '*Wood preservation products*'. Lamy no 161.
9 Competition Council, 25 March 1988 '*Processed aluminium sheets*'.
10 Competition Commission, opinions of 22 October 1980 and 11 December 1980, Receuil Lamy no 170 and 173.
11 Cass Crim 16 January 1990.
12 Opinion of the Competition Commission of 30 October 1986, case: '*ARCI Association*'.
13 Opinion of 29 March 1984, '*Mineral fibre ceilings*'.

setting a price without consideration of productivity gains resulting from progress in manufacturing methods.[14] These price-fixing practices are prohibited under Article 7. The anti-competitive agreement may also be one for the setting of profit margins.[15] Thus the Competition Commission frequently criticised concerted practices between suppliers and distributors for the purpose of braking a fall in prices and margins.[16]

3.11   Market sharing

Article 7 of the 1986 Ordinance prohibits anti-competitive agreements for the purpose of 'allocating markets or supply sources' (see section 1.2). Markets may be allocated among parties to the agreement:

(a)   by geographical area;
(b)   by customers;
(c)   or may set up a quota system for production or sale by each party to the agreement.

In all these cases, it constitutes a serious restriction on competition.

3.12   Joint ventures

3.12.1   The creation of joint subsidiaries is not in and of itself an unlawful anti-competitive agreement.[17] It is important though to determine whether the groups which set up such a structure do so with the essential purpose of avoiding competition, even partially, between themselves and precluding other companies from competing. In this case, the creation of the joint subsidiary would be prohibited under Article 7 of the Ordinance if the subsidiary becomes a vehicle to restrict competition.[18]

3.12.2   The formation of joint subsidiaries may also be subject to the provisions on review of concentrations (Article 39 of the Ordinance of 1 December 1986). On this point, see section 4.

3.13   Crisis cartels

Cartels formed to confront crises are not permitted as such.

3.14   Other forms of co-operation

3.14.1   Concerted practices the object or effect of which is to limit market access by economic players are impediments to the free play of competition.

---

14 Opinion of 9 March 1978, '*Trading in flat glass*'.
15 Opinion of 17 June 1977, '*Automobile spare parts and equipment*'.
16 Opinion of the Competition Commission of 27 September 1979, '*Household appliances and electroacoustics*', opinon of 26 May 1983 '*Plant health products market*'.
17 Paris, 17 June 1992: BOCC, 4 July 1992 p 217.
18 For example: Opinion of 28 October 1980, '*Concerted practices in water distribution*'; Opinion of May 17, 1977 '*Manufacturing and distribution of phonograph records*' and Decision of the Competition Council of 13 June 1989.

3.14.2 Boycott

A boycott consists of 'agreeing to refuse either to supply a particular customer or to purchase from a particular supplier without legitimate reason'.[19] In the face of these concerted exclusion strategies, the Competition Commission adopted a strict view, in particular with regard to trade unions which encouraged their members to boycott certain manufacturers.[20] They may bear substantial liability. The case law established by the Competition Council is based on the same principles.[1]

3.14.3 Regulation of entry into a business or entitlement to a quality mark

Restrictions on the conduct of a business Regulations governing business activities often conceal an intent to limit the number of competitors behind conditions which appear to be justified by the public interest. This may be the case when an 'accreditation card',[2] registration on a list,[3] or trade union approval[4] is necessary, or when the purchaser of an undertaking is required to join a professional group and a right of pre-emption is given to the group, admission to an association which may be refused in a discriminatory manner[5] is required or an exclusive requirements contract is imposed.

The Competition Council has vigorously condemned these collective practices which have the purpose or effect of limiting market access by economic players.[6]

Restrictions on the granting of a quality mark or label The Technical Commission on Anti-competitive Agreements[7] decided very clearly that an approval or label may be subject to the prohibition on anti-competitive agreements unless the approval procedure does not impose technical requirements other than those which are indispensable for the protection of consumers and the public. The validity of an approval procedure is also conditional on its being open to all undertakings in the market for the product in question.

3.14.4 Impediments to technical progress and innovation

These practices, which are very difficult to prove, consist in impeding the development of certain products. They were found in the electrical appliance market where the concerted actions to impede growth of competing undertakings were all the

---

19 1980 Report, p 31.
20 Opinion of 19 May 1985, '*Practices observed in the wind instrument and upright piano market*'.
 1 For example:
   – Decision of 15 March 1988: BOCC, 16 April 1988, p 96.
   – Decision of 21 June 1988: BOCC, 30 June 1988, p 172.
   – Decision of 7 November 1989: BOCC, 1 December 1989, p 25.
 2 Technical Commission on Anti-competitive Agreements, 4 January 1978, '*Professional anti-competitive agreements in the advertising field*'.
 3 Technical Commission on Anti-competitive Agreements, 17 June 1977, '*Spare parts for automobiles*'.
 4 Technical Commission on Anti-competitive Agreements, 18 May 1973, '*Petroleum vats and cisterns*'.
 5 Competition Commission, 18 November 1986, '*Trade shows in the Paris region*'.
 6 1988 Report, p 26 and 1990 Report p 32.
 7 Opinion of 18 May 1973, '*Petroleum vats and cisterns industry*'.

greater as the undertakings in question were upsetting the established order by offering innovative products.[8]

Similarly, concerted actions to impede technical progress with the goal of limiting the growth of cheaper products have been found on numerous occasions.[9]

3.14.5   Covenant not to compete

Restrictions on market access may also result from agreements or covenants not to compete when their geographical extent, scope with respect to the activities covered and duration exceed the intended objective. This objective may be either to guard against problems of competition which may arise between them, in particular when they jointly pursue projects which may well lead to economic progress,[10] or to guarantee the efficacy of the transfer of a customer base.

C   Abusive Behaviour

3.15   Unfair pricing

On this point see sections 3.7, 3.8 and 3.12.

3.16   Predatory pricing

3.16.1   The Act of 16 December 1992[11] introduced new Articles 52.1 and 52.2 into the Ordinance of 1 December 1986. The first Article defines the violation and the second imposes the sanctions. The offence of unlawful pricing is:

> 'the causing of or attempting to cause an artificial increase or decrease in the price of goods or services or public or private property by disseminating deceptive or defamatory information by any means whatsoever, issuing offers on the market which are intended to disrupt the market or by making offers higher than the prices sought by sellers or by using any other fraudulent means'.

Thus, the goal is to cause an artificial increase or decrease in the price and an attempt to do so is punishable. This practice may also constitute an anti-competitive agreement or abuse of dominant position. The existence of the offence also presupposes that the guilty party made an offer or higher offer and accompanied it with deceptive or defamatory information.

3.16.2   Sanctions

If the violator is an individual, the penalties are imprisonment of two years and/or a fine of 200,000 francs.

Legal entities may be held liable when their controlling bodies or representatives have committed the offence of unlawful pricing on their behalf.

---

8 Competition Commission, 27 September 1979, '*Electrical appliances and electroacoustics*'.
9 For example: Competition Commission, January 11, 1979, '*Industrial explosives and firing accessories*'.
10 1978 Report, JO Doc adm 6 January 1979; on excessive nature.
11 Act no 92-1336 of 16 December 1992.

The fines may be as high as 1.5 million francs when the price increase or decrease is for food products.

3.17 Refusals to supply

On this point see section 3.7.2.

3.18 Tie in sales

On this point see section 3.7.6.

4 CONCENTRATIONS, MERGERS AND ACQUISITIONS

4.1 Thresholds

4.1.1 Definition of a concentration

Under Article 39 of the Ordinance of 1 December 1986:

> 'a concentration results from any act, notwithstanding its form, which entails the transfer of title to or enjoyment of all or any part of the property, rights and obligations of an undertaking or which has the purpose or effect of enabling an undertaking or a group of undertakings to exert decisive influence, either directly or indirectly, over one or more other undertakings'.

Two elements are therefore necessary:

A transfer of title or rights This definition applies to 'all techniques for forming corporate groups in which a company becomes dependent on or dominated by another' (ie to mergers, merger-splits, partial business asset transfers, shareholding acquisitions and the creation of joint subsidiaries).

Conferring decisive influence The influence of an undertaking on another is decisive when it relates to the composition, meetings or decisions of the governing bodies of an undertaking (criterion taken from the Community regulation).[12]

4.1.2 The conditions governing review of concentrations

Under Article 38, paragraphs 1 and 2, of the Ordinance of 1 December 1986, the conditions on the exercise of review are twofold:

Conditions relating to the effects of the concentration 'Any concentration which is liable to restrict competition, in particular by the creation or strengthening of a dominant position', may be subject to review. If the transaction results in the creation or strengthening of a dominant position, there is a restriction on competition. In contrast to review of abuses of dominant position, review of concentrations focuses on the *structures*, without regard to any abuse by the undertakings in question.

12 Regulation no 4064/89/EEC: OJEC no L395, 30 December 1989 p 1.

Conditions relating to the size of the concentration: quantitative thresholds

(a)   the market share threshold: the authorities may review concentrations in which the undertakings in question have 'collectively made more than 25% of the sales, purchases or other transactions on a national market for substitutable property, products or services or on a substantial part of such market' (Article 38, paragraph 2, of the Ordinance of 1 December 1986);

(b)   the turnover threshold: the authorities may also review concentrations in which the undertakings in question have 'a total turnover, net of taxes, of more than 7 billion francs, provided that at least two of the undertakings party to the concentration have a turnover of at least 2 billion francs' (Article 38, paragraph 2, of the Ordinance of 1 December 1986).

The relevant market for the calculation of the turnover is the *national* market. Foreign activities by the undertakings party to the concentration must therefore be ignored in calculating the turnover.

4.2   Notification – procedure

4.2.1   In contrast to the provisions of Community law, notification of a concentration is optional under French law (Article 40 of the Ordinance of 1 December 1986).

Review will therefore be made either pursuant to a notification, if one is given, or through intervention by the Minister of the Economy and Finance.

4.2.2   Notification procedure

Deadlines   The notification is given to the Ministry of the Economy. Although it is optional, the notification, if made, must be given within three months from the date on which the transaction becomes final (Article 40). The notification must be made by an undertaking in question, ie by one of the undertakings party to the concentration.

Contents and requirements   Article 28 of the Decree of 29 December 1986[13] provides that the notification must include:

(a)   a copy of the instrument or draft instrument submitted in the notification and a description of the anticipated consequences of the transaction;

(b)   a list of the executive officers, directors and principal shareholders in the undertakings which are the parties to or object of the transaction;

(c)   the annual accounts for the last three financial years of the undertakings in question and the market shares held by each company;

(d)   a description of the principal concentration transactions, if any, carried out during the last three years by these undertakings;

(e)   a list of the subsidiaries, including, if applicable, for each one the percentage shareholding and a list of the undertakings which are economically related to them with respect to the transaction.

A two-month period begins to run (Article 40) from the day on which the acknowledgement of receipt is delivered (end of Article 28 of the Decree).

13 Decree no 86-1309 of 29 December 1986.

Upon expiration of this period, the planned transaction is deemed approved if the authorities have failed to respond.

This time period is increased to six months if the Minister refers the matter to the Competition Council.

Effects of the notification   When the Minister receives notification of a concentration, he may:

(a)   explicitly state that he does not object thereto;
(b)   fail to respond; in this case, the Minister's silence for a period in excess of three months following the date on which notification was given is deemed tacit approval and the Minister may no longer refer the matter to the Competition Council, unless any undertakings given in connection with the notification are not respected;
(c)   or refer the matter to the Competition Council for its opinion. In this case, the Minister of the Economy and Finance notifies the parties to the transaction (Article 29 of the Decree of 29 December 1986) of the referral.

4.2.3   Review initiated by the authorities

The Minister of the Economy and Finance alone has the power to initiate an investigation in concentration matters (on this point see section 4.4.).

4.3   Appraisal criteria

4.3.1   Restriction on competition

The following factors must be taken into account:

(a)   the national and international context of a market;
(b)   the competitiveness of the undertakings in question with respect to international competition;
(c)   the possibility that imports may affect the competitive situation on the internal market.

4.3.2   Contribution to economic progress

Article 4 of the Ordinance of 1 December 1986 provides:

'The Competition Council shall determine whether the proposed or completed concentration makes a sufficient contribution to economic progress to compensate for restrictions on competition.'

The extent of the contribution to economic progress is determined on the basis of various factors such as:

(a)   decreased costs;
(b)   increased productivity;
(c)   the innovative capabilities of the undertakings in question.

The greater the potential restriction on competition, the greater is the contribution to economic progress required by the Competition Council.

This analysis is not limited to the domestic scene if the benefits of the transaction for economic progress occur on the world market.

4.4   Powers of enforcement

4.4.1   *The Competition Council*

Referral to the Council   The Minister of the Economy and Finance alone has the power to refer matters to the Council and request its opinion. The Council may not take the initiative to review a concentration. It should also be noted that the Minister is not required to wait for the expiration of the three-month period during which the undertakings may notify the concentration in order to refer it to the Council.

Procedure before the Council   This procedure is set forth in Article 44 of the Ordinance. It is not adversarial and does not include notification of the alleged infringements. The reports on which the Council bases its decisions, as well as the documents relied on by the rapporteur, are sent to the parties. The parties then have one month to make their comments in reply. The parties may attend the Council meeting or be represented at it (Article 25) and present their comments.

Opinion of the Competition Council   The Competition Council issues[14] a reasoned opinion, which is subsequently published together with the ministerial decision. In this opinion the Council specifies whether the transaction in question may or may not be approved and indicates any measures which should be taken.[15] In cases of unlawful exploitation of a dominant position or state of economic dependency the Council may ask the Minister to enjoin the undertakings in question to cease and desist (see Ordinance, Article 43).

4.4.2   *The Minister of the Economy and Finance*

The Minister of the Economy and Finance has sole decision-making power after receiving the opinion of the Competition Council. The Council's opinion is merely advisory: it does not in any way limit the discretionary power of the Minister of the Economy and Finance. In accordance with Article 42 of the Ordinance, the Minister's decision may be:

(a)   not to carry out the proposed concentration;
(b)   to re-establish the former legal situation;
(c)   to modify or supplement the transaction;
(d)   to take any appropriate measure to ensure or establish sufficient competition.[16]

14 When notification of the transaction has been given, this opinion must be rendered before the expiration of a six-month period following the acknowledgement of receipt, in order to enable the Minister to make his decision on a timely basis.
15 See, for example: Opinion 91-D-09, of 15 October 1991: BOCC, 14 March 1992, p 84.
16 See, for example, Decision of 11 March 1992 concerning a concentration in the shaving products industry: BOCC, 14 March 1992, p 84.

The Minister may also subject completion of the transaction to certain requirements designed to ensure that a sufficient contribution to economic and social progress is made to compensate for the restrictions on competition.[17]

Before making any of these decisions, the Minister of the Economy sends the draft decision, accompanied by the Competition Council's opinion, to the parties and gives them a time period in which to make their comments (Article 30 of the Decree of 29 December 1986).

4.4.3 Sanctions

Article 44, paragraph 3, of the Ordinance of 1 December 1986 established administrative sanctions on undertakings which refuse to obey the Minister's orders. If the orders are not followed, the Minister of the Economy and Finance may impose a fine. In this case the Minister must consult with the Competition Council and may impose a fine only up to the amount determined in the Council's opinion (maximum amount of the fine set at 5% of the undertaking's turnover). The Ordinance is silent as to appeals brought against the Minister's decisions. But, like any administrative act, these ministerial decisions may be appealed on the basis of abuse of power to the administrative courts.

17 Decision of 13 April 1988 concerning a concentration in the sugar industry: BOCC, 16 April 1988.

Germany*

Oppenhoff & Rädler
Hohenstaufenring 62
50674 Cologne
Germany

Tel   ++49 221 2091 0
Fax ++49 221 2091 435

* Prepared by Peter Sambuc, Michael Oppenhoff, Dr Hanno Goltz, Dr Dirk Schroeder, Dr Wolfgang Deselaers, Anne Federle and Markus Deck.

Germany

1 GERMAN COMPETITION LAW

1.1 Background

German anti-trust law is based on the Act against Restraints of Competition (Gesetz gegen Wettbewerbsbeschränkungen, hereafter 'GWB') of 1957, as amended. The GWB applies to all restraints of competition which have an effect within the territory of the Federal Republic of Germany. Its objective is to provide comprehensive protection of competition on all levels of production, distribution and commercial services in nearly all areas of the economy. The GWB is a fairly complex and detailed Act which consists of six chapters and 106 sections. The most important sections are those relating to horizontal agreements (sections 1–14), vertical agreements (sections 15–21), merger control (section 22–24a), concerted practices (section 25 (1)), discrimination (section 26 (2)) and enforcement (sections 36–97).

1.2 Anti-competitive agreements and concerted practices

1.2.1 Under section 1 GWB, horizontal agreements, ie agreements concluded between enterprises competing on the same level of production or distribution, are void to the extent that they are likely to influence, through restraint of competition, the production or market conditions for the sale of goods or commercial services. For instance, agreements which normally fall under section 1 GWB relate to the fixing of prices, the operation of joint selling or purchasing organisations and the allocation of territories, customers, or quotas. The GWB provides some exceptions to the general prohibition of cartels laid down in section 1 GWB. First, several segments of the economy, such as the banking, insurance, and transportation industries as well as public utilities, are partially or entirely exempted from the prohibition of section 1 GWB. Second, various types of cartel agreements are exempted or may be exempted by the cartel authorities. In particular, rebate cartels, crisis cartels, export cartels, standardisation cartels, rationalisation cartels, specialisation cartels as well as certain other co-operation cartels, in particular between small and medium-sized enterprises, may qualify for exemption.

1.2.2 Pursuant to section 25(1) GWB, concerted practices of enterprises which cannot be made the subject matter of a contractual obligation are prohibited. Therefore, in practice, it does not matter whether the parties enter into an agreement in the form of a contract (violation of section 1 GWB) or whether they only informally reach a mutual understanding to co-ordinate their competitive behaviour (violation of section 25 (1) GWB). However, mere parallel behaviour is not sufficient evidence of the existence of such co-ordination.

1.3   Monopoly practices (abuse of market power)

Pursuant to sections 22(4) and 26(2) GWB, the abuse of a market dominating position is illegal. Conduct is abusive if it significantly impairs competitors, customers, or suppliers in their competitive activities without objective justification. Examples of such abuse are refusals to supply, loyalty rebates, tying practices and excessive, discriminatory or predatory pricing.

2   ENFORCEMENT

2.1   Enforcement authorities

2.1.1   Anti-trust enforcement in Germany is vested primarily in the Federal Cartel Office ('FCO'). The FCO is an independent Federal High Authority established in Berlin. It is subject to the jurisdiction of the Federal Minister of the Economy, who is empowered to address general or specific directives to it. As opposed to other competition authorities, the FCO does not have a hierarchic structure. Decisions are adopted by one of at present ten divisions, each of which has jurisdiction for specific sectors of the economy or for certain types of agreements (eg chemical industry, steel industry, licence agreements). The divisions are composed of a chairman and five or six associate members. Decisions are taken by the chairman and two associate members. Every two years the FCO publishes a report on its activities and on major developments in its field of responsibility.

2.1.2   More limited responsibilities are entrusted to the Federal Minister of the Economy and the State Cartel Offices. Unlike the FCO, the State Cartel Offices are not independent authorities, but a part of the Ministry for Economic Affairs of the respective state.

2.1.3   The Monopoly Commission is an advisory body composed of five independent members, which is responsible for rendering expert opinions. Every two years it issues an opinion on the general development of market concentration. Before deciding whether to permit a merger that has been prohibited by the FCO, the Federal Minister of the Economy must request the Monopoly Commission to render an opinion on the specific case.

2.1.4   The FCO, the Minister of the Economy and the State Cartel Offices are jointly referred to as the Cartel Authorities.

2.2   Jurisdictional rules

2.2.1   The FCO is responsible for all horizontal and vertical restraints of competition extending beyond the territory of a state. It also has jurisdiction for merger control, the approval of crisis, export and import cartels and certain other types of agreement, independent of whether the territory of one or more states is concerned.

2.2.2   The jurisdiction of the Federal Minister of the Economy is essentially limited to the granting of exceptional approvals. The Federal Minister is empowered to permit cartel agreements and mergers for reasons of overriding public interests. In addition, it may prohibit export cartels if they are prejudicial to Germany's foreign trade.

2.2.3 The State Cartel Offices are responsible for all matters not falling under the exclusive jurisdiction of the FCO or the Minister of the Economy, in particular for horizontal and vertical agreements or restrictive conduct not extending beyond the territory of the respective state.

2.3 Registration/filing or notification

2.3.1 Notifications

The GWB provides for two types of notifications. First, the Cartel Authorities may be, and under certain conditions must be, notified of mergers. Second, certain types of cartel agreements and anti-competitive recommendations must be notified in order to benefit from an exemption. A notice issued by the FCO contains detailed guidelines on the information to be provided. Notifications not complying with the requirements laid down in these guidelines are nevertheless effective, provided they contain the information required by the GWB (eg, in the case of cartels the name and place of business of the participating enterprises; the legal form and address of the cartel; the name and address of the legal or appointed representative; and the comments of certain trading partners, if applicable). Apart from a few exceptions (in particular pre-merger notifications and notifications of export cartels), a summary of the notification is published in the Federal Gazette.

2.3.2 Administrative proceedings

The Cartel Authorities may initiate proceedings on their own initiative or upon application. Formal proceedings are frequently preceded or even replaced by informal contacts between the Cartel Authorities and the parties concerned. The Cartel Authorities conduct the necessary investigations on their own initiative. They may require enterprises to submit information on their economic conditions, may examine books and records on the enterprise's premises and may seize material which could serve as evidence. As required by the German Federal Constitution, searches may only be made by order of a local court. Witnesses and experts may be requested to appear and testify before the Cartel Authorities. Participants (ie applicants, enterprises concerned by the proceedings and persons invited by the Cartel Authorities) have the right to be heard. They may request an oral hearing and are entitled to inspect the files of the Cartel Authorities. However, access to the files will be denied in so far as this is necessary to safeguard business secrets.

Before taking an unfavourable decision, the Cartel Authorities state their reasoning in a letter to the participants, allowing them to submit their observations. Prior to making a final decision, the Cartel Authorities may issue preliminary orders in order to regulate a situation temporarily. Decisions and orders of the Cartel Authorities must be served upon the participants, giving full reasoning behind such decision or order. Certain types of orders (in particular unfavourable decisions) are published in the Federal Gazette. All orders of the Cartel Authorities may be appealed, both on points of fact and law, to the Courts of Appeal, which in the case of the FCO is the Kammergericht in Berlin, where a specialised chamber deals with these matters. Decisions of the Court of Appeal may be appealed on points of law to the Federal Supreme Court, where the case will equally be heard by a chamber specialised in competition law matters. In general, the appeal suspends the effect of the disputed order until a final decision has been rendered.

2.4   Fines and other sanctions

2.4.1   The sanctions available for violations of the GWB depend upon the specific type of infringement.

2.4.2   Cartel agreements (section 1 GWB), resale price maintenance agreements (section 15 GWB) and clauses in licence agreements that exceed the scope of the licensed right (sections 20 and 21 GWB) are ineffective unless they are exempted.

2.4.3   Exclusive dealing agreements (section 18 GWB) and agreements the conclusion of which constitutes abusive conduct by a market-dominating enterprise (Section 22 GWB) may be declared to be ineffective by the Cartel Authorities.

2.4.4   Most violations of the GWB constitute administrative offences that are subject to fines. Unless expressly stated (as is the case with respect to the violation of orders issued by the Cartel Authorities and the courts), only intentional conduct may be sanctioned. Offences may be punished by fines of up to DM 1 million or three times the amount of the additional revenues obtained through the infringement, whichever is higher. The fine for negligent violations may not exceed half the maximum amount for intentional violations. Fines may be imposed not only against the author of the infringement but also against his employer, if such employer failed correctly to supervise his employees.

2.4.5   If the legal representative of a legal entity commits an offence (by his/her own action or by failing to supervise employees correctly), a separate fine may be imposed against the legal entity. In principle, fines may no longer be imposed after the lapse of a period of three years after the violation.

2.4.6   Besides or instead of imposing fines, the Cartel Authorities may also issue orders prohibiting certain types of conduct, such as the implementation of illegal concerted practices or agreements that are ineffective pursuant to the GWB. The Cartel Authorities are not normally empowered to order an enterprise to take specific measures. However, there is an exception in cases where a specific measure is the only way to ensure that the party concerned abstains from prohibited conduct.

2.4.7   Due to the suspensive effect of an appeal against an order of the Cartel Authorities, a company is free to continue anti-competitive practices until the order becomes final. In order to avoid market-dominating companies reaping unjustified benefits from this situation, the Cartel Authorities may, after the order has become final, require that such company pay an amount equivalent to the additional revenues it has reaped as a result of its abusive conduct after having been served with the order. Damages paid to third parties and administrative fines paid by the company will be deducted from this sum.

2.5   Exemptions

2.5.1   Certain types of institutions and industries are entirely or partially exempted from the application of the GWB. The GWB as a whole does not apply to the German Federal Bank, the Bank for Reconstruction, the Alcohol Monopoly and fields covered by the Treaty establishing the European Coal and Steel Community. Certain agreements concluded by operators in the field of air, sea and land transport, by (associations of) agricultural producers, by credit institutions and insurance companies, by copyright associations and by public utilities are not subject to the rules on cartel agreements, resale price maintenance agreements, exclusive dealing agreements and/or recommendations that have the same effect as agreements prohibited by the GWB. In several cases the exemption is conditional upon notification of the agreement to the Cartel Authorities.

2.5.2 In addition, the GWB also provides for the exemption of certain specific types of horizontal or vertical agreements or recommendations. Under certain conditions the prohibitions of the GWB thus do not apply to conditional cartels, rebate cartels, crisis cartels, rationalisation and specialisation cartels, co-operation agreements and joint purchasing agreements between small and medium-sized enterprises, recommendations of associations of small and medium-sized enterprises, export and import cartels, as well as resale price maintenance agreements for publications. Moreover, the FCO has declared that it will in principle not intervene against co-operation agreements between a restricted number of small and medium-sized enterprises, provided that their aggregate market share does not exceed 5% (*de minimis* exception).

2.6 Third party rights

Private parties may bring an action for damages or an injunction against an enterprise that (intentionally or negligently) violates a provision of the GWB (or an order issued by the Cartel Authorities or the courts based on such a provision), provided that this provision 'has as its purpose the protection of another person' (section 35 (1) GWB). In particular, section 1 (cartel agreements), section 15 (resale price maintenance), section 25(1) (concerted practices), section 26(1) (boycotts) and section 26(2) (discrimination) are considered to be such 'protective provisions'. By contrast, the provisions on exclusive dealing arrangements (section 18 GWB) or abusive conduct of a market-dominating enterprise (section 22(4) GWB) do not provide sufficient grounds for civil proceedings. Civil lawsuits must be filed with the respective District Courts.

3 CHECKLIST OF POTENTIAL INFRINGEMENTS

A Vertical Agreements

3.1 Introduction

The GWB rules concerning vertical restraints address specific areas, such as the restriction on the freedom to determine prices and business terms (section 15 GWB), resale price maintenance for publications (section 16 GWB), non-binding price recommendations for branded goods (section 38a GWB), exclusive dealings (section 18 GWB) and licensing agreements (section 20 GWB).

3.2 Distribution (exclusive, non-exclusive and selective)

3.2.1 In Germany, a distributor might be referred to as 'Vertragshändler', 'Eigenhändler' or 'Vertriebshändler'. Frequently, the concept of 'Vertragshändler' is applied to car dealers. In practice, distributors are very often exclusive dealers. In contrast to a commercial agent, a distributor deals in his own name and for his own account. He is usually under the obligation to market the product within the marketing concept of the producer, but at his own risk. The most important rules relating to distribution agreements are contained in sections 15 and 18 GWB.

3.2.2 Pursuant to section 15 GWB, agreements between enterprises regarding goods or commercial services are null and void to the extent that such agreements restrain the freedom of a party thereto in establishing prices or business terms in contracts which it concludes with third parties. Therefore, section 15 GWB prohibits all forms of resale price maintenance and other agreements whereby one party is restricted in its freedom to determine prices or business terms in contracts with third parties. In practice, this provision is of considerable importance, given that it applies to any agreement irrespective of whether the restraints are likely to influence market conditions to an appreciable extent. Moreover, German courts have given section 15 GWB a very wide scope of application. For instance, a restraint on a supplier not to sell to other customers at more favourable prices (a most favoured buyer clause) is subject to the prohibition laid down in section 15 GWB. The same applies to any other indirect influence on a party's freedom to fix its prices, price elements or discounts.

3.2.3 There are (only) two exemptions from the prohibition laid down in section 15 GWB which relate to resale price maintenance for publications such as books, periodicals and newspapers as well as to non-binding price recommendations.

3.2.4 Clauses of a distribution agreement which contravene section 15 GWB are automatically void. This leads to the nullity of the agreement as a whole if it cannot be implied that the partners intended the remainder of the agreement to be valid despite the invalidity of the restrictions caught by section 15 GWB.

3.2.5 Contrary to section 15 GWB, which protects the freedom of the parties with respect to terms agreed with third parties, section 18 GWB addresses the freedom of the parties to conclude other contracts at all. In particular, section 18 GWB addresses restrictions on the use or resale of the products supplied, tying agreements as well as exclusivity agreements.

3.2.6 Unlike section 15 GWB, section 18 GWB does not provide for the general prohibition or nullity of such agreements. Rather, section 18 GWB only empowers the Cartel Authorities to prohibit, inter alia, exclusive distribution agreements if they have a significant impact on the market. This condition is met only in cases where either a significant number of enterprises in the relevant market are bound in the same manner (bundle effect) and unfairly restrained in their freedom to compete, or market entry is unfairly restricted for other enterprises, or the competition for the goods involved or for other goods or commercial services is substantially impaired by the scope of such restraints. The question of whether the restrictions under scrutiny are 'unfair' or 'substantial' requires the Cartel Authorities to balance the interests of the parties to the agreement against the objective of section 18 GWB to secure the freedom of competition. In particular, the duration of the exclusivity, market structure, position of the parties on the relevant market and the foreclosure effect of the agreements need to be taken into account. For instance, exclusivity agreements between brewers and inn-keepers with a duration of more than 20 years are normally considered to constitute an 'unfair' restriction of competition. Also, exclusive distribution systems established by market-dominating enterprises (see sections 3.2.7 and 3.22 below) are more likely to be considered 'unfair', unless it can be shown that the restrictions are essential in order to maintain an economically effective distribution system. In practice, there have only been a few cases in which exclusive distribution agreements have been prohibited and declared void.

3.2.7 Sections 15 and 18 GWB also apply to selective distribution systems whereby only a selected group of dealers obtain the right to distribute certain products. The application of section 15 GWB means that the resellers must remain free to fix their prices and business terms in contracts with their customers. Pursuant to section 18(1) No 3 GWB, the Cartel Authorities may prohibit agreements by which a party is restricted in its freedom to resell the products supplied to third parties. While such restriction forms an integral part of any selective distribution system (prohibition on the resale to dealers who are not admitted to the system), section 18 GWB has so far been of almost no practical relevance with regard to selective distribution systems. Therefore, in practice, such systems are challenged only under section 26(2) GWB, pursuant to which abusive behaviour by market-dominating enterprises is prohibited (see section 3.22 below). Normally, selection of the dealers according to qualitative criteria relating, for example, to staff qualifications, showroom facilities and customer service is unobjectionable, provided that the criteria are reasonable and applied without any discrimination. The requirement of non-discrimination implies that, eg, a supplier must not restrict his deliveries to specialised small retailers if an equally well-equipped specialised department store also meets the quality requirements. As a result, a selective distribution system must not exclude certain distribution channels, given that this would keep prices at an artificially high level. Selection pursuant to quantitative criteria is more likely to constitute a violation of section 26 GWB, unless it can be shown by the supplier that there is no economically viable alternative which is less restrictive of competition.

3.2.8 The principle of non-discrimination requires the supplier to enforce his system as efficiently as possible. For instance, a supplier must take legal action against dealers who breach their contractual obligation not to supply to unauthorised dealers and/or against unauthorised dealers to the extent that they cause an authorised dealer to breach its contract with the supplier.

3.3 Exclusive purchasing

Exclusive purchasing agreements also fall under section 18 GWB and may be prohibited by the Cartel Authorities if the conditions outlined above (section 3.2.6) are met. In the absence of such prohibitory decision, exclusive purchasing agreements are normally unobjectionable under German competition law. This is not, however, the case where the agreement is used as a 'hidden cartel' by competitors, in order to restrict or eliminate (actual or potential) competition between themselves. In such circumstances, the general prohibition laid down in section 1 GWB is likely to apply (see section 3.11 below on horizontal restrictions).

3.4 Franchising

In principle, the German Cartel Authorities consider franchise systems to be a positive development in the downstream marketing of goods, given that they usually promote innovation and open markets for small and medium-sized enterprises. Nevertheless, sections 15 and 18 GWB apply to franchise agreements. Therefore, in particular any restrictions on the franchisee's freedom to determine his prices are prohibited. Non-binding price recommendations, however, are permissible. Exclusivity arrangements and restrictions on use or resale are also permissible, but subject to section 18 GWB. Finally, franchise agreements entered into by actual or potential competitors are likely to be considered to be 'hidden cartels' falling under section 1 GWB.

3.5   Intellectual property licensing

3.5.1   Pursuant to sections 20 and 21 GWB, restraints imposed on the assignee or licensee of patents, registered designs and know-how are invalid only to the extent that they exceed the scope of the respective protected right. Restraints on the exercise of the protected rights relating to the manner or field of use, quantity, territory or time are expressly considered to be within the scope of the protected rights. Therefore, such restraints are permissible, unless they restrict the licensee to a larger extent than the industrial property right foresees. For instance, a patent licensing agreement must not bind the licensee for a longer time than the duration of the patent. Also, the licensee must not be restricted from competing with the licensor or other licensees in respect of the production or distribution of competing products unless such competition is not possible for the licensee without using or disclosing the licensed technology.

3.5.2   Pursuant to section 20(2) GWB, there are five categories of restraints which may be imposed on the licensee even though they exceed the scope of the protected right. In particular, the licensor may restrict the licensee's freedom to determine the prices of the licensed products. Other exemptions concern restraints on the proper use of the licensed goods, the freedom to exploit improvements of the licensed technology (grant back licence), no-challenge clauses and the regulation of foreign markets.

3.5.3   Upon application by the parties to an agreement, the Cartel Authorities may approve agreements containing restraints which are not permitted under sections 20 and 21 GWB if it can be shown that neither the assignee or licensee nor other enterprises will be unduly restrained and that the restraint will not substantially impair competition.

3.5.4   Restraints imposed on the assignor or licensor are not privileged by sections 20 and 21 GWB and fall under the general rules in sections 15 and 18 GWB (see sections 3.2.2 and 3.2.6 above) as well as section 1 GWB. The same applies to agreements relating to the acquisition or use of industrial or intellectual property rights not covered by sections 20 and 21 GWB, such as trade marks, copyrights or design patents.

3.6   Commercial agency

3.6.1   Under German law, a commercial agent is an individual or business entity which acts in the name of the principal and is bound by his instructions but which, nevertheless, remains independent from the principal. The most important competition law issue is whether and to what extent section 15 GWB (prohibition on resale price maintenance) applies to agency agreements. As a rule, section 15 GWB does not apply as long as it is the principal who assumes the normal commercial risks relating to the sale of goods, such as the marketing and storage risks and the del credere guarantee. Losses and profits resulting from the conclusion and execution of the contracts solicited by the agent must be borne by the principal. In this respect it is not the wording of the agreement which is decisive, but the actual commercial position of the agent within the marketing and sales structure of the principal. Therefore, if these risks are neither directly nor indirectly assumed by the agent, the principal may prescribe prices and business terms of the contracts solicited by the agent.

3.6.2 Furthermore, all restrictions which form a natural part of an agency relationship are permissible and do not raise any concerns as to their compatibility with section 18 GWB. This holds true in particular with regard to non-competition clauses, given that they only reflect the agent's obligation to act in the interests of the principal.

3.7 Refusal to supply

In general, every manufacturer, distributor or retailer is free to sell to the dealers and customers of his choice. Therefore, in principle, a refusal to supply may be challenged only in cases where the supplier holds a market-dominating position within the meaning of section 26(2) GWB (see section 3.22 below). As a rule, the refusal to sell by a market-dominating enterprise is considered abusive behaviour, unless it can be shown that the refusal is justified by objective reasons relating, eg, to quality requirements or capacity.

3.8 Price restrictions

Any form of price restrictions in vertical agreements, including most favoured buyer clauses or minimum or maximum price obligations, are prohibited by section 15 GWB. Section 15 GWB extends far beyond the prohibition of traditional resale price maintenance and prohibits all restraints of a party's freedom to determine the prices, price elements or discounts in contracts with third parties.

3.9 Resale price maintenance

3.9.1 Any form of resale price maintenance is prohibited by section 15 GWB. However, pursuant to section 38a GWB, non-binding price recommendations for branded products are permissible, provided that the goods in question are in price competition with other comparable goods of other manufacturers, that the recommendations are explicitly referred to as non-binding and are made in the reasonable expectation that the recommended prices correspond to the prices which are likely to be charged by the majority of the addressees of the recommendation. Further, economic or other pressure must not be applied in order to ensure compliance with the recommendations. Under similar conditions, non-binding price recommendations even for non-branded products may be permissible if they are made by associations of small or medium-sized enterprises and serve to improve the competitiveness of the members of the association in relation to large enterprises.

3.9.2   The Cartel Authorities may prohibit non-binding price recommendations if such recommendations are applied in an abusive way, in particular, in order to keep prices at an artificially high level without any reasonable justification.

3.10   Tie in sales

Pursuant to section 18(1) No 4 GWB, the Cartel Authorities may prohibit agreements which require a party to purchase goods or commercial services which are, by their nature or according to commercial practice, not related to the goods or services needed by the purchaser, provided that such restrictions have a significant impact on market conditions (for details, see section 3.2.6 above). For instance, the obligation imposed on numerous petrol station owners to purchase not only gasoline but also automobile care products from the gasoline supplier was declared an unjustified tie-in under section 18 GWB. However, in practice, the requirements of section 18 GWB are seldom met, with the result that tying agreements may normally only be challenged if the rules on abusive behaviour apply (see section 3.19 below).

B   Horizontal Restrictions

3.11   Introduction

3.11.1   Pursuant to section 1 GWB, agreements entered into by enterprises or associations of enterprises for a common purpose and resolutions of associations of enterprises are invalid in so far as they are likely to influence, through restraint of competition, production or market conditions regarding the trade in goods or commercial services. Therefore, in order for an agreement to be caught by this general prohibition, the following conditions must be met.

3.11.2   Section 1 GWB only applies to 'enterprises'. However, this term is broadly interpreted and comprises all individuals, partnerships, corporations or other legal entities engaged in business activities relating to the sale of goods or the performance of commercial services. Accordingly, if and to the extent that state and other public bodies pursue such economic activities, they are also subject to section 1 GWB.

3.11.3   The requirement of a 'common purpose' is understood to exclude vertical agreements from the scope of section 1 GWB. Therefore, in practice, this condition is met where the parties to the agreement are actual or potential competitors.

3.11.4   There is 'restraint of competition' where an agreement restricts the freedom of at least one of the parties from determining his competitive behaviour. There may even be a restraint if only the position of third parties is affected (for example, if barriers to market entry are created or strengthened by the agreement). Intra-group agreements, however, do not normally fall within the scope of section 1 GWB. The same applies to all agreements concluded between small or medium-sized enterprises with a combined market share of no more than 5%, given that they do not normally restrict competition to an appreciable extent (*de minimis* exception).

3.12 Information exchange

Agreements whereby competitors exchange information on prices, price elements, terms and conditions of sale or other market data, which are normally considered confidential, violate section 1 GBW if the information exchanged permits the identification of suppliers or customers or discloses the terms of individual transactions. Such agreements tend to reduce competition even if they do not contain any restriction as to the parties' freedom to determine their prices and business terms in contracts with third parties. On the other hand, so-called non-identifying procedures providing average prices or other global market statistics, from which no conclusions about individual transactions can be drawn, are normally unobjectionable.

3.13 Joint buying and selling

3.13.1 Joint purchasing organisations established by competitors tend to prevent, at least partially, their members from individually negotiating terms and conditions with their suppliers, irrespective of whether they are contractually free to do so. The economic objective of securing better terms and prices by building up market power can normally be achieved only if the participants abstain from entering into individual negotiations with their suppliers. Therefore, joint purchasing organisations are normally caught by section 1 GWB. However, according to section 5c GWB, there is an exception for purchasing cartels which are established by small or medium-sized enterprises. Enterprises with a combined market share of no more than 10 or 15% normally qualify for this exception.

3.13.2 Joint selling organisations are normally held to contravene section 1 GWB even if their members remain contractually free to sell directly to their customers. In principle, such systems only make economic sense if the participants at least implicitly agree to sell their products only through the joint selling organisation.

3.14 Fixing prices and conditions of sale

3.14.1 The classic cartel falling within section 1 GWB is the fixing of prices for goods or services. The prohibition of such cartels not only applies to direct pricing arrangements but also to any other agreements restricting the parties' freedom to determine prices, such as agreements relating to price elements, price ranges or pricing ratios between various products.

3.14.2 Condition cartels, in turn, are normally compatible with German anti-trust law provided that they are notified to the Cartel Authorities. Pursuant to section 2 GWB, the prohibition laid down in section 1 GWB does not apply to agreements whose object is the uniform application of general business terms, delivery terms or payment terms, including cash discounts. No part of such standard terms and conditions may, however, relate to prices or elements thereof, except for the establishment of uniform discounts.

3.15   Market sharing

Agreements whereby competitors allocate product or geographic markets, customers, or quotas are generally found to be incompatible with Section 1 GWB. In practice, there may be an exception only in cases where such agreements form part of a major transaction such as the establishment of a joint venture or the transfer of assets or know-how and where it can be established that the restrictions are reasonably necessary for the implementation of the transaction in question. For instance if a business is sold, the seller may agree to a non-compete clause for a reasonable time.

3.16   Joint ventures

3.16.1   The formation of a joint venture by competitors is subject not only to the merger control rules but also to section 1 GWB. The question of whether the formation of a joint venture constitutes a 'restraint of competition' within the meaning of section 1 GWB depends on the circumstances of each case. As a rule, so-called concentrative joint ventures are less likely to fall under section 1 GWB than co-operative joint ventures. In order for a joint venture to be considered concentrative, it must, in principle, be in a position to exercise its own commercial policy and perform all the functions of an autonomous economic entity in a market other than that of the parent companies' or neighbouring, upstream or downstream markets. In particular, these elements normally exist if the parent companies only pursue capitalistic interests. On the other hand, if the commercial policy of the joint venture remains in the hands of the parents or if the joint venture is dependent on its parents for the maintenance and development of its business, there is a high risk that the joint venture is being used by the parent companies merely as a vehicle to co-ordinate their competitive behaviour ('hidden cartel'). Therefore, such co-operative joint ventures are more likely to violate section 1 GWB.

3.16.2   When assessing agreements supplementing the formation of the joint venture, a distinction has to be made between restraints imposed on the joint venture and restraints imposed on the parents. Restraints imposed on the joint venture, such as the obligation not to compete with the parent companies, are normally unobjectionable, given that the parents, through their position as shareholders, are free to determine the competitive behaviour of the joint venture. The situation is different with regard to provisions which restrict competition between the parent companies. Such restrictions violate section 1 GWB, unless it can be demonstrated that they are objectively necessary for the proper functioning of the joint venture. For instance, an obligation on the parent companies not to compete with each other must be limited in duration, subject matter, and geographic scope to what is necessary for the creation and operation of the joint venture.

3.17   Crisis cartels

According to section 4 GWB, the German cartel authorities may exempt crisis cartels from the prohibition in section 1 GWB, provided that the agreement is necessary to effect a systematic alignment of capacity to demand and that the agreement is made with due regard for the general economy and common welfare. So far, this exemption has been of almost no practical relevance.

3.18 Other forms of co-operation

3.18.1 Sections 2 to 8 GWB cover various types of cartel agreements which are exempted or may be exempted by the cartel authorities from the prohibition in section 1 GWB. In particular, the provisions relating to specialisation and co-operation cartels are of some practical importance.

3.18.2 Pursuant to section 5a GWB, the Cartel Authorities may approve agreements whose object is the rationalisation of economic processes by means of specialisation, provided that substantial competition in the market is not impaired. Factors to be taken into account are, inter alia, the market shares of the parties, their financial, technical and other resources, their access to the supply and sales markets, and the possibility for customers and suppliers to turn to other enterprises. Under specific circumstances, even specialisation cartels involving a market share of 50% or more may qualify for this exemption.

3.18.3 Pursuant to section 5b, co-operation cartels relating eg to joint production, research, financing, administration or advertising may be exempted if the parties are small or medium-sized enterprises. As a rule of thumb, agreements involving a market share of no more than 10 or 15% may be covered by this exemption.

3.18.4 Both specialisation and co-operation cartels may be combined with agreements controlling prices or establishing joint purchasing or selling organisations, if and to the extent that such supplementary agreements are necessary to implement the specialisation or co-operation in question.

C Abusive Behaviour

3.19 Introduction

3.19.1 Abusive behaviour in competition is regulated by the GWB and the Act Against Unfair Competition (UWG).

3.19.2 Section 1 UWG prohibits any competitive act in the course of business activities which is contrary to honest practices ('gute Sitten'). This provision applies to any enterprise which competes in business regardless of its size or position in the market.

3.19.3 The GWB deals with abusive behaviour in the context of abuse of market-dominating power. Sections 22 and 26(2) GWB contain detailed provisions on the abuse of power by enterprises which dominate the market.

3.20 Abusive behaviour in unfair competition

3.20.1 General

The broad rule of section 1 UWG prohibiting any act in competition which is considered by all reasonable members of the business community to be contrary to honest practices has been refined by jurisprudence. There is a large body of jurisprudence in the form of case law in which the courts have considered whether certain competitive acts are compatible with the honest practice rule or constitute an act of unfair competition. Unfair competition can be found wherever there is competition and has as many facets as competition itself.

The courts have defined certain categories of business conduct which must be branded as a violation of the honest practice rule. The large categories of unfair competition are solicitation of customers by dishonest practices such as exaggerated product claims, unsolicited telephone calls by sales persons, lotteries, premium gifts, misleading advertising; exploitation of a competitor's goodwill by product imitation or other deception as to origin, breach of contract or disregard of legal provisions; and, last but not least, unfair hindrances such as boycotting, predatory or below-cost pricing and degrading comparative advertising.

Examples of abusive behaviour can mostly be found in the last category of unfair hindrance.

3.20.2   Unfair hindrance

It is inherent to competition that any successful commercial transaction in a free market economy will restrict the business opportunities of competitors. In a free market economy, the players will compete in the market place and the best offer will win. The success of one competitor will adversely affect all competing enterprises, will impair their market chances and may even lead to their exclusion from the market if, in the long run, they are not able to compete. These are the natural functions of competition.

The UWG seeks to prevent unfair practices which hinder an enterprise from offering its product or services on the market so that the potential buyers will have no fair chance to consider that offer and make a free choice as to the best offer. Barriers to market entry resulting from competition based on efficiency and performance (Leistungswettbewerb) are normal and acceptable. Barriers caused by other means not based on efficiency and better performance are contrary to honest practices.

There are obvious unfair means of competition such as boycotting which will directly keep a competitor from entering the market, but there are other more subtle unfair means of hindering and restraining a competitor from fully exploiting his market chances.

The courts have, for instance, held that the mass distribution of free product samples may result in congesting the market which would unfairly hinder competitors. Another example is the free-of-charge distribution of advertising (news) papers which can constitute abusive conduct if, as a result, the existence of regular newspapers is endangered.

3.20.3   Predatory and below-cost pricing

Predatory and below-cost pricing is a chapter in itself. Price competition is the backbone of successful activity in the market. Undercutting prices is a normal reaction and is necessary to compete. Even below-cost pricing is not unfair per se.

Below-cost pricing can be a dishonest and abusive practice if it is done with the intent and for the purpose of destroying the business of a competitor and to remove him from the market. Selling certain products constantly or repeatedly under cost price without apparent reason may be an indication of using price cutting as a means of destroying a competitor and frustrating the functions of a free market.

3.20.4 Other forms of abusive conduct

The rules of fair competition as they have developed under section 1 UWG protect the individual player in the market by guaranteeing fair and honest practices in competition. These rules have to be observed by all enterprises regardless of their market power. Enterprises which are dominating the market or enjoy relatively strong market power are subject to the special rules of the GWB against abusive practices. The GWB rules are designed to preserve the free enterprise structure of the market. Having different objectives, the provisions of the UWG and the GWB on abusive conduct are applied independently and with equal rank. The rules of the GWB do not overrule the honest practice requirements of the UWG and, vice versa, market-dominating enterprises have to observe the rules of the UWG. In some instances, a certain conduct such as a boycott is prohibited as an unfair practice under section 1 UWG and also considered contrary to a competitive market structure and, therefore, contrary to GWB rules.

There are certain other interrelations. An act which has been qualified as dishonest practice under the UWG will normally be qualified as an unfair hindrance under the GWB provisions. The market-dominating enterprise is not prevented from using normal means of competition as long as it does not abuse its market power in a way which is prohibited by the GWB. There are, however, situations in which a market-strong enterprise has to be extra-careful in choosing its instruments of competition because the effect on the functioning of the market will be more detrimental if there is a strong market power. The mass distribution of free product samples or tie-in agreements by a relatively small company will have little or no effect on the market, whereas the same market strategy by a large and already-dominating company will foreclose the market for competitors and may be, therefore, considered a dishonest practice.

While the UWG deals with abusive practices as a segment of unfair competition, the relevant provisions of the GWB are directed against the abuse of market power. If the conduct of an enterprise is not or not fully controlled by the forces of competition, legal constraints are necessary. The market-dominating enterprise will have to observe rules which are designed to put it in a position 'as if' there were effective competition. The lack of competition is compensated by governmental control of behaviour.

In the German legal community, abusive behaviour is normally understood to describe abuse of market-dominating power. This will be the subject of the following discussion.

3.21 Abuse of market-dominating power

3.21.1 Definition of market domination

In order to understand the German concept of preventing abusive behaviour, it is necessary to have an understanding of the term market domination. Since this term will be discussed in more detail later in this chapter, it will suffice at this point to discuss the basic principles. According to section 22(1) GWB, an enterprise is market-dominating in so far as, in its capacity as a supplier or buyer of a certain type of goods or commercial services, it

(i) has no competitor or is not exposed to any substantial competition; or
(ii) has a paramount market position in relation to its competitors.

For this purpose, in addition to the market share, the financial resources, the access to supply or sales markets, its links with other enterprises and the barriers to the market entry of other enterprises will be taken into account.

A market-dominating position can also be enjoyed by an oligopoly if in fact no substantial competition exists between the members of the oligopoly and they are jointly not exposed to substantial competition or have a paramount market position (section 22(2) GWB).

Section 22(3) GWB provides certain presumptions for market domination. A single enterprise is presumed to be market-dominating if it has at least a one-third market share and an oligopoly is presumed to be market-dominating if three or fewer enterprises have a combined market share of 50% or five or fewer enterprises have a combined two-thirds market share. In both instances, there are certain minimum total sales requirements.

3.21.2   Abuse by market-dominating enterprises

In the event that market-dominating enterprises abuse their dominating position in the market for these or any other goods or commercial services, the Cartel Authorities may prohibit such abusive practices and declare agreements to be of no effect. Prior to such action, the Cartel Authorities must request the parties involved to discontinue the abuse to which objection is raised (section 22(4) and (5) GWB).

Section 22(4) GWB gives some examples of abusive behaviour, but other behaviour may also be found abusive by the Cartel Authorities. Pursuant to section 22(4) GWB, abuse may be present if a market-dominating enterprise which is a supplier or buyer of a certain type of goods or commercial services:

(a)   impairs the competitive possibilities of other enterprises in a manner relevant to competition on the market in the absence of facts justifying such behaviour;
(b)   demands considerations or other business terms which deviate from those which would result in all probability if effective competition existed;
(c)   demands less favourable considerations or other business terms than are demanded from similar buyers on comparable markets by the market-dominating enterprise, unless there is justification for such differentiation.

Section 22(4) No 1 GWB describes an abuse which is a hindrance to competition (so-called 'Behinderungsmißbrauch'); section 22(4) Nos 2 and 3 GWB above describe an abuse which exploits the supply or demand side of the market (so-called 'Ausbeutungsmißbrauch').

3.21.3   Methods of establishing abuse

The abusive exploitation is characterised by asking for prices and other business terms which deviate from conditions which would exist on a competitive market or which deviate from those which are demanded by the dominating enterprise itself from other similar buyers. In the latter case, abuse is established by comparing the different prices and conditions of the dominating enterprise to different categories of customers without justification for such differentiation.

In the case of abuse by deviating from conditions which would exist on a competitive market (section 22(4) No 2 GWB), the so-called 'as if' test is applied by establishing the prices and conditions as if competition were effective. This test requires a comparable competitive market ('Vergleichsmarktkonzept'). This can be another territorial market or the market which existed before it was dominated or a market for similar goods or services.

In order to establish abusive conduct, the difference between the price found on the comparative market and the price charged by the dominant enterprise must be substantial. There is a very fine line which separates permissible use of market power from misuse which can be qualified as abusive behaviour.

Other methods of finding a competitive price, such as cost control, have largely failed in practice. It appears to be next to impossible to check and verify the cost calculation of large and, in particular, international enterprises. In this context, another much contested and unsolved issue is found in the well-known *Valium* case, in respect to the significance of research and development costs in the pharmaceutical industry.

3.21.4 *Consequences of abuse*

Section 22 GWB authorises the Cartel Authorities to take action against abusive behaviour, but it does not grant individual rights and it is not a law for the protection of individual interests (section 823(2) Civil Code). It is within the Cartel Authorities' discretion to take action against alleged abusive behaviour which is brought to their attention, for instance, by a complaint of the aggrieved party.

3.22 Section 26(2) GWB

Section 26(2) GWB also deals with the abuse of market-dominating power. Market-dominating enterprises shall not unfairly hinder, directly or indirectly, another enterprise from business activities which are usually open to similar enterprises nor in the absence of facts justifying such differentiation treat such enterprise directly or indirectly in a manner different from the treatment accorded to similar enterprises.

3.22.1 *Extended scope and individual rights*

Section 26(2)(2) GWB broadens the applicability of this provision to enterprises upon which small and medium-sized enterprises depend to such an extent that sufficient and reasonable possibilities of dealing with other enterprises do not exist (relative market strength).

Section 26(3) GWB states that market-dominating and enterprises with relative market strength shall not use their market position to cause other enterprises in business activities to accord them preferential terms unless justified by factual circumstances.

In addition to the rather large number of enterprises protected by section 22(2) GWB, the importance of this provision lies in the fact that it creates individual rights and is considered a law for the protection of individual interests. Therefore, it bestows the right on any aggrieved party to bring court action for injunction and damages against abusive conduct.

3.22.2 *Dependency*

The courts have defined several broad categories of dependency on enterprises with relative market strength. In practice, the most important category is when a dependency on supply exists because a retailer has to offer certain quality products of high reputation in his assortment. In an early case, the courts found that a sports article retailer in Upper Bavaria would have no viable business without being able to offer Rossignol skis, although they amounted to only 3% of his total sales. Other examples can be found en masse in the radio and television retail trade.

3.22.3   Justification

In the light of GWB's aim to ensure free competition, the courts have applied strict standards to the reasons justifying refusal to sell and other discriminatory conduct. The refusal to sell to mail-order businesses, to department stores and even to discounters on the grounds of lack of service or damage to the goodwill of the trade-mark have not been accepted by the courts for a wide range of goods. Selective distribution with a limited number of qualified dealers is possible and enforceable, provided that strict conditions are fulfilled.

3.22.4   Horizontal relation

While section 26(2)(2) GWB protects enterprises which are vertically dependent upon a market-strong enterprise as supplier or customer, section 26(4) GWB extends the protection against unfair hindrances to the horizontal relation between competitors. An enterprise with superior market strength shall not use its power to unfairly hinder small and medium-sized competitors.

3.22.5   Rights and liabilities

In addition to the private action rights of aggrieved parties, the Cartel Authorities are authorised under section 35 GWB to issue a prohibitive order in the event that section 26 GWB is violated. The violation of section 26 GWB is a misdemeanour which is subject to an administrative fine up to DM 1,000,000 and, in addition, up to three times the extra gains derived from the violation.

There is a civil liability for damages suffered by the afflicted party, but only actual, not punitive, damages can be awarded.

4   CONCENTRATIONS, MERGERS AND ACQUISITIONS

4.1   Introduction

Mergers within the definition of the GWB need to be notified to the Federal Cartel Office (FCO) unless they are subject to European merger control. The FCO must, with some exceptions, prohibit combinations which create or reinforce a market-dominating position. Between the introduction of merger control in June 1973 and 31 December 1993, 17,260 mergers were notified and 104 mergers prohibited by the FCO. Other merger plans have been abandoned after informal discussions with the FCO or in the course of the proceedings, or have passed after the participating enterprises have agreed to measures which eliminated the anti-competitive effects. The small number of prohibitions is therefore not indicative of a minor importance or effectiveness of merger control.

4.2 Definitions, thresholds

4.2.1 For the purposes of merger control, enterprises are all individuals, partnerships, companies, corporations and other entities, whether public or private, domestic or foreign, which are engaged in business activities, including individuals owning a majority interest in an enterprise. If an enterprise is a member of a group, the total group, including enterprises under joint control, is taken into consideration on the part of that enterprise. Enterprises participating in the merger are the parties directly involved in the combination, but also all members of a group of which a participating enterprise forms part. A seller participates in the combination only to the extent of the sold assets or shares.

4.2.2 Mergers within the definition of the GWB are the following combinations:

(a) the purchase of the assets or a substantial part of the assets of an enterprise by way of acquisition, merger or otherwise. The courts have interpreted the term 'substantial part of the assets' quite broadly so that the term can also cover the purchase of assets which do not constitute a separate plant or business;

(b) the purchase of shares in another enterprise if the purchased shares, together with shares already owned by the purchaser, grant the purchaser at least 25%, or 50%, or a majority of the capital or the voting rights. The term 'shares' includes all types of participations and interests in an enterprise. An increase to a higher level of participation in the capital or voting rights is a new combination even if the purchase of shares above a lower threshold has previously been subject to merger control. A purchase of shares below the lowest threshold is also an event of combination if statutory, contractual or other arrangements grant the purchaser a position equivalent to a shareholder with more than 25% of the voting shares;

(c) if several enterprises acquire and/or own shares in an enterprise above any of these thresholds (joint venture), this is deemed to be (i) a combination of those enterprises with the joint venture, and (ii) a combination between those enterprises in the business area in which the joint venture is or will be engaged. Joint ventures can also be subject to section 1 GWB which prohibits horizontal restraints of competition; as a general guideline, this is the case if the joint venture is of a co-operative nature;

(d) agreements between enterprises by which (i) a group relationship is created, (ii) operations of one enterprise are leased in whole or to a substantial part to another enterprise, or (iii) one enterprise undertakes to conduct its business for the account of, or to transfer its profit and loss in whole or to a substantial part to, another enterprise;

(e) interlocking directorships, if not less than half of the members of the supervisory board, the management board or other management body of two or more enterprises consists of the same persons;

(f) any other arrangement which permits one or more enterprises to exercise, directly or indirectly, a controlling influence upon another enterprise;

(g) any other arrangement among enterprises of the type set forth in: (b), (e) and (f) above which does not meet the specific criteria but grants one or more enterprises, directly or indirectly, a substantial influence from a competitive point of view upon another enterprise.

4.2.3   Combinations have to be notified to the FCO if the participating enterprises had an aggregate worldwide turnover, without sales reductions and turnover tax, of DM 500 million or more in their last fiscal year. Turnover from trading activities is counted at 75% and print media turnover at twenty times the actual turnover. Instead of the turnover, one-tenth of the balance sheet total is used for banks and building societies and the premium income for insurance companies. On the seller's side, only the sold assets or the sold enterprise are taken into consideration.

In practice, only combinations pursuant to sections 4.2.2(a) and 4.2.2(b) above have gained real importance, while the other events of combination have not been of any particular significance.

4.2.4   Combinations do not need to be notified if they do not lead to a substantial strengthening of a pre-existing relationship between the participating enterprises, in particular if they concern only enterprises belonging to the same group. A further exception applies for credit institutions: the acquisition of shares for placement in the market does not constitute a combination as long as the credit institution does not exercise the voting rights (except in the first shareholders' meeting of a newly-formed enterprise) and sells the shares within one year.

4.3   Notification procedures

4.3.1   Intended combinations (except those pursuant to sub-para (g) in section 4.2.2 above) need to be notified to the FCO before completion (pre-merger notification) if (i) one enterprise or group with a turnover of DM 2 billion or more or (ii) two or more enterprises or groups with a turnover of DM 1 billion or more each form part of the combination or (iii) the combination is to be effected by legislative enactment or other sovereign act.

Upon receipt of a pre-merger notification, the FCO has one month to consider whether or not to investigate the matter, and if it advises the parties of its intention to investigate within that one-month period, a further three months to complete its review and, if warranted, issue a prohibition. In critical cases it is not uncommon for the FCO to ask the parties for further extensions if the FCO cannot complete its review within the statutory period.

As long as the initial one-month period has not elapsed without a notice of investigation from, or a statutory or voluntary extension of the investigation period without prohibition of the intended combination by the FCO, the parties are prevented from completing the transaction and any steps violating that prohibition are invalid and may subject the parties participating therein to fines. The parties can proceed with completion prior to the lapse of any applicable waiting period after they have received a release letter from the FCO confirming that the FCO has completed its review without prohibition. In practice, the FCO issues a release letter within days or weeks in uncritical cases, and even where it starts an investigation, concludes most cases well before the lapse of the extended waiting period.

The prohibition to complete a combination does not prevent the parties from entering into any type of obligatory agreement directed towards the transaction, including purchase and sale agreements, option agreements and the like.

4.3.2   Notifiable combinations which do not meet the criteria for a pre-merger notification can be notified after completion (post-merger notification). The participating companies can also pre-notify those cases, and if they elect to do so, the pre-merger notification rules apply. Even if the parties elect to pre-notify, they can proceed to a legally effective completion at any time and their pre-merger notification will then be treated by the FCO as a post-merger notification. In post-merger notification cases the prohibition period is one year.

4.3.3 Even if the participating enterprises have complied with the pre-merger notification procedure on a mandatory or voluntary basis, the FCO has to be notified once completion has occurred. This completion notice serves only statistical purposes and does not give rise to any further rights of the FCO. The FCO can only prohibit a transaction which has already passed in the pre- or post-merger notification proceedings if (i) the combination is completed in a form other than as notified, (ii) it has not been completed yet and the relevant circumstances have materially changed or (iii) the parties have induced the FCO to take no action by filing an incorrect or incomplete notification or by failing to supply pertinent information upon the FCO's request.

4.3.4 Completed transactions are published by the FCO in the Federal Gazette upon receipt of the completion notice in a pre-merger notification case or of a post-merger notification. Pre-merger notifications are not published, but the FCO is not under an obligation to keep them confidential, except for trade secrets of the parties, and generally refuses to adhere to confidentiality. In fact, where warranted the FCO uses the notified information (except for trade secrets) in the course of its investigation and answers enquiries from third parties about pending cases, and both the proceedings and such information can come to the attention of third parties and the public. On the other hand, simple pre-notifications which do not lead to investigations of the FCO do normally not become publicly known as a result of the merger control proceedings.

Publicity can be avoided by approaching the FCO on an informal basis prior to any notification, and this is frequently done in critical cases. The FCO is quite willing to discuss intended combinations informally and give its initial reaction, though on the understanding that this will not bind the FCO in subsequent formal proceedings. Informal discussions have the further advantage that critical aspects are defined and the parties have an opportunity to address them in the formal submission.

4.3.5 The obligation to notify rests with the enterprises participating in the combination and where there is a seller, also the latter. The FCO is prepared to start the proceedings on the basis of a notification of any one of these parties even if other parties have not joined yet, but in critical cases where a prohibition is possible and will have to be served upon all parties concerned, the FCO will insist upon proper representation or at least a clear definition of all parties requiring service.

4.3.6 The notification must include a description of the intended or completed combination and for each participating enterprise:

(a) the firm name or other designation and the seat or principal place of business;
(b) a description of the business;
(c) the market shares and the basis for their calculation or estimate if the shares of the participating enterprises reach 20% or more in any product or service market in Germany or a substantial part thereof. This does not only extend to markets in which several participating enterprises are engaged but also to markets in which one of the enterprises reaches that level of market share by itself. In practice, the FCO does normally not insist on the notification of

shares of the buyer in markets which are only served by the latter and are far removed from any critical market;

(d) the turnover of each participating enterprise or for banks and building societies, the balance sheet total, and for insurance companies, the premium income; and

(e) in case of the acquisition of shares, the shares already owned by the buyer and those purchased or to be purchased.

If an enterprise is a member of a group, the information must be furnished on a group-wide basis and the ownership and control relations among the group members need to be added.

The FCO can demand from each participating company detailed information about the market shares, the calculation basis and the turnover. To the extent required for its investigation the FCO can also request from the participating enterprises and third parties further information about their business affairs and can inspect their files; parties receiving such request can have its legal justification reviewed in appeal proceedings. In critical cases it is quite usual for the FCO to carry out industry-wide surveys on market definition, market characteristics, market shares and other aspects pertinent for its decision.

4.3.7 German merger control extends also to foreign combinations which have an effect in Germany. This applies irrespective of whether or not any enterprise directly participating in a combination or any direct or indirect parent company of any such enterprise resides in Germany, ie applies also in those cases in which foreign enterprises not owned by German enterprises merge outside of Germany. The FCO has issued a memorandum describing the circumstances under which the latter type of transaction can have an inland effect and needs to be notified. Such an effect exists in the opinion of the FCO in any event if several participating enterprises or groups have operations or subsidiaries in Germany, though other circumstances may also suffice.

It is disputed whether or not the pre-merger notification requirement applies to the latter type of foreign combinations as well: the FCO maintains that this is so, but the legal effectiveness of a foreign transaction is governed by the respective foreign law, and although the FCO has sent letters of admonition to the parties concerned, it has so far never imposed a fine. In any event, the rights of the FCO extend in those cases only to the German aspects and the FCO does not have the power to prevent the foreign transaction as such.

4.4   Appraisal criteria

4.4.1 The FCO must prohibit a combination if one can expect that the combination will create or reinforce a market-dominating position in any product or service market in Germany or a substantial part thereof, except if the participating enterprises show that the combination also results in improvements of the competitive conditions and that these improvements outweigh the disadvantages of the market domination. The decision of the FCO has to be based entirely on competitive considerations while questions of public policy such as the competitive position of the participating enterprise in foreign markets, the preservation of working places or the rehabilitation of a failing company cannot play any role. These factors can only be taken into consideration in the proceedings before the Federal Minister of Economics as discussed in section 4.5.4 below.

The FCO has no discretion: if there are grounds for a prohibition, the FCO must so decide, even if the engagement of the participating enterprises in the respective market forms only a small part of their overall activities. In practice, the FCO nevertheless exercises some discretion and does not totally overlook the public policy factors.

4.4.2 An enterprise is market-dominating within the definition of the GWB if it is not subject to substantial competition or enjoys a superior market position in relation to its competitors. In this latter respect, the market shares, the financial resources, the access to supply and sales markets, the relations with other enterprises, the legal or factual barriers to market entry by other enterprises, the ability to direct its supply or demand to other goods or services and the ability of the other market side to change to other competitors are of primary importance. Two or more enterprises can also be market-dominating as an oligopoly if there is no substantial competition among them and together they fulfil the conditions for market domination vis-à-vis the other competitors.

4.4.3 The creation or reinforcement of a market-dominating position can be supported by any of the criteria outlined before. Although in practice the market share has always been the most important factor, a combination of these criteria permits the FCO to address and, if warranted, prohibit not only horizontal but also vertical and conglomerate mergers. In particular, if one of the participating enterprises is found to be market-dominating by itself, it takes very little to justify the expectation that that position will be reinforced by the combination: according to a Supreme Court decision the reinforcement must be noticeable but does not have to be material. The financial resources of the buyer of a market-dominating enterprise have, for instance, been considered to reinforce that market-dominating position even if the buyer is not engaged in the same or a related market as long as he has an entrepreneurial interest. The FCO has also attempted to prevent combinations which would give the combined enterprises a superior purchasing power, but so far with rather mixed results.

4.4.4 In arriving at a decision, the FCO has to investigate all relevant aspects speaking for and against a prohibition. Except as stated in sub-para (b) below, this applies also with respect to certain statutory presumptions for market domination and reinforcement provided in the GWB, although in practice the burden of rebutting applicable presumptions rests to a large extent with the participating enterprises. The presumption pursuant to sub-para (a) below has always been the most critical one, while the others have played a lesser or no role. The presumptions are as follows:

(a) a company is presumed to be market-dominating if it has a market share of one-third or more in any product or service market; this presumption does not apply if the enterprise had a turnover of less than DM 250 million;

(b) several competitors are deemed to be market-dominating as an oligopoly if (i) three or fewer enterprises have a total market share of 50% or more or (ii) five or fewer have a market share of two-thirds or more in any product or service market; this presumption does not apply to companies with a turnover of less than DM 100 million. For merger control purposes, the onus to rebut the oligopoly presumption rests also legally with the participating enterprises, except to the extent that (i) companies with sales of less than DM 150 million are concerned or (ii) all companies participating in the combination have an aggregate market share of 15% or less;

(c)   it is presumed that a combination will create or reinforce a market-dominating position if:

    (i)   an enterprise with a turnover of DM 2 billion or more enters into a combination with another enterprise which (i) is engaged in a market in which small and medium-sized companies have a total market share of not less than two-thirds and the participating enterprises have an aggregate market share of 5% or more or (ii) is market-dominating in one or more markets with a total market volume of DM 150 million or more; or

    (ii)   the participating companies had an aggregate turnover of DM 12 billion or more and at least two of them had a turnover of DM 1 billion or more each. This does not apply if the combination concerns a joint venture which is only engaged in markets with a market volume of less than DM 750 million.

4.5   Powers of enforcement

4.5.1   The prohibition of an intended combination in a mandatory pre-merger notification case prevents completion of the transaction and thus prevents the intended combination.

In a post-merger notification case, the prohibition of the combination is only a necessary first step; once this decision has become final, the FCO has to decide on the necessary measures to remove the anti-competitive effects. This can be done by ordering the dissolution of the total combination, but also by other measures, for instance an order to dispose of certain parts of an acquired business or enterprise or other measures of a structural nature. In practice, there have been very few cases in which a completed combination has been dissolved, and the FCO relies primarily on the fact that all significant combinations require pre-merger notification and completion is prevented by the prohibition.

4.5.2   The prohibition order and, to the extent applicable, any dissolution order can be appealed against by each participating enterprise and the seller, first by an appeal to the Intermediate Court in Berlin and then by a further appeal to the Supreme Court, and will become final only upon a final court decision or the lapse of the appeal term. Practically all prohibitions in completed transaction have been appealed against, many of them successfully. Prohibitions in pre-notification cases have been appealed against less frequently, since often circumstances did not allow for a delay of the combination by several years, and the appeals had mixed results.

4.5.3   The FCO does not only have the necessary powers to enforce a final decision but can also issue preliminary injunctions in order to prevent the parties from completing an intended combination or from taking measures which would render the dissolution of a completed combination impossible or more difficult. In practice, this instrument has been used very rarely as a result of the fact that in pre-merger notification cases completion is prevented by the waiting periods and a prohibition.

4.5.4   If the FCO has prohibited a transaction, the participating companies can petition the Federal Minister of Economics before and after an appeal to permit the combination despite the prohibition on the grounds that the anti-competitive effects are outweighed in the specific case by advantages of an overall economic nature or a superior public interest; the GWB refers in this context in particular to the competitive position of the participating enterprises in foreign markets. Thus, the procedure for a Minister's approval permits to give consideration to public policy.

In practice, only very few petitions have been filed and only half of them were successful in whole or in part, most of them in the early years of merger control; there is a considerable reluctance on the part of the Minister to grant an exception for a combination with anti-competitive effects. The Minister's decision is again open to appeal.

4.5.5 Third parties can make their views about a combination known to the FCO informally, but can also become parties to the proceedings if they can show that their interests will be substantially affected by the outcome. As parties to the proceedings, they get access to the FCO and court files, except for trade secrets of the participating enterprises, and have a separate right to appeal.

4.5.6 The FCO cannot prohibit a combination, even if it fulfils the conditions for a prohibition otherwise, in the following circumstances:

(a) the participating companies and groups had an aggregate turnover of less than DM 500 million in their last fiscal year;

(b) an enterprise or group with a turnover of not more than DM 50 million in its last fiscal year merges with, or sells assets or a subsidiary to, an enterprise or group with sales of less than DM 1,000 million; if the other enterprise or group had sales of DM 1,000 million or more, the privilege is only extended to enterprises or groups with a turnover of less than DM 4 million. This rule applies in the case of print media only with significant exceptions;

(c) the relevant market had a total market volume of less than DM 10 million in the last fiscal year and concerns goods or services being offered for not less than five years;

(d) the FCO can refrain from issuing a prohibition if the participating enterprises agree in the course of the proceedings to take measures which alleviate the anti-competitive effects of the combination, such as to dispose of certain operations or subsidiaries or to sever ties with other competitors within a given time frame. The measures have to be of a structural nature, while undertakings concerning their future business, such as the future conduct of certain operations, are not apt to exclude a prohibition.

CHAPTER IX

Greece

Costas Vainanidis
Julia Pournara

Vainanidis Schina & Economou
5 Akadimias Street
106 71 Athens
Greece

Tel   ++30 1 36 34287
Fax   ++30 1 36 04611

CHAPTER IX

Greece

1 GREEK COMPETITION LAW

1.1 Background

1.1.1 In 1977, under the emerging need to control co-ordinated market behaviour more effectively and in anticipation of the country's entry into the Common Market, the Greek Parliament adopted Act 703/77 'on the control of monopolies and oligopolies and the protection of free competition'. The Report introducing the bill to Parliament referred to the achievement of two objectives: the protection of the competitive process and the harmonisation of Greek law with the principles of EC anti-trust legislation. The Act was subsequently amended by Act 1232/1982 and Ministerial Decision B 3/395, by Act 1934/1991, which was primarily aimed at the achievement of some harmonisation of Greek merger control with the relevant principles of EC Regulation 4064/89, by Act 2001/1991 and recently by Act 2296/1995. This latest amendment is expected by most interested parties to bring a positive change in the field of competition law since it introduces several significant and positive modifications concerning, for example, the merger control regime, the authorities' reorganisation and procedural rules.

1.1.2 Act 703/77, the whole spirit and substance of which is based on the EC competition rules, is concerned with the proper functioning of a mechanism in the market which will safeguard consumer interests and will secure traders' commercial freedom both in the supply and demand side of the market. Therefore, Greek anti-trust law aims at maintaining a competitive environment which will enable undertakings effectively to compete on the basis of economic considerations and will contribute to the maximisation of consumer welfare.

1.1.3 Act 703/77 is divided into seven chapters. The first regulates all substantive issues, namely restrictive practices and abuses of dominant positions as well as merger control. Chapter two deals with the institutions entrusted with the application of the law. Chapter three refers to judicial remedies and chapters four and five to procedural rules with respect to registration records, notifications, complaints and investigations. Provisions concerning sanctions and duties to be paid in case of infringement of the law follow and chapter seven contains the final provisions.

1.2 Anti-competitive agreements and concerted practices

1.2.1 Section 1 – prohibited restrictive practices

Section 1(1) of Act 703/77 prohibits agreements by undertakings, decisions by associations of undertakings and concerted practices of whatever kind, which have as their object or effect the prevention, restriction or distortion of competition within the national territory. There are, therefore, two conditions that must be satisfied for the application of this section:

(a)   the existence of an agreement, decision or concerted practice by undertakings or associations of undertakings;
(b)   which prevents, restricts or distorts competition within the national territory.

1.2.2   Undertakings and associations of undertakings

Although the notion of an undertaking for the purposes of anti-trust legislation is not defined by law, it is considered to include any natural or legal person engaged in economic or commercial activity. The Commission for the Protection of Competition dealt with this question, for the first time, in Decision 9/1981. It held that the concept of undertaking is broader, including every economic activity irrespective of whether its sole object is to gain profit or not. It also stated that the purpose of the law, ie the protection of free competition in all sectors of the economy, is of significant importance in this respect. The legal form and legal personality of the firm is immaterial,[1] as well as the issue of them being privately or state-owned.[2] Moreover, two or more undertakings will be treated as a single economic entity if they are under the same ownership or control.[3] Finally, associations of undertakings include groups of firms in the form of an association,[4] a company[5] or a joint venture.[6]

1.2.3   Agreements, decisions and concerted practices

The concept of agreement is broadly interpreted and comprises many forms of collaboration, ie not only written agreements but also those concluded orally[7] or tacitly,[8] which are legally or morally binding on the parties. Even gentlemen's agreements may be caught under this section.[9]

Greek competition authorities have also dealt with the issue of concerted practice on several occasions. By Decision 15/1981, where reference was made to the judgment of the European Court of Justice in the *Dyestuffs* case, the Commission for the Protection of Competition clarified this concept:

'in order to accept the existence of a concerted practice, it is not necessary for the parties to have drawn up a common plan with a view of adopting a certain kind of behaviour. It suffices that they inform each other in advance about the course of conduct they intend to adopt, in such a way that each party will be able to arrange its actions by virtue of its competitors following a parallel behaviour.'

1   See CPC Decision 12/1981 concerning the Association of Chartered Accountants in Greece.
2   With the exceptions provided for in section 5 of this Act.
3   See CC Opinion 29/85 where it was accepted that a distribution agreement between two companies with different legal personalities, where the subsidiary was 80% owned and controlled by the same natural persons who owned and controlled the parent company, did not fall within the scope of section 1.
4   See CC Opinion 24/1985 and CC Opinion 83/1989.
5   See CC Opinion 9/1984.
6   See CPC Decision 14/1981.
7   See CC Opinion 10/1984.
8   See CPC Decision 8/1980.
9   See CPC Decision 4/1980.

The similarity of price lists, for example, was accepted as sufficient proof of a concerted practice.[10] However, by a significant judgment[11] on this matter, the TMACFI stressed the idea that, apart from practical evidence, economic analysis is very important in establishing a concerted practice, as it may reveal that parallel conduct can possibly be explained by the oligopolistic nature of the market rather than the mental consensus of the parties. In a later Opinion[12] the CC held that the undertakings concerned were not guilty of a concerted practice to delay the execution of their contractual obligations, because their parallel conduct was justified on the similar problems which simultaneously arose in their commercial relations with the other party.

1.2.4   Anti-competitive object or effect

Section 1(1) condemns undertakings which collaborate in order to:[13]

(a)   directly or indirectly fix purchase or selling prices, or any other trading conditions;
(b)   limit or control production, disposal, technical development or investment;
(c)   share markets or sources of supply;
(d)   apply dissimilar trading conditions to equivalent transactions in such a way as to impede effective competition, in particular by unjustifiably refusing to sell, purchase or conclude any other transactions;
(e)   make the conclusion of contracts subject to acceptance by the other parties of supplementary obligations which by their nature or commercial usage have no connection with the subject of such contracts.

However, the above list is not exhaustive. Consequently, any agreement the essence and purpose of which is the restriction, prevention or distortion of competition or which is actually causing an impediment to the competitive process will be caught under section 1(1). An economic, factual and legal analysis is absolutely necessary in this respect and a number of factors must be appraised: definition of the relevant product and geographical market, barriers to entry and the overall structure of the market.[14]

1.2.5   De minimis

There are, however, agreements which will not be caught under this section if they do not actually restrict competition to an appreciable extent.[15] A share of up to 5% of the companies involved in the relevant product market will most probably be an

---

10 See CC Opinion 21/1984.
11 See judgments no 3484/1989 and 3485/1989 of the TMACFI.
12 See CC Opinion 98/1990.
13 The relevant indicative examples are a literal translation of the equivalent examples contained in Article 85(1) of the Treaty of Rome.
14 Unfortunately, there are only a few cases where competition authorities have sufficiently considered this economic and legal environment. See, for example, CPC Decision 15/81 and CC Opinions 102/91 and 109/91.
15 See, for example, CPC Decisions 1/79, 6/80, 15/81, 22/82, and CC Opinions 2/83, 31/85, 34/85, 47/86, 95/90 and 102/91.

efficient indication to this effect.[16] None the less, there are other criteria that should also be assessed and still remain to be determined by the competent authorities.[17]

1.2.6   Section 1(2) – infringing agreements shall be null and void

Section 1(2) declares that 'the agreements or decisions prohibited pursuant to the preceding paragraph shall be absolutely void unless this Act provides otherwise'. This paragraph refers to the civil sanctions in case of breach of section 1(1). In this case the agreement is deemed not to have been concluded; therefore it does not produce any legal effects without any prior decision being necessary to this end, as expressly stated in section 3.

Nevertheless, since the law provides that an individual exemption may be granted, only to duly notified agreements, in accordance with section 1, para 3, it is clear that not all notified agreements and decisions are null and void if they infringe section 1(1). However, in the case of agreements or decisions which are part of a compound contract, the provisions which can be severed from the prohibited ones shall remain valid and enforceable.[18]

1.2.7   Section 1(3) – exemptions

Section 1(3) sets forth the requirements that must be fulfilled cumulatively for prohibited agreements to benefit from individual exemption. In particular, restrictive decisions and agreements may qualify for an exemption in case they:

'(a) contribute to improving the production or distribution of goods or to promoting technical or economic progress, while allowing consumers a fair share of the resulting benefit;

(b) do not impose on the undertakings concerned restrictions beyond those which are absolutely necessary to the attainment of the above objectives;

(c) do not afford such undertakings the possibility of eliminating competition in respect of a substantial part of the relevant market.'

Since it is expressly provided in section 21(2)(a) that failure to notify a decision, agreement or concerted practice precludes the application of this section, it follows that only duly notified agreements will be eligible for an exemption. The Competition Commission has sole power to grant individual exemptions and the relevant decision may be renewed, under certain circumstances, amended or revoked by the same authority (section 10).

It should be noted that before the amendment of the law in 1991, the Minister of Commerce had the exclusive power to issue such decisions. Yet in very few cases[19] did the Minister exempt an agreement from the prohibition of section 1(1). Unfortunately, the relevant case law cannot serve as a guideline as to the policy

---

16 There are, however, cases where the *de minimis* rule was applied without reference to the exact market share, eg CC Opinion 48/86, CC Opinion 49/86 and CC Opinion 100/90.

17 See CC Opinion 102/91 where the Commission held that the firm's small market share which varied from 4.5% to 5.5% in combination with qualitative criteria led to a conclusion that the relevant practices could not appreciably affect competition. However, it did not proceed in further specifying which these criteria can be.

18 See CPC Decisions 1/79, 6/80 and 7/80.

19 In particular, see CC Opinions 10/84, 33/85, 53/87 and 78/89.

that will be followed by the competent authorities in the future, since the decisions and opinions of the competent authorities lack profound economic analysis, sufficient examination of the relevant requirements and are not adequately justified.

1.2.8 Block exemptions

Unlike EC authorities which have issued a number of block exemptions, Greek authorities have not taken any steps to this effect. Only in very few cases was reference made to EC Regulations, in particular when examining exclusive distribution systems.

1.2.9 Negative clearance

Following an application by the undertakings concerned, the competent authorities may certify that on the basis of the information available there is no contravention of sections 1(1), 2 or 2(a). The right to apply for negative clearance is of great practical importance and its abolition by Act 2000/1991 was considered to be most unfortunate. Therefore, it was correctly re-introduced by the latest amendment of the law by Act 2296/1995.

1.2.10 Notification

Greek anti-trust law establishes a general obligation to notify all agreements, decisions or concerted practices of the kind described in section 1(1), without exception. Therefore, it is clear that in cases of agreements which do not involve an infringement of the relevant competition rules, notification is unnecessary when undertakings notify their agreements or decisions, they must also file an application either for negative clearance or for individual exemption.

Sections 20 and 21 of the Act which deal with the notification of existing and new agreements respectively, depending on whether they have been concluded before or after the date of entry into force of the Act, provide that the former must be notified by the participating undertakings to the competent authorities, within four months as from the date of entry into force of Act 703/77 (ie 26 March 1978) and the latter, within 30 days as from the day on which they are concluded, taken or implemented.

Following lawful notification and until the Competition Commission delivers a decision in accordance with section 1(3), the agreements or decisions concerned shall be deemed to be provisionally valid. However, notification does not confer immunity from fines in case there is finally a finding of infringement of the law and this probably discourages undertakings from proceeding with the notification.

Failure to meet the above obligations precludes the application of section 1(3) and threatens the imposition of a fine. Additionally, the notification must, in accordance with section 22, contain all necessary information so that the competent authority may examine each particular case or carry out an inquiry into the business sectors involved or control restrictive practices of undertakings.

1.3   Abuse of market power

1.3.1   *Abuse of a dominant position*

Section 2 of Act 703/77 prohibits the abusive exploitation of a dominant position within the national market as a whole or in part. Like Article 86 of the EEC Treaty, the law does not condemn monopoly power per se but only the abuse of that power. Two elements must be established for section 2 to apply:

(a)   the existence of a dominant position within the national market as a whole or in a part thereof;
(b)   an abuse of the dominant position.

1.3.2   *Definition of dominance*

There are a number of cases where the competent authorities dealt with the definition of this term. In a significant recent Opinion, 109/91, the Competition Commission held that:

> 'an undertaking is in a dominant position when it holds a significant share of the relevant market, its financial strength is much higher than that of its competitors, it significantly affects other similar undertakings related to it at all stages of production and distribution and in conjunction with other factors, is able to determine its commercial behaviour without particularly taking under consideration the position of its competitors or purchasers and impose on its customers conditions which differ from those which would normally exist in a highly competitive market'.

The above Opinion[20] follows another leading Opinion[1] on that matter which marks an important change in relation to the authorities' approach on the establishment of a dominant position. Until then,[2] the definition of market power was mostly,[3] if not solely,[4] related to market shares held by the undertakings concerned in the relevant market, with no consideration to other criteria like barriers to entry, vertical integration, scale of activities etc. Fortunately, the above cases involve an appraisal of the aforementioned factors in the assessment of market power. In particular, in CC Opinion 64/84 account was taken of the fact that the firm's two basic competitors were large companies, perfectly vertically integrated in the market, holding 10% and 25% market share respectively. In addition, the fact that there was a variety of products offered by all these firms and that other undertakings' entry into the market was not impeded, was also considered.

However, since market power does not exist in the abstract, but only in relation

---

20 It should be noted that in this case a rather significant market share of 48% did not lead to a finding of dominance, because the company was open to strong competition from imports of same products, thus not being able to affect market conditions unilaterally.
1 See CC Opinion 64/88.
2 See, for example, CPC Decision 13/81 and CC Opinions 4/83, 9/84, 17/84, 22/84, 28/84, 30/85, 33/85, 38/86, 55/87 and 61/87.
3 See, for example, CC Opinion 28/85 where a market share of 50% to 52%, along with the firm's high annual turnover and technological lead, established its dominant position in the market.
4 See, for example, CC Opinion 3/84 where a rather small share of 30% to 35%, held by the undertaking concerned, in the relevant market, was regarded as sufficient evidence of a dominant position and CC Opinion 22/84, where a very high market share of 85% was considered as a conclusive factor for the establishment of the company's market power.

to a market, the definition of the product, geographical and temporal market is of essential importance. It is rather unfortunate that the basic tests of demand and supply side substitutability have been elaborated very little by the competition authorities. Only in exceptional cases was reference made to physical characteristics and intended use of the products concerned,[5] structure of supply[6] and demand.[7]

Even though the whole of the national territory usually constitutes the relevant geographical market, there were few cases where dominance was examined in relation to parts of Greece.[8]

1.3.3 Collective dominance

As already accepted in the case law of the Commission and the European Court of Justice, a dominant position can also be held by two or more undertakings jointly, the conduct of which may be consequently examined under this section. The Competition Commission has for the first time established the existence of a collective dominant position held by five undertakings, in Opinion 56/87.[9]

1.3.4 Abuse of economic dependence

Section 2(a) deals with another concept, which is similarly regulated by German and French anti-trust legislation and was introduced by Act 1934/1991 and slightly amended by Act 2296/1995. In particular, it provides that:

'Any abuse by one or more undertakings of a position whereby other undertakings, being buyers or suppliers of goods or services, are economically dependent on them and have no equivalent alternative solutions, is prohibited. Such an abusive exploitation of the position of economic dependence may in particular consist in imposing arbitrary trading conditions or in abruptly and unjustifiably terminating long-standing commercial relations.'

Interesting debate was actually developed as to the necessity and effectiveness of establishing this prohibition since a dilative interpretation of section 2(1), like the one followed by the EC authorities, could control the abusive behavior of undertakings which have become unavoidable trading partners for other companies which have no equivalent alternative solutions.

1.3.5 Abuse

Similar to Article 86 of the EEC Treaty, section 2 provides a non-exhaustive list of conduct which is prohibited as abusive:

'(a) directly or indirectly imposing fixed purchase or selling prices or other unfair trading conditions;
 (b) limiting production, consumption or technical development to the prejudice of consumers;

---

5 See CC Opinions 59/87 and 64/88.
6 See CC Opinion 109/91.
7 See CPC Decision 15/1981.
8 See, for example, CPC Decisions 1/83 and 24/82, where the geographical market was held to be Northern Greece and a Greek island respectively.
9 See also CC Opinion 76/89.

(c)   applying dissimilar conditions to equivalent transactions, in particular by unjustifiably refusing to sell, purchase or conclude any other transactions, thereby placing certain undertakings at a competitive disadvantage;

(d)   making the conclusion of contracts subject to acceptance by the other parties of supplementary obligations or to conclusion of supplementary contracts, which by their nature or according to commercial usage, have no connection with the subject of such contracts'.

In a number of cases that have arisen during 18 years of the application of the law, conduct held to be abusive was mostly related to pricing policies (eg, unfair and predatory prices), refusal to supply, rebates (eg, discriminatory discounts, fidelity rebates) and mergers and takeovers.

2   ENFORCEMENT

2.1   Enforcement authorities

2.1.1   For many years, the insufficient performance of the competent authorities has been considered as one of the major drawbacks of the enforcement of the law. Most of the relevant Decisions and Opinions have, for example, been heavily criticised for lacking sufficient economic analysis which is quite fundamental in anti-trust law cases. The essence of this problem was mainly linked to two factors: first, competition law is a rather technical subject which is comprised of complex legal and economic elements. Therefore, the institutions entrusted with its application should have been constituted by members with adequate knowledge and experience on the relevant matters, which was not always the case. Second, the establishment and organisation of the above administrative bodies within the Ministry of Commerce resulted in them being subjected to pressure exercised by the Minister.

The above considerations were taken into account in drafting the last amendment of the law, which consequently introduced some rather radical and positive changes in the institutional field.

2.1.2   *The Competition Commission*

This independent administrative body is the authority entrusted with the enforcement of the law and has the following exclusive powers:

(a)   to decide, at first instance, on infringements of sections 1, para 1, 2 and 2(a) of the law;

(b)   to decide on all matters related to concentrations of undertakings, in accordance with section 4 to 4(f);

(c)   to prohibit the implementation of concentrations of undertakings when they may significantly impede competition;

(d)   to decide on the applications for the issue of negative clearances;

(e)   to order interim measures provided that specific conditions are fulfilled;

(f)   to give opinions on all matters related to competition law;

(g)   to impose fines and other pecuniary sanctions provided by law.

In case of breach of sections 1, para 1, 2 and 2(a) it may proceed with the following measures towards the offending undertakings:

(a) address a recommendation to bring the infringement to an end;
(b) order the above undertakings to terminate the violation and refrain from repeating it in the future;
(c) threaten to impose a fine and/or a penalty in case of continuation or repetition of the transgression; and
(d) impose a fine and/or penalty on the above undertakings.

The Competition Commission is supported in the execution of the powers vested on it, by its Secretariat. The organisation and all matters related to the Secretariat will be regulated by Presidential Decree.

2.1.3   The Minister of Commerce

Following the last amendment of the law, the Minister of Commerce has very limited powers with respect to competition law cases. In particular, he is competent to permit, along with the Minister of National Economy and under certain conditions, a concentration prohibited by a decision of the Competition Commission (see section 4.6.2 below). He is also empowered to issue Ministerial Decisions excluding categories of agreements from the application of the law (block exemptions), following the concurrent opinion of the Competition Commission.

2.1.4   The Administrative Court of Appeal

In accordance with section 14, an appeal can be filed against the decisions delivered by the above authorities (see section 2.5.1 below).

2.1.5   The Council of State

Finally, a further appeal requesting revocation of the judgments issued by the Administrative Court of Appeal will be heard before the Council of State.

2.2   Procedural rules

2.2.1   Initiation of proceedings

An investigation can be triggered: (a) following a complaint, that can be filed by any natural or legal person, alleging infringement of sections 1(1), 2, and 2(a); (b) upon the Competition Commission's own initiative, and (c) at the request of the Minister of Commerce.

In accordance with section 8, para 14, any person who submitted a request or complaint under this Act must, upon a 30 days' advance notice, be present at the hearings before the Competition Commission related to his case, either in person or through his lawyer. The same rule shall apply to undertakings and associations of undertakings, against which proceedings have been instituted before the Competition Commission and upon a 30 days' notice in advance.

2.2.2   Time limits for decisions

In accordance with section 24, para 4, the Competition Commission must deliver its decision on the relevant complaints within six months of their filing. In exceptional cases and when further investigation should be conducted, the above time limits may be extended by two months.

2.2.3   Collecting information

Section 25 states that the Chairman of the Competition Commission or any official of the Secretariat appointed by him, may obtain information concerning the application of Act 703/77 by sending a written request to undertakings, associations of undertakings or other natural or legal persons, to public or other authorities. It further provides the sanctions to be imposed in case of delay, refusal or obstruction in supplying the information requested, ie fines[10] of up to 3,000,000 drachmae for each person liable for these offences and probable initiation of disciplinary proceedings against the civil servants or officials of public undertakings which have violated the above obligations.

2.2.4   Conduct of investigations

The powers that can be exercised by the Competition Commission when carrying out an investigation in the relevant cases, are regulated in section 26. In particular, the authorised officials of the Commission's Secretariat, having the powers of a tax inspector, may:

(a)   examine the books of any kind whatsoever, the business records or other documents of the undertakings concerned and take copies of, or extracts therefrom;

(b)   conduct investigations into their offices and other premises;

(c)   carry out domiciliary investigations, provided that section 9 of the Constitution is observed; and

(d)   take sworn or unsworn statements at their discretion.

Following the conclusion of the investigation, a report, which will be served on the undertakings concerned, is prepared.

2.3   Fines and other sanctions

2.3.1   Fines

Fines that are threatened or actually imposed[11] on the offending undertaking in the case of violation of sections 1(1), 2 and 2(a) of the present Act, may amount up to 15% of the gross income of the undertakings that committed the infringement, by reference to the year that this was committed or to the preceding year. The gravity and the duration of the violation under consideration shall be taken into account when imposing the relevant fines.

Failure to observe the obligation to notify all restrictive agreements in accordance with sections 20 and 21, may also result to the imposition of a fine. In particular, failure to notify existing agreements may result in a fine of 100,000 to

10 See CPC Decision 6/80.
11 See, for example, CPC Decisions 1/73 and 7/80 and CC Opinions 28/85 and 50/86.

200,000 drachmae, and failure to notify new agreements may result in a fine varying from 3,000,000 drachmae to 10% of the gross income of the undertakings that
committed the infringement, by reference to the year that this was committed or to
the preceding year. Finally in respect of fines provided for in case of violation of
the provisions relating to concentrations see section 4.9.

2.3.2   Penal sanctions

Section 29 describes the circumstances under which a pecuniary penalty varying
from 1,000,000 to 5,000,000 drachmae will be imposed on the natural persons
who, in accordance with section 30, are liable for observing the provisions of sections 1(1), 2 and 2(a) (eg, the administrator(s) in the case of a limited liability
company, and the members of the Board of Directors in the case of a societe
anonyme). The above penalties may be doubled in case of repetition of the violation in question.

Section 29 also provides for the imposition of pecuniary and even custodial
penalties in case of other infringements related to the investigations conducted by
the com-petent authorities.

2.4   Third party rights

2.4.1   A third party alleging a violation of the provisions of the law may choose to
proceed to the following actions:

(a)   he may file a relevant complaint with the Competition Commission;
(b)   following the filing of the said complaint, he may also request the
       Commission to order interim measures;
(c)   lodge an application with the competent ordinary civil courts requesting an
       award of damages.

2.4.2   Complaints

Section 24 provides that 'every natural or legal person may file a complaint alleging an infringement of sections 1(1) and 2'. It must be noted that the legitimate
interest of the complainant is not a prerequisite for filing a complaint. (For the procedure which will subsequently be followed see section 2.2.1.)

2.4.3   Interim measures

Following the last amendment of the law and in accordance with section 9, para 4,
the Competition Commission has sole power to order interim measures upon its
own initiative, following the application of any person who has lodged a complaint
under section 24 (or following an application by the Minister of Commerce),
where:

'(a)   an infringement of sections 1, 2 and 2a of the present Act is thought likely to occur,
       and
  (b)   it is extremely urgent to prevent a direct danger of irrecoverable damage being suf-
       fered by the applicant or being caused to the public interest.'

2.4.4   *An action for damages*

This could be held admissible on the basis of section 914 of the Greek Civil Code, since any transgression of the provisions of Act 703/77 constitutes an illegal act, provided that:

(a)   an illegal act is proved to have been negligently or intentionally committed by a natural or legal person;
(b)   this specific act directly damaged another natural or legal person; and
(c)   a causal link is established between wrongdoing and damage.

If all these conditions are fulfilled, the undertakings and associations of undertakings which violated sections 1(1), 2 and 2(a) of the present Act will be liable for compensation.

2.5   Judicial protection

2.5.1   As already mentioned, an appeal can be filed before the Athens Administrative Court of Appeal, against the decisions issued by the Competition Commission in cases of prohibited restrictive agreements and abuses of a dominant position, within 20 days from the notification thereof. However, this action does not suspend the enforcement of the Competition Commission's decisions, unless the President of the Court decides to the contrary, following a petition by the interested party and provided sufficient grounds exist.

2.5.2   Litigants that were parties to the said procedure may seek revocation of the Court's judgment by lodging a further appeal before the Council of State.

2.5.3   Cases before the above administrative courts shall be tried in accordance with the provisions of the Code of Fiscal Procedure (save where it is otherwise provided or regulated in Act 703/77).

3   CHECKLIST OF POTENTIAL INFRINGEMENTS

3.1   Introduction

From 1977 when Act 703/77 was adopted, the institutions entrusted with its enforcement dealt with a number of practices which impeded competition. However, by reviewing the relevant decisions and opinions, one could come to the disappointing conclusion that the factual and legal analysis of competition cases is woefully inadequate. Consequently, the elaboration of the concepts and elements involved, which is most of the time very poor, can not be used as a satisfactory guideline. As a result, practitioners engaged in the defence of anti-trust law cases, often face difficulties while advising their clients accordingly. Therefore, commentators have argued that more dynamic enforcement of anti-trust legislation is absolutely necessary as well as the formation of a reasonable competition policy in conformity with the interpretative lines and objectives determined by the European Commission and the European Court of Justice.

3.2 Agency

3.2.1 The main issue in relation to agency agreements is whether they could be considered as agreements between two undertakings for the purposes of competition law. The question was basically examined by the competent authorities in four, almost identical cases, namely CC Opinions 79/89, 88/90, 89/90, and 90/90.[12]

The relevant facts were similar, ie on the one hand the agent was acting in his own name but on behalf of the principal, in accordance with the latter's instructions, being paid a commission for the business he transacted and on the other hand the principal was bearing the financial risk for the relevant transactions and still possessed the title of the goods in question.

The Competition Commission stated correctly that reference can be made to section 1(1) only if the undertakings which are parties to an agreement were economically and administratively independent. However, it further held that the specific activities examined, were clearly separated from other activities carried on by the agent, who consequently was not deprived of his qualification as an independent trader. Therefore, it concluded that the compatibility of the agreements in question with competition law should be examined.

3.2.2 Although the outcome of these cases is rather contestable, they emphasise the degree of economic independence enjoyed by the agent in the context of the particular agency, thus following, in this respect, EC competition law.

3.3 Distribution

Dealing through commercial agents is therefore distinguished from a distribution agreement in that an agent basically negotiates business and enters into transactions in the name of, and on behalf of the producer or the supplier. Distribution agreements are a very common type of vertical restraint in Greek practice. Quite often they have been permitted by the competent authorities, since they were considered rather to enhance the competitive process in the market than obstruct it. Nevertheless, there are certain clauses which will certainly be held inadmissible, in particular when they confer absolute territorial protection or when they eliminate price competition.

3.4 Exclusive distribution

3.4.1 In some cases,[13] exclusive dealing agreements have been examined on the basis of the principles of Regulation 1983/83. Therefore, restrictions as to the conferring of absolute territorial protection will certainly fall within the prohibition of section 1(1) and will not qualify for an individual exemption.

3.4.2 In CC Opinion 39/86 a condition in the exclusive distributorship contract, prohibiting the distributor from selling, actively or passively, to other parties fell within section 1(1), even though it could not be established, on the merits of the case, that this contract could affect competition to an appreciable extent.

---

12 See also CC Opinion 19/84.
13 See, for example, CC Opinions 39/86, 50/87, 63/88 and 78/89.

3.5   Selective distribution

3.5.1   There are quite a number of selective distribution systems which have been examined by the competent institutions,[14] following a request by the interested parties for the issue of negative clearance. Sometimes the relevant agreements were allowed as such, or following modification of specific clauses contained therein, but in other, fewer, cases they were condemned.

3.5.2   After a review of the relevant decision practice of the Commission, it follows that the principle established by the European Court of Justice in the *Metro* cases is basically applied; therefore, the distinction between qualitative and quantitative criteria is essential to the question of whether a condition imposed on the distributor will be prohibited or not. In Opinion 96/90, the Competition Commission stated that:

> 'selective distribution systems do not fall within the ambit of section 1 para 1 if the retailers are chosen on the basis of objective criteria, related to the sufficiency of the retailer or its staff and premises, under the condition that they are laid down uniformly for all potential resellers and are not applied in a discriminatory fashion'.

An indispensable prerequisite is, of course, that the product in question qualifies for a selective distribution system.

Obligations to have specialised departments and employ trained staff, to keep stock of the products concerned, to preserve their quality standards and maintain their reputation, to display them adequately and appropriately, were occasionally held admissible. However, some Opinions applied a very significant rule, ie that, even though certain terms and conditions do not restrict competition, in the first place, they can cause such an effect when they are imposed on the same reseller, by several suppliers, for the sale of similar products. For example, an obligation to participate in the advertisement of the products concerned could restrict the distributor's freedom to deal with other products, if he had to observe the same condition in the context of another contract.

3.6   Franchising

Franchising agreements enable the franchisee to use the name and know-how of the franchisor, but still operate as an independent business. However, they were examined only cursorily by the competent authorities. Consequently, one could hardly say how relevant cases will be dealt in the future and which conditions will be considered incompatible with anti-trust law. Most probably, they will be decided by reference to the principles laid down in Regulation 4087/88.

3.7   Refusals to supply

Refusals to supply have also been examined by the competent authorities[15] in the context of abusive exploitation of dominant firms' market power. However, if an

---

14 See for example CPC Decisions 1/79 and 6/80 as well as CC Opinions 36/86, 41/86, 42/86, 48/86, 54/87, 60/88, 61/88, 79/89, 84/89 and 94/90. In most of these cases the relevant products were perfumes and cosmetics, clothes and, in two of them, cement.
15 See, for example, CPC Decision 7/80 and CC Opinions 77/89, 82/89 and 98/90.

objective justification (eg, shortage of stock, insolvent customer, compulsory legal obligations[16]) can be invoked and proved by the offending companies, the conduct in question shall not be condemned.

3.8 Price restrictions

3.8.1 *Price fixing* will be examined by the competent authorities in the context of an agreement,[17] as a practice,[18] as well as an abuse of a dominant position. In all cases they constitute a serious violation of competition law. Even recommended price lists, when they are nevertheless observed in practice by the parties concerned, will most probably not be permitted.[19]

However, there are still very few cases where the state still fixes selling prices in relation to certain products. In these cases, agreements which involve such price restrictions will be allowed, by virtue of section 36 (see section 5.3 below), even though they prevent competition.

3.8.2 *Predatory prices* were examined in a case concerning the sale of batteries in Greece. Two Opinions were accordingly issued by the Competition Commission,[20] but they were both annulled by the Minister of Commerce's decision K6-175/29, where it was stated that an undertaking would not be condemned for abusing its dominant position when selling at average total cost.

3.9 Tie in sales

3.9.1 As already mentioned, section 1(1)(e) explicitly prohibits the conclusion of contracts subject to acceptance by the other parties of supplementary obligations, which by their nature, or according to commercial usage, have no connection with the subject of such contracts.[1] Therefore, cases where, for example, a supplier would request its customers to purchase a specific product thereby permitting them to buy another one, would normally fall under this prohibition.

3.9.2 Tie in conditions can potentially constitute an infringement of section 2 of this Act, when imposed by undertakings which hold a dominant position in the market and cannot be objectively justified.

3.10 Market sharing

In Decision 1/79, the Commission for the Protection of Competition held that agreements containing clauses which prohibit exports and parallel imports of

---

16 See CC Opinions 82/89, where refusal to supply certain pharmaceutical products was not condemned, because a relevant obligation was imposed on the undertakings concerned by law.
17 See, for example, CC Opinion 97/1990, where it was held that fixed selling prices have the effect of harming the consumer, since he does not have much choice of buying at lower prices. Other similar restrictions were examined in CPC Decisions 1/79 and 19/82 and CC Opinions 4/83, 50/86, 47/86 and 63/88.
18 See CC Decision 145/12/22–7–1994.
19 See, for example, CC Opinion 83/89.
20 See CC Opinions 17/ and 18/89.
 1 The leading CC Opinion on tie ins is 56/87 which examined the distribution of fuel-oil by petrol stations in the national territory.

products have the effect of sharing markets or sources of supply. Therefore, if they can not qualify for an individual exemption, such agreements will normally fall under section 1(1)(c).

4   CONCENTRATIONS, MERGERS AND ACQUISITIONS

4.1   Introduction

4.1.1   Until 1991, concentrations were not extensively regulated and section 4 contained only the basic principle that a merger of undertakings shall not, as such, fall within the prohibition of section 1, para 1. A merger could, for the purpose of the law, consist in the establishment of a new undertaking, the absorption of one or more undertakings by another or the buying off of one or more undertakings by another. In the above cases the agreements and contracts in question were subject to notification.

4.1.2   Competition authorities have occasionally dealt with mergers in the context of section 2 of Act 703.[2] In some cases the takeover of a company by an undertaking holding a dominant position, was actually considered to constitute an abusive exploitation of its market power.[3]

4.1.3   However, as already mentioned, the relevant regime entirely changed in 1991, when the law was amended by Act 1934/1991, so that merger control could be regulated in some harmony with the corresponding provisions of Regulation 4064/89. Nevertheless, certain adaptations were then made, in order to fit the special features of a purely domestic market. These adaptations were somewhat disputable and the relevant legal framework was proved to be ineffective. Therefore, by the last amendment of Act 703/77 the merger control regime was substantially modified in conformity with all the basic rules governing the EC merger control regime, the most important change being the prior notification procedure. Nevertheless, the basic principle that concentrations of undertakings do not per se fall within the ambit of the law, remains intact.

4.2   Definition of concentration

4.2.1   Section 4 provides that a concentration shall be deemed to arise when:

'(a)   two or more undertakings of any form merge, in any way whatsoever;
(b)   one or more persons already controlling at least one undertaking, or one or more undertakings, acquire direct or indirect control of the whole or parts of one or more undertakings.'

Therefore, two cases will fall within the scope of the law, ie the change in control over one or more undertakings or parts thereof and a merger between undertakings.

2 See, for example, CC Opinions 55/87, 64/88 and 109/91.
3 See CC Opinion 101/90.

4.2.2 Undertaking

It is most likely that this concept will be interpreted by the Competition Commission in the same way as in the cases of infringement of sections 1(1) and 2, thus excluding from the application of the law concentrations between legal entities which do not carry on a commercial activity, unless the persons or the companies concerned already control at least one or more other undertakings.

4.2.3 Control

In accordance with section 4, para 3 control shall be constituted:

'by rights, contracts, or any other means which, either separately or in combination and having regard to the consideration of fact or law involved, confer the possibility of exercising decisive influence on an undertaking, in particular by: (a) ownership or the right to use all or part of the assets of an undertaking; (b) rights or contracts which confer decisive influence on the composition, voting or decisions of the organs of an undertaking'.

4.3 Post notification of concentrations

The law imposes a general obligation to formally notify the Competition Commission of every concentration between undertakings, within a month from their completion where:

(a)   the combined market share in the national market or in a significant part thereof represents at least 10% of the relevant product market; or
(b)   the combined aggregate turnover amounts at least up to the equivalent of ECU 10,000,000 in Greek Drachmae.

The post notification procedure mostly serves statistic purposes.

4.4 Prior notification of concentrations

One of the most significant modifications introduced by Act 2296/1995 was the obligation for prior notification of concentrations meeting certain thresholds. This amendement was hailed with notable satisfaction since, under the previous legal framework, an increasing number of concentrations were implemented in the Greek market without being examined by the competent authorities, even though they could in many cases affect competition significantly.

In accordance with section 4(b) all concentrations must be notified to the Competition Commission within ten working days from whichever of the following events occurs earliest: (i) the conclusion of the agreement, (ii) the announcement of the public bid or of the exchange or (iii) the acquisition of a controlling interest where:

(a)   the combined market share in the national market or a significant part thereof represents at least 25% of the relevant product market; or
(b)   the combined aggregate turnover amounts at least to the equivalent of ECU 50,000,000 in Greek Drachmae and the aggregate turnover of each of at least

two of the participating undertakings is more than the equivalent of ECU 5,000,000 in Greek Drachmae.

4.5 Control of concentrations

4.5.1 Article 4c provides that the Competition Commission may prohibit any concentration of undertakings, subject to prior notification, which may significantly impede competition in the relevant national market or a significant part of it, particularly by creating or strengthening a dominant position.

In accordance with section 4(c)(2), in making the appraisal of whether or not competition is significantly impeded, the Commission shall take into account, among other things, the structure of all the markets concerned, the actual or potential competition from undertakings located within or outside Greece, any legal or factual barriers to entry, the market position of the undertakings concerned and their economic and financial power, the alternatives available to suppliers and users, the interests of the intermediate and ultimate consumers. The technical and economic progress shall also be considered, provided that it is to the consumers' advantage and does not form an obstacle to competition.

4.5.2 Nevertheless, section 4(c)(3) provides that the Ministers of Commerce and National Economy may allow a concentration which has been prohibited by a decision of the Competition Commission, where its general financial advantages outweigh the restrictions on competition that may be caused, or where the concentration is found to be essential for the public interest.

4.6 Procedure for the preliminary control of concentrations

4.6.1 In accordance with section 4(d), the Competition Commission examines the concentration as soon as notification is received. Within one month after the above notification, one of the following may occur depending on whether the concentration under consideration falls within the ambit of section 4(b) or not. In particular:

(a) should the Commission decide on the above question in the negative, ie that the concentration does not fall within the ambit of section 4(b), it issues a relevant decision which is notified to the undertakings concerned;

(b) should it conclude that the concentration falls within the ambit of the above section, the case is introduced for a hearing before the Commission, the interested parties being informed accordingly.

Within two months from the introduction of the case before it, the Competition Commission will deliver its decision on whether or not the concentration under consideration significantly impedes free competition. In particular:

(a) if the Commission finds that after certain amendments effected by the participating undertakings, the concentration in question may not impede free competition significantly, it issues a relevant decision which may also set conditions and obligations intended to ensure that the undertakings concerned will abide by the commitments they have undertaken vis-a-vis the Commission concerning the above amendments;

(b) if the Commission concludes that the notified concentration may significantly impede free competition, it issues a decision prohibiting the implementation of said concentration.

4.6.2   Nevertheless, following an application of the undertakings concerned, the Ministers of National Economy and Commerce may allow the concentration prohibited by the Competition Commission (see section 4.5.2). The Ministers' decision may set conditions and obligations intended to ensure conditions of effective competition in the market or the actual achievement of the advantages outweighing the restrictions on competition caused by the concentration in question.

4.7   Suspension of concentrations

4.7.1   No concentration of undertakings should be implemented before the Competition Commission issues one of the above decisions. However, the Competition Commission may, on request, grant a derogation from the above obligation, in order to prevent serious damage to one or more undertakings concerned by a concentration or to a third party. This derogation may set conditions and obligations in order to ensure conditions of effective competition.

4.7.2   Where a concentration has already been implemented despite the provisions of the law or the decisions prohibiting its implementation, the Competition Commission may by decision require the undertakings involved or assets brought together to be separated or the cessation of joint control or any other action that may be appropriate in order to restore conditions of effective competition.

4.8   Calculation of market shares and aggregate turnover

4.8.1   Section 4(e) contains specific rules for the calculation of shares and turnovers. Therefore, where in the relevant sections reference is made to shares of participation, these shall comprise all market shares held by the participating undertakings, in the national market or the part of it related to the concentration.

4.8.2   Where reference is made to the aggregate turnover, this shall comprise the amounts derived from the sale of products and the provision of services falling within the undertakings' ordinary activities, in the preceding financial year, before deduction of relevant taxes.

4.8.3   Special provisions are also included for certain categories of undertakings (eg, in the case of credit institutions and other financial institutions in place of turnover that one-tenth of the total assets shall be used).

4.9   Fines

In case of infringements of the provisions regulating concentrations, the Competition Commission may impose the following fines:

(a)   in case of intentional failure to notify a concentration subject to post notification, a fine of up to 5% of the aggregate turnover of the undertakings concerned;

(b)   in case of intentional failure to notify a concentration subject to the prior notification procedure, a fine of up to 7% of the aggregate turnover of the undertakings concerned;

(c)   in case of failure to comply with the obligation to suspend the implementation of a concentration subject to prior notification until the issue of a decision by the Commission, a fine of up to 15% of the aggregate turnover of the undertakings concerned;

(d)   in case of failure to comply with the decision referred to in section 4.7.2 above, a fine of up to 15% of the aggregate turnover of the undertakings concerned.

4.10   Judicial review

All decisions taken by the Competition Commission and the Ministers of Commerce and National Economy in relation to concentrations can be the subject of an appeal before the Athens Administrative Court of Appeal, within 20 days from their notification. Parties who are litigants to the above cases, may seek revocation of the Court's judgment, by filing a further appeal before the Council of State.

5   EXEMPTIONS AND SPECIAL REGULATIONS

5.1   Categories of public undertakings

In accordance with section 5 of Act 703/77 anti-trust legislation shall also apply to public undertakings or to undertakings serving the public interest. However, market behaviour of certain categories of undertakings may escape the enforcement of the law, following the issue of relevant Decisions by the competent Ministers in each case, after an Opinion has been delivered by the Competition Commission in this respect. In particular, the exempted companies may be engaged in the production, processing, transformation or marketing of agricultural and livestock products, forestry or fishery products or may be involved in sea and air transport markets. Certain categories of undertakings engaged in the defence industry, the oil and agricultural market and in the provision of electricity services, were considered eligible for exemption by the Competition Commission.

5.2   Restrictive practices relating to exports

A specific provision is contained in section 6, where it is stated that, without prejudice to the country's international obligations, the provisions of the present Act shall not apply to agreements, decisions and concerted practices whose exclusive aim is to safeguard, promote or strengthen exports, unless the Ministers of National Economy and Commerce decide otherwise with regard to certain categories of undertakings or products.

5.3   Compulsory restrictive practices

Finally, particular reference is made in section 36 of the Act, in accordance with which special regulations which protect the freedom of competition or provide for compulsory agreements between undertakings, shall remain in force. However, since the wording of this section is rather vague, the definition of the relevant elements is still an open question. The leading case on this issue dealt with the compatibility of competition rules with the provisions regulating the selling prices of alcohol. The Competition Commission held[4] that the former should be abolished, but its decision was subsequently overruled by the competent administrative court[5] on the grounds that Act 703/77 does not override specific provisions of Acts not explicitly or implicitly repealed.

4 See CPC Decision 4/80.
5 See judgment 8059/1981 of the Three Member Athens Administrative Court of First Instance.

Ireland

John Meade

Arthur Cox
41 – 45 St Stephen's Green
Dublin 2
Ireland

Tel   ++353 1 676 4661
Fax   ++353 1 668 8906

Ireland

1 THE SUBSTANTIVE IRISH COMPETITION LAW

1.1 Introduction

1.1.1 Competition law in Ireland is contained primarily in the Competition Act 1991 ('CA'). Prior to 1991, the main source of competition law in Ireland had been the Restrictive Practices Acts of 1972 to 1987 ('RPA'). The RPA were limited in their scope and application, the most important aspects being a number of Ministerial Orders which were adopted under the RPA to regulate certain aspects of competition in particular markets, for example, the Restrictive Practices (Groceries) Order of 1987 ('GO'), which was introduced to prohibit, inter alia, below-cost selling in the grocery trade. The RPA, and all the Orders adopted under the RPA with the exception of the GO, were repealed in 1991 with the introduction of the CA.[1] Consequently, Irish competition law is now contained in the CA and the GO.

1.1.2 In addition to the CA and the GO, the Irish courts continue to apply certain competition law-related principles developed at common law under the laws of contract and tort, such as the restraint of trade doctrine and rules on the breach of confidentiality. There is also a limited form of price control in Ireland contained in the Prices Acts, 1958 to 1972 ('PA'). The PA empower the Minister for Enterprise and Employment ('the Minister') to issue Orders setting maximum prices for specified goods. With the introduction of the CA in 1991 all existing Orders lapsed and no Orders are presently in force, although the Minister retains his powers under the PA.

1.2 The Competition Act 1991 ('CA')

1.2.1 General

The CA is based upon EC competition law.[2] In particular, the competition rules which are contained in sections 4 and 5 CA are based upon Articles 85 and 86 of the EEC Treaty, respectively. In interpreting the CA in a number of cases, the Irish Competition Authority[3] has applied by analogy principles developed under EC

---

1 Sections 2(2) and 22 CA and the Competition Act 1991 (Commencement) Order 1991. Following the introduction of the CA on 1 October 1991 there was some debate as to whether these provisions had the effect of retaining the GO in force. However, it was subsequently confirmed in a High Court decision that the GO was still in force (*Masterfoods Ltd (t/a Mars Ireland) v HB Ice Cream Ltd* [1992] 3 CMLR 830, HC).
2 See Chapter I.
3 See section 2.3 below.

competition law.[4] There has been little litigation to date under the CA so it remains to be seen whether the Irish courts will adopt a similar approach, but that would appear likely.[5]

1.2.2   Section 4 – restrictive arrangements

Section 4(1) CA generally prohibits arrangements between undertakings which have the object or effect of restricting competition within Ireland or in any part of Ireland. Section 4(1) CA is based upon Articles 85(1) and 85(2) of the EEC Treaty.[6] Subject to the possibility of severing the restrictive elements of an arrangement which infringe section 4(1) CA,[7] any such arrangement is prohibited and void by virtue of section 4(1) CA unless licensed by the Competition Authority under section 4(2) CA. Section 4(2) CA is based upon Article 85(3) of the EEC Treaty.[8]

1.2.3   Section 4(1)

Section 4(1) CA provides as follows:

'Subject to the provisions of this section, all agreements between undertakings, decisions by associations of undertakings and concerted practices which have as their object or effect the prevention, restriction or distortion of competition in trade in any goods or services in the State or in any part of the State are prohibited and void . . .'

1.2.4   Undertakings

Section 3(1) CA defines an 'undertaking' as follows:

'a person being an individual, a body corporate or an unincorporated body of persons engaged for gain in the production, supply or distribution of goods or the provision of a service.'

The Irish Supreme Court has held that the word 'gain' is not equivalent to the word 'profit' so that the phrase 'engaged for gain' connotes 'merely an activity carried on or a service supplied which is done in return for a charge or payment'.[9]

The Competition Authority has held that an employee is not an undertaking for the purposes of the CA so long as he/she is employed but that where a former employee attempts to set up in business on his/her own they become an undertaking within the meaning of section 3(1) CA.[10] Similarly, individuals who own and

---

4 The preamble to the CA refers, inter alia, to the CA prohibiting 'by analogy with Articles 85 and 86 . . . the prevention, restriction or distortion of competition and the abuse of dominant positions in trade in the State'.

5 See the judgment of Costello J in *Dermot Donovan v Electricity Supply Board* (HC, 5 May 1994), where the judge stated that, in interpreting section 4 CA, the decisions of the European Commission and the European Court of Justice on the construction of Article 85 of the EEC Treaty 'should have very strong persuasive force . . . subject to any qualifications which may arise where the statutory provisions are different from the Treaty provisions.'

6 See Chapter I.

7 Section 4(7) CA.

8 See Chapter I.

9 *Deane v Voluntary Health Insurance Board* (SC, 29 July 1992).

10 Competition Authority Guide to Employment Agreements and the Competition Act (15 September 1992).

control a business are undertakings for the purposes of the CA.[11] The Competition Authority has also held that agreements between companies which form part of the one group do not fall within section 4(1) CA, at least in so far as the companies concerned do not individually determine their own market strategy.[12]

1.2.5 Arrangements

Section 4(1) CA, as it is based on Article 85(1) EEC Treaty, refers not only to agreements but also to decisions by associations of undertakings and concerted practices. Accordingly, the type of restrictive arrangements, including 'gentlemen's agreements', which have been found to constitute infringements of Article 85(1) of the EEC Treaty may also, by analogy, constitute infringements of section 4(1) CA.

1.2.6 The effect upon trade in Ireland

Section 4(1) CA applies where an arrangement has as its object or effect the prevention, restriction or distortion of competition in trade in any goods or services in Ireland or any part of Ireland. By analogy with the approach adopted under Article 85(1) of the EEC Treaty by the EC authorities, this may include arrangements which would have a potential effect on competition within Ireland as well as arrangements which actually affect competition in Ireland. This is the approach which the Competition Authority has adopted in interpreting section 4 CA.[13]

1.2.7 The restriction of competition

Examples are provided in section 4(1) CA of arrangements which infringe section 4(1) CA, namely, arrangements which:

'(a) directly or indirectly fix purchase or selling prices or any other trading conditions;
(b) limit or control production, markets, technical development or investment;
(c) share markets or sources of supply;
(d) apply dissimilar conditions to equivalent transactions with other trading parties thereby placing them at a competitive disadvantage;
(e) make the conclusion of contracts subject to acceptance by the other parties of supplementary obligations which by their nature or according to commercial usage have no connection with the subject of such contracts.'

1.2.8 De minimis

In order for Article 85(1) of the EEC Treaty to apply there must be an 'appreciable' restriction of competition so that restrictive arrangements which are *de minimis* in their effects fall outside the scope of Article 85(1) of the EEC Treaty. No such *de minimis* exception has been written into Section 4(1) CA. Furthermore, the Competition Authority has interpreted section 4(1) CA broadly and would appear opposed to a *de minimis* rule.[14] The Irish courts have yet to consider the issue.

11 See, for example, the decision of the Competition Authority in *ACT Group plc / Kindle Group Ltd* (Decision No 8 of 4 September 1992).
12 Competition Authority decision in *AGF / Irish Life Holdings plc* (Decision No 2 of 14 May 1992).
13 *Nallen / O'Toole* (Decision No 1 of 2 April 1992).
14 See, for example, the decision of the Competition Authority in *Nallen / O'Toole* (section 1.2.6 above).

1.2.9 General approach

Arrangements which infringe section 4(1) CA are prohibited and void unless licensed under section 4(2) CA. The Competition Authority has stated that in interpreting section 4(1) CA it will apply a 'rule of reason',[15] in other words, restrictions which are reasonable and ultimately benefit competition will not be taken to infringe section 4(1) CA. Such an approach would lessen the need to obtain licences under section 4(2) CA. It remains to be seen what approach will be adopted by the Irish courts in interpreting section 4(1) CA.

1.2.10 Section 4(2) licences

In general terms, section 4(2) CA, which is based on Article 85(3) of the EEC Treaty, provides that the Competition Authority may grant a licence in respect of an arrangement which, though restrictive of competition within the meaning of section 4(1) CA, benefits competition overall. Specifically, the Competition Authority may grant a licence under section 4(2) in respect of an arrangement:

'which in the opinion of the Authority, having regard to all relevant market conditions, contributes to improving the production or distribution of goods or provision of services or to promoting technical or economic progress, while allowing consumers a fair share of the resulting benefit and which does not –

(i)   impose on the undertakings concerned terms which are not indispensable to the attainment of those objectives;

(ii) afford undertakings the possibility of eliminating competition in respect of a substantial part of the products or services in question.'

Two types of licence may be granted, namely, an individual licence or a category licence.

1.2.11 Individual licences

In order to benefit from an individual licence an arrangement must be notified to the Competition Authority.[16] If the Competition Authority is of the opinion that the arrangement, or aspects of the arrangement, give rise to the application of section 4(1) CA but that the arrangement satisfies the conditions of section 4(2) CA, the Competition Authority may grant a licence permitting the arrangement. An individual licence is granted for a specified period and may be subject to conditions.[17]

---

15 Competition Authority Notice in respect of Shopping Centre Leases (2 September 1993).
16 Section 7(1) CA. Arrangements which were in existence at the commencement of the CA on 1 October 1991, and in respect of which the parties sought a licence (or a certificate – see section 1.2.13 below) were to be notified to the Competition Authority before 1 October 1992 – section 7(2) CA. The Competition Authority considers that such arrangements cannot be notified to the Competition Authority subsequent to 1 October 1992. If such arrangements were notified before that date, court proceedings cannot be taken on the basis of section 4(1) CA in respect of the arrangements involved until the Competition Authority has decided whether to grant or refuse to grant a licence or a certificate or until any appeal to the High Court from any such decision has been concluded – section 6(7) CA.
17 Section 8(1) CA.

1.2.12 Category licences

Section 4(2) CA provides the Competition Authority with the power to adopt what are termed 'category licences' in relation to categories of agreements which the Competition Authority regards as generally falling within section 4(1) CA but satisfying the conditions of section 4(2) CA. A category licence under the CA is the equivalent of a 'block' or 'group' exemption under EC competition law.[18] The effect of an arrangement falling within a category licence is that the arrangement is automatically licensed without the need individually to notify the arrangement to the Competition Authority.

To date, the Competition Authority has adopted four category licences, namely, a category licence concerning the exclusive purchasing of motor fuels,[19] which is modelled on EC block exemption Regulation 1984/83 in so far as that Regulation relates to exclusive purchasing agreements with service stations, a category licence on exclusive distribution agreements,[20] which is based on EC block exemption Regulation 1983/83 on exclusive distribution agreements, a category licence for agreements concerning the exclusive purchasing of cylinder liquified petroleum gas[1] and a category licence for franchise agreements,[2] which is modelled on EC block exemption Regulation 4087/88 on franchise agreements. It is anticipated that the Competition Authority will, in time, adopt further category licences based on analogous EC block exemption Regulations.

1.2.13 Certificates

On notification of an arrangement to the Competition Authority, the parties can also request the Competition Authority to certify that the arrangement concerned does not fall within section 4(1) CA. A certificate is the equivalent of a negative clearance for the purposes of Article 85(1) EEC Treaty,[3] and is granted under section 4(4) CA. Normally, parties to notified arrangements apply to the Competition Authority for a certificate and a licence in the alternative. As with individual licences, a certificate may only be granted following notification.[4] However, a bill has been published[5] which, if adopted, would empower the Competition Authority to grant what would be termed 'category certificates' which would ensure that an arrangement within a category certificate would be taken not to infringe section 4(1) CA without the need to notify the arrangement in question to the Competition Authority.[6]

1.2.14 Section 5 – abuse of a dominant position

Section 5(1) CA prohibits the abuse of a dominant position in Ireland or in a substantial part of Ireland. Section 5(1) CA is based upon Article 86 of the EEC

---

18 See Chapter I.
19 *Motor Fuels Category Licence* (Decision No 25 of 1 July 1993).
20 *Licence for Categories of Exclusive Distribution Agreements* (Decision No 144 of 5 November 1993).
1 *Cylinder LPG Category Licence* (Decision No 364 of 28 October 1994). This only permits exclusive purchasing obligations of a maximum of two years whereas EC Block Exemption Regulation 1984/83 would permit a maximum of five years.
2 *Category Licence for Franchise Agreements* (Decision No 372 of 17 November 1994).
3 See chapter I.
4 See section 1.2.11 above.
5 The Competition (Amendment) Bill 1994 (9 June 1994) ('the Bill').
6 Section 3 of the Bill.

Treaty.[7] Any abuse of a dominant position is prohibited – there are no approval procedures in relation to section 5(1) CA.

1.2.15   Section 5(1)

Section 5(1) CA provides as follows:

'Any abuse by one or more undertakings of a dominant position in trade for any goods or services in the State or in a substantial part of the State is prohibited.'

Accordingly, in order to establish an infringement of section 5(1) CA, it is necessary to establish:

(a)   the existence of a dominant position in goods or services in Ireland or in a substantial part of Ireland;

(b)   an abuse of that dominant position.

1.2.16   Dominant position

The term 'dominant position' is not defined in the CA and there has been little interpretation of the term to date. However, as section 5(1) CA is based on Article 86 of the EEC Treaty, the general principle developed by the European Commission and the European Court of Justice under Article 86 of the EEC Treaty, namely, that dominance involves the power to behave to an appreciable extent independently of competitors, customers and consumers,[8] may be applied by analogy by the Irish authorities under section 5(1) CA.[9]

1.2.17   In order to consider whether a company has a dominant position it is important to establish the relevant market within which the company operates, both in terms of the relevant product market and the relevant geographic market. In determining the relevant product market it is important to consider the extent to which different products are considered to be substitutes for each other, and, therefore, part of the same product market,[10] whilst the geographical market tends to be the market in which the companies involved operate.[11] A company which has a high market share in relation to its competitors in a distinct product and geographic market is likely to be considered as dominant in that market as its market share may give it considerable market power. However, market share is not the only factor to be taken into consideration; factors such as barriers to entry to the market and the possibility of supplies from overseas are also relevant.[12]

---

7   See Chapter I.

8   See Chapter I.

9   See judgment of Keane J in *Callinan v Voluntary Health Insurance Board* (HC, 22 April 1993).

10 See, for example, the Competition Authority's decision in *Irish Distillers Group plc/Cooley Distillery plc* (Decision No 285 of 25 February 1994).

11 See, for example, *Dairygold Trading Ltd / Suttons Ltd* (Competition Authority Decision No 347 of 1 July 1994).

12 See *Irish Distillers Group plc/Cooley Distillery plc* (Decision No 285 of 25 February 1994 and the Competition Authority Interim Report of the Study on the Newspaper Industry (30 March 1995)).

1.2.18   Abuse

Section 5(2) CA sets out a non-exhaustive list of examples of conduct which is regarded as abusive, namely:

'(a)   directly or indirectly imposing unfair purchase or selling prices or other unfair trading conditions;
(b)   limiting production, markets or technical development to the prejudice of consumers;
(c)   applying dissimilar conditions to equivalent transactions with other trading parties, thereby placing them at a competitive disadvantage;
(d)   making the conclusion of contracts subject to the acceptance by other parties of supplementary obligations which by their nature or according to commercial usage have no connection with the subject of such contracts.'

Apart from the examples set out in section 5(2) CA, conduct which has been held to constitute an abuse of a dominant position for the purposes of Article 86 of the EEC Treaty may also, by analogy, be considered as an abuse of a dominant position for the purposes of section 5(1) CA.

1.2.19   Certificates

Unlike the situation under EC competition law, where it is possible to notify an arrangement to the European Commission in order for the European Commission to confirm, by issuing a negative clearance, that certain conduct does not constitute an infringement of Article 86 of the EEC Treaty, it is not possible to notify the Competition Authority under the CA to seek the Competition Authority's confirmation that a particular course of conduct would not infringe section 5(1) CA. Certificates may only be issued in relation to section 4(1) CA.

1.3   The Restrictive Practices (Groceries) Order 1987 ('GO')

1.3.1   The GO regulates certain aspects of competition in grocery goods in Ireland. For the purposes of the GO, 'grocery goods' are defined as follows:

'goods for human consumption (excluding fresh fruit, fresh vegetables, fresh and frozen meat, fresh fish and frozen fish which has undergone no processing other than freezing with or without the addition of preservatives) and intoxicating liquors not for consumption on the premises and such household necessaries (other than foodstuffs) as are ordinarily sold in grocery shops, including grocery goods designated as "own-label".'[13]

1.3.2   The primary purpose of the GO is to prohibit the selling or advertising for sale of grocery goods below cost price.[14] The GO also prohibits the payment or receipt of 'hello money' where a supplier attempts to obtain preferential selling arrangements for its grocery goods in an outlet by offering the outlet cash or some other form of allowance.[15] The GO also prevents suppliers or wholesalers from imposing resale price maintenance on resellers of their grocery goods,[16] and

13 Article 2(1) GO.
14 Articles 11 and 12 GO.
15 Article 18 GO.
16 Articles 3 and 4 GO.

prohibits price fixing between suppliers, wholesalers or retailers.[17] In addition, suppliers are obliged to keep written details of their standard terms and conditions for the supply of their grocery goods and these are available for inspection by the Director of Consumer Affairs ('the Director').[18] Suppliers must not discriminate against customers in applying their standard terms and conditions.[19]

2   ENFORCEMENT

2.1   Enforcement authorities

2.1.1   The Irish courts

The principal means of enforcing the CA is through litigation in the courts. In this regard, section 6(1) CA provides as follows:

> 'Any person who is aggrieved in consequence of any agreement, decision, concerted practice or abuse which is prohibited under section 4 or 5 shall have a right of action for relief under this section against any undertaking which is or has at any material time been a party to such agreement, decision or concerted practice or has been guilty of such abuse.'

2.1.2   Litigants

A litigant must prove that it is 'aggrieved' by an alleged infringement of section 4(1) or 5(1) CA if it is to have locus standi under section 6(1) CA. There is little case law to date as to the interpretation of the term 'aggrieved' but a competitor affected by an restrictive arrangement or practice might have locus standi under section 6(1) CA.

2.1.3   The Minister for Enterprise and Employment

Under section 6(4) CA the Minister is given a right of action in the courts in respect of infringements of sections 4 and 5 CA.

2.1.4   The Competition Authority

At present the Competition Authority has no locus standi to take proceedings under the CA in the Irish courts.

2.1.5   The Director of Consumer Affairs

The Director does not have locus standi to take proceedings in the Irish courts under the CA but is responsible for the enforcement of the GO and, to this end, may undertake investigations and take court proceedings under the GO.

---

17 Articles 5 and 6 GO.
18 Articles 13 and 14 GO.
19 Articles 13, 15 and 16 GO.

2.2 Jurisdictional rules

2.2.1 The Competition Authority has exclusive jurisdiction to grant licences under section 4(2) CA; the courts do not have the power to grant a licence under the CA. In relation to certificates, whilst the Competition Authority also has the exclusive jurisdiction to grant certificates, the question whether a particular arrangement infringes section 4(1) CA may be ultimately decided in proceedings taken in the High Court under section 6 CA. In particular, if, in such proceedings, it is finally decided by a court that a particular arrangement infringes section 4(1) CA, any certificate issued by the Competition Authority in respect of that arrangement ceases to have effect from the date of the court's order.[20]

2.2.2 With regard to the relationship between EC and Irish competition law, there may be situations where a given agreement or practice would fall outside Articles 85(1) and/or 86 of the EEC Treaty but fall within sections 4(1) and/or 5(1) CA. For example, in a particular case it might be difficult to establish an appreciable restriction of competition and/or an effect on trade between Member States or the existence of a dominant position within a substantial part of the EC but it might be possible to establish a restriction of competition which would affect trade in Ireland and/or the abuse of a dominant position within a substantial part of Ireland.

2.3 Role of the Competition Authority

2.3.1 At present the primary role of the Competition Authority under the CA is to review under section 4 CA arrangements voluntarily notified to the Competition Authority by a party or parties to such arrangements in order to consider whether such arrangements can be approved in the form of a certificate or licence. There is no obligation to notify any arrangement to the Competition Authority; it is a discretionary matter for the parties involved.

2.3.2 When an arrangement is notified to the Competition Authority the Competition Authority publishes notice of the fact in an Irish newspaper in the month following notification. Third parties are then invited to submit comments to the Competition Authority. If the Competition Authority's initial review of the arrangement is favourable, it will publish a further notice in an Irish newspaper indicating its intention to take a favourable decision but inviting comments from third parties within 21 days. At this stage, third parties may obtain from the Competition Authority a non-confidential version of the notification. If, ultimately, the Competition Authority decides to approve the arrangement, it will issue either a certificate or licence. Alternatively, if the Competition Authority's initial review is not favourable, it may issue a Statement of Objections to the parties. The parties will then be given a period of time, normally 28 days, within which to reply. An Oral Hearing may be held before the Competition Authority if the parties so request. If the Competition Authority ultimately decides that the notified arrangement infringes section 4(1) CA and does not satisfy the conditions for the grant of a licence under section 4(2) CA, the Competition Authority will refuse to grant a certificate or licence. However, the Competition Authority does not have the power

---

20 Section 6(5)(a) CA. It should be noted that damages may not be awarded for infringement of section 4 CA in proceedings instituted under section 6 CA after the issue of a certificate for loss sustained while the certificate is in force – section 6(6) CA.

to declare such an arrangement prohibited and void by virtue of section 4(1) CA as only the courts can do so.

2.3.3　Apart from its role in reviewing notified arrangements under section 4 CA, the Competition Authority may be requested by the Minister to carry out an investigation into a suspected abuse of a dominant position.[1] If so requested, the Competition Authority will report to the Minister as to whether it considers that a dominant position exists and, if so, whether the dominant position is being abused.[2] Ultimately, the Minister may take action to prohibit the continuance of the dominant position or to adjust the dominant position.[3] Apart from this procedure, the Competition Authority cannot review issues on the abuse of a dominant position.

2.3.4　Under the CA, the Competition Authority does not have the power to take proceedings in the courts in relation to alleged infringements of sections 4 or 5 CA; nor does the Competition Authority have the power to consider complaints in relation to alleged infringements of sections 4 or 5 CA. However, the Bill would, if adopted in its present form, give the Competition Authority the power to take court proceedings in relation to suspected infringements of sections 4 or 5 CA and the power to consider complaints[4] to this end. An individual to be known as the Director of Competition Enforcement might also be appointed to the Competition Authority. At present, there are only three permanent members of the Competition Authority.

2.4　Damages and other sanctions

2.4.1　Proceedings based on section 4(1) CA must be taken in the High Court whilst proceedings based on section 5(1) CA may be taken in the High Court or the lower Circuit Court.[5] In any action in the Circuit Court, damages cannot exceed the Circuit Court's jurisdiction of IR £30,000.

2.4.2　Section 6(3) CA provides that the reliefs which can be granted to an 'aggrieved' plaintiff in an action under section 6(1) CA are by way of injunction or declaration and damages, including exemplary damages. The Minister can claim injunctive or declaratory relief but not damages.[6] If the bill is adopted and the Competition Authority is granted powers to pursue infringements of sections 4 or 5 in the courts, the Competition Authority, like the Minister, would not have the power to claim damages but could seek injunctive or declaratory relief.[7] It is not proposed in the bill that the Competition Authority would have the power to impose fines in relation to infringements of sections 4 or 5 CA.

1　Section 14(1) CA.
2　Section 14(2) CA.
3　Section 14(3) CA. To date, the Minister has not used these extensive powers under section 14 CA. The minister may also request the Competition Authority to undertake a survey pursuant to section 11 CA but this provision does not empower the minister to take the measures listed in section 14 CA. Section 11 CA has been used once – see Competition Authority Interim Report of the Study on the Newspaper Industry in Ireland (30 March 1995).
4　Sections 5 and 7 of the bill.
5　Sections 6(2)(a) and 6(2)(b) CA and the Competition Act 1991 (section 6(2)(b)) (Commencement) Order 1992.
6　Section 6(4) CA.
7　Section 5 of the bill.

2.5 Exemptions

Arrangements which fall under section 4(1) CA may be exempted from the prohibition in section 4(1) CA by an individual licence on notification to the Competition Authority or by the application of a category licence under section 4(2) CA.[8]

2.6 Third party rights

Section 6(1) CA specifically provides a right of action in the courts for a person who can claim to be 'aggrieved' by virtue of an infringement of sections 4 or 5 CA.[9] Whilst third parties cannot at present make complaints to the Competition Authority, they can submit critical comments to the Competition Authority on agreements which are notified to the Competition Authority. Third parties are assisted in this regard by the Competition Authority's practice to publish a monthly notice in an Irish newspaper listing the arrangements notified to the Competition Authority in the previous month. In addition, the bill would permit third parties to make a complaint to the Competition Authority with a view to requesting the Competition Authority to take proceedings under the CA.[10]

3 CHECKLIST OF POTENTIAL INFRINGEMENTS

3.1 Agency

3.1.1 The Competition Authority has taken a number of decisions under section 4 CA on agency agreements which, in effect, follow the European Commission's approach in assessing agency agreements under Article 85 EEC Treaty.[11] In particular, the Competition Authority has distinguished between an independent distributor and a commercial agent and held that agreements between principals and commercial agents do not infringe section 4(1) CA as the agent is 'integrated' into the business of the principal and, as such, can undertake no autonomous commercial behaviour. Furthermore, the Competition Authority has held that certain restrictions on an agent are fundamental to this relationship and may be placed on the agent without infringing section 4(1) CA whereas such restrictions if placed upon an independent distributor might be taken to infringe section 4(1) CA. For example, the Competition Authority has held that in an agency agreement the principal can set the resale prices for the products supplied to the agent without infringing section 4(1) CA whereas, in the case of a distribution agreement, a restriction on the distributor setting its own resale prices would constitute an infringement of section 4(1) CA and would not be likely to be permitted by the Competition Authority under section 4(2) CA.[12]

3.1.2 In a number of decisions[13] the Competition Authority held that the reseller in question was an agent rather than a distributor. In so deciding, some of the

---

8 See sections 1.2.10 to 1.2.12 above.
9 See sections 2.1.1 above.
10 Section 7 of the bill.
11 See, for example, *Conoco Consignee Agreement* (Decision No 286 of 25 February 1994).
12 See *Reflex Investments plc/Storage Technology Ltd* (Decision No 239 of 19 May 1994).
13 See, for example, *Conoco Consignee Agreement* (Decision No 286 of 25 February 1994) and *Patrick Flynn / Wardell Roberts plc* (Decision No 303 of 7 April 1994).

points the Competition Authority took into account were that the reseller concluded the sale of the products on behalf of the supplier on an ongoing basis; the reseller did not take title to the products supplied; the reseller's resale prices were set by the supplier; in one case, the reseller lodged the proceeds of sale, less a commission, to the credit of the supplier's bank account; whilst the reseller accepted some risk, in relation to stock and cash loss in one case, and bad debts in another case, and was responsible for hiring and paying employees in one case, the profits and losses from the business in question accrued to the supplier; in one case, the reseller had to obey the supplier's instructions and could undertake no autonomous behaviour in respect of the operation of the business in question.

3.1.3 The distinction between an agent and distributor is also important in that agents, but not distributors, are entitled to certain minimum rights to notice of termination and compensation on termination as a result of the European Communities (Commercial Agents) Regulations 1994 which implement in Ireland EC Directive 86/653 on self-employed commercial agents.

3.2 Distribution

3.2.1 Following the introduction of the CA in 1991 many distribution agreements were notified to the Competition Authority for its review under section 4 CA. Consequently, the Competition Authority adopted a category licence on exclusive distribution agreements.[14] The category licence is based on EC block exemption Regulation 1983/83. An exclusive distribution agreement which contains provisions which are no more restrictive than those specifically permitted in the category licence is automatically enforceable by virtue of section 4(2) CA without the need individually to notify the agreement to the Competition Authority.

3.2.2 The category licence only applies where the distributor is a reseller of goods supplied by the supplier and the distributor has been given an exclusive territory.[15] In general, the category licence permits the type of restrictions imposed on a distributor and supplier as are permitted under Regulation 1983/83, namely:

Obligations as supplier: not to appoint other distributors[16] or to supply the contract goods to users in the contract territory.[17]

Obligations as distributor: not to manufacture or distribute goods which compete with the contract goods;[18] to obtain the contract goods for resale only from the supplier;[19] to refrain, outside the contract territory, in relation to the contract goods, from seeking customers, from establishing any branch and from maintaining any distribution depot.[20]

3.2.3 The category licence provides, inter alia, that the permitted restrictions in the category licence can only last for the duration of the distribution agreement[1]

14 See section 1.2.12 above.
15 Article 1.
16 Article 1.
17 Article 2(1).
18 Article 2(2)(a).
19 Article 2(2)(b).
20 Article 2(2)(c).
 1 Article 3(i).

and that the distributor should be free to set its own resale prices[2] if the category licence is to apply. This is consistent with the European Commission's approach in the application of Article 85(1) of the EEC Treaty in general and under Regulation 1983/83 in particular.

3.3 Selective distribution

To date there has not been any decision as to whether selective distribution arrangements infringe section 4(1) CA. A selective distribution system is sometimes used by manufacturers of sophisticated or technical products and involves the manufacturer or supplier limiting the resale or distribution of their products to suitably qualified outlets. By analogy with the European Commission's approach under Article 85 of the EEC Treaty, a selective distribution system may fall outside the scope of section 4(1) CA if the selection of suitable dealers is based on objective, qualitative criteria relating to the suitability of the dealer's qualifications, premises, etc and the goods concerned are of such a nature as to necessitate a selective distribution system. However, if, in addition to objective, qualitative criteria, there are other restrictions in the form of quantitive criteria which would limit the number of dealers in a given territory section 4(1) CA may apply.

3.4 Exclusive purchasing

Exclusive purchasing agreements involve one party agreeing to purchase their entire requirements of a given product for resale from only one supplier. By analogy with EC competition law, such an agreement is likely to fall under section 4(1) CA. However, by analogy with EC Regulation 1984/83, an exclusive purchasing agreement is likely to be licensed by the Competition Authority under section 4(2) CA on notification if the exclusive purchasing obligation is for no more than five years. It is also likely, in time, that the Competition Authority will adopt a category licence modelled on EC Regulation 1984/83. The Competition Authority has already adopted a category licence in relation to the exclusive purchase of motor fuels which is modelled on EC Regulation 1984/83 in so far as the Regulation applies to exclusive purchasing agreements for service stations.[3]

3.5 Franchising

The Competition Authority has published a category licence for franchising agreements.[4] The category licence is based on EC Regulation 4087/88 and generally permits the type of restrictions on a franchisor and franchisee which are permitted under that Regulation.

2 Articles 3(f) and 3(g).
3 See section 1.2.12 above.
4 See section 1.2.12 above.

3.6   Intellectual property licensing

3.6.1   In one case,[5] the Competition Authority granted certificates in relation to a number of user agreements providing for the grant of a non-exclusive licence by the owner of certain trademarks and designs relating to the owner's Irish whiskey products in connection with the manufacture in Ireland of products incorporating the owner's whiskey products and sold using the owner's brand names.

3.6.2   The Competition Authority accepted that a trademark, particularly one related to a widely sold consumer product, can represent a very valuable asset with the right to it strongly reserved by its owner so that restrictions in a trademark user or licence agreement which are necessary to protect the trademark owner's property rights in the trademark would not be regarded as falling under section 4(1) CA. The Competition Authority also accepted that a 'no-challenge clause' did not, in the circumstances, constitute a restriction of competition within the meaning of section 4(1) CA.

3.6.3   An important consideration for the Competition Authority was that the particular user agreements notified did not involve an exclusive licence nor did they contain any prohibition on the production or marketing by the licensees of other products similar to those covered by the licences. It may be that if a trademark licence was in the form of an exclusive licence and contained a prohibition on the production or marketing by the licensees of other products similar to those covered by the licence that the Competition Authority might find that section 4(1) CA would apply but might be prepared to grant a licence under section 4(2) CA in such circumstances.

3.7   Refusals to supply

3.7.1   A refusal to supply an existing customer by a company which has a dominant position may, by analogy with case law developed under Article 86 of the EEC Treaty, constitute an abuse of a dominant position within the meaning of section 5(1) CA if the refusal to supply could not be justified on objective grounds.

3.7.2   Furthermore, where a refusal to supply is part of, or the result of, an arrangement between undertakings, such a refusal might be challenged as an infringement of section 4(1) CA.

3.8   Price restrictions

3.8.1   Both sections 4(1) and 5(2) CA include as examples of unlawful arrangements:

(a)   directly or indirectly fixing purchase or selling prices or any other trading conditions;
(b)   applying dissimilar conditions to equivalent transactions.

3.8.2   The Competition Authority's category licence on exclusive distribution agreements specifies that resale price maintenance in a distribution agreement,

---

5 *Irish Distillers* (Decision No 284 of 7 February 1994).

whereby a supplier restricts the freedom of an independent reseller to set its resale prices, involves a restriction of competition within the meaning of section 4(1) CA and that the inclusion of resale price maintenance in an exclusive distribution agreement will take the agreement outside the benefit of the category licence.[6] In addition, resale price maintenance in an exclusive distribution agreement would be unlikely to be individually licensed by the Competition Authority under section 4(2) CA.[7]

3.8.3 In *SuperToys*,[8] a case concerning arrangements between a wholesale supplier and a number of independent retailers, the Competition Authority set out its views on price fixing between competitors. The arrangements in question involved the joint purchasing of toys from suppliers and the advertising and pricing of toys. The retailers agreed to purchase a range of toys from certain suppliers with whom the wholesale supplier had negotiated terms on behalf of the retailers. In addition, the retailers agreed to support the SuperToys group promotional programme, which included distributing the SuperToys catalogue and agreeing on, and abiding by, prices quoted in the catalogue.

3.8.4 The Competition Authority took the view that the catalogue prices, which were agreed by all the retailers, infringed section 4(1) CA as they effectively involved price fixing between the retailers. Members of the retail group were required not to deviate from the prices, except in response to local competitive pressures, and not to advertise any such price deviations at the national level. The Competition Authority also indicated to the parties that these elements of the arrangements would not be permissible under section 4(2) CA. Following this, the parties amended the arrangements so that the retailers were free to resell the toys at whatever price they chose, although the supplier was still entitled to recommend resale prices. The Competition Authority granted a certificate in respect of the amended arrangements.

3.8.5 Rules of an association which prevent or restrict price competition between members of that association are also likely to infringe section 4(1) CA and are unlikely to be permitted under section 4(2) CA.[9]

3.9 Tie in sales

Tie in arrangements, whereby purchasers are obliged to take certain products or services in addition to the products or services they are purchasing, may infringe section 4(1) CA if they are not objectively justified and, if so, are unlikely to be permissible under section 4(2) CA. For example, the Competition Authority held

---

6 Articles 3(f) and 3(g).
7 See, for example, *Reflex Investments plc/Storage Technology Ltd* (Decision No 239 of 19 May 1994).
8 *SuperToys* (Decision No 304 of 21 April 1994).
9 Irish Stock Exchange Rules in relation to *Dealings in Irish Government Securities* (Decision No 335 of 10 June 1994), where the Competition Authority held that the setting of fixed minimum commissions by the Irish Stock Exchange for transactions in Irish Government securities, which had to be followed by all member firms of the Stock Exchange, infringed section 4(1) CA and did not satisfy the conditions for the grant of a licence under section 4(2) CA. On this, see also the decision of the Competition Authority in *Association of Optometrists* (Decision No 16 of 29 April 1993).

that a standard agreement offered by a package holiday company, whereby the company obliged its customers to take travel insurance offered by a particular insurance broker, infringed section 4(1) CA and was not permissible under section 4(2) CA. The Competition Authority granted a certificate when the arrangements were amended so that customers had the option of taking the particular broker's policy or making alternative arrangements. The fact that customers were obliged to take out holiday insurance did not infringe Section 4(1) CA but, rather, the obligation to take the particular policy agreed between the company and the broker.[10]

3.10   Information exchange

3.10.1   The Competition Authority has held that the exchange of commercially sensitive information by competitors is anti-competitive and any arrangement to do so infringes section 4(1) CA.[11]

3.10.2   The Competition Authority has also indicated that it would regard the mere communication in advance of information regarding price changes or pricing intentions to competitors as infringing section 4(1) CA because 'such behaviour reduces uncertainty regarding competitors' pricing intentions which is an essential element of competition'.[12]

3.11   Joint buying and selling

3.11.1   In *SuperToys,*[13] the Competition Authority considered that the notified arrangements were essentially a group purchasing scheme rather than an exclusive purchasing agreement. The intention behind the scheme was to increase the buying power of the retailers by their operating together. The Competition Authority concluded that the group purchasing element of the arrangements, in the circumstances, did not infringe section 4(1) CA. In this regard, it was relevant that the retailers could quit the scheme at any time and could also purchase competitive products from other suppliers. Also relevant was the fact that the retailers did not commit themselves to purchase all their toy requirements from the scheme and that their combined market share was relatively low.

3.11.2   On this reasoning, joint purchasing arrangements may in other circumstances fall under section 4(1) CA, particularly where members of a joint purchasing arrangement are not free to purchase competing products from other suppliers and/or are not free to quit the joint purchasing arrangement without incurring a penalty.

3.11.3   There is no decision from the Competition Authority or the Irish courts yet as to how they might consider joint sales arrangements. However, by analogy

---

10 *Falcon Holidays / Ben McArdle Ltd* (Decision No 274 of 4 February 1994).
11 *General Electric Capital Corpn / GPA Group plc* (Decision No 137 of 20 October 1993).
12 See *SuperToys* (Decsion No 304 of 21 April 1994).
13 See section 3.8.3 above.

with EC competition law, it is likely that the Competition Authority and the courts would consider that joint selling by competitors would fall under section 4(1) CA.

3.12 Market sharing

Section 4(1) CA specifies as an example of an unlawful arrangement one to 'limit or control production, markets, technical development or investment'. Consequently, an arrangement between competitors to share markets would infringe Section 4(1) CA and would be unlikely to be licensed under section 4(2) CA on notification to the Competition Authority.

3.13 Joint ventures

3.13.1 There has been no decision yet from either the Competition Authority or the Irish courts as to how joint ventures might be reviewed under section 4 CA. However, by analogy with EC competition law, a joint venture between actual or potential competitors may fall within the terms of section 4(1) CA. In deciding whether parents to a joint venture are actual or potential competitors, it is necessary to consider whether either parent on its own could have undertaken the activity that is to be carried out by the joint venture company; if so, then the joint venture might be taken to restrict competition between the parents within the meaning of section 4(1) CA.

3.13.2 If it appears that the parents to a joint venture are not actual or potential competitors, then the joint venture as a structure may not fall under section 4(1) CA. Furthermore, if the Irish authorities adopt the approach taken by their EC counterparts, any restrictions in the joint venture agreement which could be said to be ancillary to the operation of the joint venture and necessary if the joint venture is to operate successfully might also be taken to fall outside section 4(1) CA.

3.13.3 Alternatively, if a joint venture is taken to fall under section 4(1) CA, the likelihood of approval under section 4(2) CA may be influenced by the type of joint venture involved. For example, if the joint venture were to produce a new product or provide a new service, it may be more likely to be permitted. Conversely, certain types of joint venture might be scrutinised more closely, for example, joint selling or joint distribution arrangements.

4   MERGER CONTROL

4.1 Introduction

Irish mergers legislation is contained principally in the Mergers Take-Overs and Monopolies (Control) Acts 1978 and 1987, as amended ('MA'). A merger or take-over may also raise issues under the CA.

4.2 The Mergers Take-Overs and Monopolies (Control) Acts 1978 and 1987, as amended ('MA')

4.2.1 Application

Proposed mergers or takeovers which fall within the terms of the MA must be notified by each of the parties involved to the Minister for his approval.[14] The notification must be submitted within one month of an offer capable of acceptance having been made, for example, a conditional agreement having been signed.

The MA applies to mergers or takeovers as a result of which two or more enterprises, at least one of which carries on business in Ireland, come under 'common control'.[15] For the purposes of the MA, enterprises are deemed to be under 'common control' where:

(a) the decision as to how or by whom each enterprise shall be managed can be made either by the same person, or by the same group of persons acting in concert;[16] or

(b) an enterprise, whether by means of acquisition or otherwise, obtains the right in another enterprise:

   (i) to appoint or remove a majority of the board or committee of management of the second enterprise; or

   (ii) to shares of the second enterprise which carry voting rights where, after the acquisition, the voting rights in the second enterprise which are controlled by the first enterprise represent more than 25% of the voting rights in the second enterprise (provided that the acquiror did not already have more than 50% of the voting rights in the second enterprise before the acquisition).[17]

Certain threshold requirements must also be met if the MA is to apply to a proposed merger or takeover. In this regard, the MA only applies to transactions where, in the most recent financial year, the value of the gross assets of each of two or more of the enterprises to be involved in the proposal is not less than IR £10 million or the turnover of each of those two or more enterprises is not less than IR £20 million.[18] Proposed mergers or take-overs involving enterprises at least one of which is engaged in the printing or publication (or printing and publication) of one or more than one newspaper must be notified under the MA regardless of the assets and turnovers involved.[19]

In addition, certain acquisitions of assets must be notified under the MA. In this regard, where the assets, including goodwill (or a substantial part of the assets) of an enterprise are acquired by another enterprise, the acquisition will constitute a notifiable transaction for the purposes of the MA if the result of the acquisition is to place the second enterprise in a position to replace (or substantially to replace) the first enterprise in the business in which the first enterprise was engaged immediately before the acquisition and the value of those assets or the value of the

---

14 Section 5(1) MA.
15 Section 1(3)(a) MA.
16 Section 1(3)(b) MA.
17 Section 1(3)(c) MA.
18 Section 2(1)(a) MA.
19 The Mergers Take-Overs and Monopolies (Newspapers) Order 1979.

turnover generated from those assets exceeds the threshold requirements referred to above.[20]

4.2.2 Sanctions

The following sanctions may be imposed for completing a transaction which is notifiable under the MA without following the notification procedures and obtaining prior approval from the Minister, namely:

(a) title to any shares or assets involved in the transaction will not pass until the transaction has been notified and approved by the Minister;[1]

(b) the persons in control of each enterprise which failed to notify the transaction, or which notified the transaction but failed to provide information which was subsequently requested by the Minister, will be guilty of an offence and liable, on summary conviction, to a fine not exceeding IR £1,000 and, for continued contravention, to a daily default fine not exceeding £100 or, on conviction on indictment, to a fine not exceeding IR £200,000 and, for continued contravention, to a daily default fine not exceeding IR £20,000;[2] and,

(c) where a purported sale of shares is rendered invalid for failure to notify and obtain ministerial approval, the purported vendor may recover from the purported purchaser any damages that the purported vendor suffers by reason only of the invalidity, unless the purported purchaser satisfies the court that before the purported sale it had notified the purported vendor of circumstances relating to the proposed sale which gave rise to the possibility of such an invalidity.[3]

4.2.3 Notifications

The following information must be submitted on a notification under the MA: details of each of the enterprises to be involved in the proposal including ownership, current activities, numbers employed and financial performance in recent years; details of the proposed transaction and the period within which the transaction is to take place; estimated market share in Ireland of each of the enterprises involved in the sectors in which they are engaged and details of any further acquisitions that may be planned by them in the foreseeable future in these or any other sectors; reasons for the proposal in so far as each of the enterprises involved is concerned; details of any changes planned in the operation of any of the enterprises as a result of the proposed acquisition; details of any other agreement which is being entered into in conjunction with or at the same time as the proposal; details of any legal sanctions or clearances which may be necessary in other jurisdictions in relation to the proposal; details of any investigations or prosecutions instituted in respect of the enterprises concerned by other national authorities in relation to antitrust or other competition law matters.

---

20 Section 1(3)(e) MA.
1 Section 3(1) MA.
2 Section 5(3) MA.
3 Section 4 MA.

4.2.4   Criteria

In determining whether to approve a notified transaction, the Minister takes into account certain criteria listed in the MA,[4] namely:

(a)   whether the proposed acquisition would be likely to prevent or restrict competition or restrain trade in any goods or services;

(b)   the likely effect of the proposed transaction on the 'common good', in particular: the continuity of supplies or services; levels of employment; regional development; rationalisation of operations in the interests of greater efficiency; research and development; increased production; access to markets; shareholders and partners; employees; consumers.

4.2.5   Procedure

Following notification, the Minister may request further information from the parties within one month (this period runs from the date when both parties notified the transaction).[5] If so, the Minister will stipulate a time limit for the parties to reply. Following the receipt of any further information, the Minister will then either approve the transaction or refer the notification to the Competition Authority.[6]

Referrals to the Competition Authority must be made within 30 days of notification or the receipt of any further information requested by the Minister (whichever is later).[7] On referrals, the Competition Authority will investigate the proposed transaction and report to the Minister on the impact the transaction would have on the issues noted at section 4.2.4. The report should be submitted within a time limit stipulated by the Minister, which will be at least 30 days following referral by the Minister.[8] The Minister will publish the Competition Authority's report within two months of receipt.[9] Following receipt of the report, the Minister will make his decision; he may either approve the transaction or by Ministerial Order prohibit the transaction either absolutely or except on conditions specified in the Order.[10] Alternatively, a notified transaction will be deemed approved if the Minister fails to make an Order within three months of notification or the receipt of further information (whichever is later).[11]

4.3   The Competition Act 1991 ('CA')

4.3.1   Application

It is not clear under the CA whether mergers or take-overs, including transactions which are approved by the Minister under the MA, may be reviewed under

---

4   Section 8(2) MA.
5   Section 5(2) MA.
6   Sections 7(a) and 7(b) MA.
7   Section 7(b) MA.
8   Section 8(1) MA.
9   Section 17(4) CA.
10   Section 9(1)(a) MA.
11   Section 3(1)(c) MA.

sections 4 or 5 CA. However, the Competition Authority has held that a merger or take-over, including one which has been notified to, and approved by, the Minister under the MA, may be reviewed under section 4 CA.[12]

4.3.2   Criteria

On the basis of the Competition Authority's decisions, a transaction must result in 'a lessening of competition' if it is to infringe section 4(1) CA. Factors which the Competition Authority takes into account include: the level of competition in the market generally; the ease with which new competitors may enter the market; the extent to which imports may provide competition to domestic suppliers; the alternative sources of competition in the market, and, in particular, the extent to which the acquiror was a competitor of the target prior to the acquisition; the position of the target company if the proposed transaction were not to proceed, particularly, whether it would remain a competitor in the market; the bargaining power of end-users or consumers in the market; the availability of substitute products or services.[13]

The Competition Authority reviews more closely acquisitions in concentrated markets, ie where there are a small number of competitors which have large market shares between them.[14] If the Competition Authority should decide that a particular acquisition would infringe section 4(1) CA it is unlikely that the Authority would grant a licence under section 4(2) CA.[15]

The Competition Authority has not addressed in its decisions the issue as to whether it considers mergers and take-overs to be reviewable under section 5 CA. However, by analogy with EC competition law, a merger or acquisition might also be reviewable under section 5(1) CA, where the acquiror was in a dominant position prior to the acquisition, and might not be acceptable under section 5(1) CA if the effect of the acquisition were to restrict competition. The Competition Authority has indicated that it considers that mergers and acquisitions may be reviewed under section 5(1) CA.[16]

4.3.3   Restrictive covenants

It has been held by the Competition Authority that the imposition of a non-competition obligation on a vendor on the sale of a business may infringe section 4(1) CA, depending upon the nature of the restrictive covenants, in particular, the territory and business concerned and the duration of the restrictions.[17] The general rule adopted by the Competition Authority is that a non-compete obligation imposed on a vendor for a period of five years following the sale does not infringe section 4(1) CA provided the transaction involves the sale not only of assets and goodwill but also technical know-how; in the absence of the transfer of technical know-how, the maximum period permissible tends to be two years. It is also necessary, if such a provision is to fall outside section 4(1) CA, that it be confined to the type of business sold and the area in which the vendor previously competed. The Competition

12 *Woodchester Bank Ltd / UDT Bank Ltd* (Decision No 6 of 4 August 1992).
13 See, for example, *Scully Tyrrell & Co/Edberg Ltd* (Decision No 12 of 29 January 1993).
14 See *Scully Tyrrell & Co/Edberg Ltd* (Decision No 12 of 29 January 1993).
15 See *Irish Distillers Group plc/Cooley Distillery plc* (Decision No 285 of 25 February 1994).
16 Competition Authority Guide to Irish Legislation on Competition (1992).
17 See, generally, *GI Corp/General Semiconductor Industries Inc* (Decision No 10 of 23 October 1992).

Authority has also stated that if a non-compete clause infringes section 4(1) CA it is unlikely to be permitted under section 4(2) CA.[18] The Minister has indicated that in reviewing non-compete clauses under the MA he will adopt the approach the Competition Authority has taken under section 4 CA.

4.3.4   The courts

It should be noted that the Irish courts have yet to consider whether mergers or take-overs are reviewable under sections 4(1) or 5(1) CA so that it remains to be seen whether the Courts would adopt the approach taken by the Competition Authority. No transaction has yet been contested in the Courts under the CA.

4.4   Proposed changes

The bill, if adopted, would provide that mergers or take-overs within the meaning of the MA would not be reviewable under section 4 CA, regardless of the assets and turnovers involved.[19] If the bill is adopted, however, it would still appear possible that mergers or take-overs might be reviewable under section 5 CA.

---

18 See, for example, *Ipodec Ordures Usines SA / GKN United Kingdom plc* (Decision No 342 of 14 June 1994).
19 Section 2 of the bill. The proposed provision would have retrospective effect to the coming into operation of the CA on 1 October 1991.

CHAPTER XI

Italy

Davide Braghini

Studio Legale Sutti
Via Montenapoleone 8
20121 Milan
Italy

Tel ++39 2 76204 1
Fax ++39 2 76204 805

CHAPTER XI

Italy

1 ITALIAN LAW ON COMPETITION AND THE MARKET

1.1 Background

1.1.1 Italian anti-trust law is one of the most recent in Europe and is modelled on EC competition law.[1] It must be pointed out that, even though attempts to pass an anti-trust law in Italy date back to the 1950s and almost ten bills have been examined by Parliament,[2] the enactment of Law No 287/90[3] followed closely the entry into force of the EC Merger Control Regulation (No 4064/89/EEC), which completed the framework of EC competition law.

1.1.2 The constitutional basis for the Law is Article 41 of the Constitution of the Italian Republic,[4] which provides the principle of freedom for private enterprise. In any event, the introductory rules of the Law assure the supremacy of EC competition law, providing that the domestic legislation has a residual field of application and submitting the Law to interpretation in accordance with 'the principles of the European Community legal system'.[5] Even if it has been stressed that the utilisation of EC principles must only support the traditional criteria of interpretation,[6] the provision is most useful, since Italian authorities and courts have no experience in the matter while there is a substantial and consolidated body of Community case law.

---

1 The most comprehensive comments on the law are provided by V Donativi, *Introduzione della disciplina* anti-trust *nel sistema legislativo italiano. Le premesse*, Milano, 1990; R Alessi, G Olivieri, *La disciplina della concorrenza e del mercato*, Torino, 1991; G Bernini, *Un secolo di filosofia antitrust. Il modello statiunitense, la disciplina comunitaria e la normativa italiana*, Bologna, 1991; G Napoletano, *La tutela della concorrenza e del mercato in Italia*, Roma, 1992; A Frignani, R Pardolesi, A Patroni Griffi, L C Ubertazzi (edited by), *Diritto* antitrust *italiano*, Torino, 1993; V Afferni (edited by), *Concorrenza e Mercato*, Padova, 1994.

2 For a collection of the relevant bills and proposals see Capotorti, Di Sabato, Patroni Griffi, Picone, Ubertazzi, *Il fenomeno delle concentrazioni di imprese nel diritto interno ed internazionale*, 1989.

3 10 October 1990, No 287, in *Gazzetta Ufficiale della Repubblica Italiana*, 13 October 1990, No 240.

4 Article 41 of the Constitution of the Italian Republic provides that: 'Private economic enterprise is free. It must not be carried out in a way which contrasts with social utility or in such a manner as to damage human safety, freedom and dignity. The law provides appropriate programmes and controls in order for public and private economic enterprise to be directed and coordinated towards the social good'.

5 It must be pointed out that in referring to EC *principles*, the Law allows the use not only of the main rules – Articles 85 and 86 of the Treaty of Rome and Regulation No 4064/89/EEC – but also of the many implementation provisions (Regulations, Directives, Notices) and the wide case law developed by the EC Commission and Court of Justice.

6 Cf F Saja, *L'Autorità garante della concorrenza e del mercato: prime esperienze e prospettive di applicazione della legge*, in *Giurisprudenza commerciale*, 1991, I, 457.

1.2   Field of application

1.2.1   First of all, the supremacy of EC competition law is assured by adopting the so-called one-stop shop principle. Article 1.1, in fact, provides that the Law only applies to arrangements, abuses of dominant positions and mergers falling outside the field of application of EC competition law (ie Articles 65 and/or 66 of the ECSC Treaty, Articles 85 and/or 86 of the EEC Treaty, relevant EC regulations – Regulation No 4064/89/EEC – and any 'other Community acts having equivalent legal effect').[7]

Thus the Law aims to avoid overlap of jurisdiction between domestic and Community authorities and the possibility of conflicting decisions. Moreover, it seems to be a more efficient division of jurisdiction, reflecting the specialisation of each authority.

1.2.2   The provision, nevertheless, poses some considerable interpretative problems, which could only be resolved by continuous cooperation between the domestic Authority and the EC Commission.

Problems arise in border situations, particularly in cases which have trans-national importance but fall outside the scope of the EC rules (eg the so-called minor agreements). Conversely, there are internal situations which may attract the attention of the EC Commission: for example, the Commission has sometimes maintained that a part of a Member State's territory is a substantial part of the common market.[8] In fact, the Italian Guarantor Authority (*Autorità Garante della Concorrenza e del Mercato*) has already examined some cases which probably fall within the field of application of the EC rules: the Authority justified this intervention by maintaining that the Commission only has jurisdiction in cases where 'the main object or effect' of the facts under consideration 'prejudices trade between Member States'.[9]

1.2.3   With regard to procedure, Article 1.2 provides that the Guarantor Authority must inform the Commission about cases coming to its attention and falling outside the scope of the Law. There is only an obligation to stay the proceedings when the Guarantor Authority ascertains that an investigation is under way before the Commission, except in relation to 'those aspects of exclusively domestic importance' (Article 1.3). In any event, it would be better for the Guarantor Authority to stay the proceedings and to recommence them only when the Commission decides it has no interest in the matter (except that the non-application of EC law represents an affirmative policy choice of the Commission).

1.2.4   In general, it seems appropriate that the Guarantor Authority investigates border situations only when the EC law does not actually apply to the case.[10]

---

7   A Guarino, *Sul rapporto tra la nuova legge* antitrust *e la disciplina comunitaria della concorrenza*, in *Contratto e Impresa*, 1991, 644, maintains that the limitations to the Italian law are provided only by the ECSC and EEC Treaties and Regulations and Directives of the EC Council, not by Commission provisions: in any event, this literal interpretation of the rule does not seem to have been endorsed.

8   See, for example, the recent decision in the case *Monopoli Portuali*, C-179/90: *Merci Convenzionali Porto di Genova v Siderurgica Gabrielli* [1991] ECR I-5889, [1994] 4 CMLR 422, ECJ.

9   Decision *English Language Book*, in *Bollettino*, 1992, no 8, 6; cf also Decision no 1845, *SEA*, in *Bollettino*, 1994, no 11; Court of Appeal of Milan, order 05/02/92, *MYC, Red Line, MGR v AFI, Virgin Dischi, SIAE*, in *Rivista di diritto industriale*, 1992, II, 52.

10   Cf TAR Lazio, 02/11/93, No 1549, *ANIA v Guarantor Authority for Competition and the Market, Codacons, others*, in *Foro italiano*, 1994, III, 146; F Munari, Comment on Article 1, in V Afferni, *Concorrenza e Mercato*, cit, 32.

1.2.5 Extra-territorial application

The Law applies to any situations which fall within its scope and which arise in the Italian market, without reference to the nationality of the parties and to the country in which the anti-competitive behaviour and concentrations were planned.[11]

1.3 Public sector

1.3.1 The features of the Italian market, which is characterised by broad state intervention in the economy and by the existence of several legal monopolies or quasi-monopolies, recommended to the legislators the passing of a provision similar to Article 90 of the Treaty of Rome and of a special regulation for self-production, which has no equivalent in other antitrust laws.

1.3.2 Article 8 – state companies and legal monopolies

Article 8.1 does not correspond to any EC written rules but only to the principles adopted by the Commission. It provides that the Law applies to private undertakings as well as to those owned entirely or in part by the State. These principles have already been applied several times.[12]

1.3.3 Article 8.2 excludes the application of the Law to undertakings which, by operation of law, manage legal monopolies or perform services of general economic interest: the exception is limited to any transactions *closely* connected with the fulfilment of the specific task assigned to them. The provision mirrors Article 90.2 of the Treaty of Rome, but it has been observed that the Italian formulation seems to accord more importance to the exception.

The general reference to undertakings which 'act on a monopoly basis in the market' seems to allow the extension of the provision to undertakings owning an absolute intellectual property right; nevertheless, it seems more appropriate to interpret the provision restrictively, in accordance with Community principles.[13]

1.3.4 Article 9 – self-production

Article 9 contains an anomalous provision, whose inclusion in the anti-trust law has been criticised. It provides an exception for firms which produce goods or services that are reserved by legal monopoly to the State, public entities or other undertakings, for their own use or benefit, as well as for that of their controlled or controlling companies.

The subsection that follows specifies that the provision does not apply when the monopoly has been established for reasons of public policy, public safety and national defence or, moreover, in the telecommunication industry.

---

11 For example, with regard to art 2, see Guarantor Authority, Decision 12/06/91, no 94, *Mitsui/Nippon*, in *Boll*, 1991, no 4. Cf also F Munari, *Comment on Article 1*, cit, 50.

12 Cf Decision 04/03/92, no 412, *Sip-3C Communications*, in *Boll*, 1992, no 5; Decision 10/04/92, no 453, *Tirrenia Navigazione*, in *Boll*, 1992, no 7; Decision 15/05/92, no 508, *Cementir/Sacci*, in *Boll*, 1992, no 9; Decision 27/05/92, no 519, *MYC/SIAE*, in *Boll*, 1992, no 10.

13 Restrictive intepretation of the rule has been confirmed by the courts: cf Court of Appeal of Milan, Order 15/07/92, *AVIR v ENEL*, in *Società*, 1993, 64.

1.3.5 It is very important to limit correctly the field of 'one's own use', particularly with regard to self-production of services. There is self-production only when the production of a service is for the benefit of the one who produces the service; ie, the effects and the benefits of the production of the service must fall on the same producer.[14]

Moreover, this provision implies a unitary idea of group of undertakings, which is not expressly upheld by the Law.

2 ANTI-COMPETITIVE AGREEMENTS AND ABUSE OF MARKET POWER

2.1 Article 2 – restrictive arrangements

2.1.1 Article 2, which is very similar to Article 85 of the Treaty of Rome, prohibits arrangements which have as their object or effect the prevention, restriction or distortion, in a consistent way, of competition within the national market or within a relevant part thereof. Though the text is in some points different from the one of the EC rule, implementation did not show any relevant discrepancy, also thanks to the interpretation rule as in Article 1.4.

2.1.2 Arrangements

Article 2.1 contains a definition of arrangements, which are then declared prohibited and void to all purposes. The rule refers to agreements, concerted practices, resolutions of *consortia*, association between undertakings or any similar entities. This list is not exhaustive and the Italian rule can comprehend any kind of agreement considered by the Community authorities.[15]

2.1.3 Undertakings

The definition of *entrepreneur* provided by the Italian Civil Code is inappropriate for the scopes of an anti-trust regulation. Therefore, the Guarantor Authority decided to use the economic notion of undertaking which has been adopted by the EC Commission; consequently, the law has been applied also towards a sport organising association and apartment house managers.[16]

Applying EC principles of interpretation, the Guarantor Authority will regard groups of companies as a single undertaking, where the subsidiaries have no autonomy of action.

2.1.4 The restriction of competition

Article 2 requires that the affection of competition be 'consistent'. In this way the Law expressly excludes agreements having a minor importance, so acknowledging

14 The Guarantor Authority seems to bestow a wider definition of self-production: cf Decision 17/03/93, no 1017, *Aeroporti di Roma*, in *Boll*, 1993, no 6; Decision 16/03/94, no 1845, *SEA*, in *Boll*, 1994, no 11.

15 For example, in Decision 15/05/91, no 78, *Sindacato Laziale di Commercianti di prodotti petroliferi*, in *Boll*, 1991, no 3, the Guarantor Authority maintained that an informative notice of an association of undertakings on diesel supply prices had to be considered as an arrangement.

16 *Federazione Italiana Vela*, Decision 18/11/92, no 788, *AICI*, in *Boll*, 1992, no 22; cf also TAR Lazio, 02/11/93, no 1549, *ANIA v Guarantor Authority*, cit. Cf also Guarantor Authority for Competition and the Market, *Relazione Annuale al Presidente del Consiglio de Ministri per il 1994*, 126.

the so-called *de minimis* rule long affirmed by the EC Court of Justice. Nevertheless, since there is no communication similar to the Notice of the Commission on *minor agreements*, it is not possible to know when the Guarantor Authority will maintain that an arrangement is not relevant for the purposes of the Law.

Moreover, the examination of the jurisprudence of the Guarantor Authority shows that such Authority prefers to interpret Article 2 adopting a so-called *rule of reason*: the prohibition is not applied to arrangements that, on the whole, are not strongly anti-competitive, rather than granting to them the exemption provided by Article 4.

The behaviour of the Authority seems to be more flexible in situations where there are so-called *vertical agreements*, agreements in fragmented markets and also new developing markets.[17]

The restriction of the competition must affect the national market or a relevant part thereof; the Guarantor Authority maintains that also an area limited to a few *provincie* could be a relevant part of the national market, taking into account the nature of the product which is dealt in the market (eg concrete).[18]

2.1.5 Finally, a minor agreement falling outside the scope of the Law is subject to the general rules provided by the Italian Civil Code: restrictive agreements must be proved in writing and limited to a specific activity or territory, and in any case can not last longer than five years (Article 2596 of the Civil Code).

2.1.6 The list of agreements in Article 2 is illustrative only, in the same way as those types of agreements listed in Article 85 of the Treaty of Rome. By way of example, the Guarantor Authority has prohibited the following arrangements:

(a)   recommendation by an association between the main insurance companies in Italy of the recommended levels of premium and exemptions for motor vehicle insurance policies;[19]
(b)   creation of a joint venture in the concrete market by two undertakings remaining active in the same market;[20]
(c)   creation of a consortium between the main petrol companies in Italy in order to prepare national planning for a petrol distributors' network.[1]

2.1.7 Nullity

Prohibited arrangements which are not eligible for exemption under Article 4 are void to all purposes. Nullity, according to the general principle provided by the Italian Civil Code (Article 1419), does not extend to the whole agreement, unless there is evidence that the parties considered the void clauses essential for the contract they intended to enter into.

---

17 For a short outline of several cases see P Giudici, *Comment on Article 2*, in V Afferni, *Concorrenza e Mercato*, cit, 110.
18 Decision 27/05/92, no 520, *Procal*, in *Boll*, 1992, no 10; cf also TAR Lazio, 21/07/93, no 1157, *Procal v Guarantor Authority*, in *Foro italiano*, 1994, III, 147.
19 Decision 02/07/93, no 1266, *ANIA*, in *Boll*, 1993, no 15/16.
20 Decision 15/05/92, no 508, *Cementir/Sacci*, in *Boll*, 1992, no 9.
 1 Decision 23/06/93, no 1238, *Ristrutturazione rete distributori carburanti*, in *Boll*, 1993, no 14.

2.1.8   Article 4 – Exemptions

This provision also mirrors Article 85.3 of the Treaty of Rome, even if the text differs to some extent. In fact, the four requirements provided by the EC rule are joined in a single general clause. The Guarantor Authority can authorise 'for a limited period of time', arrangements which 'lead to improvements in the conditions of supply within the market creating substantial benefit for consumers'.

There follows a list of the other requirements:

(a)   increasing or improving of production or distribution, of technical or technological progress;
(b)   absence of any restriction which is not indispensable to the attainment of the above-mentioned objectives;
(c)   maintenance of some competition in the market to some extent.

The lack of any explicit reference to the pursuit of economic progress seems to be not relevant.

2.1.9   In order to grant an exemption under Article 4, the Guarantor Authority must positively appraise also 'the need to guarantee to the undertakings concerned the necessary competitiveness at the international level'. This criterion, which generally is taken into account with regard to concentration, seems to grant a preferential treatment to Italian medium-sized and small enterprises. In this way, it would be possible to compete with main multi-national groups not only developing the size of domestic companies but also by agreements.

2.1.10   A special criterion is provided by Article 25 for banks: the authority concerned (see section 3.1.5 below) can grant an exemption to promote stability of the monetary system; in any event criteria under Article 4 must be respected and the exemption is granted with the approval of the Guarantor Authority.

2.1.11   The existence of the requirements for the granting of exemptions can not be appraised by the courts.
Exemptions could be individual or block.

2.1.12   Individual exemptions

An individual exemption can be granted following a specific request by the undertakings concerned (at present there is no form). Article 4.3 provides that the Guarantor Authority has to respond within 120 days from the notification of an arrangement by the parties. It is not clear if the deadline refers to the granting of the exemption or only to the decision to start investigations in order to grant such exemption; in fact, Article 13 of the Law provides that after 120 days from the notification the Authority can not start investigations, unless the communication was not true or incomplete. In any case the lack of a decision cannot be construed to be a clearance of the arrangement.

2.1.13   Group exemptions

The Guarantor Authority, which was created in 1990, has not yet introduced any regulation for group exemptions, in the absence of a previous experience and wide knowledge of the domestic market.

Though it is not possible to implement directly current EC Regulations for group exemptions, probably the Guarantor Authority could take advantage of the *ratio* of such regulations in its appraisal of the effective restriction of the competition caused by arrangements.

2.2 Article 3 – abuse of a dominant position

2.2.1 Article 3 of the Law reproduces the contents of Article 86 of the Treaty of Rome; it prohibits:

(a) the abuse by one or more undertaking;
(b) of a dominant position within the national market or a relevant part thereof.

2.2.2 *The dominant position*

The Law does not contain a definition of dominant position.[2] By operation of the interpretation principle in Article 1.4, the Guarantor Authority can take advantage of the notion of dominant position which has been created in the application of the EC law, adapting to the extent of the national market.[3]

The rule refers to the abuse by 'one or more undertakings', so recognising the possibility of a collective dominance. Moreover, a so-called 'relative' dominant position could be considered under Article 3.

The Guarantor Authority maintains, in conformity with the principle long affirmed by the EC Court of Justice, that, though an undertaking benefits from a dominant position originated from a rule of law, such an undertaking must respect the prohibition regarding abuses, unless the provision of Article 8 applies (see section 1.3.2 above).[4]

2.2.3 As far as the *relevant market* is concerned, the Guarantor Authority will consider both the geographic and the product markets.[5] Obviously, the reference to the national market (or to a relevant part thereof) simplifies the examination, reducing the boundaries to a small area. Nevertheless, sometimes the EC Commission maintained that a part of a member state territory can also represent a relevant part of the Community market.

The Guarantor Authority has considered an airport to be a relevant part of the national market.[6]

2.2.4 *The abuse*

The list of abusive behaviour set out in Article 3 is for the purpose of illustration only, notwithstanding the text ('and moreover the following shall be prohibited')

2 A notion of dominant position is provided by Law No 67/1987, but it is a very specific provision for the appraisal of concentrations in the newspaper market (see section 7.2 below).
3 Cf Guarantor Authority for Competition and the Market, *Relazione annuale al Presidente del Consiglio dei Ministri per l'anno 1990*, in *Giurisprudenza Commerciale*, 1992, I, 173.
4 Cf Decision 04/03/92, no. 412, *Sip – 3C Communications*, in *Boll*, 1992, no 5; Decision 17/03/93, no 1017, *Aeroporti di Roma*, in *Boll*, 1993, no 6; Decision 28/10/93, no 1532, *Sistema di telefonia cellulare*, in *Boll*, 1993, no 32; Court of appeal of Rome, Order 30/03/95, *Omnitel Pronto Italia v Telecom Italia*.
5 Cf also Court of Appeal of Milan, order 23/01/92, *Carivest v Nuova Samim*, in *Giur comm*, 1992, II, 450.
6 Decision 17/03/93, no 1017, *Aeroporti di Roma*, cit.

seems to specify some typical abuses which are very similar to those set out in Article 86 of the Treaty of Rome.

By way of examples, the Guarantor Authority has established the existence of an abuse of a dominant position in the following situations:

(a)   the refusal of a company managing the legal monopoly of voice telecommunications to grant the use of its network to a private company wishing to offer some additional services for telephone calls (payment by credit card);[7]
(b)   the behaviour of a category sport association obstructing the utilisation of technical devices different from the ones it had adopted;[8]
(c)   granting fidelity discounts;[9]
(d)   the behaviour of a legal monopolist obstructing self-production (see para 1.3.4 above) by private companies.[10]

3   ENFORCEMENT

3.1   Enforcement authorities

3.1.1   In principle it is up to the Guarantor Authority for Competition and the Market to enforce the Italian anti-trust Law. The Guarantor Authority is an administrative body, which has been created on purpose by the same Law and has the features of an *Independent Regulatory Agency*. The Law, moreover, provides two exceptions for the broadcasting and publishing industry and banking undertakings, where the power to enforce the Law is entrusted to the respective pre-existent supervision authorities. This rule (Article 20) is intended to guarantee the respect of the specific interests of these industries; but the distinction risks creating some jurisdiction problems and differences in the application of the Law.

3.1.2   *Guarantor Authority for Competition and the Market*

The Guarantor Authority is a newly created Independent Regulatory Agency. It is a collective body, composed of five members, who are appointed by the Presidents of the two Chambers of the Parliament. The members of the Guarantor Authority remain in charge for seven years and can not be appointed twice.

The offices of the Guarantor Authority are divided in seven main sections:

(a)   co-ordination and secretarial;
(b)   problems of the competition (general studies);
(c)   documentation and information system;
(d)   administration;
(e)   unfair advertising;
(f)   investigations; this office is divided in three subsections:

   (i)   financial services, electronics, information technology, telecommunications, agricultural, food, mechanical industry;
   (ii)   energy, manufacturing, construction industry, public utilities;
   (iii)   transport services, commercial distribution, broadcasting, publishing industry.

7 Decision 04/03/92, no 412, *Sip – 3C Communications*, in *Boll*, 1992, no 5.
8 Decision 18/11/92, no 788, *Federazione italiana vela*, in *Boll*, 1992, no 22.
9 Decision 10/04/92, no 453, *Tirrenia Navigazione*, in *Boll*, 1992, no 7.
10 Decision 17/03/93, no 1017, *Aeroporti di Roma*, cit.

It is important to point out that this division on matters applies also to concentrations, while there is no difference of competence between arrangements, abuses of a dominant position and concentration operations.

3.1.3 Article 10.4 points out that it is up to the Guarantor Authority to maintain with the EC bodies the relationships provided by the EC law on competition. The Law does not explain if the same Guarantor Authority has also the competence directly to enforce Community competition law pursuant to Article 88 of the Treaty of Rome and Article 9 of Regulation No 17/62/EEC.

3.1.4   Broadcasting and publishing industries

Article 20 provides that the enforcement of the Law towards undertakings operating in the broadcasting and publishing industries is up to the respective guarantor authority (the Guarantor for Broadcasting and Publishing). The distinction is made by a subjective criterion: it refers to operations in which participate undertakings registered in the National Register for the Press (undertakings publishing daily newspapers, important magazines, press agencies) or in the National Register for Broadcasting Enterprises; excluded are the undertakings operating in the publishing and information industry in general.

Anyway, for anti-trust purposes the Guarantor must apply the provisions of the Law No 287/90, while the special rules for the sector (Laws No 416/81, 67/87, 223/90 – see section 7.2 below) have residual application.

Before the decision, however, the special authority must request the opinion of the Guarantor Authority for Competition and the Market, in order to assure the homogeneous application of the principle of the Law. The opinion must be given within 30 days from the request; this time being elapsed, the proceedings can continue in any case.

3.1.5   Banking industry

Also in the banking sector there is a special competence of the respective supervision authority, ie the central Bank of Italy, for the application of the Law towards banks and credit institutions. Nevertheless, the Guarantor Authority continues to have competence when the above-mentioned undertakings are involved in operations which do not strictly concern the banking activity.[11] Moreover, the Guarantor Authority has competence on all undertakings operating in the wider so-called para-banking field and in the financial industry in general. Also in this case the opinion of the Guarantor Authority must be requested. With regard to the special hypothesis of authorisation of arrangements in the banking industry see section 2.1.10 above.

3.1.6   Insurance undertakings

In the case of undertakings operating in the insurance industry the Guarantor Authority retains enforcement competence, but must request the opinion of the special supervision authority for this industry (ISVAP – Institute for Vigilance on Private and Collective Interest Insurances). The provision does not comprehend insurance brokers.

---

11 Cf Decision 20/11/91, no 222, *Istituto Bancario San Paolo di Torino/Crediop*, in *Boll*, 1991, no 12; Decison 16/12/92, no 853, *Cedito Romagnolo/Centrauto*, in *Boll*, 1992, no 24.

3.1.7   Courts

The courts are also entrusted with the power to enforce imperative rules provided by the Law. This authority can only ascertain the nullity of the arrangements affecting competition, behaviour abusing a dominant position and prohibited concentrations; moreover, it can acknowledge right to damages caused to third parties in the performance of the above-mentioned activities. See also section 3.4.5 below.

3.2   Investigation powers and procedure

3.2.1   The Guarantor Authority has wide powers to investigate, similar to those of the EC Commission. In particular, the Guarantor Authority can exercise its powers in the following situations:

(a)   notification of an arrangement by the undertakings concerned; in this case the Guarantor Authority must decide within 120 days whether to commence proceedings: this time being elapsed, proceedings can be no longer started, unless the notification has been uncompleted or not true;
(b)   complaint by any third party or by a public administration body. The Guarantor Authorithy may also investigate complaints lodged anonymously;
(c)   own motion investigation by the Guarantor Authority acting on its own initiative.

3.2.2   Investigations

Investigation powers and procedure are provided for in Article 14 of the Law and in the implementation Regulation.[12]

3.2.3   Starting investigations

When the Guarantor Authority presumes the infringement of Articles 2 and 3 of the Law, it must notify the decision to start proceedings to the undertakings concerned, as well as to any other third parties who have a *present, direct and immediate interest* and submit to the Guarantor Authority useful information for the starting of proceedings. The decision, moreover, must be published in a special gazette (*Bollettino*) edited by the Guarantor Authority, in collaboration with the Secretariat of the Prime Minister.

    The notification can also be performed by an officer of the Guarantor Authority and the decision must contain the specific indication of the allegation made towards the investigated undertakings.

3.2.4   Hearing

The decision by which the Guarantor Authority starts proceedings must also contain an indication of the time within which the investigated undertakings and the interested third parties can ask to be heard by the Authority.

    The same persons have the right to be heard at least once again before the end of

12 DPR 10/09/91 No 461 in GU 13/05/92 No 110.

the investigation: for this purpose, the Guarantor Authority must give notice to them at least 15 days before the end of proceedings.

The above-mentioned persons can intervene in the proceedings at any time, submitting remarks and statements, and have a right to be assisted by personal consultants.

3.2.5 Investigation powers

The Guarantor Authority can at any time during the investigation (also at the same time as the notification of the commencement of the proceedings):

(a) request information;
(b) make inspections;
(c) request expert opinions, statistical and economic analyses and consult experts.

These powers can be enforced against both the investigated undertakings and any other subject who is deemed to be in possession of the relevant information.

The powers of investigation are limited to the documentation relating to the activity of the undertaking, while any personal document is excluded, even if it is found at the undertaking's premises. The Guarantor Authority has the right to have a copy of the documents which are deemed to be relevant.

3.2.6 Protection of secrecy

Documents which are protected by professional secrecy (eg lawyers' correspondence) can be excluded from the Guarantor Authority's investigations. This exclusion does not extend to documents which are confidential for any other reason and in particular to industrial secrecy (unless the Guarantor Authority maintains the existence of particular reasons to justify the confidentiality).

3.2.7 The decision

The investigation will normally end with a negative decision or a decision by which the Guarantor Authority establishes the existence of an infringement of the provisions of Articles 2 or 3. In such case the Authority fixes a time within which the undertakings concerned must terminate the infringement, by adopting the measures suggested by the Authority if necessary.

Only in the event of a very serious infringement can the Guarantor Authority immediately impose a fine (see section 3.3 below).

The final decision must be notified to the undertakings concerned and published in the *Bollettino* within 20 days.

3.2.8 Appeal

Appeal against all decisions of the Guarantor Authority must be filed with the Regional Administrative Court for Lazio (TAR Lazio); there is no other competent court (Article 33.1). Therefore, decisions of this court are very important for the interpretation of the Law.

The jurisdiction of this court, in particular, also includes the appeal of decisions by which the Guarantor Authority imposes a fine;[13] moreover, with regard to these decisions, the Administrative Court also has the power to modify the amount of such fine and reduce it to the minimum, if necessary.[14]

3.3   Sanctions

3.3.1 The Guarantor Authority can impose a fine only in two cases:

(a)   when a very serious infringement has been established (Article 15.1);
(b)   when the undertakings do not observe an order to terminate the infringement within the time indicated in the decision (Article 15.2).

3.3.2 In the first case the fine can be fixed at an amount from a minimum of 1% up to a maximum of 10% of the turnover realised by each undertaking in the previous year and in the market concerned. In the case of an infringement by an undertaking which is a member of a group of companies, it seems correct to determine the fine on the basis of the turnover of each undertaking concerned.

3.3.3 In the case of lack of compliance with the decision of the Guarantor Authority, the minimum amount for the fine is twice the fine which could have been imposed under the above provision, whilst the maximum is always 10% of the turnover calculated as above.[15]

In the event that the undertaking persists in not observing the order, the Guarantor Authority can decide to suspend the activity of the undertaking for up to 30 days.

3.3.4 A fine is also provided for in the case of a refusal to provide information on request (cf section 3.2.5 above) (up to 50 million lire) and also in the event that the information or the documents supplied were false (a fine of up to 100 million lire).

3.4   Third party rights

3.4.1 The rights of all third parties who could be damaged as a result of an anti-competitive abuse are protected by the following instruments:

(a)   a complaint or report to the Guarantor Authority, in order to obtain the commencement of an investigation;
(b)   an intervention in the investigation proceedings;
(c)   an action in the courts in order to obtain a declaration of nullity of the behaviour prohibited and/or the compensation for damages suffered because of such behaviour.

---

13 Cf Court of Cassation, 05/01/94, No 52, in *Foro italiano*, 1994, I, 732.
14 Cf TAR Lazio, 21/07/93, No 1157, *Procal v Guarantor Authority for Competition and the Market*, in *Foro italiano*, 1994, III, 147.
15 It should be pointed out that, generally, the Guarantor Authority provides for the application of the minimum fine the first time it investigates a new market. For the first case in which a fine has been imposed under the provision of Article 15.2, see Decision 17/03/93, no 1017, *Aeroporti di Roma*, in *Boll*, 1993, no 6.

3.4.2 Complaints

In the case of a complaint or a report by a third party, it is not clear if the Guarantor Authority must start investigations or, alternatively, can decide to do so in accordance with its own judgment.[16]

3.4.3 Intervention in the proceedings

Firstly, the right of intervention in the investigation proceedings is granted to third parties who have a *present, direct and immediate interest* and who have submitted useful information to the Guarantor Authority for the starting of proceedings. Such third parties must receive notification of the commencement of the investigation, and can, at any time, have access to the documents relating to the investigation and submit statements, pleadings, documents and opinions to the Guarantor Authority. Moreover, they have a right to be heard before the end of the investigation.

3.4.4 The right of intervention is also granted to all subjects who have a private or public interest in the matter and also to bodies which represent widely held interests and which could suffer present, direct and immediate harm as a result of infringements of the Law. These subjects must file an application within 30 days from the publication of the starting decision in the *Bollettino*, explaining the reasons justifying their intervention. They can have access to the documents relating to the investigation at any time and submit statements, pleadings, documents and opinions to the Guarantor Authority.

3.4.5 Courts

Article 33.2 provides that the nullity of any arrangement and anti-competitive behaviour and the right to compensation for damages suffered in consequence of such abuses can be ascertained by the Court of Appeal which has jurisdiction in the territory where the infringement took place.

The wording of the rule does not exclude the Guarantor Authority from applying for a declaration of nullity of prohibited arrangements (in the event that it is no longer possible to start investigations; cf section 3.2.1 above).

3.4.6 Urgent measures

The same Court of Appeal can also order urgent measures in connection with infringements of the Law.

The courts have interpreted this rule restrictively: the Court of Appeal can only grant urgent measures which are related to a declaration of nullity and the right to damages on which the ordinary courts have jurisdiction. In this way, the jurisdiction on interim measures is strictly connected to the main jurisdiction on the matter, as it is provided for in general by the Code of Civil Procedure.[17]

16 The existence of a duty for the Guarantor Authority to start proceedings upon a formal report by a third party is maintained by M S Spolidoro, *La disciplina* antitrust *in Italia*, in *Rivista delle società*, 1990, 1292.
17 Cf Court of Appeal of Milan, Order 05/02/92, *MYC, Red Line, MGR v AFI, Virgin Dischi, SIAE*, cit; Court of Appeal of Rome, Order 14/01/93, *Gruppo Sicurezza v Aeroporti di Roma*, in *Foro it*, 1993, I, 3377.

In these cases the Court of Appeal has jurisdiction even if an urgent measure has been requested as an interim measure before the commencement of the proceedings;[18] in particular, jurisdiction belongs to the same judge having jurisdiction over the merits of the case (in accordance with the general provision of Article 669-*ter* of the Code of Civil Procedure).

Urgent measures also include, without doubt, injunction orders.

3.4.7 The Court of Appeal is not obliged to conform to any possible previous decision of the Guarantor Authority, which is an administrative body, nor must the court suspend the proceedings in the event that the Guarantor Authority is carrying on its own investigations (cf Article 295 of the Civil Procedure Code).

3.4.8 The exclusive jurisdiction provided for by Article 33.2 creates some perplexities; in fact, other inferior courts (*Tribunali*) continue to have jurisdiction over cases involving EC competition law. In particular, in cases where there is a doubt on the national or community extent of the matter, jurisdictional conflicts could arise, in which case, it seems reasonable to resolve such conflicts by giving jurisdiction to the *Tribunale*.

4   CHECKLIST OF POTENTIAL INFRINGEMENTS

4.1   Introduction

The strong similarity of Italian competition law to EC rules and, moreover, the duty of Italian authorities to interpret Law No 287/90 in conformity with principles of EC competition law (Article 1.4) means that potential cases of infringement are substantially similar to those examined under EC law. Therefore, we refer to the wider analysis of the matter contained in the chapter relating to EC law, our intention being, in the following paragraphs, to underline some of the elements which distinguish Italian law.

4.2   Agency

4.2.1 As far as agency is concerned, it is worth stressing the correct meaning of the word 'agent' according to Italian law. An agent is anyone who 'undertakes in a continuous way to promote the conclusion of contracts in a specific area' for the principal (Article 1742 Italian Civil Code); only in the event that it is expressly agreed in the contract can the agent also represent the principal and conclude contracts on his behalf.

4.2.2 The provisions of the Italian Civil Code specify that the agent shall be an independent undertaking. Moreover, the exclusivity is considered a *naturale contracti* (a typical clause of the contract); in fact, Article 1743 of the Civil Code states that:

(a)   the principal cannot use more than one agent at the same time in the same area and for the same kind of activity;

18 Cf Court of Appeal of Milan, Order 23/01/92, *Carivest v Nuova Samim*, cit.

(b)   nor can the agent be appointed to deal in the same area and in the same line of business for more than one undertaking in competition with each other.

4.2.3   Therefore, it is likely that if restrictions of competition provided for by an agency agreement do not exceed those indicated by the above-mentioned rule, they will not be challenged on the basis of Article 2 of the Law. Anti-trust regulation will be applied in any event if more restrictive provisions are added in the relationship between the parties (eg extension of the restriction of competition to more territorial areas and to different kinds of activity), or in connection with the duration of the contract and the exclusivity.

4.2.4   The restriction of competition after termination of the contract is regulated by Article 1751 bis of the Italian Civil Code in accordance with the provisions of Directive No 86/653/EEC; also in this case it is likely that where the agreement does not provide more restrictions than those contemplated by the above-mentioned provision (maximum duration of two years, limitations regarding the field of activity, clientele and territorial area for which the contract is in force) there is no reason to apply the prohibition contained in Article 2 of the Law.

4.3   Distribution

4.3.1   The Guarantor Authority demonstrated from the beginning a favourable attitude towards vertical agreements, included amongst which are, principally, exclusive distribution agreements.

Distribution agreements are not expressly provided for by the Italian Civil Code and the regulation partially derives from provisions relating to continuous supply (*somministrazione*) agreements (by a continuous supply agreement one party undertakes to supply goods periodically and continuously to the other party, according to the needs of such a party).

4.3.2   Having regard to the provisions for continuous supply agreements, two kind of exclusivity are considered, one of which could refer typically to distribution agreements.

In the event that exclusivity is provided for by the agreement for the benefit of the supplied party, Article 1568 of the Italian Civil Code provides that the supplier shall refrain from supplying in the same area, directly or indirectly, the same kind of goods which are the object of the contract. Moreover, if the party who is supplied undertakes to promote the sale of goods in the territory for which he is granted exclusivity, and then he fails to perform that obligation, he shall be liable for damages, even if he performed the contract as far as regards an agreed minimum quantity obligation.

4.3.3   As has been stated with regard to agency agreements, it is likely that if a distribution agreement does not contain more restriction than those indicated above, Article 2 of the Law will not apply. On the other hand, the Guarantor Authority may examine the duration of the distribution agreement and of the exclusivity contained therein. In fact, since the above-mentioned provision does not consider the matter and since the general limitation (five years) provided for by Article 2596 of the Civil Code does not seem to be applicable, in theory, the exclusivity could be indefinite.

4.3.4 As far as any exemption under Article 4 of the Law is concerned, it is likely that the Guarantor Authority will conform with the principles of Regulation No 1983/83/EEC, as far as they relate to intra-state situations. In fact, the Guarantor Authority has already gone further by taking into account the provisions of Regulation 1983/83 at the time of making the decision to start investigations relating to an exclusive distribution agreement.[19]

4.4 Selective distribution

No provision is contained in the Italian Civil Code with regard to selective distribution. According to Article 1.4 of the Law, the principles of EC competition law (see Chapter I) will be applicable.

4.5 Exclusive purchasing

It is worth referring to the provisions of the Italian Civil Code on continuous supply agreements as far as exclusive purchasing is concerned.

In the event that exclusivity is provided for by a contract for the benefit of the supplier, Article 1567 provides tight restrictions on the party who is supplied (exclusive purchaser): he shall not be supplied with the same kind of goods by any third party, nor can he himself, unless the parties agree differently, produce the kind of goods which are the object of the contract.

For the possibility of challenging this kind of exclusivity, see section 4.3 above on exclusive distribution.

4.6 Franchising

Franchising agreements, which normally involve several typical restrictions on competition, are not expressly regulated by the Italian legal system. On the other hand, it is worth noting that scholars often refer to Regulation No 4087/88/EEC in order to establish the basic elements of this type of contract. Therefore, it is likely that the Guarantor Authority will refer to such Regulation and to principles applied in the Community case law.

4.7 Intellectual property licensing

4.7.1 While the monopolistic position of the owner of an intellectual property right cannot normally be prohibited (unless there is an evident abuse) just because the monopoly is the essence of such a right, agreements by which the exploitation of IP rights is licensed to third parties usually contain restrictions on the activity of the licensor and the licensee, which limitations are likely to be prohibited by the anti-trust Law.

As regards the possibility that such agreements could obtain an exemption in accordance with Article 4 of the Law, it would be better to refer to what has been said on EC exemption regulations, the basic principles of which should also be applicable to domestic situations, in accordance to the provision of Article 1.4.

19 Cf Decision 26/02/92, no 402, *Vevey Europe/Res Pharma*, in *Boll* 1992, no 4.

4.7.2 The relationship between copyright and anti-trust Law has been the subject of a case before the Court of Appeal, which court, however, gave a decision which referred mainly to the powers of the courts in the application of Law No 287/90.[20]

4.8 Refusals to supply

4.8.1 The refusal to contract is considered by the Italian legal system as a typical abuse. Given the gravity of such abuse, a provision had already been introduced into the Civil Code. Article 2597 provides that an undertaking which benefits from a legal monopoly is obliged to contract on equal terms with anyone who requires the goods or services which are the subject of the monopoly.

This provision has always been applied restrictively, in relation only to monopolies expressly provided by the Law. Article 3 of the Law now provides for the sanction of refusals also by those who are in a dominant position, but who do not benefit from a legal monopoly.[1]

4.8.2 The refusal to contract, moreover, could be the effect of a restrictive arrangement: this kind of provision may easily be found in the case of *consortia* for co-ordination of trade activity.

4.9 Price restrictions

4.9.1 As with Community law, price fixing is directly considered by Articles 2 and 3 of the Law as a typical restriction of competition.

The prohibition provided by these rules has already been applied in several cases; it is worth reporting situations where prices were fixed by associations representing undertakings of a particular industry, maintaining that they were only indicating a statistical level of minimum costs.[2]

4.9.2 Discriminatory pricing is also expressly considered as a practice normally to be forbidden.

The Guarantor Authority considered some cases where the discrimination applied with regard to the different nationality of the undertakings involved;[3] these cases could also fall within the scope of EC competition law.

4.10 Tie-in sales

Imposition of tie-in clauses may be a typical abuse of a dominant position, prohibited by Article 3 of the Law. Moreover, the Guarantor Authority, in considering a case where a tie-in clause had been inserted into a standard agreement drafted by an association representing Italian gas suppliers (*Centro Italiano GPL*), prohibited the execution of the agreement in accordance with Article 2 of the Law.[4]

---

20 Cf Court of Appeal of Milan, 05/02/92, *MYC v SIAE*, cit; the essence of the case was to challenge the monopoly of SIAE, the Italian Society for Authors and Editors.
1 For an application of the rule regarding a legal monopoly, cf Decision 04/03/92, no 412, *Sip/3C Communications*, cit; for a simple dominant position cf Decision 10/04/92, no 452, *ANCIC/CERVED*, in *Boll*, 1992, no 7.
2 Cf Decision 26/08/91, no 140, *Assirevi*, in *Boll*, 1991, no 7; Decision 02/07/93, no 1266, *ANIA*, cit.
3 Cf Decision 17/03/93, no 1017, *Aeroporti di Roma*, cit.
4 Cf Decision 07/10/92, no 714, *Centro Italiano GPL*, in *Boll*, 1992, no 19.

4.11   Information exchange

Information exchange between competitors could typically be done within associations representing undertakings of a particular industry and *consortia* for development of a market.

The Guarantor Authority prohibited such exchange of information only in cases where it involved further restrictions of competition such as price fixing, market sharing, etc.[5]

4.12   Joint buying and selling

4.12.1   As stressed by EC law, this practice should not always be prohibited, and in fact its capacity to create restrictions on competition depends on the size of the undertakings involved.

4.12.2   It is worth reporting two cases where the Guarantor Authority considered an exclusive distribution agreement between two competing producers (in particular, in the milk and dairy products industry), by which agreement one of the two producers undertook to market, through a subsidiary, the products of the competitor. The Guarantor Authority stated that these agreements, even if having a partially vertical nature, were actually horizontal agreements, because the two parties were competitors. In both cases, however, Article 2 was not applied because the agreement did not involve a 'consistent' restriction of competition.[6]

4.13   Market sharing

Agreements for market sharing are invariably a restriction of competition infringing Article 2 of the Law and therefore prohibited by the Guarantor Authority.[7]

It seems interesting to note a case where such an agreement was not prohibited because it referred to foreign markets and not to the Italian one: therefore, the agreement did not fall within the scope of Article 2 of the Law.[8]

4.14   Joint ventures

4.14.1   For the differences between co-operative and concentrative joint venture, see sections 5.2.1 and 5.2.5 below.

4.14.2   A co-operative joint venture is, without doubt, a potential restriction of competition; the Guarantor Authority displayed particular severity towards this kind of arrangement because of the strong restrictions it can involve.[9]

---

5 Cf Decision 26/08/91, no 140, *Assirevi*, cit; Decision 02/07/93, no 1266, *ANIA*, cit; Decision 23/06/93, no 1238, *Ristrutturazione rete distributori carburanti*, cit.
6 Cf Decision 13/01/92, no 329, *Contal/Talat* and *Sodital/Putignano*, in *Boll*, 1992, no 1-2.
7 Cf Decision 23/06/93, no 1238, *Ristrutturazione rete distributori carburanti*, cit; Decision 27/05/92, no 520, *Procal*, in *Boll* 1992, no 10.
8 Decision 04/12/91, no 249, *Italian Group Cement*, in *Boll*, 1991, no 13.
9 Cf Decision 15/05/92, no 508, *Cementir/Sacci*, cit.

The co-operative aim could also be achieved when the competing undertakings do not have an equal interest in the joint venture.[10]

5 CONCENTRATIONS

5.1 Introduction

The control of concentration operations is regulated by the same Law and also by the Guarantor Authority for Competition and the Market (or the special agencies according to the criteria set out above – see sections 3.1.4, 3.1.5 above).

5.2 Definition of concentration

5.2.1 Article 5 defines concentration operations by distinguishing the following:

(a) mergers between undertakings;
(b) acquisition of partial or total control of undertakings;
(c) joint ventures.

There is no provision in the Law excluding concentration operations inside a group of companies. In any event, the Guarantor Authority maintains that such operations generally do not have external effects on competition; furthermore, in March 1995 the same Authority specified that certain operations between companies within a group do not need to be previously notified.[11]

Article 5.3 states that operations 'having as their main object or effect the coordination of behaviour of independent undertakings' are not deemed to be concentrations; the rules on arrangements can apply.

5.2.2 *Mergers*

It is worth noting that in this case the Guarantor Authority has decided that the undertakings concerned must notify the operation immediately after the resolution of the meeting of the members of companies which merge (see section 5.4.2 below).

5.2.3 *Acquisition of controlling interests*

Similarly to the provisions of EC law, the Italian rule states that there is acquisition of controlling interests when 'one or more subjects controlling at least one undertaking or one or more undertakings acquire *directly or indirectly, by any means'* the control of the whole or of parts of one or more undertakings.

Moreover, Article 5.2 states that there is no acquisition of control in the event of an acquisition of interests by a bank or a credit institution, at the time of their creation or of the increase in the capital of an undertaking, provided that such acquisition is made in order to sell the interests within one year and that during this

---

10 Cf Decision 17/06/92, no 563, *Cementir/Merone*, in *Boll*, 1992, no 12.
11 Cf Guarantor Authority for Competition and the Market, *Relazione annuale al Presidente del Consiglio dei Ministri per il* 1991; Notice 28/03/95, in Boll, 1995, no 12.

time the right to vote is not exercised. The provision must be interpreted restrictively and, in particular, does not apply to *holding companies.*[12]

5.2.4   The notion of *control* for the purposes of the above provisions is stated in Article 7, which mirrors the equivalent concept in EC law. It includes the situations provided for by Article 2359 of the Civil Code (control of the majority in general meetings, dominant influence by way of shares, quotas or agreements, indirect control) and extends them, to include a *determining influence*, due to any kind of rights, agreements or other legal relationships (individually or jointly, taking into account any factual or legal circumstance). It is not clear if the wording *determining influence* could have a different meaning to *dominant influence* provided for by Regulation no 4064/89/EEC. In any event, the provision also includes potential control.

The control can be held directly or indirectly by either a physical person, an undertaking, or by a group of persons or undertakings.

Upon consideration of the market situation, the Guarantor Authority can also maintain that the acquisition of the minority interests creates a concentration.[13] Further, there could be an acquisition of control, if the previous joint control becomes individual in the event of a division or *scission.*[14]

5.2.5   Joint ventures

It should be pointed out that the provision only considers the creation of a joint venture by way of creation of a *new company.* Moreover, co-operative joint ventures are excluded.[15]

5.2.6   Although the Law contains no provision on the matter, the Guarantor Authority maintains that *arrangements restricting competition ancillary* to concentration operations must be examined within the framework of the concentration.[16]

5.3   Appraisal of concentrations

5.3.1   The Guarantor Authority shall assess whether a concentration involves:

'the creation or the strengthening of a dominant position in the national market as a result of which the competition would be eliminated or *significantly and permanently* reduced'.

The assessment of the effects of the concentration is made by the Guarantor Authority at its own discretion; in fact, it seems to be a technical discretion, which must conform to the parameters fixed by the Law.

The Guarantor Authority maintains that it is very important to ascertain that the restriction of competition be *significant and permanent.*[17]

5.3.2   Article 6 provides that in its assessment the Guarantor Authority must take into account the following elements:

12 Cf Decision 29/01/92, no 354, *Fincomid/Silfin*, in *Boll*, 1992, no 1-2.
13 Cf Decision 06/11/91, no 206, *Sintesi/Bastogi*, in *Boll*, 1991, no 11.
14 Cf Decision 22/05/91, no 80, *ENI/Enimont*, in *Boll*, 1991, no 3.
15 Cf Decision 12/06/91, no 94, *Mitsui/Nippon*, in *Boll*, 1991, no 4.
16 Cf Decision 17/04/91, no 63, *Plada/Fedital*, in *Boll*, 1991, no 2.
17 Cf Decision 24/03/92, no 436, *Cereol/Continentale*, in *Boll*, 1992, no 6.

(a) the possibility of choosing supplies and users;
(b) the position in the market of the undertakings concerned;
(c) the access to sources and outlets;
(d) the market structure;
(e) the state of supply and demand;
(f) the existence of barriers to entry into the market;
(g) the competitive situation of the national industry.

The last element should not be considered as a sign of protectionism, but as an opportunity to take into account the potential competition of foreign undertakings, which have not yet entered the national market.[18]

5.3.3 For the purpose of the assessment of the situation of undertakings in the market, the Guarantor Authority established the concept of relevant market, which is divided into a territorial market and a products market. The definition is in the appendix of the form for the notification of concentration and reflects the concept used in the EC practice.

5.3.4 Article 6 contains no provision regarding the different kinds of concentration (ie vertical, horizontal or conglomerate concentration); for this reason it seems that the assessment of different concentrations has to be made according to the same principles.

5.3.5 Decision

If the Guarantor Authority ascertains that a concentration has the abovementioned effect, it can adopt two different decisions:

(a) to prohibit the concentration; or
(b) to authorise the concentration and indicate the measures necessary to avoid the restrictive effect on competition.

5.3.6 Article 18.3 provides that if the concentration operation has already been executed, the Guarantor Authority can prescribe the measures necessary to restore competition. These measures can provide for deconcentration, but also other measures which do not directly affect the concentration may be suitable; in this case, the concentration can be authorised de facto.

If the measures indicated by the Guarantor Authority are not complied with, it is not possible to enforce them. The Authority can only impose the fines provided for by the Law (section 5.6 below).

5.3.7 Special government powers

Article 25 provides for the special authorisation of a concentration which must otherwise be prohibited. The Council of Ministers can enact some general and preventive guidelines on the basis of which a concentration may be authorised 'in the substantial general interests of the national economy in the area of European integration'.

---

18 Cf Decision 10/07/91, no 113, *ENI/Enimont*, cit.

The reference to European integration prevents the application of such criteria causing a conflict with EC competition law.

The application of the guidelines is the responsibility of the Guarantor Authority, which shall verify that such authorisation does not involve the total elimination of competition or any unjustified restriction; it shall also indicate the measures necessary to restore a situation of *full competition* within a fixed time.

5.3.8   Article 25.2 also provides that the Prime Minister, by way of a reciprocal provision, can prohibit concentration operations where they involve undertakings of a foreign country which does 'not protect the independence' of undertakings by way of provisions equivalent to those adopted in Italy or which applies discriminatory provisions to acquisitions made by Italian undertakings. Moreover, this prohibition is subject to the condition that 'essential reasons concerning the national economy' are involved.

This provision must not be applied to any EC country.

5.4   Mandatory prior notification

5.4.1   The Law provides for a mandatory prior notification of concentration operations which meet at least one of the following criteria:

(a)   the total aggregate domestic turnover of all undertakings concerned is more than 500 billion lire; or
(b)   the domestic turnover of the undertaking to be acquired is more than 50 billion lire.

Since the above-mentioned criteria are alternative, the obligation to notify the concentration arises quite often.

The turnover values indicated by the Law are increased every year in accordance with the index of inflation.

5.4.2   The notification shall be a *prior* notification, but the Law does not provide any precise time. It is only provided that notification of mergers must be made immediately after the making of the relevant resolutions by the merging companies. In the case of a public takeover bid the notification shall be made at the same time as that made to *Consob*.

For the purpose of the communication, the Guarantor Authority has prepared an appropriate form, in which all the required information is set out.[19] The notification must be posted by registered mail with advice of receipt or else delivered by hand to the offices of the Guarantor Authority.[20]

5.4.3   Calculation of turnover

The Guarantor Authority has stated that the turnover shall be calculated with reference to the group to which an undertaking belongs. As no provision of the Law provides this and, moreover, there is no concept of a group for this purpose, it is maintained that such provision has to be interpreted restrictively. In particular,

19 In *Boll*, special issue of the 28/05/91. The Form is now being modified (March 1995).
20 Autorità Garante della Concorrenza e del Mercato, Via Liguria 26, 00187 Roma.

it is not possible to refer to undertakings which are connected only by the wide relationship provided for by Article 7 of the Law.

In the case of the acquisition of control, only the turnover of the acquiring and the acquired undertakings (and of any possible subsidiary and controlled company) shall be considered and not the turnover of the vendor.

5.4.4 Moreover, the turnover shall be calculated having regard to the last financial year and to the domestic market (therefore, even if the group turnover is considered, it is not possible to have regard to foreign related companies). This amount must be net of any indirect taxation and sales discounts. No exclusion is provided by the Law for inter-group transactions.

5.4.5 Article 16.2 provides special criteria for the calculation of the turnover:

(a) of banks and financial institutions: one tenth of total assets (excluding revolving accounts);
(b) of insurance companies: the value of all premiums collected.

The wording *financial institutions* does not include holding companies.

5.4.6 Notifying persons

The form states that the obligation to notify shall be complied with by:

(a) the acquiring party in the case of an acquisition;
(b) the offeror in the case of a public takeover offer;
(c) all parties concerned, who can for this purpose make a joint notification and appoint a common representative, in the case of mergers, joint ventures, and acquisitions of joint control.

The obligation to notify concentration also extends to foreign undertakings who make the relevant turnover in Italy.

5.4.7 Contents of the notification

The notification shall contain the following information:

(a) information on the parties: general corporate information, activity undertaken;
(b) information on the operation: legal name of the transaction, existence of administrative conditions or authorisations, industries concerned, economical and financial data;
(c) ownership and control: list of all undertakings and/or individuals belonging to the same group of each of the parties involved (the same are requested to produce a copy of the balance sheets for the last three years), acquisitions performed in the last three years, means of control;
(d) personal and financial connections: for each subject involved in the operation, list of the ten main shareholders (direct or indirect interests higher than 10%) and of any other interest (higher than 10% or 5% for listed companies) in other undertakings in the same market;
(e) general information on the markets involved in the operation.

More detailed information on the effects of the operation is requested only for the 'most substantial' concentrations.

5.5   Procedure

5.5.1   The procedure for the assessment of concentrations consists of two phases:

(a)   pre-investigation;
(b)   investigation, which is only carried out if at the end of the pre-investigation phase the Guarantor Authority deems that the operation can have anti-competitive effects.

5.5.2   Pre-investigation

The Guarantor Authority shall inform the Prime Minister and the Minister for Industry of a notification of a concentration within 5 days of its receipt, in order to allow them to formulate decisions (see section 5.3.7 above).

Within 30 days from notification,[1] the Guarantor Authority shall decide whether to start investigations, assessing whether the operation:

(a)   is included in the hypothesis provided for by Article 5;
(b)   does not have a Community dimension;
(c)   exceeds the limits provided for by Article 16.1.

In the case of a negative decision, the Guarantor Authority shall notify its decision on the merits to all parties concerned and to the Ministry for Industry.

5.5.3   The abovementioned 30 day limit also applies if the Guarantor Authority receives an informal notification or acts on its own initiative; in the latter case the Guarantor Authority is not obliged to inform the subjects concerned before discontinuing investigations. However, the same limit can be extended in the event that the Guarantor Authority has received an incomplete notification and immediately requested more information.

The term having elapsed, the Guarantor Authority can no longer start investigations on the matter, unless the notification was incorrect, incomplete or false. The term is halved for public takeover bids.

5.5.4   Investigation

The decision to start investigations must be notified to the undertakings concerned (or to their common representative) and shall contain the reasons for which the concentration is deemed to affect competition. The decision shall also be published in the *Bollettino*.

Otherwise, the provisions relating to the investigation of arrangements and abuses of a dominant position shall apply (see sections 3.2–3.4 above). It should be pointed out that all time limits for intervention in the proceedings are halved.

---

1 This term is peremptory: cf TAR Lazio, decision 24/03/93, no 497, *Fininvest v Garante per la radiodiffusione e l'editoria*, cit.

5.5.5 *Suspension of a concentration*

In commencing investigations, the Guarantor Authority can order the suspension of the formation of a concentration, which otherwise may be completed (notwithstanding the possible negative consequences following a final prohibitive decision). This provision does not apply to public takeover bids, for which it is provided that the acquirer shall not exercise voting rights until the end of the investigation (Article 17.2).

5.5.6 *Decision*

The investigation must be terminated within the peremptory time of 45 days from its commencement; this term can be extended by up to 30 days in the event that the Guarantor Authority cannot obtain the required information from the undertakings possessing it.

5.5.7 Article 18.2 provides that the Guarantor Authority can terminate the investigation early in the following situations:

(a) the Guarantor Authority ascertains that its intervention is not necessary; or
(b) the undertakings concerned eliminate the elements which affect competition from the concentration project and file an appropriate application for the dismissal of the matter.

In such cases the Guarantor Authority shall terminate the investigation, giving a reasoned notice to the undertakings concerned and to the Minister for Industry. Moreover, the National Commission for Corporations and the Stock Exchange can prohibit a concentrative public takeover bid.

5.5.8 With regard to the possible decisions of the Guarantor Authority in the event of a negative assessment of the operation, see section 5.3.5 above.

5.6 Sanctions

5.6.1 Besides the sanctions related to the investigation (see section 3.3.2 above), the Guarantor Authority can impose fines in the following cases:

(a) execution of a prohibited concentration;
(b) lack of compliance with the measures imposed in order to restore competition in the case of a concentration executed before the final decision of the Guarantor Authority;
(c) lack of prior notification.[2]

No sanction is provided for the non-observance of the order for the interim suspension of the concentration (see section 5.5.5 above).

5.6.2 In the cases indicated under (a) and (b) above, the fine shall be between 1% and 10% of the turnover of the business which is the object of the concentration; in

---

2 Cf Decision 31/03/93, no 1048 and 1049, *Cragnotti & Partners/Fedital*, in *Boll*, 1993, no 6.

this case it seems appropriate not to refer to the turnover of the group of undertakings concerned.

In the case indicated under (c) above the maximum fine is equal to 1% of the turnover of the undertaking which failed to make the notification. The literal interpretation of the rule (Article 19.2) does not allow the extension of the imposition of the fine to the lack of notification of a public takeover bid.

The two fines can be accumulated.

5.7   Appeal and third party rights

All decisions of the Guarantor Authority can be appealed before the Regional Administrative Court for Lazio (TAR Lazio) in Rome, like decisions on arrangements and abuses of a dominant position (see section 3.2.8 above).

As far as third party rights are concerned, the reader is also referred to the rules set out for arrangements and abuses of a dominant position (see section 3.4. above), as far as applicable.

6   CONSULTING ADVISORY ACTIVITY

6.1   Introduction

6.1.1   The Guarantor Authority also has wider general powers on market and competition regulation. These powers increase the importance of this independent agency.

6.1.2   Proposal powers

Article 21 provides that the Guarantor Authority shall investigate and report to the authorities concerned (ie Parliament, the Prime Minister, Ministers, local and territorial bodies and authorities) any situations affecting competition or the proper functioning of the market, which situations arise as a result of statutes or general administrative regulations or decisions and are justified by the requirements of the general interest.

The Guarantor Authority is entrusted with this power in order to 'contribute to a more complete protection of competition and the market'. In these cases the Guarantor Authority can also suggest the measures which it deems appropriate in order to remove such anti-competitive situations.

The Guarantor Authority can disclose to the public its reports (they are generally published in the *Bollettino*).

6.1.3   Consulting powers

Article 22 provides that the Guarantor Authority can give its opinion on proposals for laws and regulations and problems on the competition and the market. These opinions can be given either on its own initiative or upon request of any public body or entity concerned. Moreover, the Guarantor Authority, upon request of the Prime Minister, must give its advice on proposals for laws and regulations which can affect the situation of competition and the market. The opinion is not binding.

6.1.4 Annual Report

The Guarantor Authority shall prepare each year, by 30 April, a Report on the activity carried out during the previous year. The Report shall be addressed to the Prime Minister, who shall then pass it to Parliament; it is also published in the *Bollettino*. Further, the importance of the Report is due to the fact that, besides listing the decisions of the year, it contains guidelines on the Guarantor Authority's policy.

7 SPECIAL REGULATIONS

7.1 Introduction

In order to complete the outline on Italian anti-trust law, it is worth reporting some special regulations which exist for the newspaper, broadcasting and banking industries. These rules, even if aimed at protecting interests other than competition, are strictly related to the provisions of the Law.

As has been pointed out above, these provisions do not replace those of the anti-trust Law.

7.2 Newspapers

7.2.1 Law No 416/1981 provides an obligation to notify the authority concerned of transfers of interests in undertakings which must be listed in the National Register for the Press and which are higher than 10% of the capital of such undertakings; a notification is also required for shareholders' agreements and voting syndicates between companies which own daily newspapers.

Article 1 of the same law contains a notion of control which basically reflects the main concept provided for by Article 2359 of the Civil Code.

7.2.2 Law No 67/1987 provides for the nullity of concentration operations between undertakings which publish daily newspapers, and which create a dominant position in the market. A dominant position exists whenever the same subject, directly or indirectly, controls:

(a) undertakings publishing daily newspapers which have a circulation of more than 20% of the total circulation of newspapers in Italy; or
(b) undertakings publishing more than 50% of the newspapers published in the same region; or
(c) undertakings publishing newspapers which print more than 50% of newspapers published in the same region;

or is connected with undertakings publishing daily newspapers which:

(d) have a circulation exceeding 30% of the total circulation of newspapers in Italy.

7.3 Broadcasting industry

Law No 223/90 contains provisions aimed at avoiding the creation of a dominant position in the broadcasting industry. Article 15 prohibits:

(a)   the ownership of a broadcasting licence at a national level whilst controlling undertakings which publish daily newspapers with a circulation of more than 16% of the total circulation of newspapers in Italy;

(b)   the ownership of more than one broadcasting licence at a national level whilst controlling undertakings which publish daily newspapers with a circulation of more than 8% of the total circulation of newspapers in Italy;

(c)   the ownership of more than two broadcasting licences whilst controlling undertakings which publish daily newspapers with a circulation of less than 8% of the total circulation of newspapers in Italy.

7.4   Banks

7.4.1   Article 161 of the *Testo Unico* of laws on banking and credit (*Decreto Legislativo* No 385/1993) provided for the repeal of all provisions in Title V of the anti-trust Law. These provisions, which had already been modified by *Decreto Legislativo* No 481/1992, were part of an independent section of the Law and have now been replaced by the provisions of the same *Testo Unico*. This regulation is aimed at avoiding conflicts of interest between banks and industrial and commercial companies and entities which own shares in the banks.

The Bank of Italy shall enact regulations for application.

7.4.2   Article 20 of the *Testo Unico* provides a mandatory notification to the Bank of Italy of all changes in the shareholders' interests in the capital of a bank if those interests exceed the limit to be fixed by the Bank of Italy. A notification is also provided for all agreements between the shareholders of a bank or of a company controlling a bank.

7.4.3   Operations which lead to the acquisition of the control of a bank or, in any event, of an interest exceeding 5% of the capital, are subject to the prior authorisation of the Bank of Italy. Authorisation is also required for the acquisition of control of a company which owns an interest higher than 5% of the capital of a bank or which controls a bank, in any event.

Authorisation cannot be granted to subjects who, by means of controlled companies, exercise '*to a substantial degree*' a business activity different to banking or financing and who want to acquire an interest higher than 15% of the capital or to acquire control of a bank. Authorisation is also refused when there is evidence of shareholders' agreements which involve a '*substantial concentration of power for the appointment or dismissal of the majority of the directors of the bank, so affecting the sound and prudent management of the bank itself*'.

7.4.4   Article 23 refers to the notion of control provided for by Article 2359 of the Civil Code and contains a presumption of a 'dominant influence' for the purposes of banking law.

CHAPTER XII

Luxembourg

Freddy Brausch
Hermann Beythan

Loesch & Wolter
11 rue Goethe
Boîte postale 1107
L-1011
Luxembourg

Tel   ++352 4811481
Fax ++352 494944

CHAPTER XII

Luxembourg

1 LUXEMBOURG COMPETITION LAW

1.1 Background

1.1.1 The source of competition law in Luxembourg is found principally in the law of 17 June 1970 on restrictive commercial practices (the 'Law').

1.1.2 The reasons behind the Law are that the Luxembourg legislator was of the opinion that Luxembourg should have legislation providing for the possibility to prohibit anti-competitive practices that are contrary to the public interest.

1.1.3 The fact that Luxembourg's neighbouring countries had instituted competition laws that go further than only implementing the obligations arising out of the European Economic Community Treaty (the 'EEC Treaty') had also to be taken into consideration. The legislator did not want Luxembourg to 'constitute an island within the European Community'.

1.2 Anti-competitive agreements and concerted practices

1.2.1 Article 1(1) of the Law states:

'Article 1 – May give rise to the penalties provided for by this law:

(1) any agreement between undertakings, any decision by groups of undertakings and any concerted practices that have as an object or effect the prevention, the restriction or the distortion of competition in the market and that are of a nature to prejudice public interest.
(2) [. . .]'.

There are, therefore, three elements :

(a)   an agreement between undertakings or a decision by a group of undertakings or a concerted practice between undertakings;
(b)   that is of a nature to prejudice public interest;
(c)   that prevents, restricts or distorts competition on the Luxembourg market.

1.2.2   *Undertakings*

The term 'undertaking' has to be understood in the same sense as in Article 85 of the EEC Treaty.

1.2.3   *Agreements, decisions by groups, concerted practices*

The Luxembourg legislator made use of the definition of Article 65 of the European Coal and Steel Community Treaty (the 'ECSC Treaty').

Due to this broad definition all kinds of restrictive practices, whether pursuant to a written agreement or whether under an informal understanding or otherwise, fall in the scope of the Law.

With respect to examples of restrictive practices, the preparatory documents to the Law (the 'Preparatory Documents') state that one may refer to the examples given under Article 85 of the EEC Treaty and to their interpretation by the Commission of the European Communities and by EC case law.

1.2.4   *Prejudice to the public interest*

According to the Preparatory Documents, 'public interest' is defined in this context as:

> '. . . something other than an individual interest . . . of an essence superior to the interest of a group, such collective interest often being nothing else but the addition of individual interests. The public interest participates in the public order and is inherent to the economic policy, and is placed strictly on the top of the hierarchy of values in the economic field'.

1.2.5   *Restriction of competition*

This term has to be interpreted in the same way as in the EEC Treaty. One may refer directly to the interpretation of Article 85 (1) of the EEC Treaty by the Commission of the European Communities, respectively by EC case law.

1.3   Abuse of market power

1.3.1   Article 1, (2) of the Law prohibits the abuse of market power. It states:

> 'Article 1 – May give rise to the penalties provided for in this law:
>
> (1) [. . .]
> (2) the activities of one or several undertakings that exploit in an abusive manner a dominant position on the market and prejudice public interest'.

Therefore the following are required:

(a)   the existence of a dominant position of one or several undertakings;
(b)   that is of a nature to prejudice public interest;
(c)   by the abuse of the dominant position.

1.3.2   *Dominant position*

According to the Preparatory Documents, a dominant position is deemed to exist in respect of a situation in which an undertaking or a certain number of undertakings acting together control a share of the market, of a certain product, that is so important, that it is to a large extent possible for the undertaking or undertakings to determine the price and the (market) conditions, regardless of competing undertakings.

1.3.3 Public interest

Reference is made to the comments above (see section 1.2.4).

1.3.4 Abuse of a dominant position

Reference is made to Article 86 of the European Community Treaty and to the examples stated therein.

1.4 Exemptions

1.4.1 Article 2 of the Law provides for possible exemptions with respect to concerted practices as well as the abuse of a dominant position. Article 2 states:

> 'Article 2 – Are not concerned by Article 1, agreements between undertakings, decisions by groups of undertakings and concerted practices as well as the activities of one or several undertakings which dispose of a dominant position on the market:
>
> (1) that result from the application of a law or of a decree;
> (2) with respect to which the authors are able to justify that they contribute to improving the production or distribution of goods or to promote technical or economic progress whilst respecting the interest of the consumers'.

This exemption is inspired by Article 85 (3) of the EEC Treaty and by the French competition laws in force at the time of drafting the Law, namely Article 59 *ter* of the French Decree of 30 June 1945 amended by Decrees of 9 August 1953, 24 June 1958, 17 August 1959 and by the law of 2 July 1963.

1.4.2 Unlike EC competition laws the exemption may apply as well in the case of a dominant position.

1.4.3 It is up to the persons concerned to adduce proof that the dominant position respective to the restriction to competition is beneficial. This can be established only with regard to the economic and market situation at a given moment. Practices which may have been approved at an earlier stage may therefore be disallowed later. As to the justification by reason of a law or of a decree, the sole existence of a law or decree prescribing such practice is not sufficient. Moreover, it must be shown that such activities are beneficial having regard to the public interest.

2 ENFORCEMENT

2.1 Enforcement authorities

2.1.1 Article 3 of the Laws states:

> 'A Commission for restrictive commercial practices is instituted at the Ministry of Economic Affairs. This Commission is responsible for reviewing possible infringements of Article 1, for examining the justifications given pursuant to Article 2 and for providing the Minister of Economic Affairs with a motivated report on each case examined. The decisional power, however, rests with the Minister of Economic Affairs.

The Commission is composed of six members of which two are officers of the Ministry of Economic Affairs, one is an officer of the Ministry of Justice and three persons come from the private sector and are chosen by reason of known knowledge of economic matters.

The chairman of the Commission, as well as its members, are appointed by the Minister of Economic Affairs, with the exception of the representative of the Ministry of Justice who is appointed by the Minister of Justice.

[. . .]'.

The main actors are:

(a)   the Commission for Restrictive Commercial Practices;
(b)   the Minister of Economic Affairs;
(c)   the courts.

Moreover, other Ministers and the public prosecutor may intervene by their (binding) request to the Minister of Economic Affairs to take up a case.

2.1.2   *The Commission for Restrictive Commercial Practices*

The Commission examines cases submitted to it by the Minister of Economic Affairs and transmits a motivated report thereon to the Minister.

The Commission is composed of six members of which two are agents of the Ministry for Economic Affairs, one is an agent of the Ministry of Justice, the remaining members coming from the private sector.

The members of the Commission are appointed by the Minister of Economic Affairs with the exception of the member from the Ministry of Justice who is appointed by the Ministry of Justice. If a case so requires, other agents from other ministries may assist on a temporary basis.

2.1.3   *The Minister of Economic Affairs*

The Minister of Economic Affairs has the following powers:

(a)   to submit cases of suspected infringements of Article 1 of the Law to the Commission, either at his own initiative or on the request from another Minister or from the public prosecutor.
      The above constitutes the only way to submit a case to the Commission;
(b)   to decide on the outcome of a case submitted to the Commission, upon receipt of the motivated report from the Commission.
      The Minister may either decide that a practice does not infringe Article 1 of the Law or, on the contrary, that it constitutes an infringement. In such case, the Minister may prohibit the practice or address a warning or a recommendation to the presumed perpetrator.

2.1.4   *The courts*

If the presumed perpetrator does not desist from the incriminated practice, the case is submitted to the competent courts that will examine whether the practice constitutes an infringement of Article 1 of the Law and whether such infringement is justified pursuant to Article 2 of the Law.

The courts may then sanction the perpetrator by way of fines and/or imprisonment.

A presumed perpetrator may appeal the decision of the Minister of Economic Affairs before the Luxembourg Administrative Court, the 'Council of State'.

2.2 Procedural rules

2.2.1 The Commission is only competent to investigate infringements to competition law. The Commission may deal only with suspected infringements brought to its attention by the Minister of Economic Affairs. The Commission gathers upon notice given by its chairman or by the Minister of Economic Affairs.

2.2.2 It has five months to issue its report, except in cases where extensions have been granted by the Minister of Economic Affairs.

2.2.3 Decisions taken by the Commission are taken by majority vote, a quorum of four commission members, of which at least two have to be state agents, being required. Dissenting opinions are allowed. They will be stated in the report of the Commission.

2.2.4 The Ministry of Economic Affairs may then either dismiss the case, issue recommendations or prohibit the incriminated practice. The decision of the Ministry of Economic Affairs has to be brought to the attention of the persons concerned by registered mail. It may be published in the 'Mémorial', the State Gazette.

2.3 Registration/filing or notification

No particular procedures are given with respect to the registration and filing of requests. The decisions are notified to the persons concerned by registered mail.

2.4 Fines and other sanctions

Persons liable for having infringed Article 1 of the Law may be sanctioned by imprisonment of eight days to one year and/or a fine ranging from 10,000 to 1 million Luxembourg francs.

Moreover, contracts or other transactions may be declared void or voidable.

2.5 Exemptions

Exemptions are possible as described above.

2.6 Third party rights

A third party suffering damage as a result of an infringement does not dispose of a particular action. However, in certain instances, third parties may be entitled to damages by way of the ordinary civil law remedies.

3   CHECKLIST OF POTENTIAL INFRINGEMENTS

3.1   General

3.1.1   At present the activities of the Commission have been very limited (three reported cases have been brought before the Commission). Neither the proceedings before, nor the decisions of the Commission being mandatorily made public, guidelines as to potential infringements of the Law can be given only with difficulty. As a general guideline reference can be made to Articles 85 and 86 of the EEC Treaty, on which the provisions under the Law are based.

3.1.2   One of the reasons adduced for the relatively minor importance of the Law is the small size of the Luxembourg market for most products and its domination by non-Luxembourgish entities. Another main reason is that with regard to the practices the most detrimental for the consumer, special consumer protection laws, apply with thus usually no particular use for the Law.

3.1.3   Apart from the provisions of the Law – in respect of which, in the absence of Luxembourg case law and legal literature of its own on the subject matter reference must be made to Articles 85 and 86 of the EEC Treaty – legal and regulatory provisions from several other sources come into play.

The most important ones in this respect are:

(a)   the Grand Ducal Decree of 31 May 1935 on illicit speculation in the field of foodstuffs, of commodities, paper and state bonds (the 'Decree of 31 May 1935');

(b)   the Grand Ducal Decree of 9 December 1965 on pre-determined prices and refusal to supply (the 'Decree of 9 December 1965');

Noteworthy are further:

(c)   the law of 7 July 1983 on the State Office for Prices;

(d)   the Grand Ducal Decree of 15 February 1964 on prices of imported products;

(e)   the Grand Ducal Decree of 8 January 1971 on the obligation to declare price increases to the State Office for Prices;

(f)   the Grand Ducal Decree of 8 April 1986 on the obligation to inform the consumers of the prices of products and services.

3.1.4   Finally, a series of laws and decrees exist which relate to a particular product, namely Grand Ducal decrees, respectively laws relating to profit margins on the sale of imported wool for knitting; profit margins on the sale of toys; the price-control of entrance fees for events and shows; maximum prices for the rental of films and for cinema tickets; the sale of fruits and vegetables; the sale of bread; the sale of accumulators of motor vehicles; profit margins of components of central heating systems; prices for wall paper; commissions of real estate brokers; prices of furniture; prices of potatoes; prices for pharmaceutical products; prices for tobacco; prices for Luxembourgish wines; prices of imported sausages; prices for transport by taxicabs; prices for fuel for domestic heating.

3.1.5   As exemplified by the above-cited provisions, rather than trying to prohibit or to influence anti-competitive practices and thus to obtain adequate pricing by healthy competition, in particular with respect to consumer products, the Luxembourg approach is one of price control.

3.2 Vertical agreements

3.2.1 No particular Luxembourg case law exists with respect to anti-competitive practices relating to the distribution, exclusive purchasing, franchising, intellectual property licensing, commercial agency and tie-in sales from which one could deduct how the courts would interpret the Law in this respect. It can, reasonably be assumed that the courts would extensively rely on the EEC case law on the application of Articles 85 and 86 of the EEC Treaty.

3.2.2 In respect of refusals to supply, price restrictions and resale price maintenance, apart from the provisions of the Law reference may be made to the following provisions. Article 1 of the Decree of 31 May 1935 states essentially:

'Article 1 – Will be punished by emprisonment from 8 days to 5 years and a fine [. . .].

(1) Persons who by fraudulent means have caused or maintained, respectively tried to cause or to maintain an increase or decrease of the prices of foodstuffs or of other commodities or of paper or of State bonds;
(2) Persons who without the use of fraudulent means have intentionally caused or maintained, respectively tried to cause or to maintain on the national market an abnormal increase or decrease of the prices of foodstuffs or other commodities, of paper or of State bonds, either by means of prohibitions or agreements having as their object the determination of minimum or maximum sales or purchase prices or by reason of restrictions to the production or to the free circulation of products;
(3) [. . .]
(4) [. . .]'.

The Decree of 9 December 1965 states:

'(1) Article 1 – It is prohibited for anyone who by profession produces and sells goods or provides services, to resort to vertical price fixings by any means whatsoever having as their object to prescribe individually or collectively minimum sales prices for goods or minimum prices for the provision of services, or to maintain such predetermined prices.

It is also prohibited to confer the character of fixed minimum prices to recommended prices, to indicative prices, to the prices, respectively the profit margin determined by the State Office for Prices, or to maximum retail prices that are mandatorily indicated on the packaging of goods.
(2) Article 1, first paragraph, does not apply to the sale of books, newspapers and other products of the press.

Exemptions may be granted by the Minister of Economic Affairs for a determined product or service, in particular with respect to the novelty of a product or a service, to the exclusivity attached to a patent or with respect to the promotion of new products or services.

Such exemptions are limited in time.
(3) [. . .]
(4) It is prohibited for the persons referred to in Article 1 of this Decree, with the aim to circumvent the prohibitions laid down in this Article 1, to refuse to satisfy within the limits of their stock and under the conditions that conform to the market practice, the orders of purchases of goods or orders for the provision of a service, provided such orders do not have an abnormal character and that they are made bona fide.

It is also prohibited for such persons to practice habitually, for the reasons referred to above, discriminatory sales conditions that are not justified by the market practice'.

3.3   Horizontal restrictions

Reference is made to section 3.1. above, and in particular to the Decree of 31 May 1935 and the Decree of 9 December 1965.

3.4   Abusive behaviour

Reference is made to section 3.1 above, and in particular to the Decree of 31 May 1935 and the Decree of 9 December 1965.

With respect to predatory pricing, the law of November 1986 on unfair competition that prohibits, respectively restricts certain practices such as dumping or sales of products with a bonus, must be mentioned.

3.5   Concentrations, mergers and acquisitions

Presently, no specific legislation on these subjects exists, that, from a competition viewpoint, would submit concentrations, mergers and acquisitions to governmental approval. However, the Law provides for the possibility for the Minister of Economic Affairs to prohibit concentrations, mergers and acquisitions if they constitute an anti-competitive practice or an abuse of a dominant position that prejudices public interest.

CHAPTER XIII

The Netherlands

Pierre V F Bos
with the assistance of Marco M Slotboom

Trenité Van Doorne
Louizalaan 149
1050 Brussels
Belgium

Tel   ++32 2 537 5159
Fax   ++32 2 537 6961

CHAPTER XIII

The Netherlands

1 THE SUBSTANTIVE DUTCH COMPETITION LAW OF THE NETHERLANDS

1.1 Introduction

1.1.1 Dutch competition law is founded on the Economic Competition Act ('ECA')[1] which entered into force on 13 November 1958. The ECA has had a very liberal approach towards competition policy. Pursuant to the ECA anti-competitive agreements and abuses of economic dominance were and, in principle, still are permitted under the ECA, unless they are declared null and void because they run counter to 'the general interest'. This passive way of reviewing anti-competitive behaviour is known as the 'abuse system'.

1.1.2 Although the EEC Treaty entered into force in the same year as the ECA, only recently the forces of European integration and the apparent lack of efficiency of the Dutch competition law have induced the Dutch authorities to rethink their policy. Articles 85 and 86 of the EEC Treaty are based on a so-called 'prohibition system' that forbids cartels and restrictive practices unless their economic advantages outweigh the harm to competition. The exact opposite, therefore, to the Dutch competition rules.

1.1.3 Until 1993, the legislative option in the ECA to be used by the Minister of Economic Affairs to declare certain types of anti-competitive agreements null and void had only been used twice with respect to individual vertical price fixing in so far as certain goods are concerned.[2] The ECA was implemented, albeit in a lenient manner, on a case-by-case base.

1.1.4 The early 1990s saw an intensification of Dutch competition policy: three decisions, each promulgated by Royal Decree based on Section 10 of the ECA, declare null and void certain types of horizontal price fixing agreements,[3] market-sharing agreements[4] and tendering agreements.[5]

---

1 'Wet economische mededinging', 28 June 1956, Staatsblad 1958, nr 413.
2 The 1964 Vertical Price-fixing Decree ('Besluit houdende onverbindendverklaring van bepaling met betrekking tot verticale prijsbinding in mededingingsregelingen'), 1 April 1964, Staatsblad 1964, nr 11, replaced by the 1991 Vertical Price-fixing Decree ('Besluit houdende onverbindend-verklaring van bepalingen in mededingingsregelingen inzake individuele verticale prijsbinding met betrekking tot bepaalde goederen'), 11 December 1991, Staatsblad 1991, nr 713.
3 The Horizontal Price-fixing Decree ('Besluit horizontale prijsbinding'), 4 February 1993, Staatsblad 1993, nr 80.
4 The Market-sharing Arrangements Decree ('Besluit marktverdelingsregelingen'), 19 January 1994, Staatsblad 1994, nr 56.
5 The Tendering Arrangements Decree ('Besluit aanbestedingsregelingen'), 19 January 1994, Staatsblad 1994, nr 55.

1.1.5 On 2 November 1994, an amendment of the ECA was adopted in order to increase the effectiveness of the ECA and the Decrees. The most important modifications are (i) the application of the rules of the ECA to *all* undertakings[6] and (ii) the inclusion in the scope of the ECA of legally non-binding arrangements (for instance gentlemens' agreements) as opposed to legally binding arrangements.[7] This text takes into account the modifications of the ECA produced by the amendment which will enter into force by 1 September 1995.

1.1.6 Although these recent initiatives have taken Dutch competition law a step towards the aim of Europeanisation and qualitative improvement, efforts will be continued. Currently, a new Competition Act relying to a large extent on the EEC Treaty rules is being drafted. An optimistic forecast of the date of entry into force of this new legislation seems to be spring of 1998, but it could well be delayed (even far beyond that date).[8]

1.1.7 Next to the ECA and the Decrees based on the ECA, the civil law rules on tort for matters such as unfair competition[9] and in particular, consumer deception,[10] play an ancillary role.

1.2 The Economic Competition Act

1.2.1 As a result of the 2 November 1994 amendment the ECA applies to all undertakings.[11] It covers 'competition arrangements' and 'positions of economic dominance'.

1.2.2 The Minister of Economic Affairs, who is in all cases competent, and any other Minister who may also be competent for a specific subject concerned (hereinafter together referred to as the 'Minister') may determine that a competitive arrangement or a position of economic dominance has effect contrary to the general interest. The meaning of this notion is vague; it gives the Minister a very considerable amount of discretion.

1.2.3 A competition arrangement is defined as a binding or non-binding arrangement or civil law decision, in which economic competition is regulated.[12]

1.2.4 Competition arrangements are permitted unless such arrangements are declared null and void by an individual decision[13] or by Decree[14] because they run counter to the general interest. The Minister may publish details of a competition arrangement that falls foul of the general interest.[15] Under certain circumstances

---

6 Until the entry into force of the 2 November 1994 amendment, the ECA applies to owners of enterprises and a limited list of practitioners (such as doctors, notaries, architects, etc).

7 'Wet tot wijziging van de Wet economische mededinging (vergroting van de effectiviteit)', 2 November 1994, Staatsblad 1994, nr 801.

8 For more information on the new Competition Act, see Pierre Bos and Alexandra Kamerling, *U-turn in Dutch Competition Policy*, [1994] 6 European Competition Law Review, p 344 ff, at pp 349–351.

9 Section 6:162 of the Dutch Civil Code.

10 Section 6:194 of the Dutch Civil Code.

11 See footnote 6, above.

12 ECA, s 1.

13 ECA, s 19(1)(*b*).

14 ECA, s 10.

15 ECA, s 19(1)(*a*).

the Minister, on the request of an undertaking which is not a party to such arrangement, may declare a competition arrangement binding on all parties within the market concerned. Such decision may apply for a maximum period of three years.[16]

1.2.5 A situation of economic dominance is defined as being a factual or legal relation involving a predominant influence by one or more undertakings on a market for goods or services in The Netherlands.[17]

1.2.6 In case the Minister decides that a situation of economic dominance has effects contrary to the public interest, he may take the following measures:

(a) the publication of details on the dominant position;[18]
(b) the issuance of 'directives' to any natural or legal person having an economic dominant position,[19] requiring it:

  (i) to refrain from certain behaviour;
  (ii) to supply certain goods or services for ready cash to designated persons, at customary prices;
  (iii) to determine prices for certain goods or services;
  (iv) to apply specific terms of payment and delivery for certain goods or services.

1.3 The Horizontal Price-fixing Decree

1.3.1 The Horizontal Price-fixing Decree declares null and void any restrictions in an agreement between two or more undertakings which restrict their freedom to set prices when selling or purchasing goods or services.[20] Not only purely horizontal price-fixing agreements fall under the scope of the prohibition, but also vertically construed price-fixing agreements which in practice have the effect of regulating price competition between competitors. Hence the interpretation of this prohibition including so-called 'fan constructions'. These are arrangements in which undertakings agree individually with a separate entity, for instance an industry association, that this entity will fix their prices.[1]

1.3.2 Other vertical price-fixing agreements are exempted from the application of the Decree.[2] Collective vertical price-fixing agreements however are caught by the general prohibition of Section 9(e)(1)(*b*) of the ECA, while, in so far as certain goods are concerned, the 1991 Vertical Price-fixing Decree[3] applies to individual vertical price-fixing agreements.

1.3.3 The Decree allows for a number of exemptions from the general prohibition.

---

16 ECA, ss 6 and 7.
17 ECA, s 1.
18 ECA, s 24(1)(*b*).
19 ECA, s 24(1)(*b*).
20 Section 1 of the Decree.
1 See ss 1 and 2 of the Decree, see also § 3.1 of the Explanatory Memorandum (published together with the Decree).
2 Section 3(*a*) of the Decree.
3 See footnote 2, above at p 293.

1.3.4 Agreements that limit the freedom to accept prices when *purchasing* goods or services only are null and void if the undertaking concerned has more than 100 employees.[4]

1.3.5 Exemptions for *sales* agreements concern restrictions in agreements in which:

(a) agreements between sellers and their purchasers (vertical price-fixing agreements);

(b) prices are fixed for a tender;[5]

(c) restrictions are imposed on undertakings who sell to end users goods or services which are the subject matter of a joint publicity campaign (lasting up to one month); and

(d) agreements which are considered *de minimis*, ie agreements that involve no more than eight participants with an aggregate annual turnover of less than NLG 5,000,000 if their main activities involve trade in goods, and less than NLG 1,000,000 in other cases.[6]

1.3.6 Both in respect of sale and purchase arrangements, an exemption has been made for undertakings dealing directly in goods or services with the general public, where these undertakings are aimed at maintaining a franchise organisation.[7] Exemption is also granted to price-fixing restrictions in partnership agreements and price-fixing restrictions between undertakings within a corporate group.[8] As a policy consideration within the context of public energy supply, the Decree exempts any restrictions which relate to the price of electricity or natural gas.[9]

1.3.7 Exempted are further restrictions in:

(a) agreements which exclusively affect markets outside The Netherlands; and

(b) agreements which are subject to any approval or obligation under any legislation other than the ECA or which arise out of a statutory obligation.[10]

1.3.8 An exemption is granted for all agreements which have been exempted from the application of Article 85(1) of the EEC Treaty by means of an individual exemption[11] or by means of relevant block exemptions as from time to time modified.[12] These block exemptions also apply to cases in which there is no appreciable effect on interstate trade or where the restriction of competition is not noticeable within the meaning of Article 85(1) of the EEC Treaty.[13]

1.3.9 The exemptions mentioned under sections 1.3.4, 1.3.5(c) and (d) and 1.3.6 will not be applicable, if the agreements in question are prohibited under Article 85(1) of the EEC Treaty.[14]

4 Section 2(2) of the Decree.
5 See section 1.5 below.
6 Section 3 of the Decree.
7 Section 4(1)(a) of the Decree.
8 Section 4(1)(b) of the Decree.
9 Section 4(1)(c) of the Decree.
10 Sections 4(2)(a) and (b) of the Decree.
11 Section 4(1)(f) of the Decree.
12 Sections 4(1)(d) of the Decree and 8 of the Market-sharing Arrangements Decree.
13 Section 4(1)(e) of the Decree.
14 Section 5 of the Decree.

1.3.10 Individual exemptions from the prohibition of the Decree may be granted by the Minister on request, if the Minister considers that it is in the public interest. The exemption criteria are similar to those of Article 85(3) of the EEC Treaty.[15]

1.3.11 Individual exemptions may be subject to certain limitations or obligations. Notifications for exemptions must be submitted to the Minister. The burden of proving that the exemption criteria are met lies with the applicant. Until now, only few of such individual exemptions have been granted.[16]

1.4 The Market-sharing Arrangements Decree

1.4.1 The Market-sharing Arrangements Decree pertains to the mutual respect of market positions of competitors. It declares null and void any restrictions in agreements between competitors limiting their freedom:

(a) to determine the quantities of goods to be sold or purchased or the services to be performed or obtained by them;
(b) to determine their production capacities;
(c) to determine their places of establishment, their sales territories or their sources of supply; or
(d) to choose their suppliers or purchasers or the acceptance of orders for the delivery of goods or services.[17]

1.4.2 Not only horizontal agreements but also fan constructions are declared null and void.[18]

1.4.3 Market sharing can only arise where the parties concerned continue to carry out the relevant activities, albeit under restrictions. Thus, where an arrangement leads to the total prohibition on carrying out the activity concerned, there exists no market sharing under the Decree (no single market is actually shared).[19]

1.4.4 The Decree does not apply to specialisation agreements, normalisation and standardisation agreements, collective exclusive dealing, selective and exclusive distribution as well as joint purchasing.[20]

1.4.5 Moreover, the Decree exempts:

(a) agreements between undertakings of a corporate group;[1]
(b) partnership agreements;[2]

15 Section 6 of the Decree in conjunction with § 5.2 of the Explanatory Memorandum.
16 Exemptions have been given in, eg, *Nefarma*, 31 May 1994, Staatscourant 100; *Fleurop Interflora*, 29 March 1995, Staatscourant 72. The negative decisions of the Minister on notices of objection against the refusal to grant an exemption in the cases *Diners Club Benelux*, 7 February 1995, Staatscourant nr 27 and *Maasgrind Combinatie*, 7 February 1995, Staatscourant nr 29, confirm that the Minister will grant exemptions in exceptional cases only when horizontal price fixing is concerned.
17 Section 1(a) to (d) of the Decree.
18 Section 2 of the Decree.
19 According to §§ 5.1 and 5.2 of the Explanatory Memorandum (published together with the Decree). A literal interpretation of the Decree however could lead to the opposite conclusion.
20 § 4.2, § 5.1 of the Explanatory Memorandum.
1 Section 3(1)(d) of the Decree.
2 Section 3(1)(d) of the Decree.

(c)   agreements covered by the Tendering Arrangements Decree;[3]
(d)   agreements for the production and distribution of natural gas and electricity;[4]
(e)   agreements that apply to markets outside The Netherlands;[5]
(f)   agreements which are subject to any approval or obligation under any other legislation than the ECA or which arise out of a statutory obligation;[6] and
(g)   *de minimis* agreements.[7]

1.4.6   Agreements which are exempt are those which have been exempted from the application of Article 85(1) of the EEC Treaty by means of an individual exemption[8] or by means of EC block exemptions listed in the Decree and as from time to time modified.[9] These block exemptions are also declared applicable to cases where there is no appreciable interstate trade effect or where the restriction of competition is not noticeable within the meaning of Article 85(1) of the EEC Treaty.[10]

1.4.7   The exemptions mentioned under section 1.4.5(a), (b), (d) and (g) will not apply, if the agreements in question are prohibited under Article 85(1) of the EEC Treaty.[11]

1.4.8   Individual exemptions from the prohibition of the Decree may be granted by the Minister, after notification, if the exemption criteria (which are similar to those of Article 85(3) of the EEC Treaty) are met.[12]

1.5   The Tendering Arrangements Decree

1.5.1   The Tendering Arrangements Decree declares null and void all price-fixing and market-sharing agreements made in the context of a tender, regardless of the sectors in which it is applied.

1.5.2   The reason behind this Decree can be found in the EC Commission's intervention in the Dutch construction sector[13] and the subsequent partial modification to the interim measures granted by the President of the Court of First Instance.[14]

1.5.3   This Decree prohibits all clauses limiting the freedom of tenderers which involve:

---

3   Section 3(e) of the Decree. See below, under section 1.5.
4   Section 3(1)(f) of the Decree.
5   Section 3(2)(a) of the Decree.
6   Section 3(2)(b) of the Decree.
7   Section 4 of the Decree. See, above, under section 1.3.5(d).
8   Section 3(c) of the Decree.
9   Sections 3(a) and 7 of the Decree.
10 Section 3(b) of the Decree.
11 Section 5 of the Decree.
12 Section 6 of the Decree in conjunction with § 7.2 of the Explanatory Memorandum. In *Vereniging Toerbeurt*, 7 April 1995, Staatscourant 71, an agreement with respect to inland water transport has been exempted under both the Horizontal Price-fixing Decree and the Market-sharing Arrangements Decree. In *Stichting Verwarming en Sanitair*, 26 January 1995, Staatscourant nr 25 the Minister decided that the Decree did not apply to the notified agreement so that an exemption was not required.
13 Commission Decision of 5 February 1992 in the Case IV/31.571 and 32.572 – *Building and Construction Industry in the Netherlands*, OJ 1992 L92/204, confirmed by the Court of First Instance in case T-29/92, *SPO v EC Commission* of 21 February 1995 (not yet reported).
14 Decision of 16 July 1992, case T-29/92, not yet reported.

(a) the setting of prices to be submitted to a contracting authority;[15]
(b) deciding whether or not to tender;[16] and
(c) obliging tenderers to exchange information with respect to (a) and (b) both with each other as with third parties.[17]

1.5.4 This general prohibition is subject to some exemptions.

1.5.5 First, the Decree provides an exemption for the submission of tenders to a legal person which does not carry on the same or a related profession as one or more of the tenderers.[18]

1.5.6 Tender prices can be submitted confidentially to the legal entity which can confidentially compare the bids and appoint another as 'entitled undertaking which can negotiate with the contracting authority'. The appointment of an entitled undertaking is subject to three cumulative conditions:

(a) it must have submitted the only tender or the lowest tender;
(b) the tenders must be comparable; and
(c) the majority of the interested tenderers must have indicated their willingness that an entitled undertaking will be appointed to negotiate with the contracting authority.[19]

1.5.7 An entitled undertaking can also be appointed in the case of non-simultaneous order. The tenderers concerned must then receive the prior consent from the entitled undertaking and fulfil the following conditions:

(a) the tender price of the later submitted bid is similar to the previously acknowledged candidates; and
(b) the permission may only be granted if the entitled undertaking does not rely on its prior right to negotiate with the contractors over its original tender price and the execution of the order.[20]

1.5.8 Exempted are also restrictions of competition which arise in combined tender submissions if:

(a) the combined tender is arranged for a specific invitation to tender or where there has been an announcement that there will be an invitation to tender for a job to be carried out at a date to be specified in the future; and
(b) each of the participants undertakes to contribute substantially to the execution of the job.[1]

1.5.9 An exemption is granted to tender agreements in partnership agreements and between undertakings within a corporate group.[2]

---

15 Section 3 of the Decree.
16 Section 3 of the Decree.
17 Section 4(1) of the Decree.
18 Section 4(2) of the Decree.
19 Section 5 of the Decree.
20 Section 6 of the Decree.
 1 Section 8 of the Decree.
 2 Section 17(1)(d) of the Decree.

1.5.10   Like the two other Decrees, the Tendering Arrangements Decree does not apply to *de minimis* agreements.[3]

1.5.11   The Decree does not apply to agreements which affect markets outside The Netherlands or are subject to any approval or obligations under any other legislation than the ECA or which arise out of a statutory obligation.[4]

1.5.12   An exemption is granted for all agreements which have been exempted from the prohibition of Article 85(1) of the EEC Treaty or by means of an individual exemption[5] or by means of one of the listed EC block exemptions as from time to time modified.[6] These block exemptions also apply to cases where there is no appreciable interstate trade effect or where the restriction is not noticeable.[7]

1.5.13   The exemptions mentioned under sections 1.5.5 to 1.5.9 will not be applicable, if the agreements in question are prohibited under Article 85(1) of the EEC Treaty.[8]

1.5.14   It is possible to apply for an individual exemption, but this exemption will only be granted if the tendering arrangement is considered essential to the realisation of certain advantages from the point of view of the public interest.[9] Identical criteria to those of Article 85(3) apply.[10]

2   ENFORCEMENT

2.1   Enforcement authorities

2.1.1   The enforcement of Dutch competition policy is divided into administrative enforcement, criminal enforcement, and private enforcement.

2.1.2   *Administrative enforcement*

The power and responsibility to enforce the ECA are vested in the Minister. The Minister is assisted by the Economic Control Service for criminal investigation and administrative verifications. The powers of the Economic Control Service ('Economische Controle Dienst') to investigate and obtain all necessary information have been expanded by the amendment of 2 November 1994.[11]

2.1.3   Before taking a decision in the sphere of the ECA, the Minister is under a statutory obligation to obtain the opinion of the Committee on Economic Competition, which is composed of at least 12 independent and impartial experts.

---

3   Section 7(1)(e) of the Decree. See also section 1.3.5(d). In addition to the *de minimis* criteria mentioned in 1.3.5(d), at maximum eight undertakings may participate in the tendering agreement.
4   Section 7(2) of the Decree.
5   Section 7(1)(c) of the Decree.
6   Sections 7(1)(a) and 11 of the Decree.
7   Section 7(1)(b) of the Decree.
8   Section 9 of the Decree.
9   Section 10 of the Decree in conjunction with § 5.5.2 of the Explanatory Memorandum (published with the Decree).
10   In *VCMBR*, 6 January 1995, Staatscourant nr 10, the notified agreement was modified in such a way that it no longer fell within the scope of the Decree.
11   See footnote 7, above, at p 294.

Referrals to the Committee are announced in the Staatscourant.[12] There is no obligation to follow the Committee's opinion. As a result of the amendment of the ECA of 2 November 1992 the opinions of the Committee on Economic Competition will also be public.

2.1.4 The administrative enforcement of the ECA is regulated in specific provisions of the ECA itself. Since none of the three Decrees includes any specific provisions concerning their enforcement, one must rely on the general provisions of the ECA.

2.1.5 A decision of the Minister founded on the ECA can, at first instance, be disputed through a so-called notice of objection. This notice will be handled by the Minister himself. Appeal from a decision on such notice of objection lies with an appellate tribunal called 'College van Beroep voor het Bedrijfsleven'.[13] As a result of the amendment of 2 November 1992 the appeal before the 'College van Beroep voor het Bedrijfsleven' will no longer have a suspensive force. The notice of objection concerning a decision of the Minister, and the appeal from decisions of the Minister on such notice, should both be made within six weeks after the notification of the decision.

2.1.6 Anyone who is directly affected by an administrative decision based upon the ECA is entitled to appeal. Except for reversal of the decision one may claim the payment of damages from the Minister, if his decision is annulled.

2.1.7 Criminal enforcement

The compliance with individual measures of the Minister based on the ECA, as well as with the Decrees, is ensured by criminal sanctions. The rules concerning criminal enforcement are to be found in the Economic Offence Act ('EOA').[14]

2.1.8 Behaviour which executes and complies with a competition arrangement which has been declared null and void by an individual or general measure of the Minister is prohibited.[15] Undertakings with a dominant position which are subject to obligations imposed by a directive of the Minister must respect the directive.[16] Breach of these rules is an economic offence within the meaning of the EOA.[17]

2.1.19 Private enforcement

It is possible to obtain compliance under Dutch civil law: a breach of a legal obligation may constitute a separate tort.[18] Non-compliance with the measures provided for by the ECA is considered such a breach of a legal obligation. Competition arrangements which have been declared null and void under the ECA can not be enforced under civil law. Civil law is enforced by the competent District

---

12 'Commissie Economische Mededinging'. ECA, ss 7, 11, 20 and 25.
13 ECA, s 33.
14 'Wet op de Economische Delicten', 22 June 1950, Staatsblad K 258.
15 ECA, s 15 and 22.
16 ECA, s 26.
17 EOA, s 2.
18 Section 6:162 of the Dutch Civil Code.

Court. Decisions of a District Court can be appealed before the competent Court of Appeal. The Supreme Court ('Hoge Raad') can review points of law.

2.2   Registration/filing or notifications

2.2.1   The ECA provides for the obligation to report competition arrangements (except for competition arrangments falling within the scope of one of the Decrees) to the Minister.[19] The Minister will subsequently register these arrangements in a non-public register. Summaries of registrations are published in the Official Journal ('Staatscourant'). Non-compliance with the obligation to report competition arrangements is an offence within the meaning of the EOA.[20] In practice the obligation to report competition arrangements, however, is generally ignored. In view of the three above-mentioned Decrees which declare the most frequent competition arrangements null and void, in practice the number of competition arrangements to be reported is limited.

2.2.2   There is no obligation to report the existence of a dominant position.

2.2.3   Prior notification is required in order to obtain an exemption under the above-mentioned Decrees. Notifications and decisions of the Minister under the Decrees are published in the 'Staatscourant'.

2.3   Fines and other sanctions

2.3.1   Infringements of the ECA may be punished under the EOA by fines of up to NLG 100,000 if the party convicted is a legal entity, or a maximum of NLG 25,000 if the party convicted is a natural person. Terms of imprisonment climb to a maximum of six months.[1]

2.3.2   Penalties may include seizure of property obtained through a criminal offence and 'dispossession of unfairly obtained benefit' in which case profit gained from the offence must be restored.[2]

2.3.3   The courts may decide to take additional measures such as closure of the convicted person's undertaking for a term to a maximum of one year, denial of certain privileges (eg, withdrawal of a government permit), publication of the judgment and an obligation to end the unlawful situation at his expense.[3]

2.3.4   There are only a very few reports of enforcement of the provisions of the EOA,[4] which does not exclude informal settlements pursuant to prosecution.

2.3.5   Damages may be claimed by private parties under civil law in case of

19 ECA, s 2.
20 EOA, s 2.
 1 EOA, s 6.
 2 EOA, s 8.
 3 EOA, s 7.
 4 See, for instance, the decision of the Supreme Court of 27 June 1972 in the *Knorr* case (NJ 1972, 498) concerning the infringement of the 1 April 1964 Vertical Price-fixing Decree.

non-compliance with measures provided for by the ECA. Here too, no precedents have been reported yet.

2.4   Exemptions

The exemption procedure under the three Decrees has been mentioned in sections 1.3, 1.4 and 1.5.

2.5   Third party rights

The ECA does not give rights to any third party remedies. The Minister may, but is not obliged to, start an investigation in response to a complaint of third parties. A third party may for instance ask for preliminary measures to be taken by the Minister.[5] As stated, anyone who is directly affected by a decision by the Minister based upon the ECA is entitled to appeal.

3   CHECKLIST OF POTENTIAL INFRINGEMENTS

3.1   Distribution

3.1.1   No specific provision of the ECA or any of the Decrees deals with distribution. The Market-sharing Arrangements Decree or the genereal rules of the ECA concerning competition arrangements and situations of an economic dominance may apply.[6] In general distribution will not raise issues under the ECA.

3.1.2   However, the Minister has recently asked an opinion from the Committee on Economic Competition with respect to a situation of an economic dominance by an undertaking importing foreign newspapers, which would run counter to the general interest. Since the two biggest Dutch distributors of such newspapers exclusively purchase from the importing undertaking in question, its main competitor cannot – according to the Minister – compete on a sound basis with the dominant undertaking. The Minister has asked the Committee on Economic Competition for its opinion.[7]

3.2   Exclusive purchasing

No specific provision of the ECA or any of the Decrees deals with exclusive purchasing. The rules of the ECA concerning competition arrangements and situations of an economic dominance may apply.[8] Exclusive purchasing will in general not cause difficulties under the ECA.

---

5   See, for instance, *Edipress v Betapress*, 27 February 1995, Staatscourant nr 40.
6   Except for cases covered by the EC Commission's Regulation 1983/83 on the application of Article 85(3) of the Treaty to categories of exclusive distribution agreements (OJ 1983/ L 173/1), amended by corrigendum (OJ 1983/L 281/24).
7   *Edipress v Betapress*, see, above, footnote 5.
8   Except for cases covered by the EC Commission's Regulation 1984/83 on the application of Article 85(3) of the Treaty to categories of exclusive purchasing agreements (OJ 1983/ L 173/5), amended by corrigendum (OJ 1983/L 281/84).

3.3 Franchising

Under the Horizontal Price-fixing Decree an exemption from the prohibition of horizontal pricing agreements has been made for undertakings dealing directly in goods or services with the general public, where these undertakings are aimed at maintaining a franchise organisation.[9] Further, the rules of the ECA concerning competition arrangements and situations of economic dominance apply to franchising.[10]

3.4 Intellectual property licensing

No specific provision of the ECA or any of the Decrees deals with intellectual property licensing. The Horizontal Price-fixing Decree and the Market-sharing Arrangements Decree as well as the general rules of the ECA concerning competition arrangements and situations of economic dominance may apply.[11]

3.5 Refusal to supply

The rules of the ECA concerning competition arrangements and situations of economic dominance apply to refusals to supply. In six decisions under the ECA refusal to supply was considered to be an abuse of a dominant position.[12]

3.6 Price restrictions

3.6.1 Section 9(e)(1)(a) of the ECA declares all forms of collective vertical price maintenance obligations null and void. In so far as it concerns certain goods (domestic appliances, video and tape recorders, records and compact discs) individual vertical price fixing has been prohibited.[13] Generally exempted from these rules are restrictions laid down in (i) agreements between undertakings of a corporate group, (ii) partnership agreements and (iii) agreements that apply to markets outside The Netherlands.

9 Section 4(1)(d) of the Horizontal Price-fixing Decree.
10 Except for cases covered by the EC Commission's Regulation 4087/88 on the application of Article 85(3) of the Treaty to certain categories of franchise agreements (OJ 1983/ L 359/46). Note that this block exemption does not exempt horizontal price-fixing, as the Horizontal Price-fixing Decree does.
11 Except for cases covered by the EC Commission's Regulations 2349/84 on the application of Article 85(3) of the Treaty to categories of patent licensing agreements (OJ 1984/ L 219/5) and 556/89 on the application of Article 85(3) of the Treaty to categories of know-how licensing agreements (OJ 1989/L 61/1), both amended by Regulation 151/93 (OJ 1993/L 21/8). Both Regulations are likely to be replaced by one single Regulation on the application of Article 85(3) of the Treaty to categories of technology transfer agreements (see for a draft, OJ 1994/C 178/3). See the Explanatory Memorandum to the Market-sharing Arrangements Decree, § 3.3.
12 *NV Lymar*, 7 August 1961, Staatscourant nr 151; *Commissie bescherming handelsbelangen woninginrichting*, 7 March 1968; *NV Sitos*, 7 March 1968, Staatscourant nr 47; *Aardolie Belangen Gemeenschap*, 4 April 1974 , Staatscourant nr 67; *Vihamy*, 2 March 1983, Staatscourant nr 43; *Krant-op-zondag*, 27 September 1990, Staatscourant nr 48; *Postorderpharmacie* 11 May 1994, Staatscourant nr 89.
13 See the 1991 Vertical Price-fixing Decree, above, footnote 2 at p 293.

3.6.2 Horizontal agreements to fix prices fall under the scope of the Horizontal Price-fixing Decree.[14]

3.6.3 The use of suggested resale prices is not prohibited in The Netherlands, as long as the retailer has full freedom to deviate from such suggested prices.[15]

3.7 Joint purchasing and selling

In so far as joint purchasing and selling agreements lead to horizontal or collective vertical price fixing, those agreements are prohibited by the Horizontal Price-fixing Decree or Section 9(e)(1)(*a*) of the ECA.

3.8 Market sharing

Agreements between actual or potential competitors designed to share markets geographically or by reference to customers fall under the scope of the Market-sharing Arrangements Decree.[16]

3.9 Joint ventures

3.9.1 Under Dutch competition law no specific provision deals with joint ventures. The three above mentioned Decrees and, by means of the Decrees, the EC block exemptions, listed therein may apply to joint ventures.

3.9.1 The agreement establishing a joint venture whereby its parents withdraw from the markets of the joint venture is not a market-sharing arrangement.[17] Where one or more of the joint venture partners is not withdrawing from the market on which the joint venture will be active, market-sharing arrangements between the joint venture and its partner fall under the Market-sharing Arrangements Decree.[18]

3.10 Unfair pricing

No specific provision of the ECA or any of the Decrees deals with the practice of unfair pricing. The general rules of the ECA concerning competition arrangements and dominant position apply to unfair pricing.[19]

---

14 See section 1.3, above.
15 See the memorandum ('Memorie van Toelichting') of the Minister to Parliament to the 2 November 1994 amendment, 'Tweede Kamer, vergaderjaar' 1992–1993, 23306, nr 3, p 8.
16 See section 1.4, above.
17 Explanatory Memorandum to the Market-sharing Arrangements Decree, §§ 5.1 and 5.2.
18 See section 1.3, above.
19 The *Hoffmann-La Roche* case (18 July 1977, Staatscourant nr 137) based on Section 24 of the ECA involves the charging of excessively high prices; the *Bakkersconflict Haarlem* case (19 January 1960, Staatscourant nr 12) consisted of the charging of excessively low prices.

3.11   Predatory pricing

No specific provision of the ECA or any of the Decrees deals with the practice of predatory pricing. Nevertheless, the practice of predatory pricing could be an indication of the abuse of a dominant position. In the *Sijthoff* case, this statement was affirmed by the Court of Appeal at The Hague.[20]

4   MERGER CONTROL

4.1   General

4.1.1   The Dutch legislation does not contain any provisions on merger control. Consequently, as a general rule, mergers which fall below the thresholds of the EC Merger Control Regulation fall into an unsupervised 'black hole' in The Netherlands.[1]

4.1.2   In contrast to the intentions announced in 1994 by his predecessor, the current Minister has announced that the new Competition Act will include provisions on merger control. No further details with respect to these intentions have been made public yet.

4.2   Newspaper mergers

The association of Dutch publishers of newspapers has adopted a self-regulating merger control code.[2] Pursuant to this code a merger of a concentration of newspaper publishers may be prohibited, if this merger would give publishers a market of more than 30%, unless permission is granted by a special panel.

---

20 Court of Appeal of The Hague, 19 December 1985, BIE 1987, 58, page 228. See also the *Bakkersconflict Haarlem* case (see, footnote 19, above).

 1 However, the Dutch Government can request that the EC Commission review a concentration which does not meet the EC threshold levels pursuant to Article 22(3) of the EC Merger Control Regulation (the so-called 'Dutch clause'). Recently, the Dutch Government has used this provision for the first time ever (*RTL/Veronica/Endemol*, OJ 1995/C 112/4).

 2 See a memorandum of the Dutch Parliament, 'Tweede Kamer, Vergaderjaar', 1992–1993, 20984. nr 10.

CHAPTER XIV

Norway

Knut Bachke

Advokatene Kvam & Co
Observatoriegt 12
0254 Oslo
Norway

Tel   ++47 22 559870
Fax ++47 22 559707

CHAPTER XIV

Norway

1 NORWEGIAN COMPETITION LAW

1.1 Background

1.1.1 On 11 June 1993, the Norwegian Government adopted a new Norwegian Competition Act which entered into force on 1 January 1994. It is the practice for the Nordic countries to co-operate closely in drafting their laws and indeed Sweden introduced a new Competition Act at the same time as Norway and both laws have been prepared with a view to harmonisation between themselves and also with the competition laws within the European Union upon which the national laws are largely based. Norway is also, of course, a member of the European Economic Area (EEA) and as such is subject to the competition laws of the EEA as applied by the EEA Supervisory Authority and referred to in detail in the EEA Agreement – Articles 53–60.

1.1.2 The Act replaces all former legislation and regulations governing competition law in Norway and will provide the legal basis for national enforcement of competition whether or not Norway becomes a member of the European Union.

1.1.3 The Act acknowledges that its primary objective is to ensure more efficient use of resources by paving the way for effective competition. Of particular concern in Norway has been tendency towards price co-operation as between competitors in the market and the diminution of competition though the increase in concentration of economic power through mergers on both a national and international scale.

1.1.4 It was felt that the maintenance of general price controls was no longer effective as a means of enforcing competition and that there was a need for an active Competition Authority with the power to enforce competition in the market place for social as well as economic reasons. Accordingly, the new law not only introduces competition legislation, but also makes important organisational changes in the establishment of a National Competition Authority and also conferring on the police the necessary powers and resources to enforce the competition rules effectively.

1.2 Application

1.2.1 Section 1(3) of the Competition Act provides that it applies both to private businesses and also to public authorities and governmental or local agencies carrying on an economic activity. The only general exception from the competition rules are wage agreements.

1.2.2   Section 1(4) also provides, however, that the provisions of the Act must not conflict with any resolutions or regulations issued by the Norwegian Parliament (Storting). This is to allow for the fact that the Storting will set rates of tariffs for the supply of certain goods or services, eg when adopting the government budget, and the Competition Authority is not permitted to intervene in such cases.

1.3   Prohibitions

Chapter 3 of the Competition Act contains a general prohibition on anti-competitive practices and then sets out specific examples of prohibitions which are regarded as harmful to society. Unless falling within a statutory exemption, or granted special dispensation, any infringement of the Competition Rules is unlawful and may give rise to criminal liability (in addition to the possibility of civil damages).

The Act covers the provision of both goods and services.

1.4   Prohibition against price co-operation

1.4.1   Section 3(1)

Co-operation on prices between competitors or the imposition of resale prices is prohibited whether taking the form of a legally binding agreement or the form of some informal neutral understanding or concerted practice. The prohibition extends to agreements on mark-ups and discounts, although the grant of customary cash discounts of up to 3% is generally permitted.

1.4.2   It has been established by the Norwegian Supreme Court that section 3(1) is infringed without the need to prove that the co-operation has had an effect on prices. It is enough that the co-operation took place.

1.5   Prohibition on resale price maintenance – section 3(1)

Suppliers are prohibited from imposing or seeking to influence resale prices. This provision is designed to catch vertical price fixing and applies both to individual and to collective control of prices.

1.5.1   Suppliers are, however, permitted to indicate advisory or recommended resale prices (section 3(1), para 4). In such cases, however, it is essential that the expression 'advisory' is used and that the reseller does not influence the supplier in his calculation of the advisory resale price.

1.6   Prohibition against collusive tendering – section 3(2)

Agreements on common price or contract terms in connection with public or private tenders and other forms of bidding are prohibited.

1.7 Prohibition against co-operation and market sharing

1.7.1 Section 3(3)

All forms of co-operation between actual or potential competitors whether explicit or by tacit agreement or other form of common conduct is prohibited. This would include the sharing of markets, customers or quotas.

1.7.2 Section 3(4) focuses specifically on cartel agreements seeking to impose competitive controls and this prohibition is addressed specifically to directors, other officers and employees of such cartels who will render themselves individually liable to criminal prosecution for such conduct.

1.7.3 There are provisions on abuse of market power (section 6(5) and (6)).

2 ENFORCEMENT

2.1 Enforcement authorities

2.1.1 The primary responsibility for enforcement of Norwegian competition law rests with the Norwegian Competition Authority which was set up under the Act. The Competition Authority is empowered to make decisions finding an infringement which are subject to appeal to the Ministry of Administrative Affairs. The Ministry of Administrative Affairs is also responsible for the Competition Authority as Governmental Department.

2.1.2 In addition to the above, individuals and companies who find that they have suffered damage as a result of prohibited conduct are entitled to seek damages by action through the civil courts. The Competition Authority can take necessary action through the police (section 6(2)).

2.2 Jurisdictional rules

2.2.1 Section 1(5) of the Act provides that the prohibition will apply to all anti-competitive practices which have an effect or are intended to have an effect within Norway. Accordingly, it is immaterial whether the acts in question are committed by Norwegians or foreigners or whether they take place inside or outside Norway. The 'effects doctrine', familiar in the context of EC competition law, will be applied to determine whether or not the Competition Authority has jurisdiction.

2.2.2 It must be remembered, however, that the Norwegian Competition Act may be applicable in parallel with the competition provisions of the Treaty of Rome and the EEA if the anti-competitive conduct has effects both in Norway and in the EU/EEA markets. If a restraint on competition has an effect on other EU countries, the common EU rules will take precedence over the national rules. However, since the Norwegian Competition Act is intended to follow the approach adopted within the EU, it is unlikely that any problems of conflict would arise between Norwegian and the European Rules.

2.2.3 In addition to its role in applying Norwegian competition law, the Norwegian Competition Authority is also required to enforce EU/EEA law in Norway so as to ensure the co-ordination and enforcement of the various rules.

2.3   Commission investigations

2.3.1 There is a general duty for all persons and undertakings to furnish the Competition Authority with any information that it requests in pursuing its responsibilities under the Competition Act. This duty is of a general kind and the Competition Authority may make requests either orally or in writing. Such requests for information can be made at any time and do not need to be based on any specific infringement.

The Competition Authority is also entitled to require production of all kinds of documents and may also demand access to computers or other technical aids.

2.3.2 Persons who are required to furnish information must do so notwithstanding the existence of any statutory obligation of confidentiality imposed on such agencies as, eg tax and other public authorities (section 6(1)). However, the right to legal professional privilege remains effective as justification for non-disclosure of information.

2.3.3 The Competition Authority also has extensive powers to secure evidence, eg by demanding access to property and making on-the-spot enquiries. If evidence is not given voluntarily, the Competition Authority may request the court to compel production of evidence. In making such enquiries, the Competition Authorities are entitled to require the assistance of the police to ensure that evidence is secured (section 6(2)).

2.4   Fines and other sanctions

2.4.1 The Competition Authority has power to impose continuing fines against those persons and undertakings who fail to supply information (section 6(4)).

2.4.2 The Competition Authority also has power to impose fines or periods of imprisonment of up to three years for those persons guilty of violation of the prohibitions under the Competition Act and where the breach of competition law is particularly serious, a term of imprisonment of up to six years can be imposed (section 6(6)).

2.4.3 In addition to the possibility of fines and imprisonment the Act also allows for the confiscation of any unlawful gains whether in criminal proceedings or in civil proceedings (section 6(5)). Such gain may be recovered not only from the infringer, but also from any other person who has benefited from the anti-competitive restriction. A claim by the Competition Authority for the surrender of any gain may not be appealed to the Ministry of Administrative Affairs unlike other decisions under the Act. A special rule provides that the Competition Authority may within three months bring legal action against the infringing person if the demand for surrender of gains is not accepted and such demand would then be the subject of civil court proceedings.

2.5 Invalidity

2.5.1 Contracts which have been entered into and which infringe the prohibitions under the Act are void as between the parties, as are violations of resolutions adopted pursuant to the Act (section 5(1)).

2.5.2 The Norwegian law of severance would, however, apply to such contracts so that if the anti-competitive restrictions are severable from the remainder of the agreement, then the remainder of the agreement may still continue in force and effect. If, however, the deletion of the anti-competitive restrictions materially affects the fundamental terms of the contract, then the whole contract is likely to be invalid (section 36 of the Agreements Act).

2.5.3 The purpose of the above provision is to obtain a kind of double enforcement of the Act. If a party can declare himself not to be bound by an agreement which conflicts with the Competition Act, this would help to make the anti-competitive restraint ineffective. A prohibited cartel may in this way lose its significance even if the Competition Authority does not discover its existence.

2.6 Statutory exemptions

The Competition Act exempts certain forms of co-operation from the prohibitions described above:

(a) joint bidding and tendering (section 3(5)) – traders may co-operate on individual projects and submit joint bids or offers on condition that the offer describes the co-operation and the names of the co-operating parties;

(b) co-operation between a parent and its subsidiary companies or between several companies within the same group is exempted (section 3(6)). This is based on the view that companies within the same group will normally form part of the same economic unit and that they would be unlikely to compete with one another. It is important to note, however, that the definition of a group under the Competition Rules is narrower than than applied in other legislation such as the Companies Act and Partnership Act;

(c) licensing agreements in respect of registered patents are exempt (section 3(7)). This exemption arises from the desire to encourage the dissemination of technical improvements etc. The exemption is subject to the restriction that the right must be registered in order for the exception to apply so that it will not apply in the case of know-how agreements;

(d) there are further statutory exemptions made in the areas of agriculture, forestry and fishing (section 3(8)). These exemptions are based on historical and political circumstances. Industries concerned have been protected and prices controlled for many years so that continued co-operation on prices, supplier control and market sharing is permitted. Nevertheless, the exception is in conflict with the objectives of the Competition Act and it is clear that the Competition Authority will keep a close watch on the way in which these industries operate. Furthermore, there is no doubt that the industries concerned will have to change to a more competitive environment as the process towards harmonisation with the European Union progresses.

2.7　Individual exemptions

2.7.1　Apart from the statutory exemptions mentioned above, the Competition Authority may, by resolution or regulation, grant individual dispensation under section 3(9) from prohibition under the Act if:

(a) the conduct or agreement concerned actually strengthens rather than weakens competition;
(b) the efficiency gains arising more than offset the anti-competitive effects;
(c) the restriction on competition is *de minimis*;
(d) special considerations apply.

2.7.2　The Competition Authority is empowered to impose conditions on the grant of dispensation. Furthermore, the dispensation can be revoked if the conditions are not performed or the assumptions underlying the dispensation change. These dispensation criteria are very similar to those which apply in Article 85(3) of the Treaty of Rome and Article 53 of the EEA Agreement.

2.7.3　In granting dispensation, the Competition Authority must grant it for a specific period which would normally not exceed five years and can never be longer than ten years (section 1(6)).

2.8　Third party rights

If the Competition Act is infringed, those to whom the infringement has caused damage may claim compensation as an ordinary civil action independently of the Competiton Authority.

3　CHECKLIST OF POTENTIAL INFRINGEMENTS

3.1　Agency

3.1.1　An agent normally acts as an extension of his principal's sales activity and does not assume financial risk, receiving only a commission on sales. On this basis an agency agreement is not normally affected by the Competition Rules since the agent and the supplier are to be regarded as constituting a single economic unit.

3.1.2　A Norwegian Act of 19 June 1992 exists in respect of commercial agencies. The Act regulates what is understood by a commercial agent, his obligations, the principal's obligations, commissions, relationship in respect of third parties etc. Agency agreements will not normally fall within the prohibitions of the competition rules.

3.2　Distribution

3.2.1　A distribution agreement is distinguished from an agency agreement in that the distributor purchases the products for resale. It is normal for a dealer's agreement to contain restrictions which, for example, prohibit the purchase of certain goods or the marketing of goods outside of a specified sales area. Under certain conditions such regulations are deemed to promote effective competition.

3.2.2 There are block exemptions for exclusive distributors. By a decree of 4 December 1992, Norway has adopted the Commission's Regulation 1983/83 regarding exclusive distributor agreements. In the block exemption there is a listing of which competition limitations are permitted. At the same time, an indication is given of which competition limitations may not be included within a single dealer agreement in order for the block exemption to apply.

3.2.3 An agreement which is excluded from the block exemption because, for example, it contains restriction on competition outside the scope of the exemption, may be referred to the Norwegian Competition Authority for individual exemption. The Norwegian Competition Authority may grant such exemption under certain conditions.

3.3 Selective distribution

Selective distribution arises where a supplier wishes to restrict the number of dealers who may sell his goods whether to limit the quantity of outlets or to insure the quality of outlets. The application of selective sale systems under which the supplier may determine, on the basis of quantitative choice criteria, who is to be allowed to sell the supplier's goods, is not permitted under the Competition Rules. On the other hand, it is permissible to apply a selective sales system if the choice criteria are objectively motivated with regard to the specific nature of the goods.

3.4 Exclusive purchasing

In an exclusive purchasing agreement the buyer commits himself to buy products for resale only from one specific supplier. Such agreement restricts competition as other suppliers will be excluded from selling their product to such a buyer. Norwegian law provides a block exemption which is the equivalent to EC Regulation 1984/83 in respect of groups of exclusive purchase agreements regarding, for example, filling station agreements.

3.5 Franchising

A franchising agreement involves one party, the franchiser, in return for a consideration to allow another party, the franchisee, to use for example its trade mark and business methods when selling goods to the consumer. Under the terms of the agreements the franchisee undertakes to observe the franchiser's conditions and the franchisee cannot therefore act in the market in a completely independent manner. Block exemption has been granted in respect of franchise agreements. Through the decree of 4 December 1992, Norway has adopted the Commission's Regulation 4087/88 concerning franchise agreements. Provided that the franchise agreement is drawn up in accordance with the rules which apply to the block exemption, it will not contravene the Competition Rules. If the franchise agreement contains any non-permitted restrictions on competition, the agreement may be referred to the Norwegian Competition Authority for exemption.

3.6   Intellectual property licensing

3.6.1   Block exemptions have been granted for both patent licence agreements and know-how agreements via the decree of 4 December 1992 collectively, corresponding to the Commission's Regulations 2349/84 and 556/89.

3.6.2   By means of the block exemption, therefore, patent licence agreements and know-how agreements, as well as so-called mixed agreements (a combination of the two previously mentioned types), are exempted from the Competition Rules under the conditions specified in the decrees.

3.6.3   In order for the block exemption regarding know-how agreements to be valid, it is required, for example, for the agreed knowledge not to be generally known and for it to be of considerable significance for the product or service which is the object of the agreement.

3.6.4   If a licence agreement falls outside the scope of the block exemption as a result of non-permitted restrictions on competition, the agreement may be referred to the Norwegian Competition Authority for individual exemption.

3.7   Refusals to supply

A vendor normally has the right to choose whether he will or will not sell to a certain customer. Normal trade custom enables the vendor to decide whether he wishes to conclude a business transaction or not. The prohibition rules under the competition legislation may, however, be applicable if, for example, the vendor holds a dominant position in the market and refuses to supply without justification.

3.8   Price restrictions

In order for the Competition Act to be effective, it is necessary that prices be visible. This means that customers are entitled to the information they need in order to judge the competitive situation and the goods and services on offer. In sales to consumers, therefore, the seller is required by the Act to furnish wherever feasible information about his prices so that they can be easily seen (price labelling – section 4(1)). To increase price transparency still further, the Competition Act empowers the Competition Authority to publish information about any terms of co-operation which have the purpose or effect of restraining competition (section 4(2)). Accordingly, traders who enter into such co-operative agreements may find the terms of such agreements a matter of public record. Resale price maintenance, discriminatory or unfair pricing are generally prohibited by the Competition Act in the absence of special dispensation.

3.9   Tie in sales

Tie in sales refer to a situation where the supply of one product is made conditional upon the purchase of another product. The Norwegian Marketing Act contains rules which govern how tie in sales are to be carried out. A contravention of the

Marketing Act's provisions may result in the management of the company being fined and, in serious cases, imprisoned.

3.10 Information exchange

Agreements providing for the exchange of information on such matters as costs, prices, customers, investments etc may restrict competition and therefore be prohibited by the Competition Act. Exchange of confidential information might infringe the Competition Act while there will be no objection to the exchange of general information.

3.11 Joint buying and selling

Agreements between competitors to establish joint purchasing or selling can infringe the Competition Act since it might diminish the freedom to act in the market. Decisions which are taken collectively by a trade association and which directly or indirectly bind the members of the association may therefore be examined via the application of the Competition Act's rules to determine whether the decision inhibits competition.

3.12 Market sharing

Agreements to share markets is prohibited and it is unlikely that exemption could be given for such agreement.

3.13 Joint ventures

Co-operation between companies in joint venture relationship is, under normal conditions, permitted in accordance with Norwegian rules. Such co-operation, however, if it does not fall within the scope of so-called '*de minimis* rules', ie that it does not have an appreciable influence in the market, may be assessed in accordance with the Competition Rules. Co-operation with regard to questions which do not affect the sale of goods and services naturally falls outside the scope of the Competition Act's provisions.

An assessment of whether a joint venture is governed by the Competition Rules is therefore made from the starting point of the objective benefit to the market of such co-operation. It is possible that, with reference to the Competition Act's rules, exemption may be awarded in respect of limited competition joint venture agreements.

4 CONCENTRATIONS, MERGERS AND ACQUISITIONS

4.1 Section 3(11) of the Act permits the Competition Authority to intervene against company mergers or acquisitions whether the Authority finds that it would lead to or reinforce a major restraint of competition in conflict with the objectives of the Act.

4.2 The conditions for intervening under this provision are stricter than under the general competition provisions under section 3(10). Company acquisitions are normally based on economies of scale, synergy gains, strong purchasing power etc and many on those terms encourage competition. It is for the Competition Authority to investigate the likely effects of the merger or acquisition to consider the benefits and disadvantages which might flow from it before it intervenes.

4.3　All types of acquisition or merger will be caught by the Act, including those of both domestic and foreign companies and including cases in which only parts of a company's business are acquired.

4.4　The Competition Authority has power to approve a merger or acquisition subject to conditions including an order for partial divestiture but the Act imposes a statutory obligation on the Competition Authority to seek a solution by agreement with the participating undertakings rather than simply to intervene and prohibit the merger concerned.

4.5　To avoid uncertainty in the business community, the law provides that any intervention by the Competition Authority must take place within six months from the date of the acquisition or merger agreement being signed or the public bid having been made. In certain circumstances, however, this period may be extended to one year. Although pre-notification is not obligatory, anybody who wishes to establish in advance whether the Competition Authority is likely to intervene, can notify the final takeover agreement to the Competition Authority and if it does not respond within three months from receipt of the notification that it intends to intervene, it may not do so. There is a right of appeal to the civil courts in respect of a Decision of the Competition Authority.

CHAPTER XV

Portugal

Dr N Gonçalves

J Vaz Serra de Moura & Associados
Empreendimento Amoreiras
Torre 2–11 andar
1000 Lisbon
Portugal

Tel   ++351 1 3840086
Fax   ++351 1 3880051

CHAPTER XV

Portugal

1 PORTUGUESE COMPETITION LAW

1.1 Background

1.1.1 The constitution of the Portuguese Republic establishes[1] that the defence of competition represents an important objective of the Portuguese state so as to ensure balanced competition among enterprises. Over the past few years[2] major changes have occurred to the structure and functioning of the Portuguese economy brought about by the liberalisation, deregulation and privatisation of important areas of economic activity and by the process of European economic integration within the EC.

1.1.2 Portuguese competition law is very recent. Although anticipated in the constitution of the Republic[3] the basic competition law legislation is contained in the Law Decree No 422/83 of 3 December 1983. This law has been amended a number of times, most recently by Law Decree No 371/93 of 29 October 1993 which introduced a system of national competition regulation very similar to the provisions of EC competition law under Articles 85 and 86 of the EEC Treaty.

1.1.3 Portuguese competition law is applied and enforced primarily by the Competition Council which is the administrative authority responsible for the enforcement of competition law and the development of policy.

1.2 Anti-competitive agreements and concerted practices

1.2.1 Restrictive agreements

Article 2 of Law Decree 371/93 provides that agreements, decisions and concerted practices between undertakings or associations of undertakings in whatever form they may appear will be prohibited if they have as their object or effect the prevention, restriction or distortion of competition in part or the whole of the national market.

1.2.2 The restriction on competition

Article 2 contains a non-exhaustive list of prohibited practices as follows:

---

1 Article 81, paragraph (f).
2 Preamble of Law Decree number 371/93 of 29 October.
3 Approved in 1976.

321

(a) to fix directly or indirectly purchase or sale prices or to interfere in their determination by the free operation of the market by artificially causing price increases or decreases;
(b) to fix directly or indirectly other transaction conditions whether in the same or different stages of the economic progress;
(c) to limit or control production, distribution, technical development or investment;
(d) to share markets or sources of supply;
(e) to apply, in a systematic or occasional manner, discriminatory conditions as to price or otherwise;
(f) to refuse directly or indirectly to allow the purchase or sale of goods or the rendering of services;
(g) to make contracts subject to the acceptance of supplementary obligations which by their nature or according to their commercial use, do not have any connection with the object of contracts.

1.2.3   Article 2(2) provides that such prohibited agreements or decisions will be null and void except where justified by virtue of Article 8.

1.2.4   Economic balance

Article 5, which is broadly equivalent to Article 85(3) of the EEC Treaty, provides that agreements containing restrictions specified in Article 2(1) of the law will be exempted from the prohibition where the agreement contributes to the improvement of production or the distribution of goods and services or the promotion of protection of technical economical development provided:

(a) that consumers of such goods and services obtain a fair share of the resulting benefit;
(b) the agreement does not impose any restrictions which are not indispensable to the attainment of the objectives;
(c) the agreement does not allow the undertakings concerned the possibility of eliminating competition in a substantial part of the market for the goods or services in question.

1.2.5   Authorisations under Article 5(6) are granted individually following an investigation by the Competition Council.[4] Unlike EC law, the Portuguese competition law does not provide for group exemptions although if an agreement falls within one of the EC group exemptions, that will be followed by the Competition Council under the doctrine of the primacy of EC law over national law.

1.2.6   Individual authorisations

A notification in the form of a petition is submitted to the Competition Council by those undertakings seeking to benefit from an authorisation under Article 5. Such petitions are presented in duplicate and by registered letter.
    The petition must contain the following information:

---

4 Decree n1097/93 of 29 October.

(a) the name and address of the undertakings involved and the nature of their businesses;

(b) the name and address of all other undertakings which are associated with the participating undertakings in the agreement, decision or concerted practice;

(c) the market shares of the participating enterprises in the relevant market;

(d) the form by which the petitioning parties have advised other enterprises of the petition;

(e) the relevant facts and reasons which demonstrate that the agreement, decision or concerted practice does not have the object of impeding, distorting or restricting competition;

(f) the relevant facts and reasons that justify the application of the anti-competitive restrictions involved.

1.2.7 The petition must be supported with copies of all relevant documents including the statutes of incorporated undertakings who are parties to the agreement. Upon receipt of the petition, the Council will notify the General Board of Competition and Prices for a report on the implications of the notified agreement.

The Competition Council is required to respond within 90 days. If it fails to do so, the enterprises concerned may require that the subject of the petition be granted provisional validity.

Before making any decision, the Council is required to publish in the Official Gazette and in a national newspaper, details of the petition and to invite interested third parties to submit their comments within a period of not less than 30 days.

When a decision is finally adopted, it will be published in the Official Gazette.

1.3 Abuse of market power

1.3.1 Article 3 of Law Decree 371/93 prohibits the abusive exploitation by one or more enterprises of a dominant position in the national market or in a substantial part thereof. As is the case with Article 86 of the EEC Treaty, the holding of a dominant position itself is not prohibited but only the abuse of such a dominant position.

1.3.2 Article 3(2) provides that a dominant position exists when :

(a) an undertaking operates in a market without being subject to significant competition or with 'assumed preponderance' of the market as compared with its competitors;

(b) two or more enterprises act in concert in a market in circumstances where they do not suffer significant competition or hold 'assumed preponderance' as compared with third parties.

Unlike the situation in relation to Article 86 of the EEC Treaty, the Competition Council has laid down some basic criteria for identifying the existence of a dominant position. These are presumptions *juris tantum*, based on market share but are without prejudice to an individual analysis of each case.

1.3.3 In the case of paragraph (a) above, a dominant position is presumed when the enterprise has a market share of 30% or more. In the case of paragraph (b) above, a dominant position is assumed when the enterprises concerned have a national market share of 50% or more where three or less enterprises are involved. This threshold is increased to 65% where five or less enterprises are involved.

1.3.4   Abusive practices

By way of illustration earlier, the practices mentioned in section 1.2.2 above are considered to be abusive.

1.3.5   Abusive exploitation of economic dependence

Article 4 prohibits abusive exploitation of economic dependence in which a supplier or customer has no alternative but to trade with the enterprise or group of enterprises exercising a dominant position.

2   ENFORCEMENT

2.1   Enforcement authorities

2.1.1   The enforcement of Portuguese competition law is the responsibility of two agencies, one administrative and the other a body with a mixed administrative and judicial role.

2.1.2   The first of these is the General Board of Competition and Prices ('General Board') which is an administrative body established by the Ministry of Commerce and Tourism.[5] The statutory functions of the General Board are as follows:

(a)   to identify anti-competitive practices, to make recommendations for their regulation and to supervise the enforcement of decisions;
(b)   to investigate mergers and concentrations[6] subject to pre-notification;
(c)   to prepare studies and reports;
(d)   to submit proposals to the Ministry for measures to improve the functioning of competition;
(e)   to undertake the responsibilities attached to authorities of Member States by Article 87 of the EEC Treaty and by EC Regulation 4064/89 (the Merger Regulation);
(f)   to consult with international institutions on competition matters;
(g)   to impose fines[7] except where such responsibility rests with the Competition Council.

2.1.3   The General Board has the power to request any enterprise or association of enterprises to produce any information and documents necessary for the purpose of an investigation. The General Board has similar powers in relation to obtaining such evidence from public authorities, regional or local.

2.1.4   The Competition Council is the primary authority with power to investigate individual anti-competitive practices.[8] In addition, however, it has the following powers:

(a)   to undertake enquiries and prepare reports as may be requested by the

---

5 Vide Art 5 of Law Decree n 23/84 of 14 January.
6 Art 9 and 10 of Law Decree n 371/93 of 29 October.
7 On constant terms of Art 38, with an exception mentioned.
8 Art 13.

Ministry of Commerce and Tourism in relation to mergers and concentrations;

(b) to prepare statements as to competition matters as may be requested by the Ministry;

(c) to issue proposals to the Minister concerning excessive concentrations and market dominance;

(d) to participate in dialogue with international institutions on competition matters;

(e) to impose fines for breach of the competition laws.[9]

2.1.5 The President of the Competition Council is a judicially appointed magistrate with the Public Registry appointed for a term of three years by the Prime Minister.

2.1.6 Duty of secrecy

There is a statutory obligation on the part of both the General Board and the Competition Council to maintain secrecy and to respect the confidentiality obligations.[10]

2.2 Jurisdictional rules – the procedure

2.2.1 The procedure for investigating anti-competitive restrictions is set out by Law Decree No 371/93 and by Law Decree No 433/82 against the background of the general civil law procedural rules. The General Board carries out investigations and pursues enquiries and complaints concerning anti-competitive practices and may call on private or public bodies to assist including, where necessary, the police.

2.2.2 The General Board may request the Competition Council to grant an interim decision ordering the suspension of anti-competitive practices where such immediate action is justified on the facts.

2.2.3 The General Board will pursue its investigation giving those who are alleged to have infringed the Competition Rules the opportunity to defend their position both in writing and at oral hearings convened for the purpose. After completing its investigation the General Board will prepare a final report which is submitted to the Competition Council for a decision. The Council has the power to ask the General Board to provide supplementary information if required.[11]

2.2.4 The General Board has power to issue the following decisions:[12]

(a) to order that the file be closed;

---

9 Paragraph (f) of n-1 of Art 13. The Competition Council imposes fines for infraction of Art 2 (agreements, practices realised and decisions of associations), Art 3 (abuse of dominant position), Art 4 (abuse of economic dependence), Art 24, n-1 (no respect for dependence order of forbidden practice) and Art 27, n-2 (publication of the decision).
10 Art 19.
11 Art 26.
12 Art 27.

(b)   to declare the existence of anti-competitive restrictions and impose an order on the infringer to take the necessary measures to bring the practice to an end;

(c)   to impose fines.

2.2.5   The Council decision will be published in the Official Gazette and in a newspaper with a national or regional circulation according to the nature of the market affected and the seriousness of the infringement. Copies of the decision taken will also be sent to the Trade and Tourism Ministry and to the General Board of Competition and Prices.

2.2.6   There is a right of appeal from the Order of the Council of Competition to the Judicial Court of Lisbon.[13] The appeal will not have suspensory effects on the substance of the decision other than in relation to fines and if the infringing parties wish the Order to be suspended in its entirety, they would have to make a separate application to the court for this purpose.

2.3   Sanctions[14]

Without prejudice to any criminal responsibility, infringements of the Competition Rules are punishable with civil fines of between PTE 50,000 to 200 million according to the nature and circumstances of the infringement and its impact on the market.

3   CHECKLIST OF POTENTIAL INFRINGEMENTS

3.1   Agency

A commercial agency agreement would not normally fall within the Competition Rules. The Council (23) has considered that a true agency would not normally involve an agreement between undertakings who are truly independent of one another to give rise to restrictions of competition. On the other hand, the Council has noted that occasionally agreements described as agency agreements involve anti-competitive restrictions and in such cases should be examined to see if there are any infringements of competition law.

3.2   Distribution

Distribution agreements can violate Competition Rules in certain circumstances.[15] The Council has issued several decisions[16] in which it has set out the conditions which must be satisfied in order for distribution agreements to be legal. Essentially distribution agreements imposing territorial exclusivity are acceptable provided that the terms of the agreement are objectively fair, the terms of the written contracts must be objectively agreed and there must be no discrimination as between distributors.

13 Art 28.
14 Art 27.
15 Paragraph (c) of n-1 of Art 2 of Law Decree n 371/93 of 29-10.
16 Sentences '*Agua do Luso/Central de cervejas*', Activity Report – year 1987; Sentence '*Dan Cake*', Activity Report – year 1992.

3.3 Selective distribution

3.3.1 Selective distribution agreements will fall within the competition law restrictions to the extent that the manufacturer or importer restricts the quantity of distributors available in any particular area.

3.3.2 Such agreements may be authorised provided that they meet the criteria laid down under Article 5 of the law which broadly follows the EC law approach to selective distribution.[17]

3.4 Exclusive purchasing[18]

An exclusive purchasing agreement may be caught by the Competition Rules in the same way as exclusive distribution but would merit exemption under Article 5 to the extent that they do not lead to excessive market foreclosure.

3.5 Franchising

Franchising agreements could infringe Article 2 but may be eligible for exemption under Article 5 through the application of the same rules as outlined in relation to distribution agreements.

3.6 Intellectual property licensing

Such agreements must comply with the rules and principles already defined and the rules set out in the industrial property code.[19] Such licences will be permissible so long as they do not infringe the EC or national competition rules.

3.7 Refusal to supply

It will be recalled that Article 2(1)(f) of Law Decree No 371/93 identifies a refusal to supply goods or services as a specific example of an anti-competitive restriction. Article 3 also cites refusal to supply as an example of abusive exploitation of a dominant position. That such refusals constitute an anti-competitive practice has been upheld by the Council in several decisions.

3.8 Price restrictions

Resale price maintenances are generally forbidden under Portuguese law. Similarly, the setting of minimum prices or minimum margins or the application of discriminatory prices to customers at the same level of distribution are likely to cause problems under Portuguese competition law. There have been many

---

17 See Chapter I.
18 Sentences '*Unicer*' (1985), '*Centralcer*' (1986), '*EDP*' (1992), in 'the distribution and exclusive purchase in communication regulation of competition – General Board of Competition and Prices'.
19 Approved by Law Decree n 30679, 24 August 1940.

decisions taken concerning pricing restrictions.[20] The provision of guidance as to price in the form of price recommendations will not infringe the rules of competition provided that the supplier is not in a dominant position vis a vis the reseller enabling him in effect to apply the price recommendation as a price fixing measure.

3.9   Tie in sales

Any attempt to tie sales of one product with another where there is no actual commercial linkage is likely to be held an anti-competitive restriction.

3.10   Information exchange

Information exchange between competitors is not specifically envisaged as a potential violation of competition rules under Portuguese law. Nevertheless, it is likely that an agreement relating to the exchange of information that would ordinarily be considered confidential might suggest a degree of collusion between competitors with a view to price fixing or market sharing and as such constitute an infringement of Article 2.

3.11   Joint buying and selling

An agreement between companies to establish general buying or selling conditions whether or not pricing is involved is likely to infringe Article 2. Nevertheless, authorisations might be possible to the extent that the justifying criteria under Article 5 can be established.

3.12   Market sharing

The sharing of markets or sources of supply represents a typical example of an agreement or concerted practice which will infringe the competition rules and is unlikely to be granted an authorisation.

3.13   Joint ventures

There is no specific regulation governing the competition aspects of joint ventures. Each joint venture would have to be considered on its merits within the context of Article 2 and the application of Article 5.

4   CONCENTRATIONS, MERGERS AND ACQUISITIONS

4.1   Introduction

Competition law considerations arising out of the concentration of companies are regulated under Section III, Article 7 ff of the Law Decree No 371/93 of

20 Sentences '*Dyrup*' (1986), 'medicaments of free sale', '*Centralcer*' (1986).

29 October 1993. The merger of companies is dealt with by Article 97-170 of the Commercial Companies Code. The approach adopted by the Portuguese law on concentrations follows closely that of EC Regulation 4064/89.[1]

4.2 Thresholds

4.2.1 Article 7 provides that concentrations of companies must be notified to the General Board of Competition and Prices where:

(a) the concentration leads to the creation or expansion of an undertaking with a market share in excess of 30% of the relevant product market;
(b) where the concentration results in an undertaking having a turnover in excess of PTE 30,000 million in Portugal in the last financial year excluding all taxes and VAT and intergroup trading.

4.2.2 Different thresholds apply in respect of credit institutions and insurance companies.

4.2.3 Qualifying concentrations must be pre-notified before any juridical step is taken to implement the concentration and before any public announcement. No juridical step implementing a concentration will be effective unless an express or implied authorisation has been given.

4.3 Appraisal criteria

4.3.1 Notification is submitted to the General Board of Competition and Prices and must contain the following information:

(a) details of the parties to the concentration;
(b) the juridical nature and form of the concentration;
(c) the nature of the goods and services manufactured or supplied by the participants;
(d) a list of group and associated companies of the parties;
(e) identification of relevant product markets and the market shares of the parties;
(f) the turnover of the parties in Portugal;
(g) annual report and accounts of the parties for the last three financial years;
(h) details of the main competitors;
(i) details of the major customers and suppliers of the parties.

4.3.2 Within 40 days following the receipt of the notification, the General Board will present to the Ministry of Commerce and Tourism a report covering the following matters:

(a) whether or not the concentration creates or reinforces a dominant position in the national market or in a substantial part of it which is likely to distort or restrict competition;

1 See Chapter I.

(b)   whether or not the concentration is likely to affect the competitiveness of the participating enterprises;

(c)   whether the concentration meets the conditions contained in Article 5.

4.4   Definition of concentration

Article 9 defines what is a concentration of companies and the text corresponds to Article 3 of EC Regulation 4064/89. A concentration will arise where:

(a)   two or more undertakings which were previously independent merge;

(b)   where one or more persons acquire control of an undertaking;

(c)   where two or more undertakings pursue a common enterprise if that common enterprise establishes an autonomous economic entity of a lasting character which does not have as its object or effect the co-ordination of the competitive behaviour between the participating undertakings or between those and the common enterprise.

4.5   Procedure

4.5.1   In the preparation of its report, the General Board has full power to request the provision of information and documents from both of the parties to the concentration and third parties. If it seeks additional information the General Board has the power to extend the 40 day time limit within which it is to submit its report.

4.5.2   If there is a failure to notify a concentration, but the General Board commences the enquiry having notice of the concentration then the time limit within which to submit its report is extended to 90 days.

4.5.3   Tacit authorisations[2]

Following receipt of the general report from the General Board, the Ministry of Commerce and Tourism has 50 days within which to refer the case to the Competition Council for a determination as to its anti-competitive effect. If the Ministry fails to do so within that period, then the parties may assume authorisation and the concentration can proceed.

4.5.4   If the Ministry refers the case to the Competition Council, the Council must submit its opinion to the Ministry within 30 days[3] indicating whether it considers that the concentration adversely effects competition or not.

4.5.5   Decisions[4]

Within 15 days following receipt of the opinion of the Competition Council, the Ministry of Commerce and Tourism must issue a decision which will decide either:

2   Art 32.
3   Art 33.
4   Art 34.

(a)   not to oppose the concentration;
(b)   not to oppose the concentration subject to the parties accepting certain condi-
      tions and obligations deemed necessary to protect competition;
(c)   prohibit the concentration making such orders as may be necessary to restore
      the status quo if the concentration has already proceeded.

4.6   Judicial review

The decision of the Ministry may be appealed to the Administrative Supreme
Court.

4.7   Fines

The General Board of Competition and Prices has the power to impose fines for
supply of false or misleading information during an investigation or for a failure to
comply with a decision. The level of fines range between PTE 100,000 to 100
million.

Spain

Luis-Ignacio Alonso-Martinez

Prol & Asociados
Eduardo Del Palacio 4
28002 Madrid
Spain

Tel   ++34 1 563 0601
Fax ++34 1 563 0020

CHAPTER XVI

Spain

1 SPANISH COMPETITION LAW

1.1 Background

1.1.1 Article 38 of the Spanish Constitution[1] establishes the general principle of the freedom of undertakings in the market economy. Public institutions have to guarantee and protect it and the productivity of industry and commerce, according to the general requirements of the economy.

Competition, as a governing principle of the market economy, is an essential element of the Spanish economic organization model and has been considered as the first and more important manifestation of the freedom of undertaking. The defence of competition has to be considered, therefore, as compulsory according to the above-mentioned Article 38 of the Constitution.[2]

1.1.2 The Spanish competition system is a very recent one. Based primarily on European Community competition law,[3] the Spanish system has been renewed[4] in two different pieces of legislation: the Act for the Defence of Competition[5] of 1989 and the Unfair Competition Act[6] of 1991.

Both legal texts are complementary and in some cases, as we will see, used together in the interpretation of the different concepts, particularly unfair acts which could restrict competition.

1.1.3 Each law is interpreted by different administrative and jurisdictional bodies which produce case law, necessary for the application of Spanish competition law. The principal source of this case law is the Court for the Defence of Competition.

Although both Acts are comparatively recent, the Court for the Defence of Competition has produced a number of interesting decisions which are useful to interpret the Act.

In this connection, it is necessary to emphasise that the Court has followed, in most cases, the principles, ideas and interpretations of the European Court of Justice.

1.1.4 In addition, to facilitate the application of the Act, two regulations have

---

1 Constitution of 27 December 1978.
2 Preamble of the Act for the Defence of Competition.
3 Articles 85 and 86 of the Treaty of Rome and EC Regulations and Group Exemptions Regulations. See Chapter I.
4 The former Act 110/1963 of Reprehension of the Restrictions of Competition was not applied in all its extent. The court did not produce economic sanctions based on this Act until 1987, after the incorporation of Spain to the EC.
5 Act 16/1989 of 17 July 1989, herein generally called 'the Act'.
6 Act 3/1991 of 10 January 1991.

been approved: the first[7] concerns the particular and block exemptions for agreements forbidden by the Act, the procedure to be followed to obtain the authorisation and other functioning regulations; the second[8] deals with mergers and concentrations, general considerations of the thresholds, notifications of the concentrations and procedure rules.

1.2 Anti-competitive agreements and concerted practices

1.2.1 Article 1(1) – restrictive agreements

Article 1(1) of the Act prohibits all agreements, decisions or collective recommendations, concerted or consciously parallel practices (generally called 'agreements') which will produce, could produce or have the effect of a restriction, distortion or an impediment to competition in all or a part of the national market.

Note that, in contrast with EC competition law,[9] this Article does not mention that the restriction has to be produced between two 'undertakings'. This condition is inferred from the rest of the Act.

1.2.2 The restriction on competition

Article 1(1) contains a non-exhaustive list of examples of restrictive agreements:

(a) the direct or indirect fixing of prices or other trading or service conditions;
(b) the limitation or control of production, distribution, technical development or investment;
(c) the sharing of markets or sources of supply;
(d) the applying of dissimilar conditions to equivalent transactions with other trading partners thereby placing them at a competitive disadvantage;
(e) making an agreement subject to acceptance of supplementary conditions which by their nature, or according to commercial usage, have no connection with the subject of the contract.

1.2.3 Article 1(2) – infringing agreements shall be void

Article 1(2) of the Act establishes that agreements infringing Article 1(1) will be void if they are not covered by an exemption as provided by Articles 3–5 (see below).

1.2.4 Article 1(1) is not applicable to agreements in application of specific legislation

Article 2(1) of the Act establishes that the prohibitions mentioned in Article 1(1) of the Act will not be applicable to those agreements, decisions, practices and recommendations which exist as a consequence of specific legislation or regulations.

---

7 Royal Decree 157/1992 of 21 February 1992.
8 Royal Decree 1080/1992 of 11 September 1992.
9 See sections 1.2.1 and 1.2.2 of Chapter I.

1.2.5 *De minimis*

Agreements or groups of agreements may be authorised[10] when justified having regard to the general economic situation and the general interest, provided that they do not have a significant effect on competition by reason of their minor importance. This does not mean that agreements of minor economic importance are automatically considered not to be restrictive of competition. In order to qualify for *de minimis* treatment the agreement must be notified.

1.2.6 *Article 3 authorisations*

Article 3(1) of the Act establishes that agreements, decisions, recommendations and practices as described in Article 1, which contribute to improve the production or the distribution of products or services or to promoting technical or economic progress, may be authorised, provided that the agreements:

(a) will allow consumers a fair share of the resulting benefit;
(b) will not impose on the parties concerned restrictions which are not indispensable to the attainment of these objectives; and
(c) will not grant the parties concerned the possibility of eliminating competition in respect of a substantial part of the products or services in question.

Authorisation may also be granted[11] for agreements which, taking into account the special and general economic situation and the public interest, will support:

(a) the defence or promotion of exports (subject to compatibility with international treaties); or
(b) the balance between supply and demand if it can be established that there is overcapacity in the industry concerned; or
(c) a significant improvement in the social and economic conditions in depressed geographical areas or sectors; or
(d) where competition is not materially affected by reason of the agreements, minor importance.

The authorisations that can be granted to prohibited agreements can be classified into two general categories:

(i) Article 4 provides for individual authorisations to be granted by the Court;[12]
(ii) Article 5 contains provision for the introduction of group exemptions.[13]

1.2.7 *Individual authorisations*

Article 4 establishes that the Court is the only administrative body which is authorised to grant individual authorisations, for agreements, decisions, recommendations and practices prohibited by Article 1(1) in the circumstances laid down by Article 3.[14]

10 Article 3(2), letter (e).
11 Article 3(2).
12 See section 1.2.7 below.
13 See section 1.2.8 below.
14 For the requirements established by Article 3(1) see section 1.2.6 above.

The Court authorisation sets the date from which it will be effective, which cannot be earlier than the date of application for authorisation. The Court will also determine the duration of the authorisation and the conditions or obligations to which it is subject. These matters are dealt with by a hearing convened within ten days of the application attended by the interested parties and the Service for the Defence of Competition.[15]

The Court is also competent to grant renewals of authorisations.

The Court can also modify or revoke the authorisation in case of a substantial change of circumstances or if the affected undertakings do not respect the conditions and obligations set by the Court or the data furnished in order to obtain this authorisation were incorrect or incomplete.

In all these cases, the Court is required to hear the interested parties and the Service.

If the parties to an agreement do not receive a decision of the Court within three months of submitting an application for authorisation, they may consider the agreement approved on a provisional basis.

1.2.8   Group exemptions

Article 5 of the Act permits the government (on a recommendation from the Court) to authorise by exemption agreements, categories of agreements, decisions, recommendations or concerted practices satisfying the requirements of Article 3(1) when:

(a)   only two undertakings participate in them and they impose restrictions relating to the distribution and/or supply of specified products for sale or resale or are connected to the use of intellectual or industrial property rights or commercial or industrial know-how; or

(b)   the agreements have as their sole objective the setting of common standards and applying them uniformly, or specialisation in the manufacturing of specified products, or joint research and development; or

(c)   the agreements have as their sole object the increase in the efficiency and competitiveness of undertakings particularly small and medium sized undertakings.

To date the government has only published one Regulation.[16]

The government has follows criteria established by the European Community Group Exemption Regulations. The categories of agreements qualifying for group exemption and the conditions to be satisfied are the same as those contained in the EC Regulations. The group exemption covers the following categories of agreement, provided that they only affect the Spanish market:

(a)   exclusive distribution agreements meeting the conditions contained in EC Regulation 1983/83;

(b)   exclusive purchasing agreements meeting the conditions contained in EC Regulation 1984/83;

(c)   patent licensing agreements and mixed agreement of licensing and know-how provided that they meet the conditions contained in EC Regulation 2349/84;

---

15 For the nature and competences of the Service see section 2.1.2 below.
16 Royal Decree 157/1992 of 21 February 1992.

(d) distribution and post-sales service agreements of automobiles provided that they meet the conditions contained in EC Regulation 1475/95;
(e) franchise agreements provided that they satisfy the conditions of EC Regulation 4087/88;
(f) know-how agreements and mixed agreements of know-how and patent licensing different to those referred to in sub-para (c) herein provided that they respect the conditions mentioned in EC Regulation 556/89;
(g) specialisation agreements meeting the conditions mentioned in EC Regulation 417/85; and
(h) research and development agreements meeting the conditions mentioned in EC Regulation 418/85.

1.3 Abuse of market power

1.3.1 Article 6(1) of the Act forbids the abusive exploitation by one or several undertakings of a dominant position in the national market (or a part of it).

1.3.2 Abusive practices

Article 6(2) provides that an abuse may include:

(a) directly or indirectly imposing prices, or other unfair commercial conditions;
(b) limiting production, distribution or technical development causing an unjustified prejudice on other undertakings or on consumers;
(c) refusing without reason to supply goods or services;
(d) applying dissimilar commercial conditions to equivalent transactions which could place some parties at a competitive disadvantage;
(e) subjecting the grant of a contract to the acceptance of supplementary conditions not connected, according to their nature, to the object of the contract.

1.3.3 Article 6(3) provides that the prohibition in Article 6(1) extends to undertakings having a state-conferred monopoly or dominant position.

2 ENFORCEMENT

2.1 Enforcement authorities

2.1.1 The Court for the Defence of Competition

The Court is the administrative body charged with the administration of the Competition Rules.

The Court has power to order the cessation of restrictive agreements and abuses of dominant positions,[17] to impose fines,[18] to report on mergers and concentrations,[19] to determine notifications[20] and to examine Public Aids.[1]

17 Article 9.
18 Articles 10 and 11.
19 Article 14.
20 Article 15.
 1 Article 19.

The Court also has a policy role and is entitled[2] to submit reports on competition issues, to address reports to any organ of state and to report to the government on the application of national or European Community competition law as it may deem necessary from time to time.

2.1.2   *The Service for the Defence of Competition*

The Court is assisted in the authorisation procedure by the Service for the Defence of Competition ('the Service') which is a division of the Ministry of Finance. The Service is competent:[3]

(a)   to administer the authorisation procedure;
(b)   to monitor compliance with any conditions imposed by any order made under the Act;
(c)   to maintain the Registry of the Defence of Competition;
(d)   to undertake studies and research on economic areas, analysing the competitive situation and any possible restrictive practices;
(e)   to co-operate with other authorities internationally on competition matters.

2.1.3   *The 'Audiencia Nacional'*

This Court hears appeals from the Court for the Defence of Competition.

2.1.4   *The Courts of First Instance*

The Courts of First Instance are the general civil courts in Spain and are the jurisdictional authorities before whom general complaints for unfair competition have to be presented.

Possible judicial remedies against unfair competition include:

(a)   a declaration that an act is unfair;
(b)   an order requiring cessation of the unfair activity;
(c)   an order requiring that the effects of unfair competitive activity be remedied;
(d)   an order rectifying deceitful, incorrect or false information;
(e)   an order compensating by way of damages prejudice caused by negligence or fraud;
(f)   an order preventing unfair enrichment arising from an anti-competitive practice.

These courts are independent of the Service and Court for the Defence of Competition.
    Jurisdictional rules are contained in the Unfair Competition Act and are basically the same as the ordinary civil judicial procedure.
    This Act permits an application for an interim injunction to stop unfair competitive acts pending trial. An injunction can be obtained within 24 hours.

---

2 Article 26(1).
3 Article 31.

2.2   Jurisdictional rules

2.2.1   The Court for the Defence of Competition has exclusive jurisdiction on the granting of authorisations under Article 3 of the Act.

2.2.2   The Service has jurisdiction to investigate and to prepare the procedure.

2.2.3   Royal Decree 157/1992 establishes the administrative and jurisdictional rules to be followed in order to obtain a particular exemption for the anti-competitive agreements. This procedure is as follows:

(a)   an application for exemption has to be presented before the Service by the filing of an official form;

(b)   once the application has been presented, the Service publishes in the National Official Journal a brief summary of the application in order to permit third parties to make their comments within not more than 15 days;

(c)   within a maximum of 30 days following receipt of the application, the Service will give its opinion as to the application of the competition rules and the merits of an exemption. The opinion is submitted by dossier to the Court;

(d)   within five days following the reception of the dossier by the Court, it has to decide whether or not to admit it. If the Court considers the dossier incomplete, it may ask the Service to complete it;

(e)   the Court, when it agrees with the Service report and there is no third party opposition, may immediately issue a decision either that the agreement is not anti-competitive or that it can be authorised without conditions. If the Service makes opposition to the authorization or if it is necessary to condition it, the Court will summon the parties and the Service for a hearing (provided that no third parties present opposition);

(f)   a hearing will be necessary, with the participation of the interested parties and the Service, in the following cases:

   (i)   when the Service opposes the grant of authorisation and the Court accepts the view of the Service;

   (ii)   when the Service supports authorisation but the Court is opposed to it;

   (iii)   when an interested third party has presented an opposition to authorisation.

2.3   Powers of investigation

2.3.1   Powers of the Service

Section 2 of Chapter II of the Act,[4] contains the rules and procedures for the investigation and inspection powers of the Service.

2.3.2   Co-operation

Every person, company or firm is obliged to assist the Service and to provide all data and information necessary to the Service to discharge its obligations under the Act. Failure to co-operate may result in fines from 50,000 to 1,000,000 pesetas.

4 Articles 32 to 34.

2.3.3　*Investigations*

The Service may examine and obtain copies of all books and registers of companies and other documents, and, when necessary, has power to retain them for a maximum of ten days.

Obstruction of inspection by the Service can result in fines of up to 150,000 pesetas for each day being imposed.

The Service can gain access to premises only by express consent of the occupiers or by court order.

Information obtained under these powers can only be used for the purposes foreseen in the Act.

2.3.4　*The decision*

The final decision of the Court on the agreement notified to the administrative bodies will be notified to the applicant and other interested parties and will also be submitted to the Service for registration.

2.3.5　*Competition Public Registry*

The Service maintains a Competition Public Registry in which all the agreements and practices authorised by the Court and those total or partially prohibited are registered. Details of mergers and concentrations will also be inscribed in this Public Registry.[5]

2.4　Fines and other sanctions

2.4.1　*Power of the Court*

The Court is authorised[6] to fine those companies, associations, unions or groups that consciously or negligently infringe the competition rules or do not respect the conditions attached to individual authorisations.

2.4.2　*Amount*

The fines[7] that can be imposed are limited to 150 million pesetas, or 10% of the volume of sales of the previous fiscal year.

2.4.3 The amount of the fines is determined[8] taking into account the importance of the infringement and particularly:

(a)　the form and significance of the restriction to competition;
(b)　the size of the affected market;
(c)　the market share of the undertaking concerned;

5　See section 4 below.
6　Article 9.
7　Article 10(1).
8　Article 10(2).

(d)   the restrictive effect on actual or potential competitors, on other parties of the commercial system or on consumers;

(e)   the duration of the restriction;

(f)   the repetition of the forbidden acts.

2.4.4   *Other fines*

Besides the fine that can be imposed on the affected undertakings, it is also possible to impose a fine[9] up to 5 million pesetas, to the legal representatives or persons composing the managing bodies of undertakings directly involved in the infringing agreement or decision.

2.5   Exemptions

As indicated above, exemptions can be granted for prohibited agreements either by individual authorisation or group exemptions authorisations. These are dealt with in detail at sections 1.2.7 and 1.2.8 above.

2.6   Third party rights

2.6.1   Any person whether or not having a direct interest is able to lodge a complaint in respect of activities prohibited by the Act.[10] The Service is compelled to initiate proceedings if it observes that there could exist rational indicative evidence for the appreciation of such prohibited activities if such complaint is made. After the initiation of a complaint investigation, the Service may publish[11] in the National Official Journal, and, if considered appropriate, in a national or provincial large circulation newspaper, a notice giving brief details of the case inviting interested parties to submit representations within a period of 15 days. A similar note is also published[12] after an application for individual authorisation has been received.

2.6.2   In addition, third party rights can also be protected in an indirect way through reports which consumers organizations issue on all applications for individual authorisations.[13]

3   CHECKLIST OF POTENTIAL INFRINGEMENTS

3.1   Agency

3.1.1   Commercial agency agreements are not expressly covered in the Act. Nevertheless, such agreements have been examined in several decisions of the Court.

---

  9 Article 10(3).
 10 Article 36(1).
 11 Article 36(4) of the Act.
 12 Article 5 of the Royal Decree 157/1992.
 13 Article 5, para 2 of the Royal Decree 157/1992.

3.1.2   The Court has held[14] that the prohibition under Article 1 of the Act is not applicable to contracts agreed with commercial agents, commissionaires or inter-mediaries when these contracts consist of the promotion, inside the agreed territory, of business or contracts on behalf of another (ie the principal or supplier).

This is because the activity of the commercial agent is considered complementary to the sales activities of his principal and the agent does not act as an independent economic entity. In such circumstances, there is no agreement between independent undertakings which can fall within Article 1.

3.1.3   The Agency Agreement Act

This Agency Act[15] incorporates into Spanish law, the Directive on Commercial Agents.[16]

Section 4 of Chapter II of the Agency Act authorises the parties in an agency agreement to include clauses restricting or limiting the activities of the agent following termination of the contract. The agent may be restricted from competing after termination of the agreement for a maximum of two years from termination or one year if the agreement is concluded for less than one year.

The restriction of competition clause has to be expressly established in writing and can only affect the geographical area and the clients granted to the agent and only for the goods or services which are the subject of the agreement.

3.2   Distribution

3.2.1   Distribution agreements are not expressly defined by law, but basically would consist of an agreement for the purchase of products by an undertaking (distributor) from another (supplier) for the purposes of resale.

3.2.2   Forbidden agreements

As we have seen in section 1.2.2(b), the limitation of distribution is expressly referred to as an example of an anti-competitive restriction in Article 1 of the Act. This is particularly so for exclusive distribution agreements. Distribution agreements which do not contain an exclusivity clause are also included in this example when limiting distribution.

3.2.3   Special benefits

Although exclusive distribution agreements could have restrictive effects on competition, they are usually considered as having benefits in terms of improving distribution which is of benefit to consumers.

3.2.4   Group exemption

As stated above, the benefits of exclusive distribution are recognised by the fact that the group exemption Royal Decree includes an exemption for exclusive

---

14 In a decision of 25 June 1990, and more recently in one of 17 May 1993.
15 Act 12/1992 of 27 May 1992.
16 EC Directive 86/653/EEC of 18 December 1986.

distribution agreements which satisfy broadly the same conditions as those required for group exemption under EEC law.[17]

3.3 Selective distribution

3.3.1   Selective distribution is likely to be considered restrictive from a competition point of view because usually the supplier seeks to restrict the number or type of distributor for his goods.

3.3.2   Nevertheless, as in the case of EC competition law, the Court has granted authorisations for such agreements in two cases. The first one[18] authorised the selective distribution and post-sales service for automobiles (before the coming into force of the EC Regulation for the national market). The second one related to high quality watches.[19] From these decisions it is possible to determine that if the following conditions are satisfied, it is likely that a selective distribution system will be authorised:

(a)   if the system can be shown to contribute to the improvement of distribution and commercialisation because of the pre-sales advice given by dealers and there is no restriction on inter-brand competition;
(b)   if the system offers to the consumer an international guarantee and repair service;
(c)   if the system enable the dealer to provide a full range of stock incorporating the newest collections to the benefit of the consumer;
(d)   provided the system does not impose restrictions which are not indispensable to the objectives.

3.3.3   With regard to the distribution and servicing of automobiles, the EC Exemption 1475/95 will also be applicable for agreements meeting its terms.[20]

3.4 Exclusive purchasing

3.4.1   As we have mentioned for distribution agreements, exclusive purchasing agreements would usually be considered restrictive of competition because of their particular structure (the reseller can buy certain goods for resale only from the supplier) and could infringe Article 1(1) of the Act which forbids limitation of distribution. An authorisation (group or individual authorisation) would therefore be necessary.

3.4.2   Group exemption

As stated above[1] exclusive purchasing agreements which satisfy the conditions mentioned in the EC Regulation 1984/83 will be exempted. In other cases individual authorisation will have to be sought.

17 See section 1.2.8 above.
18 Decision of 19 April 1990.
19 Decision of 9 July 1990.
20 The Royal Decree 157/1992 and section 1.2.8 above.
 1 Section 1.2.8 above.

3.5   Franchising

3.5.1   As in the case of distribution and exclusive purchasing agreements, franchise agreements are usually considered to be restrictive of competition because of their particular structure (mainly the granting of a licence for the exploitation of a marketing system) and would be caught by Article 1(1) of the Act which forbids restrictions of distribution. An authorisation would therefore be necessary.

Prior to the coming into force of the EC Regulation on Franchising for the Spanish market, the Court had the opportunity to examine the franchise agreements and it considered[2] them to merit authorisation provided that they respected the freedom of franchisees to establish their retail prices and did not impose restrictions on parallel distribution of products.

3.5.2   Group exemption

Since the coming into force of the Royal Decree 157/1992, franchise agreements are now generally authorised provided that they respect the conditions set out in EC Regulation 4087/88.[3]

3.6   Intellectual property licensing

3.6.1   The same principles mentioned in sections 3.2 and 3.3 herein apply to this category of agreements. Territorial restrictions, restrictions on the use of IP rights and similar restrictions will often bring the agreement within the prohibition under Article 1(1) of the Act on the basis that they limit technical development. Such agreements would therefore require individual authorisation unless the group exemption applies.

3.6.2   Group exemption

Licensing agreements and mixed agreements of licensing and know-how will be automatically exempted, provided that they respect the conditions mentioned in EC Regulation 2349/84 or 556/89.

Royal Decree 157/92 also declares authorised agreements that, included in one of the following groups, affect only the national market and meet the conditions set by:

(a)   EC Regulation 417/85 – Specialisation Agreements;
(b)   EC Regulation 418/85 – Research and Development Agreements.[4]

3.7   Refusal to supply

3.7.1   General principle

A refusal to supply is not included in the agreements that are considered as restrictive of competition. However, in certain circumstances a refusal to supply could be

---

2 Decision of 21 March 1991.
3 Section 1.2.8 above.
4 See section 1.2.8 above.

considered restrictive. For example, a refusal to supply might be evidence of a restriction on sales in a distribution agreement, or of a market sharing cartel or some other anti-competitive practice. In this context, Article 1(1)(d) describes as prohibited agreements those which apply dissimilar conditions for equivalent transactions or which place a competitor in an disadvantageous position with another competitor.

3.7.2 Abusive behaviour

A refusal to supply is, however, expressly included as an example of abusive behaviour in Article 6 of the Act.[5] An undertaking in a dominant position which refuses to supply could be pursued under this provision.

3.8 Price restrictions

3.8.1 General prohibition

Fixing prices and conditions of sale are expressly considered as restrictive of competition under Article 1(1)(a) of the Act which refers to:

'establishing, directly or indirectly, prices or other commercial or service conditions'.

3.8.2 Court decisions

The prohibition is, therefore, clearly established by the Act and the Court has on several occasions made clear that any prior restrictions are unlikely ever to be authorised. Price concertation prevents consumers from choosing freely in the market since price is one of the main elements of the competitive process.[6]

The importance of the freedom to determine prices has been maintained by the Court in all the fields it has examined. Particularly in its trade association decisions, the Court has opposed price restriction for poultry,[7] bakers,[8] driving schools[9] and plumbers'[10] associations.

Concertation on price has also been prohibited by the Court, in relation to the provision of services[11] as well as goods and also in circumstances where several companies participate in a public tender with identical prices.[12]

3.8.3 Recommendations on price

The application of 'recommended' resale prices is considered by the Court to be little different from resale price maintenance and for that reason, declared restrictive of competition.

---

5 Article 6(c), the unjustified refusal to satisfy a demand to purchase products or to render services.
6 Decision of 26 March 1990.
7 Decision of 8 August 1990.
8 Decision of 13 September 1993.
9 Decision of 3 January 1991.
10 Decision of 5 December 1990.
11 Decision of 30 November 1989.
12 Decision of 12 July 1990.

3.8.4　*Maximum and minimum prices*

The Court has held[13] that the imposition of average recommended prices and minimum and maximum prices falls within the prohibition on fixing prices.

3.8.5　*Lists of prices*

The publication and distribution of retail price lists even for price recommendation purposes only, has also been considered as a practice whose object and effect were to restrict competition.[14] However, in selective distribution agreements, the Court has stated[15] that in some sectors of goods under trade marks their specifications, and the necessity for special post-sales service or repairs, indicate that price was not always the decisive element in competition.

3.8.6　*Predatory pricing*

Predatory pricing is expressly prohibited as an abusive behaviour in the Unfair Competition Act. Article 17 of this Act establishes the general principle of freedom for setting prices. However, sales made under cost or under purchasing price would be considered as unfair in some cases:

(a)　when it could lead consumers into error as to the level of prices of other products or services in the same establishment;

(b)　when it has the effect of discrediting the image of a product from another establishment;

(c)　when it consists of a strategy to eliminate a competitor from the market.

3.9　Tie in sales

3.9.1　Article 1(1)(e) of the Act prohibits an agreement to subordinate the completion of contracts to the acceptance of other supplementary compensations not connected to the object of those contracts either by their nature or commercial usage.

3.9.2　Tie in sales may also constitute an infringement of Article 6(e) as an abuse of a dominant position.

3.10　Information exchange

3.10.1　*General principle*

Agreements providing for information exchange are not expressly included in the examples contained in the Act as restrictive of competition but are likely to infringe Article 1 when they concern confidential information or information that could restrict the freedom of different commercial operators to decide on their competitive behaviour. Nevertheless, an individual authorisation is possible.

13　Decision of 26 March 1990.
14　Decision of 26 March 1990.
15　Decision of 9 July 1990.

3.10.2 The Court has had the opportunity to consider this issue in the case of the maintenance of a Register of Defaulters[16] for credit purposes. The Court held that although the information exchange involved in such Registers could restrict competition, they could be authorised. However, as a condition for authorisation, the Registers had to allow free access on non-discriminatory terms to all participants and leave them free to decide their commercial strategy with defaulters.[17] The Register could not provide for collective reactions.[18]

3.11 Joint buying and selling

The agreements between competitors to establish joint purchasing or selling, would be considered likely to restrict competition in the national market and would need authorisation of the Court, which will consider the possible benefits to the consumers, the possibility of the maintenance of a certain degree of competition and the need to avoid restrictions which are not indispensable.

The Court has authorised a joint export selling agreement[19] having regard to the circumstances of the national market and the difficulties of penetrating the foreign market.

3.12 Market sharing

The sharing of markets and the sharing of sources of supply are expressly considered to be restrictive of competition under Article 1(1)(c) of the Act. The Court has held that market sharing[20] is one type of agreement which more clearly restricts competition.

3.13 Joint ventures

3.13.1 No special provisions are contained in the Act nor in the Royal Decrees concerning joint ventures.

3.13.2 The Court has not yet had the opportunity to make a clear distinction on different kinds of joint ventures but it is likely that it will follow the principles and distinctions (concentrative and co-operative joint ventures) as apply under European Community law.

4 CONCENTRATIONS, MERGERS AND ACQUISITIONS

4.1 Introduction

4.1.1 Merger control on a Spanish basis is regulated by Chapter II of the Act.

16 Decision of 17 January 1992.
17 Decisions of 29 July and 30 September 1993.
18 Decision of 1 October 1993.
19 Decision of 16 October 1990. Although based in the former Competition Act the principles could be the same.
20 Decision of 26 October 1989 amongst others.

4.1.2 In application of those principles and to develop the Act in this respect, the government has adopted a Royal Decree[1] on mergers and concentrations. Annex I of this Regulation contains the required form and questions to be furnished to the competent authorities in case of a voluntary notification.

4.2 Thresholds

Any proposed or completed merger, concentration or acquisition of control of one undertaking by another person, company or group of companies can be examined by the Court when it affects or could affect the national market and particularly when it creates a dominant position or reinforces an existing one *provided that* one of the following thresholds is reached:

(a) when 25% or more of the market for a particular product or service within the national market or of a substantial part of it is purchased or increased; or
(b) when the total volume of sales in Spain of all participants in the transaction is higher than 20,000,000,000 pesetas in the previous fiscal year.

4.3 Appraisal criteria

The Court will report on whether the concentration is likely to have an adverse effect on competition in the national market.This report will include an analysis of the likely anti-competitive effects, having regard to:

(a) the delimitation of the relevant market;
(b) the structure of the market;
(c) the alternative products or services available to suppliers, distributors and consumers in the market;
(d) the financial and economic power of the companies;
(e) the impact of the concentration on demand and supply;
(f) the extent and power of competition from outside Spain.

The Court may also consider:

(a) the beneficial effects of the concentration on production or distribution;
(b) the promotion of technical or economic progress;
(c) the significance of international competition to the national industry or the consumer interest;
(d) whether the perceived benefits arising from the concentration could compensate for its anti-competitive effects.

4.4 Definition of concentration

Although there is no definition of a concentration in the Act, EC principles could be considered valid for the Spanish system. The Act only expressly mentions concentrations and taking of control of one or several companies by other companies groups but merger and takeovers whether hostile or friendly, would also be considered to be concentrations.

1 Royal Decree 1080/1992 of 11 September 1992.

4.5 Voluntary notification of concentrations

4.5.1 General principle – possibility of notification

Every merger or acquisition (even if only proposed) can be voluntarily notified to the Service of the Defence of Competition by one or several of the companies involved, prior to completion of the transaction or up to three months later. Prior notification will not interfere with the completion of the transaction even before any express or implied authorisation. It is important to emphasise that notification is not compulsory. However, notification may be desirable[2] particularly when one of the thresholds is exceeded in order to benefit from tacit authorisation and also to avoid the risk of a consummated concentration having to be undone at a later stage.

4.5.2 Tacit authorisations

It may be assumed that the Administration will not oppose a merger in two cases:

(a) if after one month of voluntary notification to the Service, the notification has not been referred to the Court; or
(b) if the Court had not issued its report within three months after the case is referred to it by the Service.

These 'tacit authorisations' are only granted to concentrations which have been voluntarily notified.

4.6 The calculation of turnover

4.6.1 Calculation of turnover

The method of calculation of the thresholds is set out in the Royal Decree 1080/1992. There are special rules for concentrations between banks and financial and insurance companies. There are also some specific rules concerning groups of companies.

4.6.2 General principle

In order to calculate the second of the thresholds of the companies participating in the transaction (20,000,000,000 pesetas by sales volume) it will be necessary to deduct from total sales, the VAT and other taxes.

4.6.3 Special rules

Moreover, in calculating sales volume it will be necessary to take into account the following special rules:

(a) for groups of companies the volume of sales for the same activity for the whole group must be added to the volume of sales of the companies

2 See sections 4.7.1 and 4.7.2 below.

participating in the transaction. Transactions between the members of the group or those made outside Spain will not be taken into account for the calculation of the volume of sales;

(b)   in the case of banks and credit institutions, the volume of sales will be replaced by one tenth part of their balance sheets;

(c)   in the case of insurance companies, the volume of sales will be substituted by the value of the gross premiums issued by the company.

4.7   Procedure

4.7.1   *Notification obligations*

As stated above, the parties are not obliged to notify a proposed or completed concentration to the competition authorities. Nevertheless, notification of the transaction may often be desirable.

4.7.2   *Advantages of notification*

This is particularly true when the transaction reaches at least one of the two thresholds mentioned in section 4.2. It is important to consider that, when one of these two limits is reached, the Ministry of Finances is entitled to ask the Court for a report on the transaction which would trigger a merger investigation.

If the thresholds are reached, it is convenient to notify the transaction voluntarily to the Court in order to benefit from the 'voluntary notification procedure' provided in the Act.

4.7.3   *Voluntary notification*

The advantages of voluntary notification are, mainly, the possibility of knowing the position of the administration about the transaction early on. Once the transaction has been notified, the Service has to decide whether to refer the case to the Court within one month and if a reference is made, the Court must report within three months. If these delays are not met, the parties are entitled to assume that the concentration has been approved.[3]

4.7.4   *Time limit for voluntary notification*

Voluntary notification of the transaction must be given prior to completion or within three months thereafter.

4.7.5   *Steps to follow for voluntary notification*

An official form must be filed, providing the competition authorities (the Service) with all relevant data necessary to determine the importance of the transaction and its effect on the market. In the case of a merger or the taking of control on an agreed basis, the information should be furnished jointly by the undertakings concerned.

---

3 See section 4.5.2 above.

When the concentration consists of the purchase by a person or undertaking acquiring control of one or several companies, the notification must be presented by the purchaser.

The take-over of publicly quoted companies is regulated by special Regulations.[4]

It is important to emphasise that voluntary notification to the Spanish authorities is not a substitute for notification to the European Commission under EC Regulation 4064/89.[5]

4.7.6   Requested information

The competition authorities will require (inter alia) the following information:

(a)   the annual accounts of the participating companies or groups;
(b)   the volume of sales and market shares;
(c)   the nature and characteristics of the transaction;
(d)   the economic area affected by the concentration;
(e)   an analysis of the pro-competitive and anti-competitive effects;
(f)   economic and juridical situation after the transaction.

To the official form, the following documents will be annexed:

(a)   a copy of the management reports and annual accounts of the last three fiscal years of all the companies participating in the concentration;
(b)   copies of the final version, or the more recent drafts of the documents related to the transaction.

It is also possible (but not compulsory) to annex to the form any analysis, or reports made in connection with the transaction.

All this information is required to complete the voluntary notification. Failure to submit a complete notification may result in the suspension of the one month time limit for the Service to decide on a reference. The notification will be considered to be confidential. The steps taken by the Service in connection with it will be considered confidential until the Finance Minister decides to refer the matter to the Court.[6]

4.8   Powers of enforcement

Once the Court has issued its report to the Finance Minister, the Government will be able to decide, with a maximum delay of three months, one of the following solutions:

(a)   not to oppose the transaction;
(b)   approve the transaction subject to conditions designed to remedy any anti-competitive effects;

4   Royal Decree 11/1991 of 26 July 1991 establishes the circumstances when the take-over becomes mandatory, the procedure to be followed and the administrative bodies concerned by this procedure (National Commission of Stock Exchange).
5   See Chapter I.
6   Article 8 of the Royal Decree 1080/1992.

(c)   to declare the concentration non-admissible. In this case the government could decide the following:

    (i)   to order a proposed merger to be cancelled;
    (ii) to order appropriate measures to re-establish effective competition including divestiture where the merger has been put into effect.

4.9   Timetable

The timetable applying in the case of voluntary notifications made by the parties is as follows:

Voluntary notification   Voluntary notification can be submitted prior to completion of the concentration or within three months thereafter. If within one month following notification, the Service has not rendered any communication or report to the Court, the parties may assume that the Administration is not opposed to the concentration.[7] If within three months following the date of the reference from the Service to the Court, the Court has not issued its report, it will also be understood that the concentration is not opposed.[8]

Delay elapsed   In cases where the relevant thresholds[9] have been reached, but the concentration had not been voluntarily notified to the Service,[10] the authorities may commence an investigation at any time within five years.[11]

Final decision   The final decision of the government has to be produced in a maximum term of three months after the Court's report. This final decision will be notified to the Service, the interested parties and published in the Official Journal.[12]

4.10   Request for information

The Act confers on the Service,[13] as we have mentioned in section 2.3 herein, the power to make 'necessary' investigations for the application of the Act and this extends to the investigation of mergers as well as restrictive practices and the abuse of market power.

4.11   Fines

If the participants in the concentration do not respect a final decision on a merger, the authorities will be entitled to impose fines up to a maximum of 10% of turnover in Spain.

---

7 Article 15 of the Act and 7(2) of the Royal Decree 1080/1992.
8 Article 15(4) of the Act.
9 See section 4.2 above.
10 According to Royal Decree 1080/1992.
11 Article 11 of the Royal Decree 1080/1992.
12 Article 15 of the Royal Decree 1080/1992.
13 Article 33.

4.12 Judicial review

The Court for the Defence of Competition is the administrative body competent to analyse mergers and to propose measures to be adopted. The final decision on the mergers rests, nevertheless, with the government. There is a right of appeal on a point of law to the Supreme Court.

CHAPTER XVII
Sweden

Mats Koffner

Advokatfirman Glimstedt
Kungsgatan 42
403 14 Gothenberg
Sweden

Tel ++46 31 172040
Fax ++46 31 7119038

CHAPTER XVII

Sweden

1 SWEDISH COMPETITION LAW

1.1 Background

1.1.1 As has been indicated by studies carried out by a Swedish commission on competition as well as the OECD and the European Commission, there has been insufficient competition in important sectors of the Swedish economy. More competition is needed in both the public and private sectors.

1.1.2 A new, more stringent Competition Act has been enacted and entered into force on 1 July 1993. The Act is modelled on the competition rules of the EC law as laid down in the Treaty of Rome. The former Competition Act was based mainly on the principle of abuse control.

1.1.3 The new legislation means that Sweden has abandoned the principle of misuse previously applicable, and now applies the principle of prohibition as laid down in the EC rules of competition.

1.1.4 An event with great impact on the competitive environment in Sweden in recent years is the Agreement on a European Economic Area (EEA). A process of deregulation aimed at broadening the scope of competitive market operations is under way in almost all sectors.

1.1.5 Many Swedish undertakings established in Europe are already subject to Community rules which, following the EEA Agreement, will be of increasing importance to Swedish industry. Under the EEA Agreement the Community's competition rules will constitute Swedish law with respect to trade in the EEA.

1.2 Anti-competitive agreements

1.2.1 It was natural to model amendments to the Swedish Competition Act on Community competition rules. Consequently the Act is modelled on Articles 85 and 86 of the Treaty of Rome and establishes prohibition against anti-competitive co-operation and abuse of a dominant position. The prohibition of anti-competitive co-operation is aimed at undertakings that have concluded an agreement with the object or result of restricting competition. The prohibition applies both to agreements between undertakings in the same stage of distribution and agreements between for example manufacturers and their distributors. The Act lists examples of co-operation that are particularly detrimental to competition.

1.2.2 Section 6 of the Competition Act lists examples of possible restriction of competition as follows:

'(a) directly or indirectly fix purchase price or selling prices or any other trading conditions;

(b) limit or control production, markets, technical development, or investment;

(c) share markets or sources of supply;

(d) apply dissimilar conditions to equivalent transactions with other trading parties, thereby placing them at a competitive disadvantage; or

(e) make the conclusion of contract subject to acceptance by the other parties of supplementary obligations which, by their nature or according to commercial usage, have no connection with the subject of such contracts'.

Undertakings may apply for exemptions from the prohibition of anti-competitive co-operation.

1.2.3 Small undertakings may also need to co-operate to enable them to compete with large undertakings. The prohibition against co-operation applies only where it has an appreciable effect on the Swedish market. This means that co-operation between small undertakings often falls outside the scope of this prohibition. In principle, they are not subject to the prohibition against anti-competitive co-operation if their market share is less than about 10%. If their annual turnover is less than SEK 10 million their market share may be somewhat larger.

1.3 Abuse of market power

1.3.1 The prohibition of abuse of a dominant position relates to behaviour affecting other undertakings or consumers. Dominant positions are not prohibited as such; the prohibition applies to uses of such a position that impede competition. The Act provides examples of behaviour that is particularly detrimental to competition. These include the imposition of unfair purchase or selling prices, limiting production and markets, refusing supplies to a trading party and other kinds of discrimination. No exemptions will be granted from this prohibition.

1.3.2 Section 19 of the Competition Act provides that any abuse by one or more undertakings of a dominant position in the Swedish market shall be prohibited. Such abuse may, in particular, consist in:

'(a) directly or indirectly imposing unfair purchase or selling prices or other unfair trading conditions;

(b) limiting production, markets or technical development to the prejudice of customers;

(c) applying dissimilar conditions to equivalent transactions with other trading parties, thereby placing them at a competitive disadvantage; or

(d) making the conclusion of contracts subject to acceptance by the other parties of supplementary obligations which, by their nature or according to commercial usage, have no connection with the subject of such contracts'.

1.3.3 The dominant position is normally related to various circumstances which one by one would not necessarily be conclusive. Facts which will be relevant are for instance financial strength, obstacles against establishing the market, access to goods, patent and other intellectual properties and also technology and other superior knowledge. Another important factor is the market share of the relevant market. Market shares between 40 and 50% are known to be obvious signs of a dominant position. If the market share increases by 65% it is assumed that it is almost impossible not to recognise the position as dominant.

1.4 The relationship with the national laws of Member States

1.4.1 Section 5 of the Competition Act states the following:

'Where both the provisions of this Act and the competition rules laid down in the European Economic Area (EEA) Act (1992:1317) are applicable in an individual case, decisions taken in pursuance of this Act must be compatible with the said provisions.

This Act shall not be applicable to the fixing of prices referred to in the European Coal and Steel Community Act (1972:762) if this conflicts with the terms of agreements provided for in section 1 of that Act.'

1.4.2 The Swedish competition rules together with the EC rules will ensure more effective competition in the Swedish market. Swedish undertakings abroad will also be subject to the same set of rules. EC competition law, including case law, will have a great impact when applying the Swedish national competition rules.

2 ENFORCEMENT

2.1 Enforcement authorities

2.1.1 On 1 July 1992, the Swedish Competition Authority was set up. Its task is to eliminate obstacles to effective competition. The Authority's functions include application of competition legislation, the preparation of proposals for changes in regulations that impede competition, the promotion of competition in the public sector and the promotion of a competition-oriented attitude in both the private and public sectors by providing information and opinion-forming activities.

2.1.2 The Swedish Competition Authority is also the national competent authority with regard to the application of the competition rules under the EEA agreement. The Authority will co-operate closely with the EFTA Surveillance Authority, whose functions in the EEA will correspond to those of the EC Commission.

2.2 Jurisdictional rules

2.2.1 The judicial process will take place at two judicial levels. The Stockholm City Court will be the court of first instance for cases relating to anti-competitive behaviour charges and mergers. Appeals against decisions by the Swedish Competition Authority on exemptions, negative clearance and the imposition of fines may be lodged with the Stockholm City Court. Appeals against decisions of the court may be lodged with the Market Court, a specialised court which will be the final court of appeal.

2.2.2 Cases involving compensation, the invalidity of agreements and awards of fines will be tried by the ordinary courts. The Stockholm City Court will, however, always be competent to try cases relating to compensation and awards of fines.

2.2.3 EEA competition rules will take precedence in cases of conflict with Swedish law. Section 5 of the Competition Act settles that all decisions taken in pursuance of the Act must be compatible with the EEA competition rules. EC competition law will take precedence in the event that it conflicts with Swedish regulations. The same shall apply to regulations within the EEA.

2.2.4 In the case of uncertainty pertaining to the judgment of competition matters, account must be taken of whether the restraint of trade agreement will be reported to both the supervisory authorities within the EEA as well as the Swedish Competition Authority.

2.3 Investigations

2.3.1 The Swedish Competition Authority is empowered to investigate and gather information about undertakings. However, decisions about investigations into individual undertakings shall be taken by the Stockholm City Court on application by the Swedish Competition Authority.

2.3.2 Undertakings must supply the Swedish Competition Authority with the necessary material to enable it to carry out its investigations. The Authority may also require municipalities and county councils to supply information concerning costs and revenues.

Investigations can be triggered by:

(a) the Swedish Competition Authority;
(b) a complaint by a third party; or
(c) notification of a particular agreement or conduct.

2.3.3 Section 45 provides:

'Where this is necessary for the performance of its duties under this Act, the Swedish Competition Authority may require:

(a) undertakings or other parties to supply information, documents or other material;
(b) persons who are likely to be in a position to provide relevant information to appear at a hearing at a time and place decided by the Authority; or
(c) a municipality or county council engaged in activities of an economic or commercial nature to account for the costs of and revenues from these activities.'

In the case of investigation of infringements section 47 provides:

'Upon application by the Swedish Competition Authority the Stockholm City Court may decide that the Authority may carry out an investigation of an undertaking to establish whether it has infringed any of the prohibitions contained in sections 6 and 19, where:

(a) there is a reason to believe that an infringement has been committed;
(b) the undertaking does not comply with an obligation imposed pursuant to section 45, point 1, or there is a risk of evidence being withheld or tampered with; and
(c) the importance of the action taken is sufficient to outweigh the interference or other inconvenience caused to the parties affected by it.

Applications for investigations shall be made in writing.'

2.3.4 The Competition Act also contains provisions that a decision pursuant to section 47 may also be taken in respect of a party other than the undertaking to be investigated. However, such a decision may only be taken where:

'(a) the conditions contained in section 47 (1), points 1 and 3, are satisfied;
(b) there is a strong indication that the party referred to in the application is in possession of evidence; and

(c) the said party does not comply with an obligation imposed pursuant to section 45, point 1, or there is a risk of evidence being withheld or tampered with'.

2.3.5 According to section 50 a decision to carry out an investigation shall specify:

'(a) the subject matter and purpose of the investigation;
(b) the date on which the investigation is to begin; and
(c) the Swedish Competition Authority's powers under section 51'.

2.3.6 The Swedish Competition Authority shall according to section 51 be empowered:

'(a) to examine the books and other business records;
(b) to take copies of or extracts from the books and business records;
(c) to ask for oral explanations on the spot; and
(d) to have access to any premises, land, means of transport and other areas'.

2.3.7 The party on whose premises the investigation is to be carried out will always have the right to summon a legal representative. In order to be able to fulfil its obligations the Swedish Competition Authority may request assistance from the enforcement service in carrying out the measures referred to in the Competition Act.

2.4 Fines and penalties

2.4.1 As is the case within the EC, restraint of trade agreements and conditions in such agreements are invalid if they conflict with the law. Violation of the law may result in severe financial consequences.

2.4.2 The Swedish Competition Authority can order an undertaking to terminate infringement of a prohibition under penalty of a fine. This obligation will be adapted to the circumstances. It may provide that an agreement, the terms of a contract or a concerted practice must not be applied.

2.4.3 Under the Act it is possible to impose a sanction – an anti-competitive behaviour charge – as a means of effectively deterring undertakings from infringing the prohibitions against anti-competitive behaviour and abuse of a dominant position. This charge will be fixed according to the gravity and duration of the infringement. The maximum sanction will be SEK 5 million or an amount that may be higher but must not exceed 10% of annual turnover. The minimum sanction will be SEK 5,000. The sanction will be awarded by Stockholm City Court at the request of the Swedish Competition Authority. The charge will have the same function as a penalty, ie it will be imposed for infringements that have already taken place.

2.4.4 The new Competition Act also contains rules laying down civil law penalties designed to deter undertakings from infringing the prohibitions. Agreements subject to the prohibition against anti-competitive behaviour will be void. An undertaking may also be ordered to pay compensation to an aggrieved party if it infringes the prohibition against anti-competitive co-operation or abuse of a dominant position.

2.4.5   Actions for the award of fines imposed pursuant to the provisions of the Competition Act shall be brought before a district or a city court by the Swedish Competition Authority. The Stockholm City Court is always competent to examine cases concerning awards of fines.

2.5   Exemptions

2.5.1   Anti-competitive co-operation may have favourable effects that compensate for its disadvantages from the point of view of competition. This is often the case with co-operation between small and medium-sized undertakings. It is therefore possible to obtain an exemption from the prohibition against anti-competitive co-operation.

2.5.2   To obtain an individual exemption an undertaking must satisfy certain conditions. The agreement must contribute to improving the production or distribution of goods or to promoting technical or economic progress. Moreover, consumers or other end users must be ensured a fair share of the resulting benefit. The restriction of competition must also be indispensable to the attainment of these objectives and must not have a significant effect on competition in the market.

2.5.3   Certain types of agreements have such favourable effects that they will as a rule satisfy the conditions for an exemption. In such cases the granting of 'block exemptions' is an appropriate procedure, making administration simpler and more efficient since the undertakings know in advance what is required of them and do not need to apply for individual exemptions.

2.5.4   The Swedish block exemptions are based on those in force in the EC for:

(a)   specialisation agreements;
(b)   research and development agreements;
(c)   exclusive distribution agreements;
(d)   exclusive purchasing agreements;
(e)   motor vehicle distribution and servicing agreements;
(f)   patent licensing agreements;
(g)   know-how licensing agreements; and
(h)   franchising agreements.

In addition a block exemption has been issued for certain forms of co-operation between chains in the retail trade. This will apply to co-operation that has favourable effects by making it possible for small undertakings to compete effectively with larger ones.

2.5.5   A substantial percentage of the agreements that are eligible for exemptions will be covered by block exemptions. But there will also be a need for individual exemptions. These will be granted by the Swedish Competition Authority upon application by the undertakings concerned. To ensure that the undertakings are notified of decisions without undue delay, the Swedish Competition Authority will have a time limit of not more than three months to decide on matters relating to exemptions.

2.6 Third party rights

A third party suffering from an infringement can:

(a) file a complaint with the Swedish Competition Authority;
(b) start proceedings in court.

Section 33 of the Competition Act provides that any party who, intentionally or negligently, infringes any of the prohibitions contained in sections 6 and 19 shall compensate the damage that is caused thereby to another undertaking or party to an agreement. The right to such compensation shall lapse if no action is brought within five years from the date when the damage was caused. The Stockholm City Court is always competent to examine cases relating to compensation.

3   CHECKLIST OF POTENTIAL INFRINGEMENTS

3.1   Agency

3.1.1   An agent acting in an agent relationship shall always serve as the extended arm of the supplier. The agent does not assume any financial risk of his own but, instead, receives commission in respect of the business which he is able to conduct between the supplier and the customer. The agency agreement is thus not normally affected by the competition rules since the agent and the supplier are to be regarded as constituting an economic unit. It is therefore important to be able to determine that the agent is acting on behalf of the supplier and that, in the business relationship which exists between the supplier and the customer, the agent does not participate with financial risk of his own. Should this indeed be the case, he may be regarded as being a retailer.

3.1.2   A Swedish Act (1991:351) exists in respect of commercial agencies. The Act regulates what is understood by a commercial agent, his obligations, the principal's obligations, commissions, relationship in respect of third parties, etc.

Agency agreements will not normally fall within the prohibitions of the competition rules.

3.2   Distribution

3.2.1   A distribution agreement is distinguished from an agency agreement in that the distributor purchases the products for resale. It is normal for a dealer's agreement to contain restrictions which, for example, prohibit the purchase of certain goods or the marketing of goods outside of a specified sales area. Under certain conditions such regulations are deemed to promote effective competition.

3.2.2   There are block exemptions for exclusive distributors. By the decree 1993:72 Sweden has adopted the Commission's Regulation 1983/83 regarding exclusive distributor agreements. The block exemption lists which competition limitations are permitted. At the same time, an indication is given of which competition limitations may not be included within a single dealer agreement in order for the block exemption to apply.

3.2.3 An agreement which is excluded from the block exemption because, for example, it contains restriction on competition outside the scope of the block exemption, may be referred to the Swedish Competition Authority for individual exemption. The Swedish Competition Authority may grant such exemption under certain conditions.

3.3   Selective distribution

3.3.1 Selective distribution arises where a supplier wishes to restrict the number of dealers who may sell his goods, whether to limit the quantity of outlets or to ensure the quality of outlets.

3.3.2 The application of selective sale systems under which the supplier may determine, on the basis of quantitative choice criteria, who is to be allowed to sell the supplier's goods, are not permitted under the competition rules. On the other hand, it is permissible to apply a selective sales system if the choice criteria are objectively motivated with regard to the specific nature of the goods.

3.4   Exclusive purchasing

In an exclusive purchasing agreement the buyer commits himself to buy products for resale only from one specific supplier. Such agreements restrict competition as other suppliers will be excluded from selling their product to such a buyer. Sweden has granted block exemptions via the decree 1993:73 and has adopted the Commission's decree No 1984/83 in respect of groups of exclusive purchase agreements regarding, for example, beer supply agreements and filling station agreements.

3.5   Franchising

A franchising agreement involves one party, the franchiser, in return for a consideration to allow another party, the franchisee, to use, for example, its trade mark and business methods when selling goods to the consumer. Under the terms of the agreements the franchisee undertakes to observe the franchiser's conditions and the franchisee cannot therefore act in the market in a completely independent manner. Block exemption has been granted in respect of franchise agreements. Through the decree 1993:79 Sweden has adopted the Commission's Regulation 4087/88 concerning franchise agreements. Provided that the franchise agreement is drawn up in accordance with the rules which apply to the block exemption, it will not contravene the competition rules. If the franchise agreement contains any non-permitted restrictions on limitation, the agreement may be referred to the Swedish Competition Authority for exemption.

3.6   Intellectual property licensing

3.6.1 Block exemptions have been granted for both patent licence agreements and know-how agreements via the decrees No 1993:77 and 1993:78 respectively, corresponding to the Commission's Regulations 2349/84 and 556/89.

3.6.2 By means of the block exemption, therefore, patent licence agreements and know-how agreements, as well as so-called mixed agreements (a combination of the two previously mentioned types), are exempted from the competition rules under the conditions specified in the decrees.

3.6.3 In order for the block exemption regarding know-how agreements to be valid, it is required, for example, for the agreed knowledge not to be generally known and for it to be of considerable significance for the product or service which is the object of the agreement.

3.6.4 If a licence agreement falls outside the scope of the block exemption as a result of a non-permitted restriction on competition, the agreement may be referred to the Swedish Competition Authority for individual exemption.

3.7 Refusals to supply

A vendor normally has the right to choose whether he will or will not sell to a certain customer. Normal trade custom enables the vendor to decide whether he wishes to conclude a business transaction or not. The prohibition rules under the competition legislation may, however, be applicable if, for example, the vendor holds a dominant position in the market and refuses to supply without justification.

3.8 Price restrictions

3.8.1 On the whole, co-operation in respect of prices is deemed to constitute a serious form of competition limitation. A discount system can inhibit competition and, if it is applied with the objective of achieving such a situation, the practice may be subject to the competition rules.

3.8.2 The Swedish competition rules prohibit the fixing of purchase of sales prices either directly or indirectly. Thus it follows that setting prices to sell at a loss, unreasonable prices, standard price lists and discounts, may be prohibited in accordance with the applicable competition rules.

3.8.3 Selling at prices which do not cover costs and which are issued by undertakings which have a dominant position with the objective of removing competitors from the market (ie predatory pricing) is a practice which contravenes the competition rules. Selling without covering costs over a short period of time, in connection with an advertising campaign for example, is usually regarded as constituting normal price competition and is thus not covered by the competition rules. Selling at unreasonably high prices may also be deemed to be in contravention of the competition rules if this is effected by companies which enjoy a position of dominance.

3.8.4 Normally the application of horizontally agreed standard price lists (ie between competitors) is not permitted. The application of vertical standard price lists on the other hand, is acceptable. The standard price list shall be understood to constitute a recommendation to follow a given price level. An agreement not to depart from the standard price list is likely to fall within the scope of the competition rules if the parties are agreed not to apply prices other than those which are indicated in the standard price list.

3.9   Tie-in sales

3.9.1   Tie-in sales refer to a situation where the supply of one product is made conditional upon the purchase of another product.

3.9.2   Such selling may conflict with the competition rules if there is insufficient connection between product A and product B to justify the need to buy product B as well. As a rule, there must be a relationship between the products as far as quality or technology is concerned in order for such tie-in sales to be permitted.

3.9.3   The Swedish Marketing Act contains rules which govern how tie-in sales are to be carried out. A contravention of the Marketing Act's provisions may result in the management of the company being fined and, in serious cases, imprisoned.

3.10   Information exchange

Agreements providing for the exchange of information on such matters as costs, prices, customers, investments etc may restrict competition and therefore be prohibited by the Competition Act. Exchange of confidential information might infringe the Competition Act while there will be no objection to the exchange of general information.

3.11   Joint buying and selling

Agreements between competitors to establish joint purchasing or selling can infringe the Competition Act since they might diminish the freedom to act in the market. Decisions which are taken collectively by a trade association and which directly or indirectly bind the members of the association may therefore be examined via the application of the Competition Act's rules to determine whether the decision inhibits competition.

3.12   Market sharing

Agreements to share markets are prohibited and it is unlikely that exemption could be given for such agreements.

3.13   Joint ventures

3.13.1   Co-operation between companies in joint venture relationships is, under normal conditions, permitted in accordance with Swedish rules. Such co-operation, however, if it does not fall within the scope of so-called '*de minimis* rules', ie that it does not have an appreciable influence in the market, may be assessed in accordance with the competition rules. Co-operation with regard to questions which do not affect the sale of goods and services, naturally falls outside of the scope of the Competition Act's provisions.

3.13.2   An assessment of whether a joint venture is governed by the competition rules is therefore made from the starting point of the objective benefit to the market of such co-operation. It is possible that, with reference to the Competition Act's rules, exemption may be awarded in respect of limited competition joint venture agreements.

4 CONCENTRATIONS, MERGERS AND ACQUISITIONS

4.1 Introduction

Acquisitions of undertakings (mergers) are an important factor in continuing structural adjustment and promote adjustment by various sectors to changing market conditions. Sweden has a small and open economy and competition is becoming keener in many sectors due to internationalisation. There are, however, still protected domestic markets with high barriers to entry where mergers result in market domination that is liable to eliminate competition.

4.2 Notification

4.2.1 Where the parties to a merger have an aggregated turnover in excess of SEK 4 billion during the latest year of account, the merger must be reported to the Swedish Competition Authority. If the party making the acquisition is a company which forms part of a group of companies with a common proprietary interest, the group's combined annual turnover shall be seen as the annual turnover of the party making the acquisition. Companies with an annual turnover below SEK 4 billion fall outside of the law's purview.

4.2.2 An acquisition involving an obligation to report may not be completed until the expiry of 30 days from the time when the acquisition was reported to the Swedish Competition Authority. This does not apply if the Swedish Competition Authority decides beforehand that either the report shall be handed in without taking action, or that particular investigations shall be initiated. In the latter instance, the Swedish Competition Authority may request that the completion of the acquisition be delayed by the Stocholm City Court until the matter has been decided.

4.2.3 Steps to prevent the merger may be taken if it is liable to have significant adverse effects in the long term. The system of control will be made more flexible by making a prohibition applicable only to part of a merger deal.

4.3 Conditions governing prohibition

In order for an acquisition to be stopped, or to be the subject of conditions, the following shall apply. The acquisition must create or intensify a dominant position which significantly inhibits, or which is likely to inhibit, the presence or development of effective competition in the Swedish market. In addition, the acquisition shall be deemed to be damaging in terms of the general public.

4.4 Procedure and fines

4.4.1 It is incumbent upon the Swedish Competition Authority to show that the indicated conditions governing prohibition are satisfied. No one else but the

Swedish Competition Authority may argue a cause in matters relating to acquisitions. Such arguments shall be submitted before the Stockholm City Court and its judgments may ultimately be appealed to the Market Court. The Swedish Competition Authority is required to bring an action within three months of the time that it decided to conduct a special examination into the reported company acquisition. Such a decision to undertake an examination shall be made by the Swedish Competition Authority within 30 days of the date that the undertaking company is referred to the Swedish Competition Authority.

4.4.2   An announced prohibition may be combined with the imposition of a fine. If the prohibition is issued in respect of a specific acquisition, the acquisition shall be deemed to be invalid.

CHAPTER XVIII

Switzerland

Philipp Kaenzig

Staiger, Schwald & Roesle
Attorneys at Law
Postbox 677
8027 Zürich
Switzerland

Tel   ++41 1 283 8686
Fax   ++41 1 283 8787

CHAPTER XVIII

Switzerland

1 SWISS COMPETITION LAW

1.1 Background

1.1.1 Anti-trust law has not, in the past, played a significant role in the planning and execution of business transactions in Switzerland. Due to a long-standing tradition of cartels, anti-competitive agreements and practices which would be unthinkable in other jurisdictions still exist in many sectors of the Swiss economy. In the past ten years, however, Swiss cartel law has been substantially amended and both the Swiss Federal Supreme Court and the Swiss Cartel Commission ('Cartel Commission') have shown that they are increasingly willing to take a more pro-competitive attitude when applying the law. It is also anticipated that Swiss anti-trust law will be totally revised within the next two or three years and will then be comparable to the laws of the EU and the national laws of many of the EU countries.

1.1.2 Swiss anti-trust and competition law is based on Art 31bis of the Swiss Federal Constitution.[1] This provision authorizes exceptions from the principle of free business and trade and provides for legislation against 'the economically or socially harmful effects of cartels or similar organisations'.

Based on Art 31bis of the Constitution, parliament has enacted the principal sources of Swiss anti-trust and competition law, namely the Federal Act on Cartels and Similar Organisations ('Cartels Act', CA) of 20 December 1985[2] and the Federal Act Against Unfair Competition ('Unfair Competition Act', FAUC) of 19 December 1986.[3] Several other federal, cantonal and even communal laws and ordinances govern various aspects of competition (such as governmental supervision of prices[4]) and are mostly intended to protect the consumer against 'unfair' practices.

1.1.3 The Cartels Act does not prohibit cartels or anti-competitive agreements as such, but declares inadmissible those cartels and anti-competitive agreements which are abusive. The Cartels Act expressly declares admissible a restraint of competition if such restraint is justified by predominant private interests worthy of protection and if its effects do not violate the interests of the public at large (Art 7 CA).

Under the concept of the Cartels Act, free and unimpaired competition is considered to be only one of various aspects by which to determine the detrimental and beneficial effects of a cartel for the economy. The Cartel Commission is therefore required to consider carefully not only free competition as such but also the effects of such competition (prices, quality, production costs and distribution costs

---

1 SR 101.
2 SR 251.
3 SR 241.
4 Federal Act on the Supervision of Prices of 20 December 1985; SR 942.20.

as well as the structure of Swiss economy) when evaluating a cartel or a similar organisation. The Cartel Commission is required to weigh against each other the useful and the harmful effects when determining the admissibility of a cartel or similar organisation (Art 29, para 2 CA). A cartel is considered to be harmful if competition is completely prevented, but not necessarily if competition is only 'significantly impaired' (Art 29, para 3 CA).

1.1.4 The above concept (in connection with unwieldy and slow enforcement rules) has, in the past, made it very difficult effectively to control restraints on competition in Switzerland. The shortcomings of current legislation have, however, been widely recognised in the past few years. Structural changes in the global economy have made it necessary to reconsider protectionist practices which have in the past been beneficial for the Swiss economy. As a result of these discussions and of increasing criticism from international organisations such as GATT and OECD[5] various motions and petitions have been submitted in parliament substantially to revise Swiss competition law. In 1992 a commission was formed by the federal council to submit a first draft for a revision of the Cartels Act.[6] In September 1993 this commission presented a preliminary draft for a revised Cartels Act which would be more compatible with the laws of the EU and of other European countries. Based on this preliminary draft, the federal council published its definite draft in the official gazette.[7] This revision must, however, still be debated in parliament and it remains to be seen to what extent the proposed changes survive this debate.

1.1.5 For the time being the Cartels Act of 20 December 1985 will remain the legal basis for Swiss anti-trust law. The Cartels Act contains private law rules (Arts 6–19 CA) which regulate the behaviour of competitors amongst each other and public law rules (Art 20ff CA) which are intended to safeguard the interests of the state and the public at large. Common to both sets of rules is the definition (Arts 1–5 CA) of cartels and other potentially anti-competitive practices ('organisations similar to a cartel').

1.2   Cartels and similar organisations

1.2.1 Article 2 of the Cartels Act defines cartels as contracts, resolutions or legally unenforceable undertakings which influence or are apt to influence the market for specific goods or services by jointly restricting competition, in particular by regulating the production, sale or purchase of goods as well as of prices and terms of business.

The definition of a cartel therefore requires two or more parties to co-ordinate their acts either by contract, resolution or 'unenforceable understandings' in order to influence the market. An industrial concern can therefore be a cartel only if its members are legal entities in their own right, free – subject to contracts, resolutions or legally unenforceable understandings – to determine their own behaviour on the market. Also, Art 2 CA applies only to horizontal contracts, resolutions and understandings between producers or dealers at the same distribution level (vertical agreements can, however, be qualified as cartels under Art 3 CA; see section 1.2.2 below).

---

5 GATT, *Mécanisme d'examen des politiques commerciales:* Suisse, Genève, août 1991 and OECD, *Etudes économiques de l'OECD:* Suisse, Paris, 1992.
6 *Studienkommission zur Revision des Kartellgesetzes.*
7 Botschaft zum Kartellgesetz, BBl 1995 I, S 468ff.

The 'aptitude to influence the market for specific goods or services' requires only that the influence is or would be perceptible, not that it is or would be significant. The market for a certain product or service includes all equivalent products or services which are considered by the average consumer when making his choice.

In order to qualify as a cartel, the members must jointly restrict competition. The enumeration in Art 2 CA of possible anti-competitive behaviour ('regulating the production, sale or purchase of goods as well as of prices and terms of business') is not exhaustive and the statute applies to all forms of behaviour which influence or are likely to influence the market.

Recommendations can, according to Art 2 CA, be treated as cartels if they obviously result in a common restriction of competition. This provision which was introduced in 1986 was, eg, applied to the form of general business conditions recommended by the Swiss Bankers' Association which the Cartels Commission held to have created an obvious common restriction of competition.[8]

1.2.2 According to Art 3 CA (vertical) agreements between suppliers and their buyers for the fixing of prices or terms of business for the resale of goods are treated as cartels if such arrangements are imposed by a cartel or a similar organisation. Article 3 CA applies only to the resale of goods and not to services. The scope of this provision includes the fixing of minimum and maximum prices, rebates or other conditions. Article 3, para 2 of the Cartels Act includes recommendations if they obviously result in resale price maintenance.

1.2.3 According to Art 4 CA an 'organisation similar to a cartel' is defined as:

'(a) an individual undertaking,
 (b) undertakings which tacitly coordinate their conduct,
 (c) the combination of undertakings by equity, participation or by other means,

insofar as they dominate or substantially influence the market for specific goods or services'.

Other than cartels, all forms of organisations similar to cartels must therefore by definition 'dominate or substantially influence the market for specific goods or services'. The central question is therefore to determine the relevant market. Paragraph 2 of Art 4 CA requires that all relevant facts concerning supply and demand must be taken into consideration in appraising the conditions of competition. In particular, the following elements are considered to be relevant:

(a) the number of competitors and their market shares;
(b) the methods of buying and selling;
(c) the financial power of the involved undertakings;
(d) the interdependence of the involved undertakings;
(e) the dependence of undertakings of the opposite market side from the organisation being appraised.

The Cartels Commission has repeatedly held that there is no single practical test effectively to determine if the market for specific goods or services is being 'substantially influenced'.[9] In applying Art 4 CA the Cartels Commission has, eg, held

8 VKKP 3/1989, 83ff.
9 VKK 1976, 121ff; VKK 1978, 212.

that a share of 59.46% of the market for billboard advertising constitutes substantial influence.[10] The Cartels Commission has also held[11] that individual undertakings (multi-national corporations) on the market for oil have the potential substantially to influence the market.

1.2.4 Article 5 CA determines that (vertical) agreements between suppliers and buyers concerning the exclusive purchase or sale of specific goods or services or concerning restrictions on their redistribution are treated as organisations similar to cartels, in so far as such agreements substantially influence the market. Article 5 CA does not require the participation of a cartel or a similar organisation and applies only when a vertical restraint has a significant influence on the market. This provision has little significance in itself since a cartel or a similar organisation will in most cases be involved if an agreement between a supplier and distributors is substantially to influence the market.

1.3   Private anti-trust law

1.3.1 Private anti-trust law governs the relationship of a cartel or a similar organisation (as defined in Arts 1–5 CA; see section 1.2 above) with third parties, especially competitors and the relationship of the members of a cartel among themselves.

1.3.2 The Cartels Act in Art 6 defines the conditions under which acts of a cartel or similar organisation qualify as unlawful restraints on competition and in Art 7 establishes exceptions justifying restraints of competition which would otherwise be inadmissible.

1.3.3 Article 6 CA declares illegal all measures of a cartel or a similar organisation if they *exclude* third parties from competing or *substantially restrain* them from entering or exercising competition. Article 6 para 2 CA contains a (non-exhaustive) list of examples of such anti-competitive measures:

(a)   the refusal to supply or the discrimination against buyers with regard to prices or terms of business;
(b)   the refusal to purchase or the discrimination against suppliers with regard to prices or terms of business or the unreasonable request for preferential prices or preferential terms of business;
(c)   the undercutting of prices or terms of business (predatory pricing); and
(d)   the discrimination against outsiders with regard to the employment of certain groups of employees.

Article 6 para 3 CA declares equally inadmissible any measures which uniformly and substantially restrain all parties from entering or exercising competition, in particular tying contracts. The law therefore not only prohibits discrimination against individual third parties but also activities which effect all third parties equally in their efforts to compete.

1.3.4 Measures taken by a cartel or similar organisation must be *aimed against third parties*. Acts of a cartel will, in most cases, meet this requirement (see section

---

10 VKK 1982, 232ff.
11 VKK 1985, 160ff.

1.2.1 above). In the case of an organisation similar to a cartel, however, acts for which there are sound and legitimate business reasons and which are not solely intended to restrain third parties in their efforts to compete, will not qualify as 'measures' in the sense of Art 6 CA; a justification under Art 7 CA is therefore not necessary.

1.3.5 The law requires a *substantial restraint* (or complete elimination) of third parties in their efforts to compete. Minor (*de minimis*) restrictions (such as imposing minor price differences of 0.5 to 1% upon distributors[12]) are permitted. The Swiss Federal Supreme Court has held[13] that the restriction must have a certain intensity which is perceived by the concerned party as a restriction because it directly or indirectly narrows the concerned party's freedom to act and requires it to take counter- or evasive measures to escape the consequences of the restriction. If the effects of the restriction are substantial with regard to the economic behaviour of the concerned party, the structure of its enterprise or the development of its business, the nature of the restriction is irrelevant.[14]

1.3.6 According to Art 7 CA a restraint of competition is admissible if it is justified by predominant private interests worthy of protection and if its effects are not contrary to the interests of the public at large. In addition, competition must not be overly impaired in relation to the desired goal as well as by the nature and implementation of the restraint of competition.

The most important justification of a restraint of competition is therefore a 'predominant private interest worthy of protection'. In order to understand this justification it is important to keep in mind that Swiss law allows the use of market power by cartels for 'legitimate business reasons'. Such legitimate business reasons can, for example, be seen in the strengthening of the cartel's position on the market, not, however, if the cartel's only aim is to exclude new competitors (Art 7, para 3 CA). An organisation similar to a cartel will rarely be able to justify a restraint of competition under Art 7 CA because its legitimate business reasons will already have been taken into account when determining if the organisation in question is taking 'measures' in the sense of Art 6 CA (see section 1.3.4 above).

In applying Art 7, para 1 CA the judge must weigh against each other the (private) interests of the parties. If a cartel refuses to supply an outsider, the interests of the cartel in keeping the outsider away from the market must therefore be weighed against the interests of the outsider in joining the market. According to Art 7, para 2 such interests (of a cartel) worthy of protection can, in particular, be:

(a) safeguarding fair and undistorted competition;
(b) creating and upholding adequate professional standards;
(c) promoting a desirable structure in a certain branch of industry or profession;
(d) implementing resale price maintenance to the extent necessary in order to guarantee the quality of goods or customer services.

The list of legitimate interests given in Art 7, para 2 CA is not exhaustive. All examples do, however, relate to the general interests of the public at large and it has therefore been maintained by various authors that a restraint of competition must contribute to the interests of the public at large in order to be justified. Other

12 BGE 91 II 319ff; BGE 101 II 147ff.
13 BGE 112 II 276.
14 BGE 99 II 233; BGE 109 II 57; VKK 1983, 40; VKK 1986, 118.

authors maintain that a restraint of competition can be justified by predominant private interests if it is without any (negative) effects to public interests. The Swiss Federal Court has not yet resolved this issue.

A further test required by Art 7 CA is that restraints on competition can be justified only if they respect the *principle of proportionality*. This requirement is met if:

(a)   the measure is apt to obtain the desirable goal;
(b)   the measure goes no further than required by the goal; and
(c)   no less restrictive alternative measures are available.

1.3.7   In applying the rules described above, the courts have held that cartelistic measures to protect fair und undistorted competition can be legitimate even if an outsider does not violate the provisions of the Federal Act against Unfair Competition. It has, for example, been held that measures of a cartel against dumping prices practised by a subsidised competitor can be legitimate.[15] Provided that professional standards are reasonable and not exclusively prompted by financial interests, it has also been held that the maintenance of sufficiently high standards in a branch of industry or profession can legitimise cartelistic measures.[16] The most important and also the most difficult justification to apply is the 'promotion of a desirable structure in a certain branch of industry or profession'. This justification can be used in connection with co-operation agreements and other concentration processes. The Federal Supreme Court has repeatedly applied this exception, especially to ensure the survival of small distributors (thereby securing the supply of economically unimportant regions of the country).[17] Finally, Art 7, para 2(d) CA expressly sanctions the implementation of resale price maintenance to the extent necessary to guarantee the quality of products or customer services. Resale price maintenance can also be justified under Art 7, para 2(a)–(c) CA.

1.4   Public anti-trust law

1.4.1   Article 29 of the Cartels Act is the central provision of public cartel law and – to a certain extent – the public law equivalent of the civil law provisions of Arts 6 and 7 CA. According to Art 29 CA the Cartel Commission investigates whether a cartel or a similar organisation is economically or socially harmful in its effects. When examining the economic or social harmfulness, the Cartel Commission must first determine the beneficial and detrimental effects of a cartel or a similar organisation and must then, if it finds a significant restraint or distortion of competition, weigh the positive and negative effects against each other (balance-method). In doing so, the Cartel Commission must take into consideration the effects on the freedom and extent of competition and all other significant effects such as those on manufacturing and distribution costs, prices, quality, supply situation, structure of the industry, country regions, competitiveness of Swiss undertakings within the country and abroad as well as the interests of the employees and consumers concerned.

It is obvious that this process is extremely complex and that there is no simple test which will allow a reliable prediction of the outcome of an investigation by the Cartel Commission. Article 29, para 3 CA simply states that 'the effects are

15   BGE 103 II 307ff/Pra 67 Nr 29.
16   VKK 1969, 321ff; VKK 1977, 250.
17   BGE 109 II 260; BGE 102 II 427ff; BGE 98 II 365ff; BGE 94 II 338.

economically or socially harmful if the examination according to para 2 reveals a preponderance of harmful effects'. Harmfulness shall, however, in any case be determined where effective competition is prevented in a market for specific goods or services, unless the examination reveals that the prevention of competition is *indispensable* for predominant reasons of public interest.

1.4.2   As in its private law provisions, the public law provisions of the Cartels Act declare illegal only the *abuse* of cartelistic measures. However, the Cartel Commission views the effects of a cartel only with regard to the interests of the public at large. The Cartel Commission cannot, when determining the economically or socially harmful effects of a cartel, consider merely private interests. Also, the Cartel Commission does not consider the effects of a cartel on third parties (such as outsiders) but on free competition as such. Free competition can therefore be 'considerably impared' (Art 29, para 2 CA) even without measures which 'substantially restrain third parties' from competing (Art 6, para 1 CA).

1.4.3   Article 29, para 3 CA determines that the effects of a cartel or a similar organisation are generally to be considered economically or socially harmful if the procedure in accordance with Art 29, para 2 CA shows a balance of harmful effects. In particular, the economic or social harmfulness *is presumed* when it is found that 'effective competition is prevented in a market for specific goods or services'. This provision therefore applies only where free competition does not exist as a result of cartelistic measures.[18] Even if the prevention of effective competition is affirmed, Art 29, para 3 CA allows for a justification of this prevention if it is 'indispensable for predominant reasons of public interest'.

1.4.4   The Cartels Act does not provide for preventive merger control. Article 30 CA does, however, allow the Cartel Commission to investigate (in the sense of Art 29 CA) mergers which create or reinforce a position which decisively influences the market (in the sense of Art 4, para 1 CA; see section 1.2.3 above) and where there are indications of economically or socially harmful effects.

If the Cartel Commission orders such an investigation of a merger, this investigation is conducted in accordance with Art 29, para 2 and 3 CA (see section 1.4.1 above).

1.5   Price control

1.5.1   Based on Art 31septies of the Swiss Federal Constitution, the Federal Act on the supervision of prices (Price Supervision Act, PSA) was enacted on 1 July 1986. According to Art 3 PSA the Federal Council elects a Supervisor of Prices who alone is competent to determine if prices increased or maintained by cartels or similar organisations are abusive (Art 16, para 2 PSA). This provision restricts the Cartel Commission's jurisdiction under Art 29 CA (see section 1.4 above). However, prices maintained by a cartel or a similar organisation which are not abusive in the sense of the Price Supervision Act can be the result of a socially harmful cartel or similar organisation, and the Cartel Commission is, in such cases, authorised to conduct an investigation and to make recommendations. The difference between the two statutes is that the Price Supervision Act is aimed against the symptoms (abusive prices) while the Cartel Act is aimed at the origins of socially harmful

18 VKK 1984, 293.

effects. Therefore, the supervisor of prices can order a reduction of prices, while the Cartel Commission can recommend the annulment of cartelistic agreements which result in prices which are not a result of a functioning competitive environment.

1.5.2 The Price Supervision Act applies to prices for goods and services (including credits[19]) determined by cartels or similar organisations in the sense of Arts 2–5 CA (Arts 1 and 2 PSA).

1.5.3 The Federal Council elects a Federal Supervisor of Prices whose responsibility it is to *prevent* and *eliminate* the abusive increase and the abusive maintenance of prices (Art 4 PSA).

1.5.4 The abusiveness of prices is established in accordance with the principles developed by the Cartels Act. The abusiveness of prices can be determined if the prices in a specific market are not the result of effective competition (Art 12, para 1 PSA). Effective competition is presumed if the consumer has the possibility to chose other equivalent goods or services without undue effort (Art 12, para 2 PSA). When evaluating the abusiveness of prices, the supervisor of prices must consider:

(a) the development of prices in comparable markets;
(b) the necessity of making reasonable profits;
(c) the development of costs;
(d) special achievements and services of offeror;
(e) special circumstances on the market (eg if demand by far exceeds supply in a specific market, a very high price can be justified if it is the result of effective competition).

1.6 Unfair competition

1.6.1 The purpose of the Federal Act against Unfair Competition is to ensure fair and undistorted competition in the interest of all parties (Art 1 FAUC). The intent of the Unfair Competition Act is therefore to guarantee fairness in the market place and to ensure the quality of competition.

1.6.2 Article 2 FAUC sets up the general rule that any conduct or business practice which is deceptive or otherwise violates the *principle of good faith* and which effects the relationship between competitors or between sellers and consumers is unfair and illegal. The scope of intentionally unfair trade practices covered by the general clause is very broad. Nevertheless, the courts have seldom based their decisions on Art 2 FAUC, relying in most cases on the specific provisions of the Unfair Competition Act. The general clause is nevertheless important as a guideline for the interpretation of the specific provisions of the Unfair Competition Act. Also, Art 2 makes clear that any conduct, including the conduct of third parties not directly involved in competition, may be qualified as unfair competition in the sense of the Unfair Competition Act. In a recent decision the Swiss Federal Court has held that a journalist can commit unfair competition if he disseminates information which is deceptive and affects the relationship between competitors.[20]

19 Amendment of 1 October 1991; AS 1991, P 2092.
20 BGE 117 IV 193 ('Bernina').

1.6.3 Article 3 FAUC contains a list of twelve specific *advertisement and sales methods* which constitute unfair competition. There are five groups of such specific acts which can be summarised as follows:

(a) *false and misleading information about the goods and services of others* (Art 3(a) and (d) FAUC). These provisions protect competitors against advertisement and sales methods which are derogatory or could lead to confusion with the goods and services of a third party;

(b) a second group of provisions (Art 3(b), (c) and (i) FAUC) declares illegal *false or misleading statements about one's own goods and services.* Any deception with regard to the company name, trade marks, products, work, performance, prices and business dealings is regarded as unfair and therefore illegal. The same applies to the misuse of academic or professional credentials;

(c) Article 3(e) FAUC deals with *comparative advertisement and sales methods.* This provision declares it illegal to compare oneself, one's products, works, performances or prices with the products, works, performances or prices of others if such comparison is in any way false, misleading or unnecessarily derogatory;

(d) Article 4(f), (g) and (h) deal with *other unfair sales methods.* Price undercutting can be regarded as an unfair practice if special attention is drawn to the price in advertisements, thereby misleading the customer about the competitiveness of the seller and the seller's competitors (especially if price undercutting is limited to a few selected goods and the consumer is led to believe that the low prices apply to all or a major part of the seller's merchandise). This provision (Art 3(f) FAUC) has been applied to a 'video-club' which offered its members three video cassettes at a very reduced price but at the same time required its members to purchase further videos at market price for the following three years.[1]

According to Art 3(g) FAUC premiums and gifts in connection with the sale of merchandise can be unfair and therefore illegal if they are apt to deceive the customer about the effective value of the goods offered. The offer of price reductions and gifts for a limited period of time is further regulated by the Federal Ordinance on Sales[2] which makes practically any sale in the non-food sector subject to regulatory approval.

Article 3(h) FAUC declares 'aggressive sales practices' which are apt to impair the customer's freedom of choice to be unfair and therefore illegal. This provision applies if psychological coercion is exercised against the consumer. Examples for such aggressive methods are sales at private parties, door-to-door sales, bus-tour sales and lotteries which (either explicitly or by psychological coercion) require the participants to purchase goods in order to participate. Lotteries are additionally regulated by the Federal Statute on Lotteries;[3]

(e) a final group of 'unfair' advertising and sales practices (Art 3(k), (l) and (m) FAUC) are prohibited primarily for *consumer protection* reasons. These provisions concern the advertisement for instalment sales or consumer credits and the use of unclear or misleading general business conditions or form contracts. Additional consumer protection has been introduced in the past few

1 SMI, Volume 1, 1990, 219ff.
2 SR 241.1.
3 SR 935.51.

years by a Federal Act on Consumer Credits[4] and revisions of the Swiss Code of Obligations.

1.6.4   Article 4 FAUC prohibits the *interference with contractual relations of third parties*. This provision primarily prohibits the bribing of employees and agents of competitors in order to induce such persons to perform their work in a manner inconsistent with their obligations and especially to disclose manufacturing or business secrets of their employer or principal (Art 4(b) and (c) FAUC). In a more general manner Art 4(a) and (d) FAUC also declare unfair and illegal any conduct by a third party which induces contracting parties to breach a contract so that the third party may enter into a similar contract himself.

1.6.5   Article 5 FAUC prohibits the *unauthorised exploitation of the work of third parties*. This provision is intended to prohibit unfair acts which are not covered by legislation on patents, copyrights or other intellectual property rights. Article 5(a) FAUC prohibits the *direct* exploitation of a third party's intellectual or industrial achievements (especially bids, calculations and blueprints not protected by copyright) by a party to whom these intellectual or industrial achievements were entrusted for another purpose.

Article 5(b) FAUC prohibits the *indirect* exploitation by a third party who knows that the person passing on the intellectual or industrial achievements was not authorised to do so. Finally, Art 5(c) FAUC prohibits the appropriation and exploitation by use of technical reproduction procedures of the marketable work or product of a third party without making an appropriate effort of one's own. Since the protection granted by special laws (such as the Federal Copyright Act[5] overrides the general provision of Art 5(c) FAUC, there is very little room for the application of this provision.

1.6.6   Article 6 prohibits the *exploitation of industrial and trade secrets which have been illegally obtained*. Such secrets are also protected by a large number of special laws and by Art 273 of the Swiss Penal Code.[6]

1.6.7   Article 7 FAUC declares unfair and illegal the *non-compliance with employment regulations* which are imposed upon competitors by law or contract or which conform with trade or local usage. Article 8 FAUC prohibits the use of abusive or misleading general business conditions or form contracts. For various reasons, competitors have been reluctant to bring actions based on these two provisions, so that both provisions have gained very little practical importance.

2   ENFORCEMENT

2.1   Enforcement authorities and jurisdictional rules under the Cartels Act

2.1.1   Private actions under the Cartels Act may be brought by a competitor who is restricted in his freedom of competition or threatened by such a restriction. Private actions may also be brought by professional or trade associations whose purpose is to promote the interests of their members and whose members

4   BB1 1993 III 788.
5   SR 231.1.
6   SR 311.0.

themselves have standing to sue (Art 8 CA). In general, private actions cannot be brought by consumers or consumer organisations. Private actions are brought before a cantonal court in the first instance (Art 10 CA). This court's decision is subject to an appeal to the Federal Supreme Court (Art 11 CA).

In a private action the plaintiff may request:

(a) a declaratory judgment declaring the restraint of competition to be illegal;
(b) an injunction requiring the illegal condition to be set aside;
(c) an injunction to discontinue an illegal measure;
(d) an award for damages caused in a wilful or negligent manner;
(e) an award of satisfaction in the sense of Art 49 of the Swiss Code of Obligations.[7]

A party that can show prima facie evidence of a restraint of competition may also request a preliminary injunction against the party exercising the restraint of competition (Art 13 CA).

The Cartels Act has provided the courts with various effective measures to ensure the enforcement of judgments. The court may order that:

(a) obligations of the members of a cartel not be binding with respect to the party restrained in competition;
(b) the plaintiff either be allowed to participate in a cartel with corresponding rights and obligations or be admitted into an association;
(c) contracts be totally or partially invalidated;
(d) a common purchasing or selling organisation of a cartel or of an undertaking which constitutes an organisation similar to a cartel enter into fair and customary contract with the party restrained in competition.

The court may also authorise the prevailing party to have the judgment published at the cost of the other party.

2.1.2 Investigations by the Cartel Commission are initiated by order of the Federal Department of Economic Affairs or by the Cartel Commission itself. In the course of its investigation the Cartel Commission may call on expert witnesses and request information and documents from any person who can contribute to the determination of the facts. If the facts cannot be determined in this manner, the Cartel Commission is entitled to issue orders to the persons concerned and to third parties requiring their attendance as witnesses and the surrender of documents. Such an order of the Cartel Commission is subject to an appeal to the Swiss Federal Supreme Court (Arts 31, 35 and 38 CA).

If the Cartel Commission in the course of its investigation ascertains an economically or socially harmful effect, it recommends to the persons concerned either to modify or revoke cartel provisions or arrangements falling within the scope of the Cartel Act. It may also recommend to the persons concerned that they refrain from specific practices. The persons receiving such a recommendation from the Cartel Commission must declare in writing within a fixed time limit whether or not they will comply with the recommendation (Art 32 CA). If recommendations of the Cartel Commission are rejected by the persons concerned, the Federal Department of Economic Affairs may, at the Cartel Commission's request and after hearing the

7 SR 220.

parties, issue binding orders (Art 37 CA). Such orders of the Federal Department of Economic Affairs are subject to an appeal to the Swiss Federal Supreme Court.

2.1.3 The Cartels Act provides for penal sanctions in the case of intentional non-compliance with either accepted recommendations of the Cartel Commission or final orders of the Federal Department of Economic Affairs (respectively judgments of the Federal Supreme Court rendered upon appeal). The maximum fine provided by law is SFrs 100,000 (Art 39 CA).

2.2 Enforcement authorities and jurisdictional rules under the Price Supervision Act

2.2.1 Anyone who considers the increase or maintenance of a price to be abusive (and the result of cartelistic behaviour) may make a complaint in writing to the Federal Supervisor of Prices. Based on such a complaint or on his own observations, the Supervisor of Prices will then establish if there are indications for abusive pricing (Arts 7 and 8 PSA). Cartels, similar organisations and public authorities are obliged by Art 17 PSA to provide the Supervisor of Prices with all necessary information and documents (Arts 17 and 18 PSA).

If the Supervisor of Prices determines that the prices in a market are abusive, he attempts to find an amicable solution with the parties concerned. If such a solution cannot be found, the Supervisor of Prices may order that a price increase be partly or totally cancelled or that an existing price be reduced (Arts 9 and 10 PSA). Such an order of the Supervisor of Prices is subject to an appeal to the Federal Department of Economic Affairs. The decision of the Federal Department of Economic Affairs is subject to an appeal to the Federal Supreme Court (Art 20 PSA). Swiss national or regional organisations which are dedicated according to their charters to the protection of consumers also have the right of appeal in accordance with Art 20 PSA.

2.2.2 Under Art 6 PSA a cartel or similar organisation intending to increase its prices may submit the intended price increase to the supervisor of prices. The supervisor of prices must then declare (within 30 days) if he considers the increase to be 'uncritical' (Art 6 PSA). Until today it cannot be said that much use has been made of this possibility.

2.2.3 The penal sanctions provided by the Price Supervision Act are the same as under the Cartels Act (maximum fine of SFrs 100,000).

2.3 Enforcement authorities and jurisdictional rules under the Unfair Competition Act

2.3.1 An action based on unfair competition may be brought by any person who is threatened or impaired in his economic interests by unfair competition. An action may not only be brought by a competitor or a trade and business association which is authorised to protect the economic interests of its members but also by consumers and by Swiss national or regional organisations which are dedicated according to their charters to the protection of consumers.

Private actions are brought before the ordinary courts at the domicile of the defendant or – if the defendant has its domicile outside of Switzerland – before the courts where the unfair acts were committed or where they were effective (Art 129 of the Swiss Private International Law Statute[8]).

The plaintiff may request that the court:

(a) enjoin a threatening injury by unfair competition;
(b) remove (by injunction) an existing injury by unfair competition;
(c) determine that an injury is the result of illegal conduct;
(d) award damages and satisfaction in accordance with Art 49 of the Swiss Code of Obligations;
(e) order that the judgment be published at the cost of the defendant.

A provisional injunction is available if the plaintiff has prima facie evidence of a violation and can also show that the detrimental effects of the violation will be harder to remedy at a future date.

2.3.2 Complaints against unfair competition can also be made to the 'Swiss Commission for Fairness in Advertising'. This Commission is organised as a foundation and is supported by virtually all Swiss professional associations in any way connected with advertisement (including the media). Although the Commission cannot threaten any legal sanctions, its orders to desist from unfair competition are mostly observed. In case of non-compliance, the party concerned could be threatend with expulsion from his professional association and would also risk the publication of the Commission's findings.

2.3.3 Anyone who is entitled to file a civil action under Art 9 of the Unfair Competition Act may also file a criminal complaint under Art 23 FAUC. An intentional act of unfair competition as defined in Arts 3–6 FAUC constitutes a misdemeanour punishable by imprisonment of up to three years or a fine of up to SFrs 100,000.

3 CHECKLIST OF POTENTIAL INFRINGEMENTS

A Vertical Agreements

3.1 Vertical agreements in general

In most cases, no clear test will be available in order to determine if a certain type of vertical restriction is admissible or not. When evaluating a vertical restriction, it is therefore necessary first to determine if the vertical restriction is imposed by a cartel or a similar organisation. If so, it will then be necessary to apply the provisions of Arts 6 and 7 CA in order to determine if the vertical restriction excludes or substantially restrains third parties from entering or exercising competition (see section 1.3.3 above) and to establish if no justification by predominant private interests worthy of protection is available (see section 1.3.6 above). The following check-list can therefore only serve to determine if certain vertical agreements or restrictions can qualify as measures of a cartel or a similar organisation which are apt to exclude or substantially restrain third parties from competing.

---

8 SR 291.

3.2   Distribution agreements

3.2.1   Exclusive distribution agreements are treated as organisations similar to cartels in so far as such agreements substantially influence the market (Art 5 CA; see section 1.2.3 above). If such distributorship agreement exercises an unlawful restraint on competition (Art 6 CA) and if no justification is available under Art 7 CA such a distributorship agreement may therefore be illegal.

Article 5 CA applies to all forms of *exclusive* distributorship agreements (exclusive sales and purchase agreements) as well as to agreements by which a distributor assumes the obligation to sell goods only in accordance with the terms and conditions dictated by the supplier. Article 5 CA can also apply to so-called *selective* distributorship agreements whereby the supplier agrees to supply only those distributors that meet certain objective criteria.

3.2.2   In view of the definition of restraints of competition (Art 6 and 29 CA) and the justifications available under Art 7 and 29 CA, exclusive and selective distributorship agreements in most cases will not be problematic under current Swiss legislation even if they do have substantial influence on the market.

3.3   Franchising agreements

Franchising agreements regularly contain exclusivity provisions and therefore fall under Art 5 CA in so far as they substantially influence the market. The same comments apply as to distributorship agreements.

3.4   Intellectual property licensing

3.4.1   According to Art 44, para 3 CA effects on competition which result *exclusively* from rights granted under federal legislation concerning industrial property and copyrights will not fall within the scope of the Cartels Act. In principle, the Cartels Act therefore does not apply to licensing agreements (including know-how licences).

3.4.2   The Cartels Act does, however, apply when a cartel, or a similar organisation that owns industrial property rights or copyrights, abuses its rights in order to restrict third parties in competition or in order to cause economically or socially harmful effects (eg, if the owner of a famous trade mark licenses the products protected by this trade mark only together with other products which the distributor does not need or want (tying contract; Art 6, para 3 CA)). However, contractual clauses for which there are sound business reasons (including the determination of prices, restriction to a certain territory, non-competition clauses etc) are permissible in licensing agreements.

3.5   Commercial agency

According to Art 418a of the Swiss Federal Code of Obligations an agent is a person who assumes the obligation to negotiate business transactions for one or more principals on a continuous basis or to conclude agreements on their behalf and for their account without being an employee of the principal. The agent therefore does not act in his own name and for his own account (and risk) and can only assist the principal in his distribution activities. An agency agreement as such can not therefore fall under the Cartels Act.

3.6 Refusal to supply

The refusal to supply is expressly mentioned in Art 6, para 2(a) CA as a measure which is apt to exclude or restrict third parties in exercising competition (see sections 1.3.3–1.3.5 above). If such a refusal to supply restricts the concerned party with regard to the structure of its enterprise or the development of its business by requiring it to take counter- or evasive measures (Art 6 CA), such a refusal to supply will constitute a violation of the Cartels Act in so far as no justification under Art 7 CA applies.

3.7 Resale price maintenance

Resale price maintenance imposed by a cartel or a similar organisation is treated as a cartel (Art 3 CA) and can therefore fall under both the provisions of the Cartels Act and the Price Supervision Act.

3.8 Other (vertical) price restrictions

Discriminatory pricing is expressly mentioned in Art 6, para 2(a) CA as a measure which – if exercised by a cartel or by a similar organisation – can substantially restrain third parties from entering or exercising competition. Again, it is important to take into account that there may be sound business reasons for applying different prices to different buyers so that price discrimination can very well be justified under Art 7 CA.

3.9 Tie-in sales

Tie-in sales are expressly mentioned in Art 6, para 3 CA as 'measures which uniformly and substantially restrain third parties from entering or exercising competition'. In order to fall under Art 6 CA, tie-in sales therefore need not discriminate against third parties. Again, however, tie-in sales can be justified for legitimate reasons in the sense of Art 7 CA.

B Horizontal Restrictions

3.10 Horizontal restrictions in general

Most horizontal restrictions of competition will qualify as cartels or similar organisations in accordance with Art 2 or 4 CA. As such, they can very well be permissible. Again, in applying the Cartels Act, it will therefore be necessary to determine if these cartels take measures which exclude or substantially restrain third parties from competing or if these cartels or similar organisations cause economically or socially harmful effects (Arts 6 and 7, respectively Art 29 CA).

3.11   Information exchange

The exchange of information as such is not restricted under Swiss law (subject to certain exceptions demanded by banking secrecy and similar legislation). However, the exchange of information can lead to 'unenforceable understandings' in the sense of Art 2 CA which are apt to influence the market for specific goods or services and therefore be treated as a cartel in accordance with Art 2 CA (see section 1.2.1 above).

3.12   Joint buying and selling

Agreements between competitors to pool their purchasing or selling activities can be cartels if they are apt to influence the market for specific goods. Such cartels can, of course, be economically or socially harmful in the sense of Art 29 CA and may restrain competitors in the sense of Art 6 CA.

3.13   Fixing prices and conditions of sale

Agreements regarding the fixing of prices and conditions of sale will constitute a cartel if they are apt to influence the market for specific goods or services. A large number of Swiss cartels provide for such measures. If these measures exclude or substantially restrain third parties from entering or exercising competition (Art 6 CA), such measures are inadmissible subject to justification under Art 7 CA.

3.14   Market sharing

Agreements providing for market sharing are also classic examples of cartels in accordance with Art 2 CA. Clearly, such agreements can be economically and socially harmful in the sense of Art 29 CA and will therefore only be permissible if the balance method shows a preponderance of beneficial effects (such as ensuring the supply of all regions of the country with important goods or services).

3.15   Joint ventures and other forms of co-operation

Again, a joint venture or, for that matter, virtually any other form of co-operation between entities on the same level can constitute a cartel. As such, it is not per se inadmissible, if it does not exclude or substantially restrain third parties from competing or result in economically or socially harmful effects.

4   CONCENTRATIONS, MERGERS AND ACQUISITIONS

4.1   Background

As mentioned above (see section 1.4.4 above) the Cartels Act does not provide for preventative merger control. Subject to the rules of the Association of Swiss Stock Exchanges which will be replaced as of 1 January 1996 by the new Federal Act on Stock Exchanges (which are mainly intended to protect the interests of minority shareholders against unfair treatment by the offeror in a take over) no notification procedures whatsoever apply to mergers and acquisitions in Switzerland. The introduction of notification and authorisation procedures is, however, a central issue of the current efforts to revise Swiss anti-trust law and it is to be expected that Switzerland will adopt procedures which are comparable to the procedures within the European Union (see section 5 below).

4.2 Repressive merger control

4.2.1 Repressive merger control is currently provided for in Art 30 of the Cartels Act. According to this provision, the Cartel Commission may order an investigation in accordance with Art 29 CA if a 'concentration' reinforces or creates a position which decisively influences the market and if there are indications of economically or socially harmful effects.

4.2.2 According to Art 30, para 2 CA a 'concentration' is defined as any affiliation, particularly a merger, a consolidation in a holding company or the acquisition of participations resulting in a dominating influence.

4.2.3 In order for the Cartel Commission to initiate an investigation, two requirements must be met:

(a) a position which substantially influences the market must be created or reinforced. Substantial influence in the sense of Art 4 CA (see section 1.2.3 above) is therefore required;
(b) there must be indications for economically or socially harmful effects.

The requirements for an immediate investigation of a merger by the Cartel Commission are therefore stricter than the requirements for an investigation into an established cartel under Art 29 CA. Since the Cartel Commission must evaluate future developments, the question, if indications for economically or socially harmful effects exist, will be hypothetical at this stage. However, if a position is created which substantially influences the market, the Cartel Commission can always, at a later date, initiate an investigation in accordance with Art 29 CA and examine the actual economically or socially harmful effects resulting from the concentration process. The same applies if an organisation similar to a cartel is involved in a concentration process and the result is a reinforcement of a position which already substantially influences the market. For these reasons, investigations in accordance with Art 30 CA have been very rare in the past.

4.2.4 If the Cartel Commission does initiate an investigation, this investigation must be conducted in accordance with the rules of Art 29, paras 2 and 3 CA (see section 1.4 above).

5 REVISION OF THE CARTELS ACT

5.1 Revision proceedings

5.1.1 The act of legislation is a long and complicated process in Switzerland. The preliminary draft for a revised Cartels Act submitted by the Commission for the Revision of the Cartels Act (see section 1.1.4 above) was presented in September

1993. It was then sent to all interested parties (including the executive bodies of all cantons, industrial and commercial associations, consumer organisations etc) who were invited to submit their comments.

5.1.2 In a second stage, the Federal Council considered the comments made by the interested parties and then submitted a definite draft ('draft') to parliament. This definite draft will be debated by a commission consisting of members of the major factions represented in parliament. This commission will submit its findings and its proposals to both chambers of parliament. Both chambers of parliament will then separately debate the proposed revision and subsequently attempt to resolve any differences remaining between the two chambers. In most cases, a draft will, by this stage, have been substantially altered (and watered down). After the new law is approved by parliament, 50,000 Swiss citizens may still by way of a referendum attempt to defeat the new legislative act.

5.1.3 Obviously, this procedure makes it very difficult to predict how the revised Cartels Act will look when it is finally put into effect. The following main points of the current draft may therefore be substantially amended or even deleted in the final version.

5.2　Major changes proposed by the draft for a new Cartels Act

5.2.1 According to Art 1 of the draft, the purpose of the Cartels Act is to prevent socially and economically harmful effects of cartels and other restraints on competition in order to encourage effective competition. The draft contains a clearer and less complicated definition of cartels and other restrictions of competition than the current Cartels Act (Art 4 of the draft).

5.2.2 The material Private and Public Anti-trust Law Provisions of the draft are substantially the same as the corresponding provisions of the current Cartels Act as applied by the Federal Supreme Court. These provisions have, however, been unified and the draft proposes much clearer tests to determine the social and economical harmfulness of a cartel. The major effects of the new law in this area should therefore be that it will be less complicated to apply the rules which already exist under current legislation (also, consumer organisations would be given the right to file complaints).

5.2.3 Article 5 of the draft states that cartels and vertical agreements are harmful if they cannot be justified by reasons of economical efficiency. Reasons of economical efficiency are defined in Art 5, para 2 of the draft.

Article 5, para 3 of the draft defines cartels which are presumed to prevent competition (and can not therefore be justified):

(a) cartels which directly or indirectly fix prices;
(b) cartels which restrict the supply of products;
(c) market-sharing cartels.

Article 7 of the draft prohibits the abuse of market power and contains an extensive list of measures which can constitute an abuse of market power.

Finally, Article 8 of the draft can be used to justify cartels and measures taken by undertakings with market power if they are indispensable in view of the interests of the public at large.

5.2.4 The draft contains more efficient procedural rules than the current Cartels Act. A newly created 'Competition-Council' would be in charge of conducting investigations. The powers of the Competition-Council would be significantly greater than the powers of the current Cartel Commission and would allow for more efficient and less time-consuming investigations. If the Secretary of the Competition-Council determines that a restriction of competition is inadmissible, he attempts to reach an amicable solution with the parties concerned, which solution is subject to the approval of the Competition Council. If no such solution can be found, the Competition-Council would be authorised to issue binding orders (and not recommendations like the current Cartel Commission). Such orders would be subject to an appeal to the Appeal-Commission and finally to the Federal Supreme Court, whose decision would be final.

5.2.5 Finally, the draft provides for preventive merger control. Notification and approval of concentrations would be required if the aggregate turnover of the parties concerned exceeds SFrs 2,000,000,000 and if the aggregate turnover in Switzerland equals at least SFrs 500,000,000. Article 10 of the draft provides for approval if the merger does not create or strengthen a dominant position which is apt significantly to impair effective competition or, alternatively, if such a dominant position is created which at the same time significantly improves effective competition in another area of the market. Concentrations must be notified to the Secretary of the Competition-Council before they are consummated. The Secretary for the Competition-Council must then, within 30 days, determine if approval can be given in a summary procedure. If there are indications that the concentration is inadmissible, the Competition-Council must conduct a detailed investigation, which investigation must be concluded (by a decision of the Competition Council) within four months.

CHAPTER XIX

United Kingdom

Julian Maitland-Walker

Charles Russell Solicitors
8–10 New Fetter Lane
London EC4A 1RS
England

Tel ++44 171 203 5000
Fax ++44 171 203 0200

United Kingdom

1 THE SUBSTANTIVE UK COMPETITION LAW

1.1 Background

1.1.1 The United Kingdom has yet to have a codified system of competition law although in recent years various proposals for introducing a new competition law adopting an approach similar to Articles 85 and 86 of the EEC Treaty have been canvassed by the Department of Trade and Industry. So far, however, no date for legislation has been set.[1]

1.1.2 In the meantime, UK competition law is currently founded on four separate statutes:

(a)   the Restrictive Trade Practices Act 1976 ('RTPA');
(b)   the Resale Prices Act 1976 ('RPA');
(c)   the Competition Act 1980 ('CA');
(d)   the Fair Trading Act 1973 ('FTA').

1.1.3 As an adjunct to these statutory provisions, there exist the residual common law rules established through jurisprudence under contract, in the form of the restraint of trade doctrine[2] and in tort, for such matters as breach of confidence, passing off, injurious falsehood or inducement to breach of contract.

1.2 The Restrictive Trade Practices Act 1976 ('RTPA')

1.2.1 The RTPA requires that certain types of agreement must be registered with the Office of Fair Trading (OFT), the UK Competition Authority,[3] which is required to maintain a register of agreements which are subject to registration which must be available for public inspection.[4] Failure to register a registerable agreement before implementation will render the agreement void or at least those

---

1 In March 1988, the UK government published a Green Paper on 'Review of Restrictive Trade Practices Policy' (Cm 331) and in 1989 a White Paper 'Opening Markets: New Policy on Restrictive Trade Practices' (Cm 727). In November 1992 a Green Paper on 'Abuse of Market Power' (Cm 2100) was published and a White Paper possibly co-ordinating new legislation on both restrictive trade practices and abuse of market power is awaited.

2 This doctrine is based on the principle that the court will not enforce a contract which is an unreasonable restraint of trade on the basis that to do so would be contrary to public policy. This is principally applied to non-compete restrictions.

3 See section 2.1.1 below.

4 There is a confidential section of the register for those agreements containing business secrets, know-how etc but the OFT has to be satisfied that they are genuinely confidential before permitting admission to the confidential section.

restrictions which are within the RTPA. It may also give rise to third party claims in damages for breach of statutory duty.

1.2.2 Agreements relating to goods or services or information agreements relating to goods or services will be registerable where they contain 'relevant restrictions'.[5]

1.2.3 Section 6(1) RTPA provides as follows:

'This Act applies to agreements (whenever made) between two or more persons carrying on business within the United Kingdom in the production or supply of goods, or in the application to goods of any process of manufacture, whether with or without other parties, being agreements under which restrictions are accepted by two or more parties in respect of any of the following matters–

(a) the prices to be charged, quoted or paid for goods supplied, offered or acquired, or for the application of any process of manufacture of goods;

(b) the prices to be recommended or suggested or the prices to be charged or quoted in respect of the resale of goods supplied;

(c) the terms or conditions on or subject to which goods are to be supplied or acquired or any such process is to be applied to goods;

(d) the quantities or descriptions of goods to be produced, supplied or acquired;

(e) the processes of manufacture to be applied to any goods, or the quantities or descriptions of goods to which any such process is to be applied; or

(f) the persons or classes of persons to, for or from whom, or the areas or places in or from which, goods are to be supplied or acquired, or any such process applied'.

1.2.4 Agreements

All agreements, arrangements or understandings whether or not legally enforceable will be covered.[6] Section 8 (goods) and section 16 (services) indicate that the activities of trade associations may constitute agreements between the association and its members and the members amongst themselves under the RTPA.

1.2.5 Two or more persons

Section 43(2) RTPA provides that for these purposes 'interconnected bodies corporate or individuals in partnership with each other', shall be treated as one person.

1.2.6 Carrying on business in the UK

An agreement will only be registerable if at least two parties are carrying on business in the UK irrespective of whether they are the parties who actually accept the relevant restrictions under the agreement and irrespective of the fact that the business carried on may have no connection whatsoever with the relevant restrictions.

5 There are separate sections of the RTPA dealing with each category of agreement: section 6 (goods), section 7 (information agreements as to goods), section 11 (services) and section 12 (information agreements as to services). Each category is treated entirely separately so that an agreement falling partly in one category and partly in another may not be registerable. In the interests of brevity, the text will focus on the provisions relating to goods.

6 Section 43(1) RTPA.

A party to an agreement which has a subsidiary in the UK[7] or is represented by an agent[8] is not carrying on business in the UK. What is required is a fixed place of business within the UK coupled with trading from it.

1.2.7 Relevant restrictions

Those restrictions identified in the list set out in section 6(1) are relevant restrictions in relation to goods and similar restrictions are identified as relevant restrictions in relation to the other categories of agreements relating to services and information agreements. It is important to stress that one or more relevant restriction must be accepted by at least two parties to the agreement for it to be registerable. For example, an agreement which imposes relevant restrictions as to goods on one party and as to services on another party, will not be registerable since the requirements of neither section 6 (goods) nor section 11 (services) are satisfied.[9]

1.2.8 Provisions to be disregarded

Section 9(3) and (4) RTPA provide as follows:

'(3) In determining whether an agreement for the supply of goods or for the application of any process of manufacture to goods is an agreement to which this Act applies by virtue of this Part, no account shall be taken of any term which relates exclusively to the goods supplied, or to which the process is applied, in pursuance of the agreement.

(4) Where any such restrictions as are described in section 6(1) above are accepted or any such information provisions as are described in section 7(1) above are made as between two or more persons by whom, or two or more persons to or for whom, goods are to be supplied, or the process applied, in pursuance of the agreement, sub-section (3) above shall not apply to those restrictions or to those information provisions unless accepted or made in pursuance of a previous agreement –

(a) in respect of which particulars have been registered under this Act; or
(b) which is exempt from registration by virtue of an order under section 29 (agreements important to the national economy) or section 30 (agreements holding down prices) below.'

Accordingly many restrictions which impose vertical restraints, eg as between a supplier and his distributor or licensor and licensee, are not treated as relevant restrictions. On the other hand, section 9(4) shows that where such restrictions are applied as horizontal restrictions, eg as between actual or potential competitors ('persons by whom ... or to whom ... goods are supplied') then they will be treated as relevant restrictions for the purposes of RTPA.

Section 9 also provides for the exclusion of restriction between coal and steel producers on the basis that these are covered by the European Coal and Steel

---

7 *Registrar of Restrictive Trading Agreements v Schweppes Ltd (No 2)* [1971] 2 All ER 1473.
8 RTPA, s 43(4).
9 Agreements in which restrictions are accepted by only one party may nevertheless fall to be examined under the Competition Act 1980 (see section 1.4 below) or the monopoly provisions of the Fair Trading Act 1973 (see section 1.5 below).
10 RTPA, s 9(1) and (2).

Treaty,[10] restrictions involving application of technical standards[11] and restrictions relating to employment and conditions of employment.[12]

1.2.9   Exempt agreements

Schedule 3 RTPA sets out a list of types of agreement which are exempt from registration. In order to be exempted, the agreement must fall entirely within one of the paragraphs. The exemptions include:

Schedule 3(2)   — certain types of exclusive dealing;
Schedule 3(3–5) — certain types of intellectual property licensing;
Schedule 3(6)   — agreements containing restrictions which have no impact on the UK domestic market.

In addition, section 29 empowers the Secretary of State for Trade and Industry to introduce additional exemptions for agreements which are of substantial importance to the economy, promote efficiency or productivity, which contain no unnecessary restrictions and which are in the public interest. These criteria are similar to those contained in Article 85(3) of the EEC Treaty[13] and have been used in a number of cases recently, particularly in relation to agreements involving joint ventures and research and development.

1.2.10   Registration

Particulars of an agreement registerable under the RTPA must be furnished to the Director General of Fair Trading[14] who maintains a public register of such agreements. The RTPA requires that registration must take place *before* implementation of the restriction and within three months of the date of the agreement. For that reason it is normal to incorporate in the agreement a clause suspending the effect of any restrictions within the RTPA until such time as they have been registered.

1.2.11   'Fail safe' furnishing

If the parties are uncertain as to whether an agreement is registerable they may 'furnish' particulars to the Director General while reserving the issue of registration. The OFT has introduced new 'fast track' procedures for processing such applications quickly.

1.2.12   Reference to the Restrictive Trade Practices Court

Section 1(2) of the RTPA requires that the Director General of Fair Trading has an obligation to refer a restrictive agreement to the Restrictive Practices Court (RPC) to invite the RPC to determine whether or not the restrictive agreement operates in the public interest. Before such a reference is made, the OFT will consider the

11 RTPA, s 9(5).
12 RTPA, s 9(6).
13 See Chapter I.
14 RTPA, ss 1 and 24.

issue of *de minimis* under section 21[15] and will also invite the parties to remove the offending restrictions from the agreement. If they are not prepared to do so and assuming section 21 is not applicable, the OFT must refer the agreement to the RPC.

1.2.13 The 'Gateways'

The RPC will review a restriction agreement with the presumption that it operates against the public interest. Section 10[16] sets out those factors which may be used to justify a restrictive agreement, known as 'Gateways' through which particular restrictions may receive judicial approval. These Gateways may be summarised as follows:

(a) that the restriction is necessary to protect the public against injury;
(b) that the removal of the restriction would deny to the public specific and substantial benefits;
(c) that the restriction is necessary to counteract restrictions on competition in the market perpetrated by others;
(d) that the restriction is necessary to enable parties to the agreement to negotiate the supply or purchase of goods from third parties controlling a 'preponderant part' of the market;
(e) that the removal of the restriction would be likely to have a 'serious and persistent adverse effect' on the level of unemployment in an area or industry;
(f) that the removal of the restriction would prejudice UK export earning;
(g) that the restriction is necessary to maintain other restrictions which have already been cleared by RPC;
(h) that the restriction does not materially restrict or discourage competition.

In addition to being satisfied as to the application of one or more of these Gateways, section 10 requires that the RPC must be satisfied that the restriction:

'. . . is not unreasonable having regard to the balance between those circumstances and any detriment to the public . . . resulting . . . from the operation of the restriction . . .'

This is often described as the 'tailpiece' condition.

1.2.14 Powers of the court

If the RPC concludes that the agreement satisfies the requirements of section 10, it will make a declaration that the restrictions are not contrary to the public interest. Such a declaration is open to appeal by either the OFT or the parties with leave. If the RPC finds that the agreement contains restrictions contrary to the public interest, it will make a declaration to that effect. The court also has wide powers to require that individual restrictions or indeed the whole agreement should cease to be implemented, impose injunctions or obtain undertakings from the parties restraining them from making other agreements 'to the like effect'. The RPC has *no* power to impose fines or other penalties on parties implementing an agreement falling within RTPA at lease on its initial order. Subsequently, however, parties

---

15 See section 2.5.3 below.
16 Section 19 contains similar Gateways for agreements relating to services.

may be subject to criminal sanctions involving both fines and imprisonment for beach of the terms of a court order.[17]

1.3   The Resale Prices Act 1976 ('RPA')

1.3.1   The RPA prohibits both collective resale price maintenance and individual *minimum* price maintenance, thus dealing with pricing restrictions both on a horizontal level (ie between competitors) and on a vertical level (ie between suppliers and dealer).

1.3.2   *Collective resale price maintenance*

It is unlawful for any two or more persons[18] 'carrying on business in the United Kingdom' whether as suppliers or dealers in goods[19] to make or carry out an agreement by which they undertake to impose directly or indirectly (eg by way of refusal to supply or the imposition of penalties) resale prices. 'Resale' is defined to include hire purchase and conditional sale agreements.[20] The agreement need not necessarily be legally enforceable and a 'recommendation' as to resale prices between suppliers or between dealers will be unlawful as if it were an agreement on retail prices.[1]

1.3.3   *Individual minimum resale price maintenance*

The imposition of minimum resale prices by a supplier on a dealer whether directly or indirectly is unlawful and any such contractual provisions are void and unenforceable. The prohibition is limited to the imposition of *minimum* resale prices so that suppliers remain free to notify to dealers prices 'recommended as appropriate for the resale of goods supplied . . .'.[2] Similarly, the RPA does not prevent a supplier from imposing *maximum* resale prices although this might constitute an infringement of other provisions of English competition law[3] and also possibly EC competition law.[4] Note also that the prohibition relates only to sales to a dealer so that the imposition of price restrictions on an agent will not be prohibited.

1.3.4   *Exemptions*

Section 14 ff of RPA allows for applications to the Restrictive Trade Practices Court for individual exemption in respect of individual minimum resale price maintenance. There is no exemption procedure for collective resale price agreements. Section 14 sets out a series of 'Gateways' similar in form to those of the RTPA which may be used in justifying exemption. In practice, however, exemp-

---

17 See section 2.4 below.
18 Includes incorporated persons and trade associations.
19 The RPA does not apply to services although RPA in relation to services may be caught under the monopoly provisions of the Fair Trading Act 1973 or the Competition Act 1980 (see sections 1.4 and 1.5 below).
20 RPA, s 7.
 1 RPA, s 3.
 2 RTPA, s 9(2).
 3 Competition Act 1980 and the Fair Trading Act 1973. See sections 1.4 and 1.5 below.
 4 See Chapter I.

tions are rare with exemptions having been given only in relation to books[5] and medicines.[6]

1.4 Competition Act 1980 ('CA')

1.4.1 The CA gives the Director General of Fair Trading power to investigate any undertaking which he considers may be engaging in an anti-competitive practice. Having established the existence of an anti-competitive practice, the Director General may seek undertakings from the perpetrator to terminate the anti-competitive conduct. If he is unsuccessful in resolving the problem in that way the Director General has power under the CA to refer the matter to the Monopolies and Mergers Commission ('MMC') to consider whether the conduct complained of operates against the public interest. The MMC is required to report to the Secretary of State for Trade and Industry with its findings and recommendations and the Secretary of State has power to order the undertaking concerned to cease its anti-competitive conduct or take such other action he considers expedient to remedy the anti-competitive conduct.

1.4.2 Section 2(1) of the CA provides that a person engages in an anti-competitive practice if:

'... in the course of a business that person pursues a course of conduct which of itself or when taken together with a course of conduct pursued by persons associated with him has or is intended to have or is likely to have the effect of restricting, distorting or preventing competition in connection with the production, supply or acquisition of goods in the United Kingdom or any part of it or the supply or securing of services in the United Kingdom or any part of it.'

1.4.3 Unlike the RTPA, the CA is not directed only to agreements or concerted practices but can apply to unilateral conduct which whether independently or when taken with conduct of associated enterprises leads to the restriction, distortion or prevention of competition. The definition of anti-competitive practices is widely drawn and adopts the 'effects' orientated approach of Article 85 of the EEC Treaty. Although not expressed, full investigation under CA by the OFT or the MMC invariably involves companies or associations with substantial market power albeit in relatively localised markets.

1.4.4 Whilst the application of 'effects' test as applied in EC Competition law is adopted, the similarity of the procedure ends there. There are no sanctions in the form of fines or other measures for offending conduct fall within section2(1) CA save for the possibility of an OFT and MMC investigation with perhaps action by the Secretary of State in appropriate circumstances.

1.4.5 The approach adopted in enforcing CA characterises the informal striving for consensus which is present in most areas of UK competition law. Initially the OFT will seek to agree a solution to any identified competition law difficulty through negotiations. If this proves unsuccessful a formal investigation may ensue leading to a 'competition' reference to the MMC.[7] If the MMC considers that the public interest is or may be harmed, the Secretary of State may request the Director

---

5 *Re Net Book Agreement, 1957* [1962] 3 All ER 751.
6 *Re Medicaments Reference (No 2)* [1971] 1 All ER 12.
7 CA, s 5(1).

General to seek undertakings from the firm concerned and only as a last resort will the Secretary of State exercise his power to make orders prohibiting the continuance of anti-competitive conduct.[8] The vast majority of investigations conducted by the Director General either on his own motion or in response to complaints are settled informally either by a finding that no anti-competitive practice has been established or appropriate undertakings agreed.[8a] Between 1980 and 1989 the Director General published only 24 reports of which only 16 resulted in a reference to the MMC. Of these, the MMC submitted a report on six, out of which anti-competitive conduct against the public interest was established in only three.

1.4.6   Exclusions

The Secretary of State has power to exclude certain courses of conduct from the provisions of CA and has done so under the Anti-Competitive Practices (Exclusions) Order 1980. This Order excludes contractual restrictions relating to exports from the UK, the provision of certain transport services and certain specified financial arrangements. The Order also contains an important *de minimis* exemption. The CA will not apply to businesses with an annual turnover of less than £5 million and a market share of less than 25% of any relevant market. It is important to note, however, that the relevant market may be highly localised to apply to a single region or perhaps a single city in which one firm may predominate although it may have no market at all outside its local operations.

1.5   Fair Trading Act 1973 ('FTA')

1.5.1   The FTA is a consolidating statute which coordinates and consolidates much of the earlier legislation on monopolies and mergers. Part I (sections 1–12) sets out (inter alia) the functions and responsibilities of the Director General of Fair Trading and the MMC. Part IV (sections 44–56) deals with monopoly references and Part V (sections 57–77) deals with mergers.[9]

1.5.2   Monopoly references

The FTA empowers the Secretary of State and the Director General to refer 'monopoly situations' to the MMC for investigation. As an alternative to a reference, the Director General may accept undertakings if he thinks they would be sufficient to deal with the adverse effects of the monopoly position.[9a]

1.5.3   'Monopoly situation'

A monopoly situation is not dependent upon the existence of market dominance. Section 6(1)(a)[10] provides that a monopoly situation will exist where at least 25%

---

8   CA, s 10.
8a   Formal undertakings may now be sought under s 12 of the Deregulation and Contracting Out Act 1994.
9   See section 4 below.
9a   Section 7(1) of the Deregulation and Contracting Out Act 1994.
10   Sections 7 and 8 contain virtually identical provisions to section 6 in relation to services and exports respectively.

of goods of any description are supplied in the UK by the same person, firm or group of firms.

1.5.4 *'Complex monopoly situation'*

Section 6(1)(c) further provides that a complex monopoly situation will exist where at least 25% of goods of any description are supplied in the UK by:

> 'any two or more persons (not being a group of interconnected bodies corporate) who whether voluntarily or not, and whether by agreement or not, so conduct their respective affairs . . . to prevent, restrict or distort competition . . .'

Accordingly, the FTA covers not only unilateral conduct by an enterprise with significant market power but also concerted market 'behaviour' by one or more independent enterprises with collective market power.

1.5.5 The geographical boundaries of the relevant market for the determination of market share is not necessarily the national market. It is possible for a very localised market to be identified in appropriate areas, eg the area of Greater London,[11] Central Scotland[12] and Northern Ireland.[13]

1.5.6 Terms of reference

The terms of reference submitted to the MMC are largely a matter of the discretion of the Secretary of State or the Director General, whichever is the requesting authority. The MMC's brief can be limited in scope but most frequently it will be required to examine all the evidence and determine whether or not any facts which it establishes operate against the public interest.

1.5.7 *'Public interest'*

Section 84 of the FTA defines the public interest criteria to be applied as follows:

> '(1) In determining for any purposes to which this section applies whether any particular matter operates, or may be expected to operate, against the public interest, the Commission shall take into account all matters which appear to them in the particular circumstances to be relevant and, among other things, shall have regard to the desirability –
>
> > (a) of maintaining and promoting effective competition between persons supplying goods and services in the United Kingdom;
> > (b) of promoting the interests of consumers, purchasers and other users of goods and services in the United Kingdom in respect of the prices charged for them and in respect of their quality and the variety of goods and services supplied;
> > (c) of promoting, through competition, the reduction of costs and the development and use of new techniques and new products, and of facilitating the entry of new competitors into existing markets;
> > (d) of maintaining and promoting the balanced distribution of industry and employment in the United Kingdom; and

---

11 *Buildings in the GLC area*, HCP (1954/55) 264.
12 *Sand and Gravel in Central Scotland*, HCP (1955/56) 222.
13 *Holiday Caravan Sites in Northern Ireland* (Cmnd 8966) 1983.

(e) of maintaining and promoting competitive activity in markets outside the
United Kingdom on the part of producers of goods, and of suppliers of goods
and services, in the United Kingdom.'

1.5.8   The MMC Report

When completed the Report is sent to the Secretary of State and Director General.
It must also be presented to Parliament. If the MMC finds that there is no harm to
the public interest, that is an end of the matter and no formal action can be taken.
If, on the other hand, the MMC finds that the facts established indicate harm to the
public interest, the MMC may recommend remedial action. What action (if any) is
taken is a matter for the absolute discretion of the Secretary of State. The Secretary
of State has wide power to order termination of agreements, alteration of price
structures, the prohibition of takeovers etc.

2   ENFORCEMENT

2.1   Enforcement authorities

2.1.1   Office of Fair Trading (OFT)

The OFT is the primary administrative authority for competition matters in the
UK. It is presided over by the Director General of Fair Trading with a staff of
under 400 comprising both lawyers and economists. The OFT has many roles
ranging from receiving and investigating agreements registered with it under the
RTPA and maintaining the RTPA register, to the receipt and investigation of complaints under CA and FTA to general information gathering in relation to
monopolies and mergers. The OFT produces an Annual Report on Competition
containing summary reports on its activities over the previous year and discussing
policy issues for the future.

2.1.2   Monopolies & Mergers Commission (MMC)

The MMC does not initiate investigations but has an advisory function investigating cases referred to it either by the OFT or the Secretary of State. The MMC is
considerably smaller than the OFT with 32 Commission members supported by
about 110 officials.

2.1.3   Secretary of State

The Secretary of State for Trade and Industry is the cabinet minister with
responsibility for competition matters and has political responsibility for the
OFT and MMC. As has been seen, he has wide power to refer monopoly and
merger cases to the MMC and has ultimate power to order remedial measures to
curtail anti-competitive practices which are perceived to operate against the
public interest.

2.1.4 Restrictive Practices Court

Provides the judicial forum for the determination of cases under the RTPA and RPA.

2.1.5 High Court and county court

The ordinary courts of the land have power within their jurisdictional limit to apply the common law competition measures such as the restraint of trade doctrine, the economic torts, passing off etc. The national courts also have power to rule on voidness under the RTPA and of action under the EC rules of competition.[14]

2.2 Jurisdictional rules

2.2.1 Each of the competition regulatory laws described above has a specific line of jurisdictional authority so that the OFT has exclusive jurisdiction to receive RTPA registration and to decide upon whether to refer to the RTP. Similarly the OFT has power to investigate and refer cases to the MMC under the CA and the monopoly provisions of FTA, such power running concurrently with the power of the Secretary of State in such cases. The Secretary of State has exclusive power to order a reference to the MMC in cases of newspaper mergers and general mergers, although in the latter case, such references are made on the advice of the Merger Panel of the OFT.

2.2.2 The ordinary civil courts have jurisdiction in relation to the common law action on restraint of trade and in respect of the economic torts. The National Courts also have power to determine the consequences of invalidity arising out of a failure to register under the RTPA and in respect of European competition law. However, the ordinary civil courts have no jurisdiction to assess the benefits of a restrictive agreement or a merger or to assess public interest issues which are matters reserved to the OFT, MMC and RPC as appropriate.

2.3 OFT investigation

2.3.1 RTPA investigations

As indicated above, particulars of registerable agreements must be furnished to the OFT which maintains a public register of such agreements. If the parties have doubts as to the registerability of an agreement they may make a fail safe furnishing seeking OFT guidance.[15] The OFT has a responsibility to consider the agreement and to decide whether a reference to the RPC should be made or whether section 21(2) should be applied, effectively discharging the OFT obligation to refer. In this context, the OFT has a wide general power to seek information of any person or association[16] and may also require that evidence under oath be given before the RPC.[17] Failure to comply with a request for information is a criminal offence and can lead to the imposition of a fine. Making a false or reckless

14 See Chapter I.
15 See section 1.2.11 above.
16 RTPA, s 36.
17 RTPA, s 37.

statement, supplying a false document or suppressing or destroying documents can also lead to fines and even imprisonment.[18]

2.3.2   CA investigations

Section 3 CA gives the Director General authority to investigate alleged anti-competitive conduct which comes to his attention. Before doing so he is required to notify the Secretary of State and the person or persons who are to be investigated. The Director General may require any person to produce documents or provide such other information as may be required for the purposes of an investigation but no person can be compelled to comply with any requirement that he could not be compelled to comply with in ordinary civil proceedings and there are similar provisions in relation to fines and imprisonment for failure to cooperate, supplying false information or suppressing documents as with FTA.

2.3.3   Monopoly and merger references

Similar powers of investigation and similar sanctions for non-compliance are conferred on the MMC in relation to references under the FTA whether in relation to monopolies or mergers. The Director General also has power to seek information prior to such references where appropriate.

2.4   Fines and other sanctions

2.4.1   In contrast to the EC Rules of Competition, there are no fines imposed for a breach of UK competition law.[19] Fines and sentences of imprisonment may be imposed for contempt, where a breach of an Order of the Secretary of State has occurred or there has been a breach of an undertaking or an injunction.

2.4.2   Failure to register a registerable agreement under the RTPA renders the agreement void and unenforceable.

2.4.3   Failure to register a registerable agreement and the operation of collective resale price maintenance under the RPA does give rise to third parties suffering loss by reason of such agreements to seek damages for breach of statutory duty.

2.5   Exemptions

2.5.1   There is no formal procedure for exemption of restrictive agreements under UK national law. However, parties to an agreement which may be registerable under the RTPA may notify it to the Director General on the basis of a 'fail safe furnishing'.

2.5.2   In addition, in cases of registerable agreements, the Director General has a discretion under section 21(1) RTPA not to take proceedings before the RPC:

---

18 RTPA, s 38.
19 Note that the current proposals for modification to UK national competition laws envisage the introduction of civil fines for breach.

'(a) in respect of an agreement if and for so long as he thinks it appropriate so to do having regard to the operation of any directly applicable Community provision and to the purpose and effect of any authorisation or exemption granted in relation to such a provision;

(b) where an agreement –

(i) of which particulars are entered or filed in the register pursuant to this Act has been determined (whether by effluxion of time or otherwise); or

(ii) has been so determined in respect of all restrictions accepted or information provisions made under that agreement.'

2.5.3 Under section 21(2) RTPA the Secretary of State may also direct the Director General not to take proceedings before the RPC in respect of an agreement where, following representations of the Director General, he concludes that:

'... the restriction accepted or information provisions made under an agreement ... are not of such significance as to call for investigation by the Court.'

2.5.4 Exemption in respect of individual minimum resale price maintenance for goods may also be obtained on application to the RPC under section 14 RPA.[20]

2.6 Third party rights

2.6.1 As has been seen above, the RTPA and RPA impose statutory obligations. In relation to the RTPA there is an obligation to register registerable agreements; in the case of the RPA there is a prohibition on entering into collective or individual minimum resale price maintenance. A breach of such statutory duty gives rise to a remedy in damages by third parties suffering loss before the English courts.

2.6.2 On the other hand, the CA and the monopoly provisions of the FTA do not give rise to any third party remedies since the legislation is designed to trigger an opportunity for the investigation of anti-competitive practices by the OFT or the MMC rather than impose any immediate prohibition. The possibility of any remedy for a third party would therefore only arise in the event of breach of any order of the Secretary of State issued in connection with such investigation.

3 CHECKLIST OF POTENTIAL INFRINGEMENTS

3.1 Agency

3.1.1 An agency agreement containing relevant restrictions will fall within RTPA unless the agent is not a distinct commercial enterprise. In order for the RTPA to apply there must be at least two parties who either produce, supply or process goods. A commercial agent who operates as no more than a salesman for his supplier albeit in a self-employed capacity, will not constitute a separate party for these purposes. A similar approach has been adopted in relation to investigation under CA in '*Yellow Pages*'.[1] The OFT found that sales agents for advertising in BT's Yellow Pages directory were no more than an extension of BT's 'own resources' and did not buy or sell anything on their own behalf so that competition

---

20 See section 1.3.4 above.

1 10 October 1992.

between them would be a duplication of sales effort within the BT Yellow Pages marketing system.

3.1.2　The Commercial Agents (Council Directive) Regulations 1993 adopt the special rules contained in the Commercial Agency Directive 86/653[2] as to the agent's minimum rights to notice on termination and to compensation. These Regulations also limit a post termination restraint of trade ban to two years limited to the agent's area of activity. Such a restriction must also be in writing to be enforceable.

3.2　Distribution

3.2.1　The exclusive dealing exemption under Schedule 3(2)[3] RTPA provides that the following restrictions are not treated as relevant restrictions for the purpose of the Act:

(a)　restriction on supplier supplying other dealers in territory;
(b)　restriction on dealer purchasing competing products or services from third parties.[4]

In addition, section 9(3) RTPA[5] permits the disregard of any restriction which relates 'exclusively to the goods supplied'. Accordingly, restrictions typically found in distribution agreements such as a restriction on sales out of territory, obligation to maintain stock, minimum purchase etc will not be caught by RTPA.

3.2.2　Distribution agreements exempted by RTPA may nevertheless be considered under CA but a similar approach towards restriction is likely unless the market shares of the parties or the circumstances of the market are such that restrictions ordinarily permissible in distribution might operate against the public interest.[6]

3.3　Selective distribution

The maintenance of limits on the number of dealers to be appointed to a distributor network is not a matter for consideration under the RTPA beyond the normal distribution issues considered in section 3.2 above. Selective distribution has however, been considered in the context of an investigation under the CA. In 'Raleigh'[7] both the OFT and MMC concluded that the selective distribution system operated was too restrictive. Although qualitative criteria for admission to the network (eg suitable premises, qualified staff, pre- and post-sales service, stocking requirements etc) were admissible, it was felt that Raleigh should be required to justify any refusal to supply a dealer and should supply discount stores who met its qualitative criteria. This is not to suggest, however, that the imposition of qualitative restrictions would never be accepted. It seems that the OFT at least is prepared to accept qualitative restriction on appointment to the network where such restric-

2　31/12/86 OJ L382/17.
3　Schedule 3(10) for services.
4　Note this does not include a restriction on the dealer manufacturing competing products. Such a restriction would therefore fall within RTPA.
5　RTPA, s 18 (services).
6　See *British Airports Authority* (exclusive car services to Gatwick Airport) 22 February 1984.
7　*Raleigh* 27 February 1981 (OFT Report); (1981–82) HC 67 (MMC Report).
8　*Sandersons* 27 August 1981.

tions are considered necessary to protect the brand name and ensure that outlets are economically viable so long as inter brand competition remains healthy.[8]

3.4 Exclusive purchasing

Most restrictions commonly found in exclusive purchasing agreements will be exempted from the RTPA either through Schedule 3(2) or section 9 RTPA.[9] Under the CA, exclusive purchasing may give rise to difficulties where it can be shown to lead to market foreclosure or impede price competition.[10]

3.5 Franchising

A franchise agreement will often contain a variety of potentially 'relevant' RTPA restrictions or the franchisee relating to, eg the method of selling the contract goods or services, the protection of the franchisor's know-how etc. If relevant restrictions are accepted by more than one party then the franchise agreement may be registerable. On the other hand, many such restrictions, at least on the franchisee, are likely to be exempted by the dealing exemption under Schedule 3(2) or the licensing exemption under Schedule 3(4).[11] Furthermore, the section 9 or 18 criteria may also be applicable. Even if exempted under RTPA, a franchise agreement may still fall within the CA in cases involving a significant market share. In such cases, the criteria applied will be similar to those previously expressed in relation to exclusive dealing generally.

3.6 Intellectual property licensing

3.6.1 The grant of an industrial property licence including a patent, copyright or trade mark does not of itself constitute the supply of goods or services within the RTPA[12] and does not in any event give rise to a restriction since it does not impose upon the licensee a restriction on anything he was permitted to do before. However, licensing agreements in respect of any form of intellectual property, eg patents, trade marks or copyright, may be caught by the RTPA if the licence contains ancillary 'relevant' restrictions accepted by two parties. Schedule 3 contains specific exemptions for various forms of intellectual property licensing including trade mark licenses (Schedule 3(4) and Schedule 4(4), patents (Schedule 3(5A)) and registered design and copyright (Schedule 3(5A). In addition, there are the exemptions in respect of restrictions relating to the goods or services provided under section 9 and 18 RTPA. In relation to the CA there are also circumstances in which restrictions in a licence might be found to operate against the public interest but in general terms the OFT and the MMC have tended to look at licensing in a favourable light in view of the fact that it implies technology transfer, which is fundamentally pro-competitive.

---

9 See section 3.2 above.
10 See *Car Parts* HC 318 (February 1982).
11 Note that an agreement will only benefit from a Schedule 3 exemption if it falls wholly within one of the paragraphs set out therein. It is not possible to claim exemption by satisfying conditions in more than one of such categories.
12 *Ravenseft Properties Ltd v Director General of Fair Trading* [1977] 1 All ER 47.

3.6.2 It should be noted that in relation patents, English law provides specific anti-competitive provisions. Section 44 of the Patent Act 1977 prohibits certain forms of tying restrictions in patent licences and section 48 of the Patent Act 1977 gives the Comptroller General of Patents a right to grant compulsory patent licences in specific circumstance where he considers that the licensor is using patent protection for anti-competitive purposes.

3.7 Refusals to supply

3.7.1 A refusal to supply will not directly raise issues under the Restrictive Trade Practices Act, which is concerned with the existence of relevant restrictions in agreements rather than unilateral market behaviour. On the other hand, the refusal may be the market manifestation of an agreement between undertakings not to supply third parties and such an agreement could, of course, involve relevant restrictions which if imposed on two or more parties might give rise to RTPA issues.

3.7.2 More usually, a refusal to supply might trigger an investigation under the CA or the monopoly provisions of the FTA where significant market power can be identified. In such cases, the Secretary of State or the OFT may well be persuaded to refer a refusal to supply to the MMC if they consider that the refusal operates against the public interest.[13]

3.8 Price restrictions

3.8.1 Individual or collective resale price maintenance will constitute a direct infringement of the RPA.[14] This will not, however, prevent a supplier publishing recommended retail prices nor will it preclude the imposition of maximum prices under the RPA, although there is a continuing doubt as to whether the imposition of maximum prices might, in appropriate circumstances, constitute an infringement of the CA of the monopoly provisions of the FTA.

3.8.2 Price discounting which cannot be justified on objective grounds, eg by reference to volume, continuity of supplies or production efficiencies, may be called into question under the CA or the monopoly provisions of the FTA.

3.9 Tie in sales

The imposition, in a contract for the supply of goods or services, of an obligation to buy other goods and services may constitute a relevant restriction under the RTPA and give rise to the obligation to register if the criteria for the application of the RTPA are applicable. Even if the RTPA is not applicable in a particular case, tie in sales may well give rise to a reference to the MMC under the CA or MMC.

13 See *Raleigh*, note 7 above.
14 See section 1.3 above.

3.10 Information exchange

3.10.1 As indicated above, the RTPA contains specific provisions with regard to information agreements as to both goods and services and agreements providing for the exchange of information in relation to the production of supply of goods or services are likely to be registerable under the RTPA where such agreements are bi-lateral or multi-lateral or where they are operated through a trade association.

3.10.2 Even information agreements operating in one direction only or involving exchange of information in circumstances in which the RTPA would not be applicable (eg where only one party is carrying on business in the UK) might be caught under the CA or the monopoly provisions of the FTA and be the subject of an MMC reference in appropriate cases.

3.11 Joint buying or selling

A simple agreement under which the parties agree on joint buying or joint selling would not, of itself, cause difficulties under UK competition law. However, such agreements will usually be associated with a restriction on the parties buying or selling otherwise than through the joint agency and restricting the right to negotiate individually. Such supplementary restrictions would bring such an agreement within the terms of the RTPA. In such cases, however, the OFT is unlikely to find that the agreement operates against the public interest unless the market shares of the participating enterprises are such that the operation of the agreement is likely to interfere with the structure of competition in the market, whether on the supply or the demand side.

3.12 Market sharing

Agreements between actual or potential competitors designed to share markets geographically or by reference to customers or to fix prices will invariably fall within the RTPA and are likely to be referred to the RPC. It is most unlikely that such agreements would be found to operate in the public interest and the RPC have condemned such agreements and imposed undertakings on parties to such agreements on several occasions.[15]

3.13 Joint ventures

Joint ventures frequently involve the acceptance of relevant restrictions by participants which are likely to result in the need for registration under the RTPA. Even if the RTPA is not applicable, joint ventures may qualify for examination under the CA or the monopoly provisions of the FTA. The UK Competition Authorities generally take a fairly benign view of joint ventures, particularly those involving joint research and development and technology exchange, so long as they can be satisfied that the maintenance of competition in the long term is not prejudiced.

---

15 See for example *Re Permanent Magnet Association's Agreement* (1962) LR 3 RP 119.

4   MERGER CONTROL

4.1   Introduction

The FTA sets out rules governing the control of mergers other than major multinational mergers having a 'Community dimension' which are dealt with by the Merger Task Force of the European Commission under the terms of EC Regulation 4064/89.[16] UK merger control has two sets of rules:

rules governing newspaper mergers   (Sections 52–62 FTA)
rules governing all other mergers   (Sections 63–75 FTA).

4.2   Newspaper mergers

4.2.1   Any merger in which a newspaper proprietor acquires newspaper or newspaper assets which will result in the acquirer having newspapers with an average daily circulation of 500,000 or more including those taken over, requires pre-merger consent of the Secretary of State. An acquisition by a non-newspaper proprietor would only be eligible for examination under the general merger rule. Magazines, periodicals and trade journals are expressly excluded from the definition of newspaper.[17]

4.2.2   Where a newspaper merger has been notified, the Secretary of State would normally refer the case to the MMC for a report. Exceptionally, however, he may give consent without a reference where there is urgency, where the circulation of the newspaper being acquired is less than 25,000 per day or where the MMC has failed to make its report within the appointed time limit. Where a reference has been made to the MMC it may be given up to three months to respond with an extension only allowed in exceptional circumstances. In practice the MMC is currently allowed only two months in most cases. Following receipt of the MMC Report, the Secretary of State has a full discretion as to whether or not to consent to the merger.

4.3   Rules governing general mergers

Unlike newspaper mergers there is no automatic merger reference. The Secretary of State, on advice from the OFT, will decide whether to make a reference to the MMC. Mergers considered likely to give rise to a significant impact on the economy whether national or local will be considered for a reference. In practice very few mergers are actually referred. The Secretary of State is only permitted to stop a merger if two thirds of the MMC find that it will operate against the public interest and even in those cases, the Secretary of State is entitled to exercise a discretion not to do so.

4.4   Definition of a merger

Section 64 FTA provides that a merger occurs where two or more enterprises 'cease to be distinct'. The definition is very wide and will encompass transfer of

16 See Chapter I.
17 FTA, s 57 (1)(a).

ownership and transfer of control and effective management. Section 63(2) defines 'enterprise' as consisting of the activities or part of the activities of a business. In order to constitute a merger, therefore, it is not sufficient simply for assets to be transferred. The whole enterprise including assets, possibly personnel and goodwill would have to be included.

4.5   Merger jurisdiction

At least one of the enterprises involved in the merger must be carrying on business in the UK or be under the control of a body incorporated in the UK. Furthermore, the reference must be made within six months of the merger or within six months of it having come to the Secretary of State's notice.[18]

4.6   Qualifying mergers

Section 64 provides that the Secretary of State may refer mergers which result either in:

(a)   the creation or strengthening of a monopoly situation (ie a market share of 25% or more); or

(b)   the takeover of assets worth £70 million or more.[19]

Curiously, the value of assets is based on gross as opposed to net value. There are provisions for dealing with a series of transactions leading to a full merger or the acquisition of an enterprise on a piecemeal basis.

4.7   Pre merger notification

4.7.1   There is no legal obligation to pre notify a proposed merger but a party may seek informal clearance ('confidential guidance') of the OFT to determine whether or not a reference to the MMC is likely. Such applications are dealt with in the OFT through an internal committee known as the Merger Panel. Confidential guidance normally takes about three to four weeks and frequently the OFT will advise that a reference to the MMC is unlikely, in which case the merger may proceed. If the OFT conclude that a reference is probable, then the parties will often decide to abandon the merger rather than become involved in the cost and uncertainty of an MMC reference.

4.7.2   Where the OFT investigates a merger either on notification or on its own initiative and irrespective of whether a reference to the MMC is made, the acquiring person or company is required to pay a fee of £5,000 where the value of assets taken over does not exceed £30 million, £10,000 where such assets are between £30–100 million and £15,000 where the assets exceed £100 million.[20]

18   Section 64(4) FTA, s 64(4).
19   This figure was raised by the Merger References (increase in volume of assets) Order 1994 SI 1994/72.
20   Merger (Fees) Regulation 1990, SI 1990/1660.

4.8   The MMC report

4.8.1   Where a reference is made to the MMC it is required to report within a particular period of time.[1] It must decide whether the merger qualifies for
investigation and also whether it operates against the public interest. Article 84(1)
provides that in determining the public interest the MMC may take account of all
matters which appear to it to be relevant and highlights particular issues of importance such as:

(a)   the maintenance and promotion of effective competition;
(b)   the promotion of the interests of consumers both as to price quality and vari-
      ety of goods or services;
(c)   the promotion of industrial and competitive efficiency;
(d)   maintaining and promoting the balanced distribution of industry and employ-
      ment;
(e)   maintaining and promoting competitive activity in markets outside UK
      amongst UK exporters.

4.8.2   To assist it in the preparation of its report, the MMC has power to call upon
the attendance of witnesses to give evidence, including evidence under oath. The
MMC also has power to require the production of documents. Persons failing to
attend hearings, failing to produce documents or falsifying or destroying documents are liable to criminal sanctions.

4.8.3   The MMC report when completed is sent to the Secretary of State with a
copy to the OFT. If the MMC finding is that the merger does not operate against
the public interest that is an end of the matter. If, however, the MMC finds that the
public interest is harmed by the merger then subject to a two-thirds majority of the
MMC taking that view, the Secretary of State has power to order that the merger
be prohibited and if it has already taken place, that the enterprises be 'demerged',
but such cases are rare. In practice, the Secretary of State will call upon the OFT to
consult with the parties in order to restore the competitive environment within the
market in the most effective and practical way. The Secretary of State is not in any
event obliged to follow the MMC recommendation and may decide not to oppose
the merger.

---

1 Not more than six months nor less than three months: FTA, s 70.

Index